TO —

MW01241112

From Charlene with
gratitude and happiness
to work with you.
These angels will guide
you and protect you
fr ever! many blossings

Marie-Ange

The Bible of Angels

Translation by Jacob Worrel

Garrett Strommen translations
http://www.Strommentutoring.com
4450 Clarissa Ave
Los Angeles, CA 90027

Design: Marc Lumer
Marc Lumer Design
341 N. Genesee Ave
Los Angeles, CA 90036
http://marclumerdesign.com

Printed in the USA

WORLD OF ANGELS INC.
theworldofangels.com

ISBN: 978-0-615-47697-1

I dedicate this Bible of Angels to all the people who want to connect with the holy angels and enjoy their miracles.

God bless all of you!

Marie-Ange Faugérolas

Marie-Ange Faugérolas

The Bible of Angels

World of Angels

Publishing

Contents

Chapter 23

⟫Acknowledgments⟪

I would like to thank my celestial companions and all those who inspired this book. I've had a happy and productive time in their company.

My heart and thoughts go out to archangel Raphael, to whom I dedicate this book. I shall be eternally grateful to him for giving me the joy of writing and living so happily amongst angels.

I would like to thank my five children for their love and unconditional support.

I would like thank my grandmother for having chosen my first name, which destined me to write this "Bible of Angels".

I would like to thank Jacob Worrel for his outstanding translations, his inspiration from the angels and his kindness.

I would like to thank Garrett Strommen for his professionalism in his work on the "Bible of Angels."

Marie-Ange Faugérolas

Introduction

Angels are our protectors and our guides. They possess real powers, and when we call upon their services, they are only too happy to step in, providing us with love and compassion. Invoking the angels, or soliciting their reliable help, allows us to obtain results beyond all hope. I have confirmed it at various points in my life. That is why I have written this book with the encouragements and support of these celestial messengers. Angels are not imaginary creatures from an invisible world. They manifest themselves in the human world and participate in real interventions. They can change destiny, open the doors of the future, and transform negative energies into positive ones. Don't hesitate to invoke them or pray to receive their advice. Angels are loving and watchful. They bring about powerful and efficient help.

This Bible of angels will allow you to get to know the world of angels better: their origins, their history, their hierarchical organization. You will find in it a number of practical rituals, prayers, and meditations. You will learn how to get in touch with the angels and how to use their powers in order to live happily and successfully.

This Bible of angels will also allow you to familiarize yourself with the angels by using crystals, perfumes, oils, and colors that attract the angels. Calling upon angels isn't complicated or difficult. Anyone can summon the messengers of God. Being sincere in your requests and welcoming them with open arms is all that is needed.

1 - The Presence of Angels

Because of the touch of angels, we experience the joy of never feeling lonely. Their presence is reassuring, and the first apparition of an angel will create the most incredible well-being.

2 - How to Know if an Angel is Nearby?

The coming of an angel brings about a feeling of lightness, of joy, and a spirit teeming with projects. Oftentimes, the angels begin to manifest themselves through pleasant physical and emotional sensations. Once someone is accustomed to these sensations, they can appear in dreams, in visions, and then in physical encounters. Whatever their ways of communicating may be, they will bring the happiness and certitude of not being alone.

Angels accompany humans throughout their existence. They don't judge their actions and are compassionate for their past mistakes. They are guides toward the future and infallible protectors.

We can invoke them to obtain comfort in times of personal crisis or when confronted with sentimental or professional problems. The coming of an angel is an event that can happen at any moment when we invoke them regularly.

Celestial creatures make apparitions, but they are often reserved for people accustomed to receiving the angelic touch. The most common manifestations are signs, surprising circumstances, unexpected encounters, or happy coincidences.

It isn't necessary to experience personal drama in order to call upon the angels. We can invoke them when we're tired or depressed. They bring about a renewal of energy and lightheartedness.

We can incite the angels to manifest themselves regularly by installing an altar for the angels in a privileged corner of the house. Rituals and meditations are also an excellent way of getting in touch with angels.

Angels are celestial creatures, messengers of God. Their influence on destiny is always positive. We can count on their help and support in all situations, because they are enlightened by divine love. Depending on the person and the circumstances, they warn of approaching dangers, send signs to light the way, or provoke actual miracles and surprises that can truly transform existence. Opening your heart to the angels allows for us to be graced with divinity, and never again must we feel alone.

3 - How to Recognize the Help of Angels?

The messages of angels frequently come to us in the form of repetitive images or signs. Sometimes, angels manifest themselves in the form of recurring visions of animals or objects. Other times, it's when two different people say the same thing. Whatever the circumstances, the state of openness that we find ourselves in will influence these forms of manifestations and angelic contact.

The help of angels always brings about a sensation of psychological comfort, physical well-being, and security. Their reassuring presence discourages us from committing mistakes we may otherwise make out of fear and insecurity.

Angels remove negative influences and protect polluted or unpleasant environments. Their presence favors emotional and personal fulfillment.

We recognize their assistance through miraculous encounters with soul mates, positive relationship changes, or when new and enriching situations present themselves unexpectedly.

4 - How to Feel the Presence of Angels?

The coming of an angel is a privileged moment that must be organized in advance. Start out by making yourself comfortable in a calm spot where you won't be disturbed. Close your eyes. Open your hands, with your palms turned toward the sky. Breathe slowly. After a few moments of relaxation, you will feel a tingling and a sensation of invisible matter in the pit of your hands. A soft breeze is caressing your face and a delicate hand is resting upon your shoulder. The beating of a wing stirs the air.

You are in a white light and love inundates your heart. An angel is at your disposal. Ask him for help or express your desires. Don't hesitate, ask, say a command!

5 - We Are Never Alone with Angels

Contrary to popular belief, we aren't born alone and we don't die alone. The birth angels accompany us throughout the entirety of our existence. They are assisted by the guardian angels who lean over our cradles just after our birth. The latter don't intervene directly in our lives, but rather content themselves by watching over our actions and gestures with a protective gaze. When we solicit them, they come running to our rescue. We can also invoke particular angels in situations that call for a specialized angel (see *The Angel That You Need*, p. 553).

God entrusted guardian angels with a mission of accompaniment. They honor it with conscientiousness and promptness. Even people who don't think of angels, who never solicit them, or quite simply don't believe in them, are always accompanied by celestial messengers. Guardian angels don't interfere in the existence of a protected person. But when we solicit their assistance directly, the angels prove themselves more efficient. They can even accomplish miracles!

On numerous occasions, I have called upon the angels in dramatic personal situations. The angels quickly intervened and transformed my life. Angelic experiences are truly mind-blowing. Don't be afraid to call upon celestial messengers. They are at your service. They are the divine voice and light, the divine love. Make use of their competence. Use their powers and offer yourself a happy fate. Let them guide you. And, most importantly, ask, solicit, pray. The angels will answer every one of your calls.

6 - How to Let Yourself Be Guided by Angels?

Before going to bed at night, let your thoughts wander. Loosen your body and enter into a state of deep well-being. As soon as you start to doze off, call upon the angels and ask them to guide you and answer the questions that you're asking yourself. You can also ask them to bring you success, prosperity, as well as personal fulfillment. The following day, or several days later, you will have new ideas, and changes will start to happen in your life.

The experience of angels is extraordinary. Feeling their presence is a wonderful joy. Abandoning yourself to their goodness and love opens up the spirit and gives new dimension to existence. Allowing them to accompany you through life leads to love and self-fulfillment. Everyone who has invoked the angels and cried out for their help has always received what they've asked for, in every possible domain. The invocation of the angels is an act of absolute faith and trust in the power of those sent by God.

This Bible of the angels was written with the angels' pen and the author's heart. Let the celestial messengers offer all their good will and guide you toward love, happiness, and success!

Chapter 1

Unlock the Heaven's Gate

It's very simple and rewarding to connect with your angels. These loving creatures will always give you a supernatural help. Whether you need love, healing, prosperity or even if you need to be saved from any circumstance.

The angels belong to another dimension where they move simply with energy.

Angels do not have bodies, they don't need them. Their energy is so powerful they can appear to us using any shape they desire in order to inspire goodness and bliss into us.

The human energy doesn't have a very high frequency. Every prayer, every ritual helps to enhance our own energy for us to call upon the angels. We can get connected to their pure and divine energy when we raise our awareness, when we are loving and caring. In so doing, we can even see the angels, receive their messages and experience miracles in our lives !

Energy is the path that leads to the angels. We can increase this energy thanks to rituals, ceremonies, prayers, meditation, visualizations, or just thanks to our honest desire to grow!

1 - The Key to the Heaven's Gate

The angels belong to another dimension and their energy is superior to ours. It flows from the same source as ours; the energy that God pours on every single life!

Have faith in God and angels and trust yourself. Be good and caring and whatever your religious beliefs are, you are ready to open the gate of Heaven !

The celestial messengers of God will strongly help you for ever !

2 - Beware the Demons

In the angelic dimension, there is, as in ours, a dreadful dark side. Facing each other, angels and demons struggle for power. The bright energy of the angels serves God and the dark energy of the demons serves the fallen angel that the Bibles names Satan. In the ancient tradition, he has hundreds of names including Lucifer, but whatever his name is, he represents the energy of destruction, division, harm and fear.

The powerful energy of the demons will endure as long as the same dark energy still exists on earth and elsewhere in the Universe. One day it will come to an end according to that universal rule of victory of light upon darkness.

Be the one, be the ones who will make the balance tilt on the right side of love, pureness and blessing.

Be the one, be the ones who will enlighten the world with your beauty, your goodwill and your awareness!

Chapter 2

Angels are the messengers of God according to the Bible, Old Testament, the Poetic Books (Psalm 103:20): "Praise the LORD, you his angels, you mighty ones who do his bidding, who obey his word."

Raphael or Absolute Love

Angels often appear when we least expect them to. For many years, I have worked with angels, meditated with angels, written with angels, and shared with many people the joy of angelic connection.

These celestial messengers can bring great importance to our lives. I work with white feathers that I found in nature, which I stick onto the screen of my computer. I have several angel statuettes that are always near me when I write. I regularly recite prayers, make requests, or perform angelic ceremonies with my children. The angels have always answered my call and given me what I've asked for. I've gone through terrible family ordeals, deaths, separations, and painful relationships. In every situation of my existence, angels came to my help. They always gave their love and support. They gave me their love of life and the ability to overcome hardship. They also allowed me to experience love, and to appreciate it as the most beautiful emotion of all.

The greatest proof of angelic love I have had the privilege of experiencing came to me one summer night, when I was laying in bed, on the verge of falling asleep. My eyelids were closed. In the distance, I saw a cloud of shining white light. In the middle of this cloud, I saw a face. I couldn't distinguish its traits. But it came closer to me, and I saw the face of an angel, of such astonishing beauty, no human could ever equal it. I felt immense joy. I felt radiant with love and goodness. A smile lit up this celestial face, and the name of Raphael suddenly overwhelmed my spirit.

This miraculous encounter with the angel of my life will remain with me until I draw my last breath. Every day, I think of this angelic apparition and thank Raphael for being there for me.

Being connected to the celestial plane and meeting the angel of your life is a wonderful gift. It allows us to become aware of the mission we must accomplish in order to realize who we are and to transmit the angelic message.

My particular love for archangel Raphael and the grace he has given me have sharply transformed my existence. Miracles have led me toward a new direction in life, toward new horizons, toward other people, and have allowed me to feel true happiness.

Angels are messengers of love and goodness. By being open and wanting to connect ourselves to the celestial plane, we are capable of questioning old ways of thinking, ideas, limits, and fears. And when doubt settles in, disturbing your relationship with angels, it's essential that you reconnect through meditations, prayers, requests, or any other form of communication you wish to establish with angels. Every moment of weakness, grief, or distress is taken into account by angels.

Angels are living proof of humanity, compassion, and love. Confide in them. Discuss the state of your soul, your fears and anxieties with them. They will never leave you in doubt or in difficulty. Ask, and you shall receive. The angelic plane is a vast ocean of love, goodness, wisdom, and energy. Dive into this ocean. You will find strength, courage, happiness, love, and health.

Chapter 3

Who Are the Angels?

God created the angels. Their name comes from the Greek word Aggelos, which means "messenger." Time and time again, their role as messengers of God is described in the Bible when the angels are sent by God to bring help to the mortals. The highest ranked angels in the celestial hierarchy have important powers in the world of physical matter. They act upon events, upon time, upon people. The angels closest to humans are the birth angels and the guardian angels. The latter are protectors, guides, and angels of circumstance. We can call upon them for specific problems. The high-rank angels lend assistance to people, and value people that elevate their consciousness, their faith, and their confidence in love, goodness, and beauty. Extremely powerful angels are also capable of healing sickness and disease, and provoking major transformations in the lives of humans.

People living with a special connection to angels benefit from a life of romantic fulfillment, professional and financial success, and possess greater confidence.

The powers of the angels are infinite. They are free to act at their own discretion and depend upon neither reason nor the physical constraints of matter. The angels live on an invisible plane. They are not susceptible to the passing of time. The distance between the divine plane and the terrestrial plane has no material existence for the divine messengers. Their movements happen at a speed inconceivable to humans. They can be in several places at once.

Their appearance in the physical world is adapted to human reason. We often see them clad in white tunics, radiating with light. But they can appear to those they are protecting with seemingly human, though astonishingly beautiful, physical traits. As celestial creatures, angels are the emanations of the love and light of God, and always have a supernatural beauty.

When God created the angels, he bestowed upon them his infinite love. In return, angels stand in complete worship before their Creator. In the Old Testament, it says: "And they prostrated before the throne and they worshipped God." The angels offer us their love because they have received the infinite love of their Creator. They are greatly aware of their responsibilities toward humans, and respect their liberty, and never judge their actions. In the image of the love of God, their goodness and compassion are unconditional.

The power of angels is superior to that of men. Examples of angelic might aren't lacking. To protect Daniel, a single angel had the strength to close the jaws of the lions. A single angel rolled the stone off the sepulcher of Jesus on the day of His Resurrection. A single angel came by night and opened the doors of the public prison to liberate the apostles.

1 - Do Not Confuse the Angels with God

Angels are the messengers of God, not God. They bring you miraculous help, but beware of worshipping them like idols because they have done something for you or helped you find your soul mate.

Thank the angels, respect their love, their light, their beauty. But know that there is a love, a light, and a beauty that surpasses theirs. Angels carry all of the heart's virtues, but they are also the servants of the Creator who created love, light, and beauty. In the Bible, the Poetic Books (Psalm 103:20), it says: "Praise the LORD, you his angels, you mighty ones who do his bidding, who obey his word."

This verse admirably illustrates the angelic and divine reality. While having faith in angels, it's also necessary to keep in mind that they are the servants and manifestation of God.

2 - How Many Angels Are There?

God created angels, but to this day, no one has been successful at counting them. The Bible claims that a variety of angels exist. In Revelation (5:11), John notes: "The number of them was myriads of myriads, and thousands of thousands."

Each angel has several names depending on different eras, traditions, and cultures. Today, a great number of angels have been attested in different traditions. A synthesis of their names allows for agreement on the terms by which they should be called and avoids confusion. The birth angels can be identified as the 72 angels of Kabbalah, whose names are no longer argued over.

3 - The Angels Have a Mission

The Creator bestowed the important mission of being an intermediary between the terrestrial and celestials planes upon angels. The different functions attributed to angels must help humanity elevate its consciousness and move toward progress.

The angels can accomplish several activities at once and can thus make themselves available to assist several people at the same time. There are angels that specialize in certain fields or domains. They are organized in a hierarchy and consist of superior angels and servant angels. This hierarchy makes them powerful and efficient; no angel acts on his own. The archangels are the heads of the angels and plan the missions of their subordinates.

Each angel has specifically defined functions, qualities, and responsibilities depending on his position in the celestial organization. One of the many functions of angels is the accompaniment of the dead during their great moment of passage. The psychopompic angels help souls depart from their bodies, and conduct them toward the light. This particular function of elevating the soul reinforces the aerial and celestial symbolism attributed to angels.

Angels have also been assigned the mission of guiding humans toward their individual fate. People who have elevated their consciousness, and who are connected to the subtle plane of the angels, tend to find the right path in the labyrinth of existence.

Nothing is done at random in the great divine organization.

4 - The Planes of Energy

We are evolving in a material universe driven by the laws of physics. The angels move about on a subtler plane without the constraints of time and space. God rests above all planes in an immaterial and infinite world. Energy circulates between the three terrestrial, celestial, and divine planes of existence. This energy is the very essence of life. The three planes of energy are interactive and hierarchical. God communicates with the angels, and the angels communicate with humans.

Opening up one's spirit grants humans access to the plane of angels from the terrestrial plane of matter. The divine plane is accessible to saints, great mystics, and to beings whose awakening lies above ordinary consciousness.

When they descend upon the terrestrial plane, angels contribute to the preservation of life. They dedicate themselves to the awakening of consciousness and to the vibratory elevation of energy on the terrestrial plane. The transformation of the lower material plane is part of the divine plan for the evolution of life. The awakening of people's consciousness is the main objective of angels. This awakening must make men responsible, incite them to respect nature, and act for the common good. Action transforms negative situations into positive realities. When the purpose behind your actions becomes the common good, the celestial messengers will give you wings to help you go further on the path of goodness and generosity.

When someone embarks on a personal, professional, humanitarian or spiritual mission, angels are compelled to make the task easier by offering concrete help that will aid in its accomplishment.

Before intervening in our existence, angels begin by bringing us joy. This joy is the motor of our actions. And as soon as we start to act toward achieving our destiny, the celestial messengers convince us that this mission brings meaning to our lives. We then focus on the result. The angels stimulate our imaginations so that we can reach our goals. They never fault in bringing us success and their help always comes at the right moment.

5 – The Right Moment

The angels' efficiency is impressive. In moments of need, they suggest great ideas, they help you meet the right person, or inspire you to make the right decisions. Angels don't ask you to wait. Their support is immediate. They neither depend upon matter, space nor time.

6 – Abundance

The principal mission of angels contributes to the evolution of humanity toward love, success and happiness.

Their power grants access to material abundance. Nothing is impossible with the support of the angels. They accomplish miracles because they belong to a plane higher than ours. They master matter and their ability to adapt to it is impressive. In order to obtain greater prodigality from the angels, be good to those around you. Generosity and charity are the primary preoccupation of angels. The more you let your money circulate, the more you shall receive. The desire to accumulate generates worry and the anxiety of never having enough. When angels bring money into your home, share these blessings with the people you love, and the angels will bring you more.

For angels, money is not an issue. There is always some at their disposal. The majority of very rich people on this Earth give back to others in the form of gifts and legacies. Why not you? Ask and you shall receive.

7 - *The Protection of Life*

Taking care of individuals is the mission of guardian angels. The high-rank archangels in the celestial hierarchy are in charge of preserving life. They must protect humanity and ensure their perennial durability. This explains why we need angels more than ever today.

The survival of the planet is threatened by nuclear power, chemical products, and ecological disasters. Interest in angels is resurging again thanks to the angels themselves. Their increasing influence awakens dormant consciences and opens up the eyes of people blinded by materialism and indifference to the evils of the planet.

The angels have given us a sign that it is time to take control and react, and they awaken responsibility in each of us to participate in the future of the world. They support and encourage all the initiatives that undertake the protection of the Earth and its ecological system. They also help doctors, researchers, and scientists of all kind.

The progress of humanity is an absolute priority of the angels. Anything that elevates mankind concerns them, and they favor any and all projects that lead us in the direction of goodness and knowledge.

8 - *Angels Dwell in Action*

Angels have the ambition and design to move humanity toward progress. They are active, swift, and willing no matter the location or time you solicit them. They respond immediately to any urgent request.

They are in the midst of tackling the heavy responsibility of awakening people's consciousness in this very moment. They receive an influx of important work, but the angels are capable of taking on several tasks at once. Their sphere of influence extends to all three planes. They feed off of the love of God in the divine plane. They hunt the fallen angels that pollute the angelic plane, and intervene for the sake of humans. Their actions are particularly efficient and quick thanks to their capability for immediate movement from one place to another, as well as their ubiquity.

9 - How to Feel the Actions of Angels?

When an invisible presence whispers advice on how to make a decision, and you find this decision to be just and unshakeable, the angels are your advisors. Decisions taken according the angels' advice always lead to success. In contrast, choices that stem from anxiety and insecurity are guided by the mind, which one should be wary of; calling upon the angels will clarify the situation.

The actions of angels are fair, and have fair ramifications on your existence.

10 - The Angels and Divinity

The development of clairvoyance and intuition is part of the angels' mission. The celestial messengers help us see the future and feel what is good for us. This allows us to set objectives for the future and illuminates the path toward happiness. Prophets and visionaries have had access to the angelic plane and they have brought back narratives and texts of high spiritual value.

With the angels, the elevation of our consciousness and clairvoyance is within reach for each and every one of us.

11 - How to See the Future with Angels?

Find a quiet and comfortable place. Dim lighting and silence encourage mediumship. Breathe in and out slowly. Relax. Call the angels. Don't control your spirit. The angels will come to you once you let go of your mind. With a little practice, you will start to feel the events of the near future, and then those of the more distant future. Generally, the visions that the angels propose are intended to provide us with a pleasant view of the future. But they may also confront us with negative situations we have until now refused to see. They then unveil solutions that will prove to be beneficial in the near future.

The results of the first few sessions of solicitation come in the form of visions, images, or symbols. For all requests related to reading the future, essential oils, crystals, incense, and angelic perfumes will ease your voyage toward the celestial plane.

12 - The Duty of Angels

The messengers of God have a duty to strive for excellence and their influence never ceases to grow. They work for the good of humans from a higher plane. They are the ones who announce joyous occasions and spur development of romantic relationships. The Annunciation of Mary's pregnancy by archangel Gabriel, and the intervention of archangel Raphael that allowed Tobias to marry Sarah, are among the most significant events in the history of angels.

The angels encourage goodness and generosity in every life situation. They act upon celebrities and other influential people who take part in humanitarian and ecological deeds.

The duty of angels is to manifest themselves through the generous actions of saints, to promote the visions of prophets like Isaiah, Jeremy, and Ezekial, and to let people of strong spirituality, whose hearts radiate love and goodness, shine.

Angels encourage professional vocations, charitable enterprises, and munificent organizations. They facilitate any enterprise or discovery that leads to the progress of humanity. They strive for the elevation of the human condition, and for the regression of sickness and poverty.

Angels carry the heavy responsibility of saving humanity before it self-destructs.

13 - Do the Angels Have Enemies?

The messengers of God battle fallen angels, demons, evil geniuses, and malignant creatures that evolve on the angelic plane. They are the soldiers of good fighting against the forces of evil.

In the Bible, the angels' armies under Michael's command are continuously up against countless demons that foster corruption, cowardice, avarice, and lust. The angels are in charge of saving lost souls and deceased beings that are incapable of reaching the light because of loaded karma.

The celestial messengers circulate in a higher plane. They come and go in the human plane, but they never descend upon the shadows of the lower material planes where their light and effulgence would be absorbed like in a black hole.

Angels never penetrate the darkest areas of the lower plane. They neither go to Hell, nor to Gehenna, where children were once sacrificed to the false god Moloch. Nor do they venture into Sheol or Tartarus, the netherlands according to Judaism and Greek mythology.

But by no means does this render their task easier. Even though they refuse contact with the lowest forms of energy, angels must confront countless demons in order to keep them away from humans. They are the shield against negative energies.

Hermes Trismegistus once said: "As above, so below." The celestial plane is as Manichean as the material plane. Battles between angels and demons never cease to occur there, and Archangel Michael bravely takes on the devil. In the New Testament, Epistles of Paul, Ephesians (6:11), it says: "Put on the full armor of God, so that you can take your stand against the devil's schemes."

Fighting the devil's armies and his dark angels represents an important part of the mission shouldered by the messengers of God. These battles not only take place on the celestial plane, but in the material one as well. Beings that radiate goodness are often attacked by evil-doers. Light creates envy and jealousy. The angels protect us from these attacks and light ultimately triumphs. They control the abuse of power and keep bloodthirsty tyrants from becoming the masters of the world. In the Bible, it says that the devil, or the "prince of that world," will never reign over the creatures of light.

God will not allow the devil to enslave humans. In the New Testament (Matthew 25:41), God says: "Depart from me, ye cursed, into the everlasting fire prepared for the devil and his angels."

14 – How Does One Fight on the Side of the Angels Against the Forces of Evil?

If you're feeling weak, depressed, discouraged, and if you're losing confidence in yourself, the cause may be negative entities looking to take possession of your energy. In this case, build an angelic altar. Light incense, candles, and pray. Rituals against evil and malignant beings are particularly efficient, but they must be followed rigorously. Turn to the practical rituals of this Bible of angels, and rest assured that the angels will always come to the rescue.

Angels are pure. They reject injustice and evil. When you choose beauty, goodness, and generosity, angels keep evil spirits away. Angels protect you from negative influences so that you can be happy, in good health, and in abundance of the things you need. Solicit them as soon as you feel preyed upon by energies that drain you of your strength and love of life. Don't let evil cast a shadow around you. Call upon the angels and their light of love. Don't forget that light always triumphs over darkness. The angels are soldiers of good. They are at war against demons, against evil, and garner respect for the divine order of things.

15 – The Fallen Angels

All angels, including the fallen angels, were created by God. They are, without exception, the work of the Creator. In the Bible (Isaiah 45:7), God says: "I form the light and created darkness: I make peace and create evil: I, the LORD, do all these things."

God created evil because it is an energy that allows for good to exist. Without evil, good would not be able to grow and evolve. God did not create a neutral world. It's a world of positive and negative energy. Angels are on the side of light and love, which is why they will never deceive you.

In the Bible (1 Kings 22:19), it says: "I saw the Lord sitting on His throne, and all the host of heaven standing by Him on His right hand and on His left." The distribution of good and rebel angels corresponds to the symbolism of right and left. The good angels stand "to the right of the Father." To the left of God are the malignant creatures. God is in the center of the world. He is all-powerful, over good as well as evil.

Angels have never committed a sin. They are the messengers and worshippers of God. They are pure.

The armies of fallen angels are commanded by Satan, but God remains the ultimate authority. God will always behold absolute power of life and death over his celestial servants. In the New Testament (Luke 11:18), it says: "If Satan also be divided against himself, how shall his kingdom stand?" The armies on the left are divided and committed to destruction. Also in the Bible (Revelation 20:10), John adds: "And they shall suffer torment day and night, century upon century." In the Epistles of Jacques lies the confirmation that god is All-Powerful (Jacques 2:19): "Thou believest that there is one God? You do well. The demons too believe it, and they shudder." The forces of evil have no reason to rejoice! The God of the Bible promises them the flames and torments of hell.

Yet, the good angels have nothing to fear. God sends them his love and protects them from destruction.

According to Hermetic doctrine, the terrestrial world is made in the image of the celestial world, a world where the incessant struggle of good against evil rages on.

16 - Angels in the House

In a great number of homes, people living in the company of celestial messengers collect angel statuettes, decorative objects of angels, and paintings depicting angels. This practice isn't merely a commercial trend, it corresponds to a spiritual reality: people bringing the concrete manifestation of the reality of angels into their homes in material form. It's no superstition; it's a genuine practice devoted to angels that demonstrates faith in the wonderful source of goodness and efficiency of angels.

Welcoming an angel in your home is as important as the ceremonies of the Lar gods for the Romans of Antiquity. Having an angel in the house protects the locality and its occupants. Their arrival must be heralded with rituals and prayers. When you buy statuettes of angels, you change the energy of the locality. Seize the opportunity to air out your rooms and let in the light. Burn incense and light candles. The arrival of angels is always a celebration!

Angels are happy to be solicited from all parts. That is why you should never hesitate to invoke them or pray for them to help you. They rejoice at the opportunity of honoring their catalog of commands! People who welcome angels into their homes open themselves up to the luminous energy of the messengers of God.

17 - The Origin of Angels

Since ancient times, we have encountered winged creatures in Sumer, in Babylonia, in Susa, in Elam, in Egypt, and in Greece.

The first narratives that attest to the existence of angels were written by prophets and visionaries telling their angelic experience and describing the winged creatures.

The Bible officially confirms the existence of angels. The numerous references in Genesis date the creation of angels at the beginning of the seven days of the creation of the world. In the book of Job, angels were conceived before men and before the stars. Thus, it seems as though angels were created by God on the second day of the creation of the world.

The Mazdean religion of ancient Iran, where the cult of Ahura Mazda predominates, created the amesha spenta, which means "immortal benefactors." There are seven of them and their function is to be the divine messengers amongst humans. We find here one of the origins of the main activity of the messengers of God in Christianity.

The Bible informs us of the functions of angels and their important role in major events throughout history. But ancient texts remain obscure on many names. The Book of Revelation by John, the Epistles of Paul, or the Book of Tobit, which tells the story of archangel Raphael, are the richest writings on the origins of angels.

Another very interesting source of information on the origin of angels exists: the Book of Enoch I and the Book of Enoch II, also known as "The Book of the Secrets of Enoch." These two volumes, rediscovered in a Slavic version, are part of the so-called extra-canonical texts that don't fit into the religions of the Bible

Enoch the patriarch is not unknown. The Bible clearly identifies him (Jude 1:14): "It was also about these that Enoch, the seventh from Adam, prophesized, saying: Behold, the Lord cometh with thousands upon thousands of his saints…"

Enoch is Noah's great Grandfather. He is mentioned by this title in the Old Testament of the orthodox Ethiopean Church. Jews and Christians alike consider the Book of Enoch to be apocryphal, probably because he arrived very late in the Occidental world thanks to a Scottish voyager that brought him over from Ethiopia in the XVIII century. The original version of the Book of Enoch is written in Aramaic, and the first fragments were discovered in 1976, in Qumran, in the manuscripts of the Dead Sea. Today, the Book of Enoch is regarded as an authority in the field of angels.

The Zoroastrian oracles are also a source of information on angels and the constitution of their celestial hierarchy. These oracles originated in the times of Antiquity, and were discovered in fragments in an edition dated to the XVI century.

Texts in the tradition of Kabbalah and Jewish Mysticism, the Talmud, and the Sefer Yetzirah, are additional sources of valuable information on angels. The Sefer Ha Zohar (Book of Splendor), commonly known as "Zohar," and written in Aramaic, offers precious knowledge about angels.

There are also texts that evoke angels disputed by the Catholic Church: the writings of Dionysius the Areopagite. His ideas on the celestial hierarchy remain a reference, along with the books of Hermes Trismegistus, and the writings of Corpus Hermeticum of 1557.

Other texts offer precious information on the origin of angels. They belong to the gnostic mystical gospels, the Assyrian and Babylonian texts, the Biblical narratives of Sodom and Gomorrah and, curiously enough, certain books of magic. The latter mention angels as much as demons and tell the tale of the fallen angels.

18 – Where Are the Angels?

Voltaire once said: "We don't know precisely where angels dwell; in the air, in the void, in the planets, God did not want us to be informed."

According to the image-makers of the Middle Ages, angels move about in the sky, and God remains in the clouds. Tradition places angels in the skies. These descriptions may seem outdated today, and yet, they retain their symbolic value.

Nowadays, one can imagine that angels live in a real world beyond our perception, in a subtle and superior plane filled with energy, where they move about with great speed, continuously crossing from plane to plane. The angels rise to the highest plane in order to report to God, and descend to the lower plane of matter when they wish to come closer to humans. They are quick and always available. Their arrival for the sake of humans is instantaneous.

Saint Thomas Aquinas said that angels do not possess the gift of ubiquity. But this statement is called into question by several examples of simultaneous voyages by angels, from great distances. They are sent to different places all over the planet, in different planes of energy. In consequence, they find themselves in different locations at once.

Angels are pure spirits and thus have no limits or temporal-constraints. Distances don't matter. This is why they are so fast and efficient and can receive orders directly from God or high-rank archangels in the celestial hierarchy as they intervene for the sake of humans.

19 – Are Angels Immortal?

Angels are creatures of God. God has the power of life and death over angels. Most of them are eternal because God decided it should be that way.

A XII century Jewish theologian said that there are two kinds of angels: "Some are created at a specific moment from subtle elements of matter. Some are eternal."

John of Damascus (VII century), the doctor of the Greek Church, said that angels are eternal "only thanks to grace, not nature." Besides angels created directly by God, some exceptions exist, like Enoch the patriarch becoming the angel Metatron, or Elijah becoming the angel Sandalphon. The latter two benefit from the same privileges as divine angels. Their eternity depends upon the divine grace of God. The seraphs and cherubs that bathe in light and divine love are guaranteed to live for all eternity and, like the great archangels, are the closest angels to the Lord.

The same cannot be said of the fallen angels that are fated to disappear one day. The Bible says that God will plunge them, along with their leader Satan, into the eternal flames of hell.

20 - Why Do We Call Upon Angels?

Who has never felt the need to call out for help? Who has never felt great solitude, despair, or grief? At any given moment of our lives, an angel is ready to step up and save us. Angels are faithful companions, capable of helping us under any circumstance. Their interventions are equally remarkable for personal matters or to surmount professional and sentimental difficulties. The angels are a great help when it comes to healing illnesses or depression. They intervene when there's a lack of artistic inspiration or to heal emotional wounds. They are our guides when we need a new direction in life.

Angels assist us when we desire more success, or when we take on great changes in our existence. They protect travelers and support people who are moving.

They give wonderful advice that leads us toward love and harmonious relationships. They encourage material abundance and success in all fields.

Angels are always in favor of spiritual elevation and making individual progress. Many artists have worked in the company of angels and their beautiful, luminous energy.

Their love and compassion envelops us in a positive aura that keeps negative influences and harmful people at bay.

Angels make genuine miracles happen in our lives when we call upon them.

21 - The Feng Shui of Angels

People with elevated consciousness communicate easily with angels. Their vibratory field easily connects with the messengers of God. But for those who have never called upon the angels, it's important to respect certain rules that will help establish a quality connection with the higher plane. In any case, practicing Feng shui facilitates making first contact.

The ancient Chinese invented Feng shui (which literally translates to "the wind and water"). For millenniums, the Chinese have been building their cities and habitations by following the rules of this traditional art. The goal of Feng shui isn't to obtain a particular style of architecture or to organize the arrangement of a room, but rather to balance different energies so as to encourage the well-being and prosperity of the occupants in a location.

For the Chinese, the passage of energy (Qi) is essential to the fulfillment of all living beings. This is why you can use the symbolism of Feng shui to enlighten your environment, thereby rendering it more welcoming to angels.

Feng shui primarily consists of liberating your home from messiness and encumbrance. When energy circulates, angels can be at ease and visit you and evolve around you.

Put the most cumbersome pieces of furniture against the wall so as to avoid blocking the circulation of energy. Don't pile up furniture. Don't leave papers, books or magazines lying about. Energy circulates properly in rooms that have been cleared and aired out. Space and light encourage the coming of angels. The energy of angels is luminous. Offer them a place dignified of their presence. Avoid dark colors, somber pieces of furniture, and brown curtains.

Angels feel at ease with pastel colors, gold, silver, and white. Bouquets of fresh flowers, especially roses, please angels. Encourage their arrival in places where you feel relaxed yourself.

Clarify your living space and work space, leaving it open to energy. And what you do for angels shall be equally profitable for you. The tidying up of encumbered spaces increases your well-being and receptiveness.

22 - *Famous People and Angels*

The role of angels extends beyond personal matters. The greats of this world are also under the influence of angels. Certain writers, painters, sculptors, and musicians created their work under the protection of angels.

The famous Michelangelo once said: "I saw an angel in the marble and only carved in order to set him free." Is this not the most beautiful homage that can be given to our celestial companions?

Aristotle said that angels are Intelligences. Socrates was accompanied by his "daemon," a protective angel that helped him make the right decisions.

Saint Hildegard of Bingen (1098-1179), Benedictine abbess and great mystic, wrote numerous texts on angels that were a source of inspiration to future writers. She said: "happy angels...do not part from the love and praise of God."

The Swedish writer and philosopher Emmanuel Swedenborg (1688-1772) was a man of science before he discovered the mystical world of angels. For many years, he traveled throughout Europe and met with the most distinguished men of his time, like Leibnitz and Newton. His spiritual influence was considerable. His books on spirituality recount his visions of the celestial world and his conversations with angels. Enlightened spirit, scientist and mystic, Swedenborg influenced a great number of writers and musicians like Goethe, Wagner, Nerval, and Berlioz. He said: "I have been given the gift of being able to speak with spirits and angels."

In Paradise Lost (1667), writer John Milton evokes the role of angels in the myth of Adam and Eve.

The composer Haydn was inspired by the Bible and by Milton's book when he wrote his musical piece entitled The Creation. In the catalogue of German archives, the partition of this piece is written under the evocative name: "an angel"!

The famous Handel (1685-1759) also met with angels. The following account is a wonderful testimony of the reality of angels. After experiencing great success, the composer, whose creativity was waning, fell into a period of doubt, desperation and drunkenness. One day, he received a manuscript from the librettist Jennens. Handel was not moved by the text and refused to give it any attention. But, unable to sleep one night, he felt inspired and started composing again. His biographer Stefan Zweig recalls that Handel had heard: "an answer given by God, the voice of an angel, who, from the heights of the heavens, resounded in his desolate heart." It was thus that, under the influence of the Creator and his angels, the composer wrote Messiah in three weeks.

In his strange novel, Seraphita, Balzac describes the unification of a being transformed into a seraph that rises up toward heaven accompanied by angels. This text was directly inspired by Swedenborg and achieved considerable success.

In the XX century, in 1943, in occupied Hungary, the young Gitta Mallasz transcribed the last words spoken by her friend Hanna before she died. These words were directly inspired by the voice of an angel. The book Talking with Angels, which recounts these dialogues, was also extraordinarily successful. Gitta Mallasz said: "I was in front of powerful beings, far away and yet very near, united to us by an ineffable link of love."

23 - Feeling the Presence of Angels

Angels have an important mission here on Earth. They must protect us, guide us, give us the love of life, and respond to our questions. They take on these tasks with generosity and love.

People with elevated consciousness can feel the presence of angels and use their clairvoyance to see them. But it's sometimes difficult to feel their presence when connecting to the angelic plane for the first time. Often, angels come to us, and we don't see them. Here are some simple methods that will enable you to feel their presence:

- *A sensation of well-being washes over you even if you find yourself in a stressful environment.*

- *An unexpected breeze blows through a closed room.*

- *A white feather comes out of a pillow.*

- *You hear the word angel on the radio or television.*

- *Someone calls you "my angel" in an unusual manner.*

- *A ray of sunlight pierces through the clouds and lands on you.*

- *You smell a sweet perfume.*

- *You hear celestial voices and music.*

- *You feel a tingling sensation in your back.*

- *An invisible hand rests on your shoulder.*

- *At night, before going to bed, you close your eyes, and angels appear to you.*

- *Your tastes change. You prefer light over dark, luminosity over gloominess. You often wear white.*

- *Hold a crystal in your hand that corresponds to an angel, and you will feel the warmth of the crystal.*

- *Think of angels before going to bed. They will come to you in your sleep.*

The next day, you will remember dreams of angels, water, the sky, or clouds.

- *Wear jewelry or crystals attributed to angels. You will feel protected by the presence of your angel.*

- *Leave a picture of an angel in the glove box of your car.*

- *Often think about angels. They will come to visit you more frequently.*

- *Listen to soft music and meditate. You will feel enveloped in the warmth and softness of their wings.*

- *Close your eyes and visualize a host of angels flying before you.*

Chapter 4

The Appearance of Angels

Ancient texts allow for a better understanding of who these celestial messengers really are and what exact functions they serve toward God and toward humans. Angelology also teaches us how angels appear to humans.

1 - Angelology

Angelology is the study of angels.

The Sefer Ha Zohar (Book of Splendor) is one of the texts of Kabbalah written in Aramaic. This text, with descriptions of angels and the configuration of the higher plane where the divine messengers evolve, is a reference in angelology. According to the Zohar, seven different celestial regions exist. This structure of heaven cut into seven planes establishes a hierarchy of angels and describes their attribution in relation of their elevation and proximity to God (see *Angelic Hierarchy*, p. 121). The Zohar specifies that in order to communicate with men, angels appear to them in human form. This fact is corroborated by the great visions of the prophets of the Bible.

Another essential text of angelology, the vision of Enoch, describes cherubs as "identical to a flaming fire and willingly taking on a human appearance."

Saint Francoise Romaine (1384-1440) has visions inspired by God and the celestial world at the moment of creation. She sees: "angels flaking like snow and dividing into choirs."

These visions allow us to establish a portrait of angels and to better understand how the messengers of God appear to humans.

2 – The Beauty of Angels

Visionaries' testimonies confirm that angels coat themselves in a beautiful appearance to intervene for the sake of humans. The messengers of God honor their Creator by displaying figures of great beauty, and certain distinctive characteristics recur.

Angels are beings of light. Their aura is white or, more rarely, a light color. Their presence emits a sparkling ray, and the goodness and love they received from God emanates from them.

Saint Thomas Aquinas said: "Angels need an assumed body. Not for themselves, but on our account."

The Talmud specifies that they have: "bodies made of superior substance, meaning, fire, water, and an even more subtle substance, light; at last the spirit sheds its material coating."

Angels have the power to manipulate the elements of matter, fashioning them to their convenience. When they leave the angelic plane, they take on a human appearance consistent with their inner beauty.

Numerous testimonies attest to the fact that angels wear white, luminous clothes. In the Book of Revelation, John describes them as dressed in pure linen, bursting with golden belts.

In the New Testament (Matthew 28:3), the angel is described in the following way: "His appearance was like lightning and his clothes were as white as snow." White, a symbol of purity, constantly appears in the observation of angels. Some visionaries see them haloed by a golden, silver, or bluish light.

Ezekiel confirms that their beauty goes beyond anything conceivable to Man.

3 - The Supernatural Powers of Angels

Angels can go through doors or walls and are capable of passing through fire without burning themselves. They don't grow old or suffer from any illnesses, and cannot die. Angels use matter to take on human form, but they experience neither weakness nor corruption.

Dionysius the Areopagite sees angels with: "eyes, ears, hair, a face, hands, shoulders, wings, arms, a back, and feet." And when angels don't take on human form, they are made of light, fire, and energy. The angel that appears to Moses manifests himself in "a flame of fire gushing out of the midst of a bush."

Often, the messengers of God are haloed in light and carry precious stones. In the Annunciation, the angel takes on a human appearance to deliver the divine message to the young Mary. Angels are spiritual entities. Their human appearance is never an incarnation. As soon as their message is delivered to humans, they regain their spiritual essence void of all material contingency. Angels never reproduce themselves and do not take part in the material world.

Their powers are truly supernatural because they act beyond matter, as well as the limits of time and space. Angels can therefore bring immediate relief to the physical and psychological ills of humans. They are also capable of intervening in the lives of men in order to provoke changes of destiny, professional success, personal upheaval, romantic encounters, and an awakening of planetary consciousness.

4 - The Gender of Angels

The winged geniuses are masculine in Assyro-Babylonian and Chaldean tradition. Wings, often associated with the virility of a beard and hair, are a symbol of power. In this tradition of the peoples of the Near East, we find the first origins of the representation of angels.

In the Bible, the cohorts of angels are gathered into armies of divine soldiers. It seems impossible to attribute any femininity whatsoever to them. Traditional representations of angels usually depict creatures of masculine gender. Angels are young men when they enter the plane of matter to make themselves visible to humans.

Religious art describes angels as eternally beardless adolescents. Their youth symbolizes the absence of corruption of the flesh as well as eternal life. The absence of a beard proves that they belong to the celestial world. Angels are both soldiers of the celestial army and pure spirits. They don't have the symbolic attributes of terrestrial power, the beard and pilosity.

The Book of Tobit describes archangel Raphael as "a young man." The angel that delivers the message of the Resurrection to the saintly women that stood before the tomb of Jesus is also "a young man dressed in a white robe." The gospel of Mark describes angels as young men dressed in white robes too.

Angelology recognizes several iconographical representations of the angel Gabriel as a woman. But these representations are rare and directly associated with the angel's specific functions. Gabriel, who comes to announce Mary's divine pregnancy, appears modestly before the young women in feminine form. This feminine representation remains an exception in angelic iconography. It's absolutely certain, and without mystery, that according to tradition, to the Bible, and to the very essence of angels, that they are of masculine gender. Angels belong to the armies of good and fight against the armies of fallen angels led by Satan. In the tradition of the ancient Near East, these angelic soldiers cannot, under any circumstances, be women.

5 - Angels' Wings

The winged geniuses of the civilizations of the Near-East, and the winged statues from Ancient Greece like the Winged Victory of Samothrace have had a considerable influence on the representation of angels.

Winged beings can be found on the walls of the Assyrian palace of Ashurbanipal. These geniuses are strength, energy, and virile power incarnate. In Susa, winged sphinxes also adorn the walls of the palace of Darius I.

The Egyptian goddesses Isis and Nephthys beat their wings at the bedside of the deceased Osiris in order to breathe life back into him.

The symbolism of wings is important. The movement of a wing produces a powerful sound that reaffirms the presence of a winged creature in the material world. Plato once said: "The force of a wing, by nature, is the ability to rise up and drive what is heavy toward the heights where the race of gods dwell. Of all the appendages of the body, wings are the most divine."

Wings are material embodiments of the freedom of God's messengers when they evolve in the human plane. Thus, they can move about in the terrestrial world with the attributes of the celestial world.

The Taoist Immortals have the power to fly and can therefore attain the Island of the Immortals. Buddhist saints course through the air.

Generally, the wings of angels are enormous and extend up high from their shoulders, lending them an air of majesty, power and beauty. Wings allow angels to move at the speed of their choice. The wing is an attribute of power and freedom. People who are in touch with angels often hear the sound of their wings fluttering.

Angels' wings are most often white or golden, and more rarely blue, red, or iridescent, riddled with eyes like the feathers of a peacock. Artists compete in their attempts to represent the beauty of angels, their aura and spiritual dimension, with utmost originality.

In Islam, angel Gabriel, answering to the name of Djibril, tells Muhammad the secrets of the religion and the omnipotence of God. It is believed that Djibril had 140 pairs of wings.

In Paradise Lost, Milton describes archangel Raphael flying at full speed with his wings extended.

The main characteristic of angelic flight is its speed. In the Bible (Daniel 9:21), angels shuttle themselves from the angelic plane to the terrestrial plane, between the glory of heaven and Earth, in the blink of an eye. According to certain sources, each Cherub has two wings. The Seraphim have six.

The Jews of Kabbalah call angels "ebra," a word that means "wing." But not all angels have wings. There are wingless angels, though they are rarer in religious iconography. Their symbolism is very particular, as it stresses their temporary power and influence over matter. Manoah's wife once met a man (an angel who had no wings) and said to her husband that he had the appearance of an angel.

Angels that ascend Jacob's ladder are often wingless, yet they still embody the role of messenger between heaven and Earth through the symbolism of the ladder.

6 – Humanization of Angels

Humanized angels often have wings, but they lose their role as divine messengers. They are no longer luminous entities coming from the angelic plane. They lose their celestial identity in exchange for a purely materialistic and temporary function.

The humanization of angels developed at the end of the Middle Ages when they took on a more decorative, rather than spiritual, role. The depictions of angels no longer had the divine and sacred essence of the angels of the great cathedrals of Reims and Strasbourg (France).

During the Renaissance, sculptures of angels were commonly erected around the tombs of nobles. The humanized angel became the symbol of the legitimacy of temporary power. He became the servant, the page, or the symbol of prestige and glorification of the great people of this world. The humanized angel became an iconographic representation devoid of spirituality.

7 – The Round-Faced Angels

In pagan art, love is portrayed through two small winged creatures embodied by Eros and Cupid. Their iconography heavily influenced the depiction of round-faced angels in Western art. The latter appear during the Renaissance in the form of the Putti angels, wearing beads, and with round cheeks, small wings, and the body of a child.

The round-faced angels exemplify the evolution of angels into purely decorative beings in the XVII and XVIII century. In this era, angels lost their real role as divine messengers and were imprisoned in caricature. The round-faced angels swapped eternal beauty for a decorative and desecrated figure. In 1726, the council of Fermo banned the depiction of naked angels. Through this intervention, angels rediscover their primary role as divine messengers.

Chapter 5

The Angels in Tradition

Angels don't all have the same origins and functions. Despite what they have in common with the Near East and Assyro-Babylonian culture, angels differ depending on the tradition.

1 - Greco-Roman Angels

In Greek mythology, there aren't what we call angels, but there are messengers of the gods. The most famous among them is Hermes. He is depicted as a man wearing winged sandals, which is symbolic of the angels' capacity for instantaneous movement. Hermes is not only the messenger of the gods, but also the interpreter of divine will. What's more, he protects heroes and performs divinations with small gemstones. Hermes saves his father Zeus' in the battle pitting him against the monster Typhon. He saves Ulysses on two occasions. These interventions are reminiscent of the guardian angels' role. In Roman mythology, Hermes is associated with Mercury, and attributed with winged sandals, a helmet, and the caduceus. As the messenger of the gods, he is responsible for bringing news.

On an Attic red-figure bobbin from 450 B.C., a painting of a young man standing up, with two big wings in his back, represents Eros. The symbol of the wings is for beings who communicate with the gods and who move from the terrestrial plane to the celestial plane.

To Socrates, the winged Eros is an intermediary between God and men. He presents "prayers to the heavens and the sacrifices they offer" and returns to earth with "the orders of the Gods and remuneration for the sacrifices they offered."

The Roman version of Eros is Cupid, usually depicted as a chubby child with two wings on his back and a bow and arrow. He is the messenger of the gods in regards to sending love.

2 - The Angels of Jewish Tradition

Jewish tradition frequently refers to the patriarchs of the Bible. The latter have influenced Jewish thinking since Abraham. In the Pentateuch (Exodus 6:3), God says: "I appeared to Abraham, to Isaac, and to Jacob as God Almighty, but by my name the LORD I did not make myself known to them." After Abraham, Moses establishes a second alliance between a patriarch and God on Mount Sinai. He receives the 10 commandments and the call of God by the angel in the burning bush (Exodus 3:2.4): "The angels of the LORD appeared to him in the flames of the fire from within the bush. He looked, and behold, the bush was burning, yet it was not consumed. God called to him from the midst of the bush..." The angel's role is fully accomplished here. The angel is God's call. The angel is God's messenger. Ezekiel's visions, Isaiah's visions, and Jacob's vision of the ladder testify to the existence of the celestial hierarchy and the power of angels in Jewish tradition.

Following the Jews' exile to Babylon, Jewish tradition was influenced by the Babylonians and their representations of angels as winged creatures. From this point onward, the directory of angels increases considerably. Angels take on human form, and are endowed with wings and other specific attributes depending on their function and rank in the celestial hierarchy. Persian tradition also influenced Jewish tradition by adding a new category of destructive angels and angels that defy God.

3 - The Angels of Kabbalah

Angelology owes a lot to Kabbalah for the fundamental texts in the Zohar and the Sefer Yetzirah. The latter is called the Book of Creation and is attributed to Abraham the patriarch. These writings are the source of Jewish mysticism, which defines the functions of angels. In the Zohar, it says: "Were the angels sent to Earth not able to take human clothes? Otherwise would the world not have been able to receive them?"

In Kabbalah, guardian angels watch over the patriarchs of the Bible. Adam is protected by angel Raziel, Shem is protected by angel Jophiel, angel Zaphkiel watches over Noah, Abraham is under the protection of Tsadkiel, Raphel watches over Isaac, and Peliel over Jacob. Metatron is the guardian angel of Moses. Malashiel guards Eliah (future archangel Sandalphon), while Michael protects Salomon.

The angels have specific functions like those of the angel of death, the angel of mercy, or the angel of judgment. Their human appearance, as described in the Zohar, defines them as messengers sent to Earth. But in Kabbalah, the angels are not only messengers. They are responsible for doing justice and making fairness reign. The Zohar also evokes the angel of the sun, who is "designated to direct and guide the sun."

The angels of wrath and punishment are responsible for judging and punishing evil beings. The angels of death are compassionate when they accompany the deceased on the day of their great journey.

4 - Islamic Angels

According to Islamic tradition, God created angels with light, the Djinn with fire, and men with clay.

The Koran describes angels in the following way:

"Praise God, the Creator of the heavens and the earth, whose messengers are the angels, endowed with two, three or four wings."

In Islamic tradition, angels are messengers of God to the prophets, Abraham the patriarch, to Zechariah, or to Mary, the mother of Jesus. They are the protectors of Adam's descendants. The angels of Islam occupy very different functions. They are guardian angels, scribe angels, and angels of final Judgment like Michael, who assures "the weighing of acts." The mission of Azrael, the angel of death, who is also called "Malak-Al-Mawt," is to bring the deceased into the Other world. To assist him in this mission, he has the angels of Mercy and Scourge.

There are many angels in Islamic tradition. The Koran says that: "Only the Lord can delineate their number."

The angels are in the service of Allah, but they are not judged in the same way that humans are during the final Judgment.

Gabriel is the most famous angel in Islamic tradition because he dictated the Koran to Muhammad. The Prophet mentions Gabriel (Djibril) three times in the Koran. Djibril leads Muhammad to the celestial world and guides him toward the throne of God.

The Koran says: "Piety and goodness consists of believing in Allah, the final day, the Angels, the Book and the prophets..."

5 - The Buddhist Angels

The historical Buddha, Siddhartha Gautama, lived in the VI century B.C. His three major teachings are: impersonality (nothing is independent of oneself), impermanence (everything is changing), and dissatisfaction (desire brings sufferance). Man is subject to his desires and suffers. Spiritual liberation and the end of attachments liberate man from his desires and his suffering and lead him toward illumination, which is attained by the sages of Buddhism, the bodhisattvas. The illuminated do not enter Nirvana, they choose to remain accessible to humans so that they can help them attain illumination as well. The bodhisattvas come to humans in the form of light or apparitions during meditation.

Before becoming pregnant with the future Buddha, Queen Maya, or Mayadevi, ("devi" meaning "goddess") dreamed that the four gods guarding the East carried her bed across the Himalayas. In the palace of gold where she had been brought, she conceived a bodhisattva, who came from heaven, in the form of a young, white elephant with six tusks that held a white lotus flower in its trunk. This lotus flower entered her body. During her entire pregnancy, Mayadevi remained under the protection of the four guardians of the East.

6 - *The Hindu Angels*

The Hindu texts, the Vedas (from Sanskrit), meaning "knowledge," form a body of work that comes from Vedism, the religion that preceded Hinduism. For Hindus, God Brahma is the creator of the Hindu religion. He belongs to the Trimurti, the triad of divinities that hatched from an egg with Vishnu and Shiva.

Brahma is the representative of Brahman, the eternal, the immutable, the ineffable.

Hindu tradition affirms that the Vedas exists since the dawn of time and that they were passed down orally from priests. The sacred writings of the Vedas are composed of four major texts: the Rig-Veda, the Yajur-Veda, the Sama-Veda and the Atharva-Veda.

The hymns, prayers and rituals addressed to the half-gods of Hinduism, the devas, are gathered in the Rig-Veda.

The devas are beneficent protectors. They are "beings of light." We know the names of the 33 devas that belong to the world of Indra. Similarly to angels, each deva has a specific assignment. Some are linked to an element, bhuta. Others are linked to a sense, indriya, others to a name, nama, and others to a sound, mantra. Others are linked to a color, rasa, a diagram, yantra, or a symbol, linga.

7 - *The Christian Angels*

The primary role of Christian angels is to be messengers of God, the intermediaries between the Lord and men. The Bible evokes angels on many occasions in the framework of a specific function. The angels of the high spheres are luminous beings because they are close to the Lord. But this doesn't keep them from treating human affairs with the utmost importance. Thus, Gabriel went to Mary to announce her pregnancy.

Raphael, filled with divine light, saved Tobias and protected his love with Sara. In the book of Tobit, Raphael says: "I am Raphael, one of the seven angels who enter and serve before the glory of the Lord."

Christian iconography reproduces depictions of angels on church frescoes, paintings, altarpieces, statuaries, and illuminated manuscripts. This abundance of iconography demonstrates Christians' high consideration and unfailing belief in the reality of angels. During his 40 days in the desert, Jesus: "was with the wild beasts, and the angels served him."

The apostles were rescued from jail by angels: "Suddenly, the angel of the Lord appeared and the cell was inundated with light. He struck Peter on the side and woke him up." Thanks to this miraculous evasion, Peter says: "Now, I know without a doubt that the Lord sent his angel."

Paul also testifies that the angels are unfailing protectors: "Last night, an angel of the God to whom I belong and whom I serve stood beside me and said: do not be afraid, Paul!" In his Epistle to the Colossians, Paul describes the court of angels who serve God, and in his Epistle to the Hebrews, he affirms that God is superior to angels.

In contrast with the Old Testament where angels are often called "man," the New Testament references "angels of the Lord." Peter evokes the celestial hierarchy (1 Peter 3:22): "Who has gone into heaven and is at God's right hand, with angels, authorities and powers having been subjected to him."

In the City of God, Saint Augustine (354-430) doesn't doubt the role and power of angels: "God would not have created only a single angel if he had not known to what good he could make them serve."

Pope Gregory I (540-590), doctor of the Church and theologian, helped the liturgy of mass evolve and affirmed the reality of angels. He said one day upon seeing young strangers: "They have the faces of angels, and should be counted among the angels of the heavens."

Saint Bernard (1090-1153) demonstrates his faith in angels in his Sermon XI on the Psalms: "We owe them much affection for their benevolence and the favors that we receive from their charity."

The greatest recognition of angels in the Catholic Church takes place in 1670, when Pope Clement X officially chooses October 2nd as the date to celebrate the Holy Guardian Angels.

8 - The Mormon Angels

The Mormons constitute one of the Christian churches, the Church of Jesus Christ of Latter-day Saints, also called the "Mormon Church." It was founded in 1830, in Lafayette (USA), by Joseph Smith (1805-1844). Visionary and prophet, Joseph Smith wanted to restore Christianity to its origins. His writings were inspired by a revelation from angel Moroni in 1820. Mormons founded their own teaching of the Bible, but essentially taught the Book of Mormon, inspired by the prophet Moroni (V century A.D.), identified as an angel. The Book of Mormon was transcribed by Joseph Smith in 1823 from gold plates according to the instructions of angel Moroni. This book evokes the history of God's people in America during ancient times.

Mormons identify Moroni as the angel that John saw flying (Revelation 14:6): "...He had the eternal gospel to proclaim to those who live on earth: to every nation, tribe, language and people."

Angel Moroni remains the symbol of the Mormon Church, and is often depicted in their churches.

9 - The American-Indian Thunderbird

The American-Indian thunderbird legend has a certain amount of similarities with the angels. The thunderbird can be found in North-American tribes and is often depicted on totem poles. The name of this wonderful bird comes from the sound of its wings in flight. Its wingspan is impressive. The Lakota Indians, a Sioux tribe, call the thunderbird "Wakinyan." The etymology of Wakinyan divulges the role of this great sacred bird in American Indian civilizations. The word "wakinyan" is composed of the word "kinyan," meaning "winged," and "wakin," meaning "sacred." This wonderful animal serves the Great Spirit in the same way that the angels serve the All-Mighty. Angels are messengers of God. The Thunderbird brings messages from the Great Spirit to men.

According to legend, the Thunderbird lives with his family in the sky. He is the leader of birds and celestial creatures. Angel Uriel is the angel of lightning. The Thunderbird is responsible for lightning, and lightning bolts burst from his eyes. He is the master of thunder, but he brings help to humans.

The Namgi people (located on the west coast of British Columbia) tell the tale of the history of their ancestor Namxxelagigu. He underwent great hardship and suffering by transporting enormous wooden beams used for construction. The Thunderbird came to his rescue, alleviating the man of his burden by transporting the beams in its claws. Following this episode, the Thunderbird shed its skin and its wings to take human form.

10 - Angels in Art

Artists have always depicted angels as wonderful celestial creatures. Their function as messengers of God is an indicator of the respect and admiration that angels inspire in artists. The symbolism of angels is almost constant in statuary and pictorial representations. Angels appear young because youth embodies beauty, potential, and lightness. Wings bestow upon angels their celestial vocation. Statues and paintings that depict angels are never caricatures. Their function as divine messengers has always protected them from criticism. Angels are naturally kept away from ugliness and violence. Literature does not caricaturize the celestial creatures either.

Angels are part of the collective consciousness, and benefit from divine protection as incarnations of beauty in its most absolute form.

In art, angels represent an esthetic principal linked to their function of idealized divine messengers. And even when angels are used toward powerful ends, they incarnate the beauty and elegance of a celestial courtier.

Medieval sculptors made the most beautiful representations of angels in stone. The smiling angel at the Reims cathedral is the greatest example. Emile Male (1862-1954), the famous historian of medieval art describes the angels in the following manner: "The long white robe of the VIII century, this beautiful, becoming tunic from no particular country or time period, seems to be the clothing of eternal life."

Michelangelo and the painters of the Italian renaissance, and then those of the French renaissance, praised the angels. The oriental paintings of the XVI century also depicted angels of astonishing beauty, which Hosein Naqqash's painting (kept in Paris, at the Guimet museum) of Raphael and the fish illustrates.

In the chapel of the palace of Versailles, built in the first years of the XVIII century, the altarpiece of the high altar is an ode to the angels, an apologia of the power of celestial beings. This arrangement of evident symbolic value compares the celestial world to the terrestrial world, where the king is dominant. In the center of the arrangement, a triangle with the name of God diffuses its rays of divine light; at the top of the arrangement, a monumental angel accompanied by a young angel extending its wings. The other angels and the golden Cherubim, all beautifully sculpted, dominate the altarpiece. In this arrangement, the angels have lost their sacred energy and their function as divine messengers. They are celestial courtiers serving a king who symbolizes God.

Other examples of altarpieces or sculptures en ronde-bosse from the XVIII century confirm that angels lost their spiritual power to become profane courtiers of kings, princes, and noblemen in private chapels. But this function attributed to angels will not last long because it's merely an iconographic trend, and the true spiritual power of angels returns in the XIX century. In 1847, Eugene Delacroix undertakes the decoration of the chapel of the Saint-Sulpice church in Paris. The paintings of Delacroix depict scenes from the Old and New Testament, where angels are often portrayed. The mythical scenes of archangel Michael slaying the dragon or Jacob wrestling with the angel can be found there. Finished in 1861, the Chapel of Angels is today one of the most celebrated works of art dedicated to the angels and their sublime and spiritual function.

Symbolist painter Gustave Moreau (1826-1898) was passionate about angels. His colorful, symbolist canvasses depict the angels in their celestial function, with a delicate and evanescent feminine appearance.

Art has always celebrated the beauty of angels, lending the divine messengers eternal and immortal value.

11 – The Annunciation

Before the announcement to Mary, the Bible tells of another miraculous maternity. It is announced to Sarah, wife of Abraham (Genesis 18:13-14): "The LORD said to Abraham, 'Why did Sarah laugh and say, will I really have a child now that I am old?" Is there anything too hard for the LORD? I will return to you at the appointed time next year and Sarah will have a son."

The New Testament tells the tale of archangel Gabriel's announcement to the young virgin Mary. After her divine maternity, Mary gives birth to Jesus, the son of God (Luke 1, 26-28): "In the sixth month, God sent the angel Gabriel to Nazareth, a town in Galilee, to a virgin pledged to be married to a man named Joseph, a descendant of David. The virgin's name was Mary. The angel went to her and said, 'Greetings, you who are highly favored! The Lord is with you."

For Catholics and Orthodox Christians, this annunciation represents the message that foretells of the divine and miraculous coming of Jesus, the son of God.

The text of the Gospel in its original Greek version notes that archangel Gabriel salutes Mary by saying the word "Xaipe," meaning "Rejoice!"

Leonardo da Vinci, Botticelli, and Titian praised the Annunciation and perpetuated the belief in Mary's virginity (Luke 1:34-35): "Mary asked the angel, 'But how can this happen since I am a virgin?' The angel replied 'The Holy Spirit will come upon you, and the power of the

Highest will overshadow you. So the baby to be born will be holy, and he will be called the Son of God."

12 - The Great Angelic Visions

Prophets and visionaries laid the foundations of angelology. Their descriptions of the angelic world allowed for the elaboration of the celestial hierarchy. Dionysius the Areopagite was largely inspired from visionary prophets when he wrote the remarkably well-documented text, The Celestial Hierarchy.

Ezekiel

The prophet and visionary Ezekiel describes the throne of God and his Cherubim with exceptional detail (Ezekiel 1, 6-11. 24): "Each of them had four faces and four wings. Their legs were straight; their feet, like the hooves of a calf, gleamed like burnished bronze. Under each of their four wings were human hands. And the four had their faces and wings thus. Their wings touched one another. Each one went straight ahead; they did not turn as they moved. Each had the face of a man in front, the face of a lion on the right side, the face of an ox on the left side, and the face of an eagle on the back. Such were their faces. Their wings were stretched upward; two of the wings were joined one to another, and two covered their bodies. When the creatures moved, I heard the sound of their wings, like the roar of rushing waters, like the voice of the Almighty, like the tumult of an army. When they stood still, they lowered their wings."

Isaiah

Isaiah describes the throne of God and the hovering Cherubim in detail (Isaiah 6:1-2): "...I saw the Lord seated on a throne, high and exalted. The train of his robe filled the Temple. Above him were Seraphim. Each one had six wings: with two wings they covered their faces, with two they covered their feet, and with two they flew."

Daniel

Daniel's visions describe the Lord's throne specifically, providing details about the Throne angels and the Dominations (Daniel 7:6-9): "After that, I looked and there before me was another beast, one that looked like a leopard. And on its back it had four wings like those of a bird. The beast had four heads, and dominion was given to it. I watched as Thrones were put into place and the Ancient One sat down: his clothing was as white as snow, and the hair on his head like pure wool; his throne was flaming with fire, and its wheels were all ablaze."

Enoch

Enoch the patriarch (who becomes archangel Metatron) also has a vision of the divine throne (Enoch XIV, 18:22): "I looked and saw a lofty throne that looked like crystal. The wheel was shining like the sun, as was the mountains of the Cherubim. Rivers of flaming fire flowed at the foot of the throne, and I couldn't bear to watch. The supreme Glory sat thereon and His coat was brighter than the sun and whiter than snow. No angel could approach this palace, or see the Face, because of the splendor and glory. No flesh could see the Face. With flaming fire all around, a great fire rose to Her; none approached Him. All around, myriads upon myriads stood before him."

Elijah

The prophet Elijah, who becomes archangel Sandalphon, offers precious information on the ascension to heaven (2 Kings, 2:11-12): "As they were walking along and talking together, suddenly a chariot of fire and horses of fire appeared and separated the two of them; Elijah was carried up by a whirlwind into heaven. Elisha saw this and cried out: 'My father! My father! The chariots and horsemen of Israel!' And Elisha saw him no more."

Zechariah

Zechariah sees the angel of the Lord: "And the angel that was talking to me came forward while another angel came to meet him." Zechariah is accustomed to seeing angels. He speaks to them with confidence and humility. He adds: "The angel who talked with me returned to wake me, like a man who is awakened from his sleep. He asked me, 'What do you see?' I answered, 'I have a vision: it's a chandelier made entirely of gold, with a bowl at the top, and up high, seven lamps with spouts for each lamp; at its sides, two olive trees, one on the right of the bowl and one on its left.' Then I asked the angel, 'What does this represent, my Lord?' He answered, 'Do you not know?' 'No, my Lord,' I replied. So he said to me: 'They are the two men selected for oil, those that stand before the Master of the whole earth.'"

John

The Apocalypse is the most well-known celestial vision. All of the prophetic visions are part of the Old Testament; the Apocalypse, however, is in the New Testament.

John evokes the celestial hierarchy when he sees the divine throne (Revelation 4:1-8): "After this I looked, and behold, I saw a door standing open in heaven. And the first voice, which I had heard speaking to me like a trumpet, said: 'Come up here, and I will show you what must happen after this'. At once, I was seized by the Spirit, and there before me was a throne in heaven with someone sitting on it. And the one who sat there had the appearance of jasper and carnelian. The glow of an emerald encircled his throne like a rainbow. Surrounding the throne were twenty four other thrones, and seated on them were twenty four elders, dressed in white, with crowns on their heads. From this throne came flashes of lightning, rumblings and peals of thunder. Seven flaming lamps were burning in front of the throne. These are the seven spirits of God. And before the throne was a shiny sea of glass, sparkling like crystal. In the center and around the throne were four animals covered with eyes, in front and in back. The first animal was like a lion, the second like an ox, the third had a human face, and the fourth was like an eagle in flight. Each of these four animals had six wings covered with eyes, all around and within. Day and night, they never ceased from saying: Holy, holy, holy is the Lord, the Almighty, who was, who is, and who is coming!"

Hildegard of Bingen

The vision of Saint Hildegard of Bingen was transcribed around 1180. The original copy of this vision was destroyed during World War II. Only one copy, made in 1925, remains. In 1141, Saint Hildegard received divine instructions encouraging her to accept and transcribe her visions. Hildegard of Bingen saw the angels: "This multitude of angels has a reason for existing that's linked to God more than men, to whom they rarely appear. Yet, certain angels that serve men reveal themselves through signs, when it pleases God."

Joan of Arc (1412-1431)

At the age of 13, Joan of Arc is extremely pious. She already hears voices telling her to liberate France from the English and to help the Dauphin take the throne. These celestial voices are the voices of Saint Margaret, Saint Catherine, and archangel Michael. During her trial, Joan of Arc did not want to reveal the details of the voices and visions that came to her. She merely said: "I saw them with my own eyes, as I see you now."

13 - The Destructive Angels

In the Books of Enoch or the Apocalypse of Moses, the angels of destruction are called "angels of Punishment." These angels are in charge of doing justice. Enoch says that they are "the sword of God." These angels are very numerous. According to Jewish legends, there are 90 000 of them. Some authors believe that the angels of destruction obey the orders of God, while others believe that they belong to the armies of Satan. In the Zohar, (I, 63 a), Rabbi Judah says: "Destructive angels are at the heart of punishment." In one Jewish legend, destructive angels whip men who have sinned "with chains of fire." Destructive angels are responsible for chastising the wicked and punishing the guilty.

14 - The Fallen Angels

The Old Testament doesn't mention the fallen angels. They appear in the New Testament, and more specifically, John's Book of Revelation (Revelation 12:7-9): "Then there was a war in heaven: Michael and his angels fighting against the dragon. And the dragon fought back, but he was not strong enough, and they lost their place in heaven. This great dragon was hurled down, that ancient serpent called the devil, or Satan, who leads the whole world astray. He was hurled to the earth and his angels with him."

Satan is the most powerful of the fallen angels. In Hebrew, Satan means "adversary." The New Testament often evokes Satan and his crimes. He is given different names: the prince of darkness, the prince of this world, the enemy of God, the prince of the power of the air. Before being guilty of wanting to compete with God, Satan was the head of the Seraphim choir and the choir of the Virtues. Satan had six wings. According to Thomas Aquinas, Satan was the "first angel to have sinned."

Rabbinic tradition depicts Satan as "the ugly one."

In the New Testament, Satan is error and evil incarnate. He isn't destined to reign over the world and will not resuscitate at the end of days because Satan is the fallen angel that divides and separates. According to the Gospel of Luke, Satan is responsible for his own demise (Luke 11:18): "If Satan is divided against himself, how can his kingdom stand?"

Satan is the angel that committed the greatest sin of pride (Isaiah 14:13-14): "You said in your heart: 'I will ascend to heaven; I will raise my throne above the stars of God; I will sit enthroned on the mount of assembly, on the utmost heights of the sacred mountain. I will be like the Highest.'"

Satan is not only the adversary of God, but also the enemy of men. Satan doesn't hesitate to say that men are also subjected to his power. In (Job 2:4), it says: "Satan replied to the Lord, 'Skin for skin! A man will give all he has for his own life.'"

According to the Book of Enoch, other angels have sinned as well. Two hundred angels were seduced by women and mated with them, giving birth to giants and monstrous creatures that enslave men and devour each other. These giants are "three thousand cubits" in size according to the Book of Enoch.

God does not tolerate angels who leave the celestial plane to enter the material world and mingle with the humans. An angel that falls to Earth becomes a fallen angel. The fallen angels were all created by God. By nature, they are divine and therefore good and full of love. But when they descend to Earth, they become evil through their own mistakes. God promises them an undesirable fate (Jude 1:6): "The angels who broke rank, and who abandoned their home, these he has kept in darkness, bound with everlasting chains for judgment on the Great Day."

The fallen angels belong to the army of the "Kingdom of Satan." The good and luminous angels belong to the army of the "Kingdom of God." The rebel angels did not all fall into the material world. Some haunt the celestial plane, trying to make their law reign by undermining the omnipotence of God. They are the cause of the principals that crack the Earth: good and evil, and war and peace. The hierarchical and structured angelic plane follows the same Manichean principals as the ones that humans follow on Earth.

Saint Augustine states: "The genuine cause of the bliss of good angels is that they attach themselves to the sovereign one, and the genuine cause of the misery of the bad angels is that they have turned their backs on this sovereign Being and turned to themselves. This vice, is it not what we call pride?"

15 - An Evil in Exchange for a Good

Saint Paul claims that the struggle of humans does not consist of battling other humans, but "the Stewards of that world of darkness, against spirits of evil that inhabit celestial spaces."

The angelic plane is not entirely at rest. It's swarmed by demons and fallen angels subordinate to Satan that attempt to undo the work of God. But no one can arrogate the right to prevent God from reigning over the celestial world and the terrestrial world.

The angels loyal to God are made of goodness and love. They carry the light obtained from God. But when humans or fallen angels create mischief, the angels of God intervene (2 Kings 19:35): "That night, the angel of the LORD went out and struck down a hundred and eighty five thousand men in the Assyrian camp. When the people got up the next morning, there were corpses everywhere!" Divine punishment is manifested through immediate violent action. The angels of justice have a mandate from the All-Mighty to destroy his enemies. But sometimes, punishment is not enough. The Lord desires vengeance (Psalm 35:6): "May their path be dark and slippery, when the angel of the LORD pursues them." After vengeance, the Lord curses those that don't embrace God's cause (Judges 5:23): "'Curse Meroz,' said the angel of the LORD. 'Curse its people bitterly, because they did not come to help the LORD, to help the LORD against the mighty warriors.'"

Love and divine light is cast upon beings that deserve it. The Lord is discerning and he punishes those who oppose him. Divine law cannot be appeased (Galatians 3:19): "What, then, was the purpose of the law? It was added because of the transgressions, until the descendant came about to whom the promise pertained. It was put into place through angels by means of a mediator." The effects of divine law are inescapable (Revelation 15:1): "I saw in heaven another great and marvelous sign: seven angels with the seven last plagues, with which God's wrath was completed." After justice, the vengeance, and wrath of God, comes the time for war between good and evil. The angels are the weapons of

God. The Bible calls them "the army of the Lord." In the celestial plane, God fights to ensure that his authority and law are respected. Love and goodness are made of light, but also strength and energy. Defending values is a permanent and necessary task in the domain of the divine. Respect for God must be permanent and without fault. Angels carry the divine message, and some are authorized to destroy fallen angels, demons, and humans that don't obey the law. Thus, the concept of an evil in exchange for a good is constant in the Bible. Angels resemble the knights Templar, a military order of monk-soldiers. They fight to defend the values and law of the Lord. He is a judicial officer, a defender of innocents, and a slayer of rebel angels. Angels are celestial beings of infinite power. Their wings are useful appendages that help them move. But in their true role, angels are not round-faced angels. They are, above all, guardians of the law and divine values, and soldiers that obey the commands of their superior (Romans 13:5): "Therefore it is necessary to submit, not only to avoid God's wrath, but also for the sake of conscience." Paul underlines everyone's individual responsibility to be respectful of God's law. Celestial or terrestrial beings that act according to the precepts of God receive love and light. The opponents and rebels are doomed to suffer punishment and destruction. The authority of God is final (Psalm 103:19-21): "The LORD has established his throne in heaven, and his kingdom rules over all. Praise the LORD, you his angels, you mighty ones who do his bidding, who obey his word. Praise the LORD, all his heavenly hosts, you his servants who do his will."

There is no paradox in the Bible pertaining to the question of good and evil. The postulate relies on good, an absolute truth that must by all means triumph over evil. The wicked always end up paying for their abominations. Terrestrial or celestial beings that follow Satan and his divisiveness are bound for Hell.

Archangel Michael is the head of the Lord's army. He leads the fight against the forces of darkness and evil. He commands respect for divine law and light. He is often portrayed with armor and a sword that symbolizes his fighting spirit and power. Archangel Michael is the quintessential warrior, whose name means "the one who is like God." Angels aren't celestial or ethereal energies. They are formidable warriors, powerful and effective. For this reason, invoking angels isn't insignificant.

16 - The Angels of the Deceased

Psychopompic angels fulfill particular functions. Their role is to accompany someone in their last moments, and lead their soul beyond death.

The angel of death comes from Jewish tradition, where angels accompany the deceased to Paradise. A psychopompic angel is in charge of the soul that just left its body, and thus has great responsibility. It must transport the indestructible, eternal, and infinite part of a man toward the light.

Shortly before his death, Joseph the carpenter received a visit from his guardian angel who warned him that the end was near. Then, "the angels took his soul and put it in a fine silk tissue."

In the story Charlemagne's life, archangel Michael carried away Roland's soul.

Christian tradition says that the angels of death prepare for their task by surrounding the dying person's bed with a reassuring presence.

Amongst all the psychopompic angels, archangel Michael appears the most in writing. It is said that he brought the souls of Adam and Eve before God. Apparently, he also led the soul of the Virgin to the Lord.

17 - Attributes of Angels

The diverse attributes of angels is impressive. The Seraphim are often gratified with three pairs of red wings. The Cherubim have four blue wings. In the Bible (Genesis 3:24), it says: "…he placed on the east side of the garden of Eden Cherubim and a flaming sword flashing back and forth to guard the way to the tree of life."

The Thrones are often depicted as the divine chariot's wheels of fire with innumerable eyes. The Dominations are sometimes portrayed as helmeted women (like the Greek goddess Athena), holding a sword in one hand and a scepter in the other. The Virtues, emblems of knowledge, hold a book in their hands. The Principalities appear as warriors. The archangels differentiate themselves from each other based on their functions and particular attributes. Michael is a war-chief. He is at the head of the celestial army, and so he is often depicted with a sword or a lance. Gabriel is the messenger of the Annunciation. He is sometimes portrayed with a lantern that lights the way. Raphael, the healer, holds a vase filled with ointments in his hand. In his other role, the pilgrims' angel, he holds a stick, a gourd, a satchel and wears sandals. Uriel, the protector of Paradise, brandishes a sword.

In the cathedral of Strasbourg, 12 statues represent the 4 evangelists, the 4 angels sounding the trumpet, and the angels carrying the instruments of the passion of Christ: the cross, the crown of thorns, a lance, and nails.

The angels wear coats made of gemstones. Sometimes, they have stars in their hands and hold chandeliers made of gold.

Some angels are characterized with swords, axes, blades, white roses, censers, lanterns, or various musical instruments.

Saint Mechtilde speaks of the hierarchy as "a psaltery with ten strings."

The first angels of Christianity have halos and wear tunics covered with a long coat. At the end of the Middle-Ages, their Greek style tunics become robes with belts made of gold and other gemstones.

The angels are sometimes described wearing "capes embroidered with gemstones." Their refined appearance lives up to their image as the messengers of God. In medieval iconography, soberness is one of the criteria for beauty and purity. The magnificent Renaissance era representations personify the power of angels, their grandeur, and their belonging to the celestial plane. The angels are always powerful and often winged, but sometimes they appear without wings. The recurring thread in the iconography of angels, however, remains beauty.

18 - The Language of Angels

Paul says (1 Corinthians 13:1): "If I speak in the tongues of men and angels, but have not love, I am only a resounding gong or a clanging cymbal." The cymbal is a metaphor that illustrates very well the empty resonance that loveless beings produce. The sound may resonate, but it has no final effect. By this, Paul means to say that words coming from someone filled with love will produce the effect of love.

Thomas Aquinas doesn't think that angels share a common language: "The angels, being pure spirits, do not need a language to communicate with each other."

No one really knows how the angels communicate amongst themselves, but it's very likely that they communicate through telepathy. Nevertheless, one may assume that guardian angels and the angels that appear to men are capable of expressing themselves in various languages. Angels have a universal knowledge of the languages and dialects of humans.

Thomas Aquinas believes that "the angelic form of expression, being intellectual, is unrelated to time and place...It cannot be perceived by everyone, only the person to whom it is addressed." According to Thomas Aquinas, angels don't correspond with God, since God created all concepts and ideas and therefore has nothing to hear. The angels communicate with God only to receive his instructions, his orders, or to give praise. The angels are capable of transmitting the illumination they received from God, which is the language of the higher angels to the lower angels.

The different religions of the Bible claim that the language of angels is the same as their own language. Rabbinic tradition says that God spoke Hebrew when he created the Garden of Eden. Muslims believe he spoke Arabic. Swedenborg also adheres to the theory that Hebrew is the language of angels.

John Dee (1527-1609), mathematician and occultist, studied magic for a long time and set out to determine the language of angels in order to communicate with them. The British occultist convinced many people that the alphabet established in the texts of Enoch allows for communication with angels. According to John Dee, the original language of the angels is called the "celestial language." Unfortunately for the occultists convinced of the operative function of the language of angels in magic, it turns out that the pseudo-Enochian language is closer to English than the supposed language of angels.

It appears as though the language of angels doesn't belong to any tradition, people, or religion. The idea of an angelic language attributed to one human language or another goes against the universal quality of angels. The universality of angels allows them to express themselves to men in the language of their choice, as the great number of people all around the world who claim to have communicated with angels demonstrates.

Angels most likely communicate through telepathy, without need for vocal support since they are pure spirits. To help them carry out their terrestrial functions, God endowed the angels with the power of linguistic adaptation when talking to humans. This is what enables them to receive invocations and prayers of all traditions, of all religions, and from individuals from all four corners of the world.

19 - Expressions That Use the Word Angel

Angels have an important place in the collective consciousness. They incarnate the highest moral values, which corresponds to their activity as celestial messengers. The expressions using the word angel come from tradition, the respect they inspire, and the inherent beauty of their function.

- *To be someone's guardian angel.*

- *The patience of an angel.*

- *As beautiful as an angel.*

- *To sleep like an angel.*

- *To be with the angels.*

- *To laugh with the angels.*

- *An angel passes by.*

- *Discussing the gender of angels (endless discussions).*

- *Angel hair (vermicelli pasta).*

- *To be an angel (of goodness, an angel of softness…).*

- *My angel.*

- *Half-angel half-demon.*

Chapter 6

The Angels in Kabbalah

Kabbalah deals with the symbolic and spiritual interpretation of Biblical texts. It's also concerned with the symbolism behind the letters of the Hebrew alphabet. Kabbalah holds a lot of information on the angels, their history, and their relationship with God.

1 - What is Kabbalah?

Kabbalah is one of the sources of angelology. "Kabbalah" is the Hebrew word for "reception." In this sense, the Kabbalist receives the teachings of tradition, a set of esoteric Jewish doctrines that originated in the books of Enoch, the Book of Jubilees, the books of Esdras, the Sefer Yetzirah, the Zohar...

In Kabbalah, the mystical Jew seeks to crack the secrets of divinity through texts. He is initiated, and must fulfill certain moral conditions and follow the commandments. A Kabbalist called the "Mekubal" recites prayers, fasts, and chants psalms. According to G. Casaril, his soul must: "cross the seven heavens and the seven palaces, breaking the hostility of the Archons."

In Kabbalah, the angels are creatures of divine essence. They play an important role in Judaic tradition, which the texts evoking angels show.

In the Bible (Genesis 3:24), a cherub forbids Adam and Eve from returning to Paradise after the fall: "After he drove the man out, he placed on the east side of the garden of Eden Cherubim and a flaming sword flashing back and forth to guard the way to the tree of life."

An angel advises Jacob, grandson of Abraham, to leave Laban and return to his homeland. Jacob spends a night wrestling with the angel, Old Testament (Genesis 32:25): "When the man saw that he could not overpower him, he touched Jacob's hip and wrenched it out of its socket." According to tradition, the stranger wrestling with Jacob is recognized as an angel. Jacob grows from this struggle with the angel and from that that point on carries the name of Israel.

Moses sees the angel in the form of a "flame of fire gushing from an ardent bush." The angels don't abandon Moses. They lead him and his people outside of Egypt.

After the exodus, the angels frequently intervene to protect the chosen people. In the Old Testament, the Book of Numbers talks about the encounter between Balaam and the angel. The king of Moab, preoccupied by the arrival of the Hebrews at the border of his kingdom, summons Balaam the diviner in order to know the future. Balaam heads for the palace on a donkey, but he is stopped en route by an angel, Old Testament (Numbers 22:27): "The donkey saw the angel of the Lord; she lay down under Balaam, who grew angry and beat her with his staff."

The angels frequently intervene after the deportation and exile of the Jews to Babylon. In narratives of Israel's captivity, there are a growing number of angels. The visions of prophets Isaiah and Ezekiel describe the angels. The books of Tobit and Daniel are fundamental sources of Hebrew angelology.

When Adam is in the Garden of Eden, he receives the book of supreme wisdom from archangel Raziel. In the Zohar, it says that the book contained the wisdom of the 72 kinds of knowledge, Virtue, and Power.

The directory of birth angels corresponds to the 72 main angels of Kabbalah.

2 - Gematria

The Kabbalists use gematria, a Biblical exegesis establishing a link between letters and numbers. Each consonant of the Hebrew alphabet corresponds to a numeric value.

Name	Numeric Value	Character
Alef	1	א
Bet	2	ב
Gimel	3	ג
Dalet	4	ד
He	5	ה
Vav	6	ו
Zayin	7	ז
Chet	8	ח
Tet	9	ט
Yod	10	י
Kaf	20	כ
Lamed	30	ל
Mem	40	מ
Nun	50	נ
Samech	60	ס
Ayin	70	ע
Pe	80	פ
Tzade	90	צ
Qof	100	ק
Resh	200	ר
Shin	300	ש
Tav	400	ת

Rabbinic tradition notes that the great temple of Jerusalem was built in the exact location where Jacob dreamed up the vision of the ladder to heaven. Upon awakening, Jacob cried: "Surely, the Lord is in this place."

Through the use of gematria, the sum of this sentence is 541, the same numeric value of the word Israel.

Words with the same number have the same spiritual essence, the same vibration, and the same energy. Nothing is left up to chance in angelology and gematria is the key to knowledge of the angels. The organization of the angelic plane is constructed with the law of the 7 orders, of the 9 choirs, of the 3 triads, and of the 10 Sefirot.

3 - Prayer and Sound

Kabbalists stress the importance of reciting prayers aloud. The sound of a prayer creates a vibration that allows for the transmission of waves from the material plane to the angelic plane.

In the New Testament (Gospel of John 1:1), John says: "In the beginning was the Word, and the Word was with God, and the Word was God." The Hindu Vedas are written with similar terms: "In the beginning was Brahman, with whom was the word."

Sound transports the energies of the people who emit them. Sound is associated with the heart, emotion, and the aura of each person. Sound is unique. It's the essence and the principal of every being. It's the vibratory emanation of life and breath.

According to Kabbalah and Jewish mysticism, prayers addressed to angels are situated on four planes. The first plane is the physical sound of words. The second plane can be understood through gematria, or in other words, the numerical sense of the word. The third plane is the vibratory plane of breath. The fourth plane is the plane of emotion. These four planes bestow an elevated and particularly operative sense upon the meaning of prayer.

4 - Creation

Kabbalah has elaborated the physical principals of creation. The physical plane is the plane of matter. The angelic plane is situated above matter, and above the angelic plane is God, often called the unknowable, pure, perfect, eternal, infinite and absolute "Spirit of God." Before creating the world and matter, God crossed the three non-manifested planes.

The three non-manifested veils

    The first veil is Ein: negation.

    The second veil is Ein Sof: the infinite.

    The third veil is Ein Sof Aur: light.

The uncreated, the infinite, and the undifferentiated are situated in the plane of light. This state is a void filled with all of the possibilities of creation. From this plane, God separated yin from yang, light from darkness, masculine from feminine.

After provoking the eruption of his creative power, God created an essential point containing the first principal that can be found at the top of the tree of the Sefirot under the name of "Keter." This point of union between divine forces and the manifested world come close to the actual astrophysics of the birth of the Universe.

Before the Big Bang, the totality of the Universe's creation and information would have been contained in a particle or in an indefinable All. The idea of the All can be found in the doctrine of Greek philosopher Anaxagoras.

5 - The Creator

The Divine One never penetrates the world of matter himself. He uses his messengers, angels or archangels, to communicate with humans. The function of great prophets, visionaries, Kabbalists, and the initiated serves to establish vibratory connections between the celestial plane and the material plane in order to allow for the circulation of divine energy.

The tree of the Sefirot is the concrete and symbolic manifestation of this vibratory bridge from one plane to the other.

The Creator is indefinable. In Kabbalah, he is YHWH, the unknowable and indescribable planner of what is manifested. In India, in the Avadhuta Gita, he is: "The Unique, unborn and immortal."

6 - The Tree of the Sefirot

The tree of the Sefirot appeared in rabbinic texts at the beginning of our era. Its tradition was inspired from the Egyptian Djed pillar, the original Assyrian Asherah, and the Java-Aleim of Chaldean tradition.

The tree of the Sefirot is of infinite spiritual wealth. It represents the ebb and flow of energy between divinity and matter. Energies are exchanged in each Sefirah, the name of which corresponds to an archangel and a color. This tree of life is comprised of the spiritual means of establishing an exchange between the divine plane, the angelic plane, and the material plane. It was made from a geometric structure in space, even if at first glance, it appears flat.

The tree of the Sefirot is located on several planes, and that's why it's so complex. Imagine a spinning geometric figure in space. It produces and absorbs energy. It emits and absorbs colors. It is arranged in columns, in triads, in 10 wheels of energy that correspond with the vibration of an archangel. The Kabbalist searches his whole life, in the geometric figure of the tree of life, for the path of initiation toward God. He purifies himself through it. He studies its symbolism, its colors, its angelic links. He searches for the origin of creation through the manifestation of divinity. He finds joy and personal fulfillment through it. The tree of the Sefirot is an inexhaustible source of active spirituality. The people who work with angels meditate with the Sefirot, pray, and carry out rituals in relation to the vibration of each Sefirah and the corresponding archangel. Each of the 10 Sefirot symbolize the incarnation of the forces of superior will. It's the principal manifested by God.

Figure 1: The Tree of the Sefirot

Keter (Metatron)

Binah (Tsaphkiel)   Hokhmah (Raziel)

Geburah (Kamael)   Chesed (Tsadkiel)

Tiphereth (Michael)

Hod (Raphael)   Netzach (Haniel)

Yesod (Gabriel)

Malkuth (Sandalphon)

7 - *The 10 Sefirot*

Keter (crown): Archangel Metatron

Hokhmah (wisdom): Archangel Raziel

Binah (intelligence): Archangel Tsaphkiel

Daath (knowledge): No archangel. Don't invoke this entity, which isn't a Sefirah. It's a passage, often represented as a vortex, toward the highest triangle of the Sefirotic tree.

Chesed (mercy): Archangel Tsadkiel

Geburah (power): Archangel Kamael

Tiphereth (beauty): Archangel Michael

Netzach (victory): Archangel Haniel)

Hod (glory, splendor): Archangel Raphael

Yesod (foundation): Archangel Gabriel

Malkuth (kingdom): Archangel Sandalphon

8 - The Colors of the 10 Sefirot's Archangels

Keter

Metatron

Visualize the union with God

Pure white

Hokhmah

Raziel

Feel the force of life

Silver, grayish-white

Binah

Tsaphkiel

Visualize our sufferance

Black

Daath

Cross the vortex

Dark gray

Chesed

Tsadkiel

Feel the love

Blue

Geburah

Kamael

See your power
Red

Tiphereth
Michael
See the harmony
Orange, gold

Netzach
Haniel
See the beauty
Green

Hod
Raphael
See the glory
Yellow

Yesod
Gabriel
Admire the organization of the world
Mauve

Malkuth
Sandalphon
See your guardian angel
Brown

9 - Escalating the Spheres

The 10 Sefirot of the tree of life correspond to wheels of energy that allow the initiated, and the Kabbalist, to travel the path of initiation toward communication with the angels and with God.

With each progression in the Sefirot comes a new step of initiation and elevation with the help and support of the archangels. You can meditate in search of personal elevation with the Sefirotic tree thanks to the archangels. You will go from Malkuth to Keter looking for grace, beauty, goodness, and compassion. The archangels will be your guides and your support.

10 – The Three Columns

The three columns constitute the tree of the Sefirot.

The columns to the right and left symbolize the columns of Salomon's Temple in Jerusalem. Freemasons attach an important symbolic function to them in the progression of the initiated toward self-knowledge.

The column in the center is dominated by Keter, the Sefirah of the manifestation of divinity in matter. It's the column of consciousness, and of elevation toward God.

The right column is mercy. Her name is Yakin. She is black. At the top, you will find the Sefirah of Hokhmah, in the center, Chesed, and at the bottom, Netzach.

The left column is rigor. Her name is Boaz. She is white. At the top, you will find Binah, in the center, Geburah, and at the bottom, Hod.

The third column in the center is consciousness and equilibrium. At the top, you will find Keter. Below, Tiphereth, and at the bottom, Yesod and Malkuth. Kabbalists believe that this column is the path that leads the initiated toward God. It allows him to progress from the material plane of the Sefirah of Malkuth toward the plane of the Sefirah of Keter, which is the center of the manifestation of divinity.

Figure 2: The Three Columns

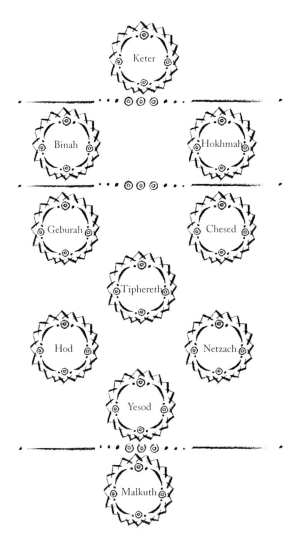

11 - Meditation of the Elevation of Consciousness
(Approximately 45 minutes)

This meditation is done by working on the central column of consciousness. It brings you out of the material plane in company of the archangels. Progressively, you rise toward the vibratory plane of the

Sefirah of Keter where God manifests himself. It's a deeply spiritual exercise that requires great psychological availability and the earnest desire to elevate one's consciousness.

Prior purification is desirable. You will find the rituals of purification for places and people on page 251.

This meditation must imperatively be done in a calm place where you won't be disturbed. Any interruption during the meditation might freeze the energies.

Material
- *A white candle and three golden candles.*
- *Angelic music.*
- *A stick of myrrh incense.*
- *A meditation rug.*

Meditation

1. Place the golden candles in a triangle and the white candle in the center of the triangle. Light the candles and burn the incense.
2. Lay down on the meditation rug.
3. Begin anatomic relaxation.
4. Close your eyes. Breathe slowly.
5. Visualize the archangels of the column of consciousness. Let their energy envelop you in love.
6. You are in the Sefirah of Malkuth at the bottom of the column of consciousness. It's dark. The angels are lighting candles. Light begins to enter into you. Your body is light. Your spirit is empty of thought. You focus your attention on your desire to rise. Archangel Sandalphon gives you his hand. He leads you through a candlelit tunnel. You arrive at the Sefirah of Yesod. The circle where you end up is bathed in mauve light. You feel a great sensation of peace. Archangel Sandalphon is replaced by archangel Gabriel, who gives you his hand. He leads you through an

illuminated mauve tunnel toward Tiphereth. The circle you arrive at is illuminated with golden light. You feel great happiness.

7. Archangel Gabriel is replaced by archangel Michael, who takes your hand and leads you toward Keter. You are thrust upward. You rise with great speed, spinning in a vortex illuminated with golden light. The speed increases. You rise higher. Your body dissolves in the speed. You enter into a blinding white light. Archangel Metatron extends his hand toward you and his touch plunges you into a state of complete well-being.

8. You are in Keter, the crown, the center, the vision of God. You are in a higher energy. You are in the absolute consciousness, in the infinite. Light enters you. You are light. You are consciousness. Your body does not exist anymore. The archangels are with you. Sandalphon, Gabriel, Michael, and Metatron smile upon you.

9. Enjoy this wonderful moment and just relax.

10. The archangels take you by the hand and bring you back to earth.

11. You reintegrate your body.

12. Slowly regain ordinary consciousness.

Effects of the Meditation

This meditation is recommended for people who wish to elevate their consciousness, to act for the sake of humanity, or to enter a state of goodness, absent of judgment. This meditation brings great serenity and inner peace. The archangels' powerful energy lends new perspectives to people who practice it regularly.

12 - The Three Triads

The three triads are the three triangles that make up the Sefirotic tree of life, and include nine Sefirot. They don't include Malkuth, who is the base of the tree.

Each triad consists of a masculine or feminine principal. A man who climbs the Sefirotic tree will end up with balanced energies. He increases his strength with the forces of masculine energy while using the intuition and divination of the feminine energies. As he climbs the ladder toward divinity, his consciousness progresses at each step.

First Triad

The first lower triad includes: Yesod, Hod, and Netzach.

These three Sefirot represent the passage from the material plane to the intermediate plane. The immaturity of childhood is left behind in order to gain the maturity of the initiated. The brutal forces of Neztach's instinct (masculine) confront Hod, the Sefirah of intuition and femininity. The man harmonizes his energies by becoming aware of his duality. He acquires power and penetrates into the Sefirah of Yesod, where he becomes initiated.

Second Triad

The second triad in the center includes: Tiphereth, Geburah, and Chesed.

The man who crosses this triad assimilates the elements of the world manifested in life. He balances the protective forces of his father Chesed and the authority of his mother Geburah. He finds equilibrium between these two Sefirot and heads for Tiphereth, where he is greeted by archangel Michael. The Sefirah Tiphereth is associated with the Sun. The initiated enters the light that illuminates his personal and terrestrial balance before the final escalation toward the last triad of divinity.

Third Triad

The third triad includes: Hokhmah, Binah, and Keter.

This triad is called the "spiritual triangle." These three Sefirot are the least accessible to the human spirit. They elevate consciousness to a very high level. Archangels Tsaphkiel, Raziel, and Metatron carry the initiated toward celestial light, the supreme illumination of the encounter with Keter, the point of divine manifestation.

Figure 3: The Three Triads

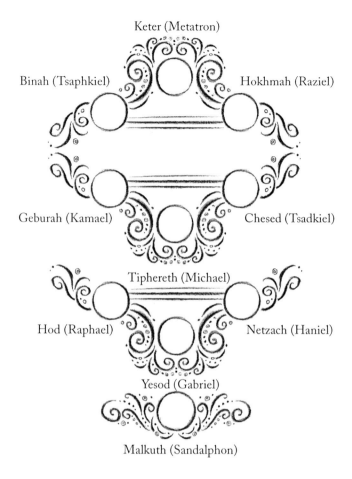

Keter (Metatron)

Binah (Tsaphkiel)   Hokhmah (Raziel)

Geburah (Kamael)   Chesed (Tsadkiel)

Tiphereth (Michael)

Hod (Raphael)   Netzach (Haniel)

Yesod (Gabriel)

Malkuth (Sandalphon)

13 – The Four Worlds

The Sefirotic tree of life offers a vision of the initiatory journey through four worlds that correspond to the four letters YHWH.

Kabbalah describes these four worlds as the inner structure of the Universe, from the material plane all the way to the divine plane. The geometric figure of the Sefirotic tree spins in space, and turns over like an hourglass, inversing the top with the bottom. Keter can be found at the bottom, while Malkuth is at the top, creating a new order of divinity. When Keter becomes Malkuth, divine essence enters into matter. When Malkuth becomes Keter, matter transcends and becomes divine essence.

First World

The first lower world is Assiah, the world of matter and manifestation. It's located in Malkuth. It's the world of action and crystallization, where humans can be found. In this world, matter is degraded and corrupted. Human consciousness is in the initial stage of awakening.

Second World

The second world is Yetzirah. It regroups six Sefirot: Yesod, Netzach, Hod, Tiphereth, Geburah, Chesed. It's the world of formation, modeling, and construction.

Emotions are formed in this world, and the first plane above matter, in the lower part of the angelic plane, can be penetrated. Angels are represented here as pure spirits enveloped in light. In this world, the initiated first enters into communication with the angels. He feels emotion and experiences the first joys of consciousness.

Third World

The third world is Briah. It's composed of Hokhmah and Binah. It's the world of creation where men harmonize physical and emotional elements with consciousness in order to elevate even higher. Ideas are formed here.

Fourth World

The fourth world is the higher world of Atziluth. It contains only Keter. It's the world of emanations or the world of archetypes. It's here that men envision God. God is manifested in this world by an abstract, infinite, eternal, and absolute presence. In this world, nothing can be divided, unity is complete. God exists in the fourth world transcendentally.

14 – The Three Thresholds

The Sefirotic tree of life is a path that leads the initiated toward elevation. At each Sefirah, he receives the support of an archangel that endows him with light. On the path of elevation, the initiated must cross three thresholds that correspond to the three states of consciousness.

First Threshold

The first stage above Malkuth is called the threshold.

It's the first step in the elevation of consciousness, which follows the letting-go of matter. Malkuth and the material world are now behind the initiated. He achieves elevation by passing the threshold of the angelic plane's first degree.

Second threshold

The second threshold is situated above Tiphereth. It's the threshold of the chasm. The initiated is thrust into the unknown world of the angelic plane. He has lost his bearings and tries to connect to his consciousness.

Third Threshold

The third threshold is situated all the way at the top of the tree of the Sefirot. The initiated must now cross the abyss that separates him from the world where divinity is manifested. He will solicit the support of archangels Tsaphkiel, Raziel, and Metatron in order to overcome this difficult step that grants access to the higher plane.

Figure 4: The Three Thresholds

The Abyss

The Chasm

The Threshold

15 - The 22 Paths and the 32 Ways of Wisdom

The Sefirotic tree is divided into 10 Sefirot. Each Sefirah has its own symbolic meaning, color, and corresponding archangel. The seven lower Sefirot are distinguished from the higher triad dominated by Keter, which separates the manifested world from the world of divine essence. There is also a more complex division that multiplies the roads from one Sefirah to the next: the 22 paths. The latter regroups 3 horizontal paths, 3 vertical paths, and 12 oblique paths.

To Kabbalists, the maze of 22 paths represents a long road to cross. Divine energy flows between the paths and allows for an increase in knowledge at each new step.

Each path corresponds to one of the 22 letters of the Hebrew alphabet and one of the blades of the 22 Major Arcana of the tarot. The 10 Sefirot and the 22 paths correspond to the 32 ways of wisdom, which are individual ways of intelligence in all of its forms.

Between the 32 ways of wisdom and the 10 Sefirot, there are 50 doors of intelligence. Doors 41 through 49 are the openings to the world of the 9 choirs of angels. The last doors grant access to Ein Sof, great God.

Figure 5: The 22 Paths and the 32 Ways of Wisdom

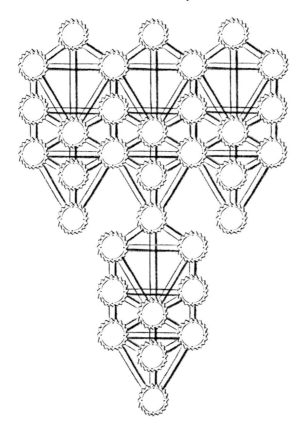

16 – The Energy of the Sefirot

The 10 spheres of the Sefirot are energetic centers with corresponding archangels and colors. These centers of energy represent the Chakras.

Malkuth is Muladhara, the first root Chakra.

Hod and Netzach are Swadhisthana, the second sacral Chakra

Tiphereth is Manipura, the third solar plexus Chakra.

Geburah and Chesed are Anahata, the heart Chakra.

Daaeth is Vishuddha, the throat Chakra.

Binah and Hokhmah are Ajna, the third eye Chakra.

Keter is Sahasrara, the crown Chakra.

Figure 6: Sefirot

Sefirot		Chakras	
Keter			7
Binah	Hokhmah		6
Geburah	Chesed		5
Tiphereth			4
Hod	Netzach		3
Yesod			2
Malkuth			1

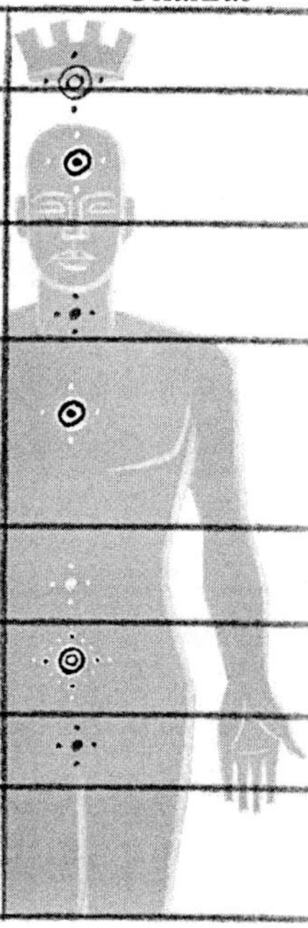

The links between the Chakras and the Sefirot underline the universal aspect of the Sefirotic tree. In each Sefirah, there is energy, and the same energy can be found in the corresponding Chakra, in the form of wheels of energy. This energy is active in the microcosm of humanity through the Chakras and it acts in the macrocosm of the angelic plane where the archangels associated with each Sefirah evolve.

The Sefirot provide wonderful support for meditation and visualization, and Kabbalists haven't finished studying the various combinations and links. In Judaic tradition, the mystic and Kabbalist Rabbi Luria (1534-1572) laid the foundation of a new doctrine. Given that the sins of man slow down the arrival of the Messiah, Rabbi Luria created purification rites that accelerate his coming. His doctrine explains the process of the creation of the world and the catastrophe that followed.

The "Tsimtsoum," which means the "contraction," is the event that preceded creation. The world was contracted by the Lord in order to create the void, a space conducive to creation and the divine emanations of the Sefirot (sacred sparks). The archetype of the universal man, Adam Kadmon, is incarnated in the geometric shape represented by the Sefirot.

According to the Rabbi Luria's doctrine, the Sefirot are vases that contain creation in all its manifestation. They are its sacred receptacles. They represent the image of man in the individual macrocosm and they symbolize the manifested Universe of divine creation.

Rabbi Luria's doctrine establishes that the Sefirot experienced a catastrophe. The creation of primordial man provoked Chevirat hakelim, the breaking of the vases. Since this disaster, men must shoulder the responsibility of the damages by submitting to "Tiqoun," which means the "reparation." It calls upon everyone to repair the vases and restore unity to creation with the goal of setting in motion the coming of the Messiah.

Today, this reparation can be accomplished by praying to the archangels of the Sefirot and through a visualization of purification.

17 - Visualization of the Divine Light

This visualization of the divine light will help you find inner harmony, personal unity, and it will allow you to connect to the higher angelic plane.

Visualization

(Approximately 10 minutes)

For this visualization, you must be dressed in white. Choose a calm and temperate environment.

Material

- *A photocopy of the Sefirotic tree with the names of the archangels.*

- *A transparent or rutile quartz crystal.*

- *Grains of myrrh (in this case, you will need a perfume burner or incense charcoal tablets) or a stick of myrrh.*

- *White clothes.*

Visualization

1. Begin by burning the myrrh.
2. Sit down in a comfortable chair. Relax, and breathe slowly.
3. Stare at the Sefirotic tree like a Mandala. Let its energy enter in you. You feel a tingling in your body, in your legs, in your arms.
4. Pick up the quartz crystal with your left hand. Hold it very tight in your closed fist. Stare at the Sefirot. Then, move the crystal into your right hand and hold it up against your heart.
5. Visualize a ray of white light entering the crystal and penetrating your heart. Your heart is filled with a burst of light. You feel a sensation of joy and well-being.
6. Inhale deeply three times, absorbing all the light in your heart. Then, breathe out to release the light.
7. Thank the archangels of the Sefirot individually. Start with Malkuth.

Follow the path of the Sefirotic tree, beginning with the Sefirah on the left, and then moving to the right, until you reach Keter. Make sure you say the name of the angel as well as the corresponding Sefirah.

8. At the end of the visualization, clean your crystal by soaking it in warm water mixed with a pinch of cooking salt.

Effects of the Visualization

The visualization of the divine light is a deep cleansing and restoration of individual unity. It opens you up to universal Sefirotic energy, and allows for a very high quality spiritual connection with the archangels.

This visualization is for anyone who wishes to find inner balance, spiritual and physical unity, or for anyone who wishes to create an opening in any domain of their life.

Chapter 7

The Angelic Hierarchy

The winged creatures of ancient Mesopotamia, Assyro-Babylonian and Chaldean, influenced the monotheistic religious traditions of Judaism, Islam, and Christianity.

The Babylonians conceived an innumerable amount of lower divine hierarchies. In Chaldean tradition, a world of benevolent spirits is classified according to particular attributes and functions that determine their place in the hierarchy; the "Mas" and "Alap" fighting against the "Lamma."

In the city of Assur in Assyria, the kings pleaded with supernatural creatures that lived in the stone bodies of the Kirubi. On an Assyrian cylinder found in the foundation of King Esarhaddon's palace, it says: "In this palace, the genius, guardian of my royalty, perpetuates his presence forever."

Castes of celestial creatures from ancient India predate the hierarchy of angels. These groups of non-human entities, like the Yaksi, the Aditya, the Vasu, the Brahmarshi, or the Apsaras, are divided into castes according to predetermined functions. Hinduism has a hierarchy for semi-divine and celestial beings, the devas, who are servants of the supreme being.

The Tibetan Book of the Dead describes a host of peaceful entities that appear to people on their great voyage toward death.

The image of a winged creature from the seven heavens pouring brandy in the king's cup was found on a Sumerian stone.

The religious reforms of Zoroaster gave great power to the divinity Ahura Mazda, who had six entities by his side, respectively representing Justice, Right thought, Power, Application, Integrity, and Immortality.

In Islam, the term "malak" is designated for angels. The Koran (Surah XXXV:1) frequently evokes the angels and describes them in the following manner: "Praise be to Allah, Who created the heavens and the earth, Who made the angels, messengers with wings, two, or three, or four."

There are two angels for every human being; these angels are in charge of keeping track of good and bad behavior. Allah revealed the Koran to Muhammad through the intermediary of angel Djibril (archangel Gabriel). The guardian angels of the Paradise of Islam are very numerous: "Only the Lord can delineate their number."

In many religions, there are invisible subordinates to the great gods, with attributes that define their function and place in the hierarchy.

There are angels with similar roles as the ambassadors of kings. They represent the monarch and fulfill his will. As the story of Enoch the patriarch illustrates, the ambassadors are expressly chosen by the monarch or God. In the New Testament (Hebrews 11:5), it says: "By faith, Enoch was taken up so that he would not see death, and he was not found, because God had taken him; before he was taken he was commended as having pleased God."

God chooses to place his representatives where they deserve to be. God chose Enoch to fill the highest function in the celestial hierarchy and transformed the patriarch into archangel Metatron.

Enoch-Metatron governs Keter, the highest Sefirah of the Sefirotic tree. The patriarch turned archangel Metatron is called the "king of the angels" and "the prince of divine Presence." According to Kabbalah, Metatron led the children of Israel into the desert after the exodus.

Jewish tradition tells the tale of Enoch's metamorphosis into archangel Metatron. He was apparently transformed into a spirit of fire, endowed with 36 pairs of wings along with innumerable eyes. Metatron lives in the seventh heaven, the residence of God. He is "the one who occupies the throne closest to the divine throne." The Zohar says that he is "equal in size to the width of the world." In Jewish angelology, Metatron is: "the angel that pushed another angel before the flood to announce that God would destroy the world."

Each angel's place in the celestial hierarchy is based on his function. No angel, not even Metatron, can pretend to be the equal of the Lord, who is the absolute master. The angel who wanted to be God became Satan: "I will ascend to heaven, I will raise my throne above the stars of God…I will be like the Highest."

John announces, in the Book of Revelation, that at the end of days, the Dragon will be thrust downward. Not even the highest-ranked angels can rival the Highest. Angels remain messengers and servants of God, no matter what their function in the celestial hierarchy may be.

Over the course of centuries, angelology has been enriched by the experiences of prophets, visionaries, and mystics. The writings attributed to Pseudo-Dionysius the Areopagite, Syrian monk and V century theologian, are the origin of the first official hierarchy of the angels. His Celestial Hierarchy is a major work inspired by the neo-platonic philosophers, the writings of Proclos, and the authors of the Alexandrian school (Origen and Clement of Alexandria).

In Celestial Hierarchy, Dionysius the Areopagite describes the functions and privileges of angels in great detail, depending on their rank: "Like any hierarchy, there are first, second, and third powers; the sacred order of archangels is a hierarchical middle where the two extremes are harmoniously reunited." "The higher hierarchy, closer in rank to the sanctuary of divinity, governs the second through mysterious and secretive means."

The treaty of Celestial Hierarchy classifies angels into nine choirs and three orders. The first triad receives illuminations. They stand closest to God. The second triad exalts divine qualities. In the third triad, angels are the messengers of God to humans.

According to Celestial Hierarchy, this last choir "attends to the human hierarchies through the mutual intermediary of its members."

In the VI century, Pope Gregory the Great evokes the three triads of the celestial hierarchy. In Gospel Homilies, he distinguishes the highest functions of the archangels from the functions of angels.

Later, Christian philosopher and theologian Saint Thomas Aquinas (1225-1274) draws inspiration from Pseudo-Dionysius the Areopagite's Celestial Hierarchies when he writes Summa Theologica. Saint Thomas Aquinas studies the choirs of angels and elaborates on the relationship between the angelic hierarchy and God. The first hierarchy has the privilege of seeing the face of God. The second hierarchy knows God through the observation of the Universe. The third hierarchy is devoted to humans. The closer angels are to God, the purer and closer they are to perfection.

The highest choirs receive orders from God and give commands in the angelic world. The hierarchical rules are strict and never broken. The angels of the lower choir never approach the creator. They obey the higher-ranked angels.

1 – The Nine Choirs and the Three Celestial Hierarchies

The word "hierarchy" comes from the Greek "hieros," which means "sacred." Thus, hieroglyphics means sacred writing, while hierarchy means the government of sacred things. The hierarchy of angels is the government of God, and the archangels are its ministers. The angels are grouped together by field depending on their activities, dates of protection, and planetary influences. They each have their place in the angelic hierarchy. Archangels are the leaders of the angels.

The angelic plane is divided into nine celestial choirs that are organized into three celestial hierarchies.

First Hierarchy

The first celestial hierarchy stands by the Lord. Its angels receive the illumination, love, and goodness of the Creator. They are the elite of the angelic plane. They include Seraphim, Cherubs, and Thrones.

- *The Seraphim*

- *The Cherubim*

- *The Thrones*

The Seraphim

Their name comes from the Hebrew word "saraph," meaning "burning one." They are the selected elite of the angels and are the closest to God. They bathe in divine light. Their power is vast. They purify the other servants of the Lord with fire and lightning. In the Bible (Isaiah 6:2), it says: "each one had six wings: with two wings they covered their faces, with two they covered their feet, and with two they flew." The Seraphim praise the Lord; they are located above the throne.

The Seraphim and the Fallen Angel

- *Seraphiel*

- *Jehoel*

- *Metatron*

- *Uriel*

- *Nathaniel*

- *Kemuel*

- *Satan before his fall*

Before his fall, Satan (whose name comes from the Hebrew word for "adversary") was the carrier of light. In contrast to the other Seraphim, he had 12 wings. His pride, vanity, and desire to surpass the power of God provoked his fall. In the Bible (Isaiah 14:14), the madness of the angel of light's pride is described in the following way: "I will ascend above the tops of the clouds; I will make myself like the Highest." In rabbinic tradition, Satan is called: "the ugly one."

The Seraphim are the fire and the flame. They produce divine energy and command the lower angels. They praise the Almighty through the prayer of the Trisagion.

"Trisagion" means "threefold saint." This prayer is inspired by a Biblical verse (Isaiah 6:3): "And they were calling to one another: Holy, holy, holy is the LORD almighty; the whole earth is full of his glory."

Prayer of the Trisagion

You can invoke the purification, light, and goodness of the Seraphim by reciting this prayer:

> Holy God, Holy Force, Holy Immortal, have mercy on us.
> Holy God, Holy Force, Holy Immortal, have mercy on us.
> Holy God, Holy Force, Holy Immortal, have mercy on us.

The Cherubim

Their name comes from the word "akkadien Karibu," meaning "orant," the person who prays. In Hebrew, the term "Kerubim" designates "Assyro-Babylonian winged entities." The Assyrians and the Chaldeans depict them in the form of sphinxes, eagles, or winged bulls with human faces.

The prophet Ezekiel was sent to the exiled Jews in Babylon. His visions were probably inspired by Chaldean tradition (Ezekiel 1:3): "The word of the LORD came to Ezekiel, son of the priest Buzi, in the land of the Chaldeans, near the Kebar River. And there the hand of the LORD was upon him." It was also also Ezekiel who described the Cherubim in great detail (Ezekiel 10:12): "The Cherubim's entire bodies, including their backs, their hands and their wings, as well as their wheels – the wheels of all four – were an expanse of sparks."

In the Pentateuch (Genesis 3:24), the Cherubim are entrusted to guard the tree of Life and the garden of Eden: "After he drove the man out, he placed on the east side of the garden of Eden Cherubim and a flaming sword flashing back and forth to guard the way to the tree of life." God is enthroned between the Cherubim, Old Testament, the Historical Books (Samuel 4:4): "...the LORD almighty, who is enthroned between the Cherubim."

The Cherubim

- *Gabriel*

- *Cherubiel*

- *Ophaniel*

- *Uriel*

- *Zophiel*

- *Raphael*

The Cherubim are celestial spirits in charge of guarding the stars, the Moon, and the Sun. They are endowed with remarkable intelligence, great science, and exemplary wisdom. They guard the throne of God, and their vigilance is infallible because of the innumerable eyes they have been provided with.

The Ark of the Covenant, the tabernacle, and the temple of Jerusalem depict the Cherubim, who often appear in Biblical texts. The Historical Books (1 Kings 6:23): "In the inner sanctuary, he made two Cherubim of olive wood, each ten cubits high." The Cherubim have an important place in the history of angels because of their protective role, their knowledge of the celestial world, and their wisdom.

Through meditation and prayer, the Cherubim awaken consciousness and encourage the transmission of wisdom.

The Thrones

These angels carry the divine. According to texts attributed to Dionysius the Areopagite, it is said: "And the sublime and luminous name given to the Thrones means that their unmixed purity distances them of any complacency with vile things, that they elevate upwards… that they are enthroned in a stable and balanced manner, in the totality of their power, around the one that is really the Highest…that they carry God and open themselves up with alacrity to divine gifts." To this degree, they take on great responsibility.

The Angels of the Thrones
  • *Zaphkiel (head of the order of the Thrones)*

  • *Oriphiel*

  • *Zabkiel*

  • *Jophiel*

  • *Raziel*

The Thrones, the Cherubim, and the Seraphim are the three absolutely pure angelic choirs since they are the guardians, the protectors, and the watchmen of the Highest. Dionysius the Areopagite says that they are "unmixed" because they are so pure that they have been given the responsibility of protecting the divine. They imitate God in his perfection and receive his assignments. The Thrones preserve the stability and balance of the Universe. They are the wheels of Merkavah, (or Merkabah) the chariot of God. The prophet Ezekiel evokes the divine chariot (Ezekiel 10:13): "I heard the wheels being called 'the whirling wheel.'" The Thrones are burning with as much divine energy as the Seraphim, and their light shines in the cosmos.

Prayer of celestial creatures of the first hierarchy to the Highest
    Holy, holy, holy is the Lord Sabaoth, his glory fills the whole earth.

Second Hierarchy
This choir is also called the "intermediate hierarchy." Its angels are less close to God and receive less divine light than the first hierarchy. Nevertheless, they are powerful, and have no relations with humans. This intermediate hierarchy is composed of the Dominations, the Virtues, and the Powers.
  • *The Dominations*

  • *The Virtues*

- *The Powers*

The Dominations

According to Dionysius the Areopagite, the role of the Domination angels is to transmit the divine light they received from the first angelic hierarchy to the other angels and restore it with love and goodness. Their emblems are the globe and the scepter. The Dominations are Zacharael, the prince of the Dominations order, Hashmal and Zadkiel.

Some authors add fifteen other angels to this choir. The Book of Enoch references the Lordships when he evokes the Dominations.

The Domination Angels

- *Zacharael*

- *Hashmal*

- *Zadkiel*

- *Muriel*

The Domination angels turn toward the Lord, whom they absorb purity and goodness from. The transmission of this luminous teaching to the other angels is the first quality of the Dominations. Their goodness, love, and legitimate authority are expressed along with the qualities transmitted from the Highest.

The Virtues

The angels of the Virtues hierarchy transmit the values of courage and of action to humans, through the intermediary of the angels of the third hierarchy. They also have the power to provoke miracles on Earth. There is a great number of Virtues.

The main angels of this choir are: Michael, Barbiel, Uriel, and Peliel. The angels that surrounded Jesus during his ascension are the Virtues. Twelve angels and two Virtues assisted Eve during the birth of Cain.

The Virtues

- *Michael*

- *Uriel*

- *Barbiel*

- *Peliel*

- *Uzziel*

- *Gabriel*

- *Sabriel*

- *Haniel*

- *Hamaliel*

- *Tarshish*

The main role of the Virtues consists of transmitting the absolute and primordial qualities that they received from God to the angels of the lower choirs. The lower angels are in charge of then teaching these virtues to humans. Dionysius the Areopagite explains that their teaching: "proceeds toward spirits of subordinate rank, giving them the gift of virtue, in godlike fashion."

The Powers

In the Bible (1 Peter 3:22), it says: "(Jesus Christ) who has gone into heaven and is at God's right hand, with angels, authorities and powers having been subjected to him." The function of the Powers is to elevate the consciousness of angels. Among them are: Verchiel, Chamuel, and Ertrosi. Order must reign in the celestial world. The Powers keep demons away; in Paradise Lost, Milton portrays the Powers as guards.

The Powers

- *Verchiel*

- *Kamael*

- *Ertrosi*

Other than their function of holding off demons and preserving order in the angelic plane, the Powers have a similar teaching function as the two other choirs in the intermediate hierarchy. Dionysius the Areopagite explains: "In the right order, (this power) elevates itself and elevates the spirits of lower ranks toward divine realities."

Third Hierarchy

The three angelic choirs of the third hierarchy form a bridge between the angelic plane and the human plane. They are the messengers of God who have received the teaching, love and illumination of the Lord from their superiors. According to Dionysius the Areopagite, this transmission of divine knowledge is a "perfect initiation at the time of its departure, but one that is diminished in its procession toward the beings of the second rank."

The angels of the third hierarchy are comprised of the Principalities, the archangels, and the angels.

- *The Principalities*

- *The Archangels*

- *The Angels*

The Principalities

The main function of the angels in the Principalities choir consists of protecting the sacred teaching, the religious spirit, holiness, and divine love. Their vocation is to transmit the reality of God. They are also entrusted with protecting the guardian angels that guide people. They are responsible for the guardian angels' mission, for the quality of their advice and their effectiveness as guides for humans.

According to Egyptian hermetic tradition, the head of the Principalities is Suroth; the other angels are Requel, Haniel, Cerviel, and Anael. The name of this choir of angels comes from the Latin "Principalitas," meaning "primacy," which comes from the Latin "primus," meaning "first." The angels of the Principalities are converted to the Power of

God and are in charge of converting men to this power.

The Angels of the Principalities

- *Requel*

- *Haniel*

- *Cerviel*

- *Amael*

- *Suroth*

The angels of the Principalities choir must also control human affairs. They devote themselves to prosecuting the worship of idols and false gods. According to Dionysius the Areopagite, they watch over the religious conversion of humans so that "the ascension toward God, as well as the conversion, communion, and union with God can be realized."

The Archangels

The origin of the word "archangel" comes from the Greek "arkhe," meaning "commandment," and "aggelos," meaning "messenger." The archangels are the implicit leaders of the angels. Any angels above the choir of angels are archangels.

The history of archangels and their exact name remains a delicate issue. Depending on the tradition and culture, different authors spell the names of archangels differently.

The Koran mentions archangels Djibril (Gabriel) and Michael, and without naming them, the angel of Death (Azrael) and the angel of Music (Israfel).

The Book of Enoch mentions the names of the seven archangels: Uriel, Raguel, Michael, Seraqael, Gabriel, Haniel, and Raphael. The Enochian vision represents the seven archangels in front of the throne of God. They are responsible for divine creation and the harmony that must reign in the created world.

The New Testament only mentions the term archangel on two

occasions, in Jude and in the First Epistle to the Thessalonians. In the Book of Revelation (Revelation 8:2), it is written: "I saw the seven angels who stand before God."

In Kabbalistic tradition, the 10 archangels are associated with the 10 Sefirot: Sandalphon, Gabriel, Raphael, Haniel, Michael, Kamael, Tsadkiel, Tsaphkiel, Raziel, and Metatron.

In the VI century, Pope Gregory the Great writes in Gospel Homilies: "Those we call "archangels" announce the most important events. Thus, archangel Gabriel was sent to the Virgin Mary. For this appointment, to announce the greatest of all events, the incarnation of the word of God, he sent an angel of the highest rank."

The 10 Archangels of Kabbalah

- *Sandalphon*

- *Gabriel*

- *Raphael*

- *Haniel*

- *Michael*

- *Kamael*

- *Tsadkiel*

- *Tsaphkiel*

- *Raziel*

- *Metatron*

Texts of all traditions claim that angels were created by God. All, except for the two patriarchs of the Bible; they were men before they were elevated to the rank of archangel. These two exceptional men were called upon by the Lord because of their exemplary life and uncommon faith, and thus became archangels Metatron and Sandalphon.

Metatron is Enoch the patriarch's celestial name. He is called the "king of angels." Sandalphon is the name of the prophet Elijah, who was taken away on a chariot of fire before disappearing into the sky. Sandalphon is the master of celestial singing. In the Old Testament, Elijah must return to Earth before the last Judgment.

The four most popular archangels remain Michael (the angel that slays the dragon), Gabriel (the angel of the Annunciation), Raphael (who heals Tobit), and Uriel (who announces the Flood to Noah).

Invocation of the Archangels

The archangels are celestial beings of great power. They can be invoked for anything related to success or personal accomplishment. The archangels' role has grown increasingly important in recent years. They participate actively in the awakening of individual and universal consciousness. The archangels' power has a planetary influence on material success, the spiritual elevation of humanity, raising awareness about the preservation of life, and the harmony between the angelic plane and the material plane. The archangels are the alchemists of the human being. They crush negative energies. They value individual qualities that encourage love, success, and the elevation of consciousness.

The Angels

The angels are the intermediaries between men and the angelic plane. They often take human form when they appear in front of the people they are helping and protecting.

The evangelists talk about how angels appeared to the saintly women at Jesus' tomb on the morning of Easter. They saw a young man sitting on the right side, dressed in a white robe. They were stupefied, but the angel said (Matthew 28:5): "Do not be afraid, for I know you are looking for Jesus, who was crucified."

Genesis and the Pentateuch (Numbers) evoke the angels using the term "angel of the Lord." Gnostic and Kabbalistic texts mention thousands upon thousands of different angels.

The angels take on a human appearance when they meet with humans.

They fulfill an innumerable amount of functions: guardian angels, angels of air and the Earth, angels of nature and cultures, angels of dawn or rain, angels of the seasons, the cardinal directions, the zodiac signs and the planets, angels of the seven heavens, angels of destiny, angels of the four elements, the months of the year and nature, birth angels, angels of longevity, of the heart or emotion.

Their protective role extends to all fields of human evolution, like the sciences, the arts, knowledge, the law, free will, peace, moral virtues...

2 - The Guardian Angels

The guardian angels have been put in charge of the protection and security of humans by their superiors. At birth, everyone is given a guardian angel. In Christianity, guardian angels are sometimes referred to as "angels of prayer."

Your guardian angel is the intermediary between you and the angelic plane. He will call upon the angels of the highest choir of the celestial hierarchy for specific requests concerning particular subjects (see *The Angel That You Need*, p. 553).

Guardian angels assume the important responsibility of protecting us from negative energies and defending us against harmful influences. People who call upon their guardian angels can rest assured of their support and unfailing presence.

A guardian angel will never intervene in your existence if you don't ask anything of him. His role is to protect you, but he cannot force you to follow his instructions. Man is always free to act as he pleases, and can choose whether to follow or ignore the advice of angels. Guardian angels hurry to you when you call upon them.

Their functions toward humans can be summarized in four points:

1. They are our protectors.

They preserve the integrity of our body and keep us in good health. They keep negative influences away. Saint Bernard says: "Under this powerful guardianship, we have nothing to fear."

2. Guardian angels are also our support.

They console us and bring us moral assistance.

3. Their third function bestows upon them the role of a guide.

Saint Gregory claims: "Each and every one of us has a specific pedagogue that feeds us, teaches us, and leads us by the hand."

4. In their fourth function, Guardian angels are our ambassadors to God.

They are responsible for sending our good thoughts and our acts of love toward God.

In the Old Testament (Psalm 91:11), it says that God: "will command his angels to protect you wherever you go." In the Gospels (Luke 4:10), God: "will order his angels to protect and guard you…"

The poet Menander (342-292 B.C.) said that: "All men receive, upon entry into the world, a good demon that accompanies him and serves as his guide in life."

Saint-Augustine (342-430) notes: "Anything visible in this world is given the guardianship of an angel."

When Daniel was in great danger in the lion's den, it was his angel that miraculously protected him. But even though guardian angels are attached to one specific person, they can also carry out other official functions. Thus, archangel Michael was the guardian of Israel.

If you wish to call upon your guardian angel, there are many prayers you can say. This one is particularly effective.

3 - Prayer to Your Guardian Angel

Holy guardian angel, watch over me.
Holy guardian angel, who receives the light of the Lord, protect me.
Holy guardian angel, advise me.
Holy guardian angel, give me the strength to be good.

Holy guardian angel, console my sadness and grief.

Holy guardian angel, help me progress toward good and abundance.

Holy guardian angel, watch over me.

Holy guardian angel, thank you.

Amen.

4 - Amen in the Prayer

Etymologically, the word "Amen" in Hebrew can be interpreted as "Truly," "Verily," or "So be it."

The word "Amen" (Amin in Arabic) is used to affirm faith and confirm the meaning of the words in the prayer. This word is frequently used in the Hebrew Bible, in the New Testament, and the Koran.

In Jewish tradition, nine people must answer "Amen" after a public prayer in order to make the prayer effective. When praying to the angels, there is one essential rule to follow: you must always be grateful to the angels. Prayers must imperatively contain thanks in order to be effective. Respect is a fundamental value in the plane of angels. The angelic hierarchy is perfectly organized according to competence, reliability, light, goodness, and love. The more respectful you are toward angels, the more your prayers and solicitations will be effective. The same goes for the people you meet in your daily life; you must behave with them as you would with the angels. Harmony reigns in the celestial world; it must also dominate your existence if you wish to establish a connection with the angels of high vibratory frequency. The more you elevate your thoughts and behavior with others, the more help you shall receive from the angels.

When you finish saying your prayers, don't forget to say thank you and to end your invocations or solicitations with one of these phrases:

- *Let it be written and accomplished.*

- *Let it be so.*

- *Amen.*

- *I believe.*

- *Such is my faith.*

These respectful words encourage angels to act on your behalf when you finish your prayer with one of these phrases. Pick the phrase that suits you the most or that corresponds to your spiritual and religious origins.

Angels that have been thanked and encouraged to act will respond to your call and will receive satisfaction from your requests or desires.

In ancient books dealing with the relationship between humans and angels, men live in fear of angels in the same way they fear God. This relationship has changed with the awakening of consciousness. Angels are no longer feared, but highly esteemed and respected. The most sincere kind of faith is love.

5 - *The Seven Heavens*

In the Old Testament, Pentateuch (Deuteronomy 10:14), it says: "Yes, to the LORD your God belong the heavens, the highest of heavens, the earth and everything in it."

The majority of the prophets' visions, texts of the Bible, and Kabbalistic writings situate the divine world in the sky. Symbolically, the elevation of the divine creates distance from the human world, thereby fostering respect and admiration.

In the Bible, God is the Lord of the kingdom of Heaven. In China, the emperor was the "son of the sky." In the New Testament (Matthew 10:7), it says: "And proclaim as you go, 'the kingdom of heaven is near.'"

The famous motto of Genghis Khan was: "A god in heaven and Khan on earth."

Human history has always placed divinities very far and very high from human sight. The Emerald Tablet of the hermetic tradition says: "It ascends from the Earth and descends from Heaven." The communication between the terrestrial world and the celestial world favors the circulation of divine energy. The Persians often use the expression: "God from

Heaven." The Aztecs organized the celestial world into 13 heavens. The Pentateuch (Deuteronomy 4:39) says: "The LORD is God in heaven above and on earth below; there is no other." According to the Zohar, there are seven celestial regions where the hierarchy of angels is in place. These seven heavens chart out the angelic plane and delineate the celestial messengers' spheres of intervention.

First Heaven

This celestial plane is the closest to Earth. It is dark, almost without light. Only the sparkling of the stars and planetary angels can be seen. According to the Zohar, the head of these angels is Tahariel. Some believe that this heaven is the paradise where Adam and Eve lived. In Hebrew tradition, this heaven is called "Shamayim," and its governing angel is Gabriel.

Second Heaven

In this more luminous space, the higher angels watch over humans. The Zohar adds that the angels are responsible for discouraging humans from making bad decisions or giving in to temptation. Islamic tradition situates John the Baptist's place of residence in this heaven. According to the Zohar, the second heaven's angelic leader is Qadomiel. In Hebrew tradition, it is called "Raqia," and its leaders are Zachariel and Raphael.

Third Heaven

According to the Zohar, this region of space is dominated by fire and flames. The heat is unbearable. Angels that travel to the third heaven go there to punish evil people. According to Muslim tradition, Azrael, the angel of death, lives in this heaven. The three angels qualified as princes – Anahel, Jagniel, and according to the book of Moses, Rabacyel – govern this plane.

The flames of hell in the north of this heaven stand in contrast with the south where there are luminous gates. The souls of perfect beings cross through this passage in order to ascend the celestial hierarchy. In Hebrew tradition, the third heaven is called "Shehaqim."

Fourth Heaven

Governed by angel Padael, the fourth heaven is bathed in a pure and radiating white light. Angels Shamshiel, Zagzagel, Sapiel, and Michael live on its right side. These angels teach mercy and appear to humans in dreams. The Talmud specifies that the celestial city, the temple and altar of John's apocalyptic vision, is located there. John told of the miraculous apparition of the celestial city (Revelation 21:2): "I saw the holy city, the new Jerusalem, coming down from heaven..." (22:1): "Then he showed me a stream of water, bright and shining like a crystal..." Hebrew tradition calls the fourth heaven "Machonon," and Michael is the head of its angels.

Fifth Heaven

In the fifth heaven, light shines with full force. The angels there are good and powerful. They praise God eternally. Enoch portrays angel Shatqiel as the prince of this heaven. Clement of Alexandria sees "angels that are called Lords" there. The Zohar specifies that the head of the fifth heaven is called "Qadaschiel." According to Hebrew tradition, the fifth heaven is Mathey, and its main angel is Sandalphon.

Sixth Heaven

The archives of humanity and the celestial plane can be found in the sixth heaven. This plane is the closest to the divine plane. According to the Zohar, its leader Oriel watches over the operation of the angels' celestial navigation. According to Hebrew tradition, this heaven is called "Zebdul," and Zachiel is the head of its angels.

Seventh Heaven

The origin of the seventh heaven is indisputable. The Persians depicted God "sitting on a great white throne, surrounded by winged

Cherubim." The Christian angels of the highest celestial hierarchy, the choirs of the Seraphim, the Cherubim, and the Thrones, accompany God and sing his praise. God is above all the other heavens, and all the other angels. He is enthroned in the seventh heaven where the souls of the just are welcomed. Love, peace, and divine grace reign in the seventh heaven.

6 – The Ladder of Angels

The angelic hierarchy determines the angels' positions based on their level of illumination. The angelic choirs' higher and intermediate planes are not accessible to humans.

Jacob the patriarch, son of Isaac, dreamed of a ladder to heaven. The story is told in the Bible (Genesis 28:12): "He had a dream: he saw a ladder resting on the earth, with its top reaching to heaven; the angels of God were ascending and descending on it." All the way at the top of the hierarchy, above the angels, Jacob sees God (Genesis 28:13): "There above it stood the LORD, and he said: 'I am the LORD, the God of your father Abraham and the God of Isaac." Jacob's dream is not only an exceptional prophetic vision, but a confirmation of the celestial hierarchy.

God's angels ascend and descend from the heavens to establish a permanent connection between the different hierarchies of the angelic and terrestrial planes. The angels descend to Earth to bring help and support to humans. Then, they return to their higher planes in order to account for their terrestrial activities. This exchange from one plane to the other is uninterrupted, a perpetual movement of angelic activity.

In Jacob's dream, the climbing and descending of the ladder by the angels is highly symbolic. It represents the obligation to climb in order to move toward God. This initiatory road parallels the steps in the elevation of individual consciousness toward the divine.

The presence of God at the top of the ladder confirms the existence of the celestial hierarchy described by Ezekiel's vision (Ezekiel 10:4):

"The glory of God rose above the Cherubim…" or by the vision of Isaiah (Isaiah 66:1): "Thus saith the LORD: heaven is my throne and the earth my footstool."

Before she was martyred, Saint Perpetua (who died in 203, in Carthage) spoke of the visions she had during her captivity. She was thrown in an amphitheatre with a wild pack of beasts, and then killed with a blade. The visions of Perpetua are mentioned by Tertullian, and then by Saint Augustine. The young woman sees the following image: "A brazen ladder, of astonishing grandeur, reaching the sky and only wide enough for one to climb…And I climbed and I saw a giant garden."

Jacob of Serugh (who died in 521) describes the cross of the Passion of Jesus as: "a ladder laden with rungs, held up so that all terrestrial beings could be elevated by him... It is like a ladder between terrestrial beings and celestial beings."

The ladder is a symbol of movement, as is confirmed by Jacob's dream, where it is ascendant and descendent at the same time.

Mircea Eliade summarizes the symbolism of the ladder in the following way: "All upward symbolism means the Transcendence of human vocation and the penetration into new, higher cosmic levels."

John's apocalyptic vision confirms the reality of this symbolism and its importance in the angelic hierarchy (John 1:51): "He then added: 'I tell you the truth, you shall see heaven open, and the angels of God ascending and descending on the Son of Man."

7 - Angelic Places

There are sacred places particularly conducive to contact with angels of all choirs and hierarchies. These places are mountains, lakes, holy places, or ancient temples.

Listen to your heart and it will direct you toward a place that inspires you. The energies of ancient temples are particularly conducive to contact with angels because when they were considered sacred places, only priests or the initiated could enter these sanctuaries. These places are marked with sacred and divine light. The Greek temples in the south of Italy and Greece are beautiful places where you can recite prayers to angels and archangels. You can also solicit them in Egyptian temples, Buddhist temples, or in the Himalayas, where the altitude helps you climb the rungs of the spiritual ladder. Peaceful and quiet places in nature are conducive to contact with higher angels. The great lakes, forests, and anywhere along the shore are also favorable places.

Chapter 8

Find Love with the Angels

What's more wonderful than feeling love, and to live and celebrate it throughout your existence? Love gives meaning to life. It changes your outlook of others, and develops tolerance and self-esteem. People who give and receive love are fulfilled and radiant.

1 - The Power of Love

According to a French expression: "When you love, you don't count the cost." Love makes people generous. But if love transcends the heart and emotions, it also stimulates intelligence and imagination. People who are animated by their love of life, for art, or for technique, make advances for humanity. Teachers who love their job transmit their knowledge in the spirit of progress and elevation. Athletes, driven by their love for their fellow man, accomplish their exploits with joy. Children who are loved by their parents and their family are balanced and develop real self-confidence. Men and women who are in a fulfilling relationship appreciate their daily lives and look for greatness in their actions. The elderly who continue to love well into their old age stay in good shape, and transmit their goodness and wisdom. The virtues of love are infinite.

In contrast to popular opinion, human beings are all equal when it comes to love. No matter the age or quality of the person, love is always wonderful. Older people who hold hands and exchange languid looks after being together for 50 years are just as endearing as young couples.

By uniting two beings together, love exalts every individual's inner power. By loving others, we develop self-esteem and reinforce our courage and will to triumph over all obstacles. I knew people hardened by life, pessimistic or depressed, who after finding their soul mate became radiant and celebrated life with their partner.

Living out your dreams with another person is wonderful. Being supported and encouraged by the person that matters most in your eyes is extraordinary. Falling asleep on the shoulder of the person whose face, voice, and scent, gives you energy day after day is wonderful.

The laughter of love is stronger than others. The looks are softer, the gestures more delicate. Love is poetry. Love is laughter and madness. It molds the soul, giving it radiance and beauty.

Love is born from two forces that, while uniting, become more and more powerful individually. This is why humans think of love as a blessing.

Love makes you want to start new projects, to do well at work, and to improve your relationships with your family and friends. It develops personality because it makes everyone want to explore their skills, talents, and tastes. Being a wonderful person in the eyes of others is important, but that can't happen without first feeling that way about yourself.

Love is a combination of feelings, tender gestures, emotions, and projects. It inspires growth and elevation. It exalts generosity, sharing, and respect. Limits and fears fade away. The other person's comfort is so powerful that outside events have less and less influence over the two lovers. Quarrels and material difficulties become less and less important every day. Love allows you to put the hardships of life into perspective. The turbulence of love reaches the inner depths of a person. People in love flee from uncomfortable situations, negative people, or destabilizing environments. These transformations create a new inner energy that radiates outward. It is said that lovers have stars in their eyes. Love is joy.

Individual strength, in addition to a couple's strength, increases fusional energy, allowing you to start new projects with someone else, transcend everyday life, and experience true happiness.

Love has no frontier or age limit and doesn't depend upon logic or reproductive instincts. Loving your children is natural. And yet, some parents don't love their children, while some adoptive parents feel great love for their non-biological children. Love escapes reason, which is why it can accomplish miracles. Many people have seen their existence transform because of a romantic encounter.

2 - The Love of the Angels

According to Biblical tradition, God conceived the angels on the second day of Creation. God gave them a specific mission by organizing the celestial world into a three-tiered hierarchy with nine choirs of angels. The angels of love are very numerous, and belong to different choirs of angels or archangels. Some are very highly ranked in the celestial hierarchy, like Seraphiel or Cherubiel, from the Seraphim and Cherubim order, the two closest orders to the Creator. Others belong to choirs of angels closer to the terrestrial plane. The closer an angel is to the terrestrial plane, the easier it is to contact them, since their vibration is lower than the great archangels that surround God and watch over the divine throne.

The angels have an immense task, since they are in charge of watching over the love, emotions, and generosity of humans. Increased awareness of the presence of angels that exists today is no coincidence. It's God's will to help the growing human population evolve, and learn to respect and love one another.

The source of angelic love comes directly from God. This love is absolutely pure. The angels that radiate this wonderful love distribute it abundantly. All requests concerning romantic relationships or the meeting of a soul mate are fulfilled by the angels, who want to make you happy more than anything. God's love contributes to the emotional and spiritual elevation of all beings that wish to open themselves up and make progress toward strength and joy.

Angelic assistance is manifested at every level: in the love between spouses, family love, or the love between two people. The love of the angels is an unconditional love and its results always go beyond expectations. It's not recommended to use the angels' love against a person's will, or to attract love from someone who doesn't want to commit themselves to you. In this case, angelic gifts may turn against you. The person who you wish to seduce may disappear from your environment and you will be forever attached to them through a burning and destructive passion. The love of angels, if used with respect, produces miracles. Love triumphs in every situation.

Some people have asked me to work with the angels of love to restore harmony to their relationship. They made altars and said prayers, and the results of their solicitations were extraordinary. Couples that felt profound and sincere love for one another came together as if it was the first day that they met, while couples that couldn't admit that they didn't love each other anymore or never loved each other at all, made their peace and broke up. Everyone found balance, and the majority of them found a partner. Angels dictate neither law nor morality; it's their love that is right and that has right consequences.

3 - Illumination Ritual of Seraphiel
(Approximately 40 minutes)

This ritual puts you in touch with the radiant vibration of Seraphiel's love. It should be performed in a ceremonial manner with great respect for the archangel. You should be alone in a meditation room where you won't be disturbed.

You can ask the archangel anything of importance to you regarding the field of love. You can request to meet your soul mate, to experience a sentimental relationship, or to feel passion. You can also ask to inspire love in the person you like, or to recover emotionally from a painful relationship, break up, or mourning period. You can also ask for them to open your heart to love, to heal you from old wounds, to find hope in love, or to be trusting. Seraphiel encourages the renewal of love through the elevation of the spirit and the soul. Seraphiel sends the love that's asked of him. Don't hesitate to ask for a lot. Receive his compassion and goodness. Seraphiel will cover you with love and will accomplish miracles in your life.

Material

- *Comfortable white clothes*

- *A meditation cushion*

- *A seraphinite gemstone (optional)*

- *A white candle on a white or silver candlestick*

- *Four pillar white candles*

- *A white or transparent chalice filled with cooking salt*

- *A white or transparent chalice filled with water*

- *A white rose*

- *A stick of myrrh incense*

Meditation

1. It's best to purify yourself by taking a shower before the meditation.
2. Wear white clothes.
3. Burn the incense.
4. Place the four white candles to form a 3 by 3 foot square. Place the candlestick with the white candle inside the square, facing north. Leave the matchbox by this candle.
5. If you have a seraphinite, place it in front of the candlestick.
6. Place the chalice filled with cooking salt to the right of the candlestick. Place the chalice filled with water to the left of the candlestick.
7. Place the meditation cushion in the center of the square.
8. Pluck the petals off of the rose and place them in the shape of a corolla

around the candlestick.

9. When you light the candle, you will be connected to Seraphiel. (Don't light it before being ready to enter into the archangel's energy.)

10. Sit down on the meditation cushion. Light the four candles of the square. Take in three big breaths and then exhale as deeply as you can.

11. Relax. Let Seraphiel's angelic energy inundate you slowly. You feel a sensation of peace and well-being. You feel at ease, but your heart increases its beating.

12. Light the candle in the candlestick. Close your eyes.

13. You are in Seraphiel's vibration of love. You feel as though you're floating. Seraphiel's light envelops you in a shining white aura like a diamond.

14. Burning hot wings envelop your body. You feel safe, you are loved, you are helped.

15. Your heart is beating very fast. Seraphiel's energy of love enters through the higher Chakra in the center of your head. You are illuminated from the inside. You shine with the force of a thousand fires. You are transformed into light. Your closed eyes are blinded by your own light.

16. Let the light act. Let Seraphiel's love act as much as you need it to. Enjoy this wonderful moment.

17. The light fades. It goes out softly. Once you've regained your bodily senses, open your eyes.

18. Put out the candle in the candlestick.

19. Slowly regain normal consciousness.

Effects of the Ritual

This highly spiritual ritual is for anyone who wants to meet their soul mate or have a romantic encounter. It's recommended for people coming out of a painful relationship or who can't get over a death.

4 - Angels and Emotion

Emotions are the most beautiful and most elevated feelings felt by human beings. To achieve personal fulfillment, it's necessary to express one's emotions. Pent up emotion creates inner pain that can bring about sickness and psychological disorders. The angels' help is essential for the expression of emotion. Angels are creatures of love and light. They feel the highest emotion of absolute and unconditional love for human beings, and this love is radiant and infinite. The unconditional love of angels emanates from the Creator, which is why it's reassuring and protective. Men must follow the angels' example by elevating the quality of their spirituality and feelings.

Making others happy brings great good, and those who give benefit just as much as those who receive. The angels are prepared to show us the way, and to guide us on our path toward generosity, sharing, and love.

Liberating your emotions transforms your way of acting and thinking. People who open themselves to emotion are more prone to giving compliments, smiling, and expressing their satisfaction and admiration for others. By doing this, your joy in life increases, your health improves, and your relationships with others can be harmonious and happy.

5 - Meditation to Liberate Your Emotions
(Approximately 20 minutes)

This meditation puts you in touch with angelic energy, and its benefits are immediate.

Material

- *Two silver candles.*

- *Two golden candles.*

- *Incense sticks: copal, jasmine, olibanum, myrrh.*

- *A white chalice filled with water.*

- *Cooking salt.*

- *A meditation cushion.*

Meditation

1. Make yourself comfortable in a calm and quiet room.
2. Make a large circle of cooking salt on the floor. Outside of the circle, light the incense and put down the chalice filled with water.
3. On the inside of the circle, place the silver candles to the west and to the north, and the golden candles to the south and to the east.
4. Put a white cushion in the center of this square of candles, which you will sit on during the meditation.
5. Breathe slowly. Begin general relaxation.
6. Call upon an angel of love (see *Find Love with the Angels*, page 145), or if you prefer, your guardian angel.

Holy angel (call him by name)

Open my heart,

Liberate my emotions,

I shall be eternally grateful,

Let it be accomplished.

7. Visualize your heart opening up like a green lotus with 12 petals. Let the angelic vibration enter into you. Feel the beneficent warmth and the white light illuminating the heart Chakra. Enjoy this privileged moment with your angel.
8. Breathe slowly. Regain ordinary consciousness.

Effects of the Meditation

By connecting us with the angels of love, this meditation opens the door to our heart and makes us aware of the infinite love of the Creator, which remains in us even though it's all too often repressed.

The meditation to liberate your emotions is recommended for shy, overly anxious, or introverted people who lack self-confidence. It's also recommended for anyone who represses their emotions.

6 – *Meditation to Chase Away Negative Emotions*

(Approximately 20 minutes)

Chasing away negative emotions that weaken energy will allow you to take control of yourself and the direction of your life. This meditation provides an indispensable cleansing of negativity. The successive layers of past suffering and old traumatisms are extenuated over the course of the meditations. Angels bring solid support and a will to persevere throughout these active changes, which open up new perspectives of the future. Meditation séances are genuinely therapeutic. The angels help us let go of fear, anxiety, sadness or grief. Invoking them brings great comfort and the strength to deal with the most difficult situations.

Material

- *Two white candles.*

- *Two purple candles.*

- *A piece of white cotton with seven drops of Vetiver essential oil.*

- *Copal, camphor, nag champa, or sage incense.*

- *Cooking salt.*

- *A white pillow.*

Meditation

1. Make yourself comfortable in a quiet and calm room.

2. Make a large circle on the floor with the cooking salt. On the outside of the circle, light the incense and put down the cotton dipped in Vetiver essential oil.

3. On the inside of the circle, place the white candles to the east and to the south, and the purple candles to the north and to the west.

4. Put a white cushion in the center of this square of candles, which you will sit on during the meditation.

5. Call upon the angel of mercy (see *The Angel That You Need*, page 553), or your guardian angel, and say:

> Holy angel (call him by name)

Cleanse my heart of negative feelings

And emotions that bring me pain,

Let the light of love and hope shine in my heart.

I shall be eternally grateful,

Amen.

6. Picture your heart as a lotus with 12 green petals that are opening slowly. Take deep breaths and exhale vigorously.

7. A cloud of black dust is released from your heart, and rises toward the sky.

8. The lotus of your heart closes slowly.

9. Breathe slowly. Take a rest.

10. Regain ordinary consciousness.

Effects of the Meditation

The benefits of this meditation are immediate. Negative feelings are stomped out, and fear and anxiety are quickly extenuated.

If you're going through a difficult time in your life, it's recommended that you do this meditation three times a week, on Monday, Wednesday, and Saturday.

This meditation is for anyone who feels fear and anxiety, or for pessimistic people who lack hope.

7 - Developing Self-esteem with the Angels

It's difficult to love a person if you don't love yourself. When we expect love from others, or hope that they will give us what we need, we enter into the illusion of a romantic relationship. The other person will not relieve our anxieties or heal us of our emotional problems. Understanding this is important in order to ask the angels for the emotional healing necessary to begin a new relationship.

Having a lover or soul mate is a gift. Romantic relationships are a celebration of joy and happiness. People are often disappointed by love because they hope to meet an extraordinary person with all the qualities they find desirable. But it's unlikely to meet someone like that if you aren't an irreproachable person yourself. Before asking the angels for a romantic encounter, first ask yourself whether you're ready to begin a new relationship.

The love of the angels makes miracles happen, but these miracles will come much quicker if you are ready to experience them. Often, fear inhibits emotions and relationships that started out with excellent prospects end with aggressive reproaches. Sometimes, the two lovers are selfish out of fear of losing their identity. In certain cases, jealousy alters beauty and love. Other times, envy and attachment to material goods can disrupt a relationship.

The angels help us become aware of what we really are so that we can have a happy and fulfilling relationship. How can we bring happiness to a relationship if we are morose and depressed? How can we give love if we lack self-confidence, are insecure, and shy? How can we share our emotions when our hearts are empty and sad? We can only give what we have. It seems inconsiderate to dream of love when we feel self-hatred or when we aren't satisfied with the way we look. Self-confidence is the key to finding love. Love increases this confidence, but without a solid foundation, everything will one day crumble. Having a successful romantic relationship or marriage depends upon your own self-esteem. Whatever childhood handicaps or emotional problems you may have, it's always possible to discover the love of life and self-esteem by working with angels. Let me remind you that the angels are our best friends, our advisors, and our guides. Their mission is to make us feel love and happiness.

Angels of love are the most powerful angels. They contribute to individual elevation in order to increase the vibratory rate of humanity. The main mission God entrusted to the angels is to transmit love and make it circulate like energy. Summon the angels of love. Solicit their precious help to learn how to love yourself. This self-love begins by respecting what you are and wanting to improve yourself. Start by accepting yourself as you are. Look at your qualities instead of worrying about your faults. Focus on everything that is positive in you.

Zarubiel is the holy angel of Beauty. The very few people who have seen him are really blessed. His supernatural beauty and the diamonds on his wings are absolutely amazing. He is very close to God and his immense power does miracles. You can pray Zarubiel and perform this ritual if you desperately feel that you will never find love. Zarubiel will enlighten your beauty and your seduction and you will find love within a couple a months.

8 - *Ritual of Zarubiel's Beauty*
(Approximately 20 minutes)

Don't eat for two hours before performing this ritual: you will feel more free and lighter with an empty stomach. This is a good moment to work on your physique. Performing this ritual in the middle of the afternoon is preferable. Avoid periods of darkness.

Material

- *A round mirror*

- *A few drops of your favorite perfume*

- *A pink rose*

- *A white candle*

- *A stick of jasmine incense*

- *A piece of non-lined paper, cut into squares*

- *A black pen*

- *A pink ribbon*

Ritual

1. Light the candle and burn the incense.

2. It's best if you place your material on a table. You will sit in front of this table. Start by plucking the petals off of the rose. Place these petals around the mirror (which should be standing up vertically) where you

can see your face. Keep one petal and crush it between your fingers to perfume your hands.

3. Pour seven drops of your favorite perfume onto the paper.

4. Look at your face in the mirror and contemplate for a few minutes. Quietly ask Zarubiel to make your inner beauty appear on your face. Close your eyes for one or two minutes. Empty your spirit.

5. Open your eyes. You will find that your face has changed. Your eyes are brighter, and your traits are softer. You like what you are.

6. Thank Zarubiel.

7. Grab the pen and write the following words onto the piece of paper:

> Holy archangel Zarubiel
>
> I'm committing myself to preserve my shine and radiance,
>
> I'm committing myself to perfect my inner and outer beauty,
>
> I'm committing myself to staying in good health.
>
> I thank you for helping me be self-confident,
>
> For helping me respect and love myself for the love of my
>
> soul mate,
>
> Let it be so.

8. Roll up the piece of paper. Seal it with hot wax from the white candle, and then wrap it with the pink ribbon.

Keep the scroll near you, in the drawer of your nightstand, in your desk, or any other personal place. This document is a commitment that you took with Zarubiel: respect it. After a few weeks of taking particular care of yourself, you will receive compliments from your family, your friends, and you will be ready to live better. After performing this ritual, you can also pray to Zarubiel regularly and thank him.

You can also get in touch with Zarubiel at sunrise, when rising energies stimulate nature.

This prayer will help you establish a broad relationship with the angel of beauty. Through the energy of Zarubiel's love, you will receive advice on how to improve your physical appearance and how to value your beauty. Zarubiel is an angel of great beauty. His wings are extraordinarily white and shine as if they were covered in diamonds.

9 - Prayer to Zarubiel

Holy archangel Zarubiel,

Let my inner beauty show itself,

Open up my heart so that my beauty can radiate,

Make my traits smooth and embellish my face.

Advise me on how to dress in harmony with who I am,

Help me emphasize my body's attractive traits and respect my health.

I'm committing myself to celebrate my beauty and well-being,

Let it be so.

10 - How the Angels Help You Find Love

When we connect with angels, our anxieties and fears diminish, and existential questions fade away behind the certainty of being loved by angels and by God. We start to feel the security of angelic love. Events in our life are beyond control. We entrust our destiny to angels through effort and action in the spirit of elevation. The famous adage "Help yourself, and Heaven will help you" reflects the absolute reality of the relation between humans and angels. The more positively you act, the more the angels will become your allies, your friends, and most of all, your guides.

When you start feeling angelic love, your existence changes completely. Every thought for the angels, every ritual performed with faith, and every prayer will bring you closer to angelic energy and make you feel the love and protection of angels. Love is a synonym for security, which is why asking for and accepting the love of angels will bring you security. By opening your heart to them, angels will lead you on the path of your greatest destiny. Accept their gifts with faith: don't doubt their interventions. Sometimes, the first manifestations of angels can create stress for certain people. This stress comes from the presence of the supernatural in a rational universe. Rest assured, you will quickly become accustomed to receiving angelic messages.

11 – How Do Angels of Love Materialize?

1. Through a Loving Presence:

- *You feel a hand resting on your shoulder.*

- *You find a white feather.*

- *You feel a very pleasant breeze.*

- *You feel safe, even under stressful conditions.*

- *You feel a sensation of inner peace.*

- *You feel light and joyful.*

- *You radiate happiness for no particular reason.*

- *You feel a tingling in your hands or body while also feeling a sensation of well-being.*

2. Through Your Feeling of Openness and Your Desire to Love:

- *You are animated with a supernatural energy that helps you move forward in life.*

- *Your desire to love makes you want to tackle life head-on.*

- *You feel your heart getting bigger every time you think about love.*

- *You feel a sensation of openness at the top of your skull.*

- *You visualize the person you are going to love.*

- *You have the same dream about love several times.*

- *Images of your future life with the person you will love overwhelm your spirit.*

- *Intuition pushes you to do things that surprise you.*

3. Through an Encounter:
- *An incredible and unexpected situation triggers your encounter with your soul mate.*

- *Exceptional circumstances allow you to meet a person who seduces you.*

- *You change environment or work, leading you to meet the person you will share your life with.*

- *A friend suddenly becomes a love interest.*

- *You unexpectedly find your soul mate while traveling.*

- *The unplanned change of a project allows you to find love.*

Angels generally manifest themselves in unexpected ways. They can shake up your life by letting you meet your soul mate or the person you will share your life with in just a few minutes. Their appearance in your existence is a source of joy. Don't ever forget to thank them.

Make your requests for love clear. The angels won't know how to make you happy if you aren't precise. Create a sketch or portrait of the person you wish to meet. Make your explanation to the angels simple and concise, whether you want to experience a beautiful love story, whether you wish to meet your soul mate, or whether you simply want to have an adventure. The angels don't require a lifelong commitment. Their main preoccupation is to make you happy and to help you make progress. Someone who wants to have love affairs isn't ready to experience long-lasting love. Angels will lead that type of person toward people that will foster psychological and spiritual evolution.

Angelic interventions are always beneficial for you, simply trust them and call upon them, they will bring you love and happiness!

12 - Meeting Your Soul Mate Through Angels

Many people dream of meeting their soul mate. But who exactly is this soul mate that haunts your days and nights? Who is this mysterious person you will want to share a romantic and passionate life with? You may sometimes ask yourself whether meeting this person is just a fantasy or a dream. Do soul mates really exist? How can we recognize them? How can we find them? Is there a specific age to meet them?

Yes, soul mates exist. Yes, there is someone on Earth who was made for you. Yes, there is someone who feels the same emotions and desires as you, and who shares the same dreams as you. And yet, this person may be very different from you, and they may live on the other side of the world, making it even less likely for you to come together. The probability of meeting your soul mate at a time and location that's convenient for you is very small. This is why it's very rare for people to meet their soul mates, and why many people simply don't believe in soul mates.

Another problem with meeting your soul mate is that people aren't always ready to commit to lifelong love. It all depends on personal evolution. People whose personalities have been developed very young are more apt to have a precocious encounter with their soul mate. Others need to experiment in life. This condition also applies to your soul mate, making this special encounter all the more random.

But how can we recognize our soul mates? Through a flash of intuition. An encounter with a soul mate provokes a feeling of physical discomfort, cold sweats, or shaking. These manifestations accompany an absolute and irrational certainty of having met your other half. Your soul mate feels the same sensations as you. This supernatural emotion is bewildering and one's next action depends upon one's circumstances. Nonetheless, a feeling of certainty remains. Soul mates don't waste their chance encounters: they must make it happen.

The person that suits you the most in the world is in complete harmony with your emotions, your most secret desires, and even your dreams. They know how to read you, just as you know how to read them. And so, both of your books must be open at the same time if you want the encounter to happen. The challenges and the seemingly random nature of a reunion with your soul mate discourage many people in search of their other half. Fantasies about meeting a soul mate end up becoming regular romantic relationships.

But rest assured, if you feel a profound desire to find your soul mate and to share your life with them, and if you're ready, don't hesitate to solicit the angels. They will fulfill your wish and your existence will be forever changed.

People who live with their soul mates can testify to the absolute beauty of this love, which lasts beyond death. There's no need to demonstrate their happiness. Through their love, they have transcended. They are radiant and their love is reflected around them.

Fortunately, angels encourage us to look for our better half because, through this discovery, we become happy and filled with joy. Angels are not afraid of the low probabilities of meeting a soul mate, or the limits and fears of humans: they are clairvoyant. Through their extraordinary knowledge of souls, they can access everyone's will and desires, and determine whether people are sincere in their quest. They enjoy changing a person's destiny, if that's what they truly want. So, if you really want to meet your soul mate, don't hesitate to call upon the angels. Ask them to set you up with an encounter, and the miracle will happen!

13 – How to Meet Your Soul Mate

Meeting your soul mate can't be prepared. Certain circumstances, or coincidences, often present themselves when you least expect them to. But this magical encounter with a soul mate will happen quicker and more comfortably if you just let go, and if you are confident and relaxed. Anyone can meet their other half if they truly want to. Angels always encourage love and provoke situations favorable to its development. They will support you one hundred percent as long as your request isn't merely the result of an emotional need or the pain of feeling lonely. Meeting your soul mate is a gift that comes when you are truly ready, in other words when you have positive energy, without expectations or requirements.

Here is a list of advice for meeting your soul mate:

- *The angels to invoke are:*

- *Anael*

- *Raphael*

- *Seraphiel*

- *Metatron*

- *Cherubiel*

- *Pick the angel you feel most comfortable with and invoke him every night before going to bed and in the morning when you wake up.*

- *Be open-minded.*

- *Be tolerant and bear no judgment.*

- *Don't be afraid of meeting a person whose origins, social status, or nationality doesn't correspond to what you imagined.*

- *Make a physical portrait of your soul mate. You can't love a person you aren't attracted to!*

- *Don't picture the encounter.*

- *Let yourself go: don't think about the encounter too much.*

- *Live happily and without expectations: sadness or impatience blocks energies.*

- *Enjoy life.*

- *Mind your physical appearance.*

- *And most of all, be confident and have faith in the angels.*

It's essential that you prepare yourself for the encounter with your soul mate by embodying an atmosphere of positive energy. In a certain way, meeting your soul mate is like two magnets coming together. Think about this image; it will help you enter into the energy of the encounter. You will attract your other half if you are charming and seductive. Everyone is capable of seducing their soul mate. This other soul was made for you. Don't wait for your clone or double. Your soul mate is a mirror image of your emotions, not your way of life or way of thinking. You are unique, and so is your soul mate. Everyone possesses an individuality that must be recognized. Respect yourself as much as you respect your other half. Stay what you are: don't change for the sake of pleasing someone else. Stay seductive, beautiful, happy, and trust the angels. Your soul mate will be attracted to you because you correspond to what they are and what they feel. A stranger can sometimes throw you off because of their differences. Being open-minded and tolerant is recommended in order to accept this stranger inhabited by the soul of your other half.

Don't try and calculate the probabilities of meeting this person. Take your mind off of the encounter. Be in a good mood. Be simple, natural, and seductive. Your seductiveness and attraction will come from your lightheartedness and the concern your have for your appearance. Keep the angels' love in your heart and let your inner beauty shine.

Think of how invaluable love is. The word is so strong that language has no other equivalent; there is only one word to express it. Love is unique and includes all the qualities of the human soul. It surpasses the limits of reason and logic. Wanting to meet your soul mate means committing yourself to a powerful energy of the celestial vibration, one inspired by angels.

The following ritual solicits angels to help you meet your soul mate. It increases your receptiveness to the powerful energies of love. I recommend performing it four times. The first time, do it on the eve of a full moon to make use of rising energies. The other days can be chosen at your convenience, depending on your spirit's openness and availability. Don't perform this ritual if you are tired, demoralized, or troubled with doubt. This ritual is a highly magical operation. It will not comfort or reassure you. It's active and effective in guiding you toward your other half. You should be ready to experience this love. It grants access to the angelic vibratory plane and to the mysteries of eternal love.

14 - Ritual to Meet Your Soul Mate

(Approximately 20 minutes)

It's recommended that you purify yourself by taking a shower before the ritual. Wash your hair. Do your hair. Look your best. If you can, wear white clothes. You will invoke five great archangels and you must show respect and admiration. Be seductive and attractive, as you would be on the day of your encounter with your soul mate.

Material

- *An altar*

- *A stick of jasmine incense*

- *A pink candle*

- *Four white candles*

- *A red rose*

- *A drawing with two stars (you and your soul mate)*

- *A piece of white fabric measuring approximately 12 by 12 inches*

- *A white or transparent chalice filled with cooking salt*

- *Five pieces of white non-lined paper*

- *A black pen*

Ritual

1. After you're dressed, showered, perfumed, and your hair is done, write the archangels' name on each piece of paper. Archangel Anael, Archangel Cherubiel, Archangel Seraphiel, Archangel Raphael, Archangel Metatron.

2. Stretch out the white fabric over the altar.

3. Make the following shape by placing the archangels names in the following manner:

Archangel Seraphiel   Archangel Metatron

Archangel Raphael   Archangel Cherubiel

Archangel Anael

4. Place a white candle under each name, except for Anael, who gets the pink candle.

5. Place the two drawings or photos of stars under Anael's name.

6. Pluck the petals off of the red rose and place them around the two stars in the shape of a heart.

7. Burn the incense.

8. Place the chalice filled with cooking salt to the right of the altar.

9. Light the candles.

10. Stand up in front of the angelic shape that you just made, with your palms against each other over your heart in a position of prayer. Invoke the angels by saying their names aloud in the following order: Very holy archangel Seraphiel, very holy archangel Metatron, very holy archangel Raphael, very holy archangel Cherubiel, very holy archangel Anael, and then say:

> Very holy archangels,
> Watch over me,
> Open up my heart to my soul mate's love,
> Open up my soul mate's heart to love,
> Let love reunite us,
> Let our love last forever,
> Protect us,
> Give us your infinite love,
> Let happiness and joy radiate in our hearts,
> I shall be eternally grateful,
> Amen.

11. Reunite the two stars and place your open palms over them. Inhale the angelic energy, and then exhale slowly.

12. Keep your hands above the stars and say the following words:

May the very holy archangels Seraphiel, Metatron, Cherubiel, Raphael, and

Anael bless these two beings who will love each other forever.

13. Now open your palms and turn them toward the sky, in a sign of offering. Thank the archangels by saying the following words:

Very holy archangels,

I shall be eternally grateful.

At the end of this ritual, I advise you to drink verbena or linden tea, and then take a rest.

15 - Achieving Happiness in your Love Life Through the Angels

How to make love last?

Most people in love ask the same questions concerning the length of love. Following the joy of the first encounter, the excitement of the first dates, and the exaltation of emotion and physical love, a real relationship starts to take form. This foundational step in the relationship is a delicate moment that is often marred by tension, conflicting opinions, or adaptation issues. In this case, the angels' help can be invaluable. You can consult them to ask for help or judicious advice.

For other couples, starting a new life together is a happy and joyous time. Yet, problems can come up in everyday life or in the pursuit of building a life together. The angels help is also very valuable in this case.

The length of a relationship depends on how much each person is invested, as well as their willingness to make it last. Angels are of remarkable assistance when it comes to two people in search of a strong relationship where love, tolerance, and mutual respect are common goals.

No one is perfect, and sometimes one person in a relationship feels fragile because of family, professional, or health problems. The couple's balance risks being disrupted. The person without problems must show compassion and tolerance to support the other person during this difficult time. Too often, couples break up because of these unfortunate circumstances. Summoning the angels in moments like these will allow you to surmount any obstacle and to rebuild long-lasting happiness.

Sometimes, couples are torn apart because of one of the partners' infidelity. The appropriate thing to do here is to evaluate the situation. If a lack of love provoked this infidelity, it's best to end the relationship. The decision to stick together often isn't motivated by love, but by the fear of being alone, fear of abandonment, or a profound feeling of insecurity. In some cases, infidelity is caused by one of the two partners' particularly unpleasant behavior. In spite of being in love, frustration and deception provoke the desire to find pleasure and joy elsewhere. Angels help these couples rebalance their energies and find harmony. They resuscitate their love through forgiveness and understanding of each others' mistakes.

Below I unveil several angelic guidelines inspired directly by angels on how to make love last. Then, I propose doing an angelic ceremony with the person you love. It deals with any relationship problems, allowing you to rediscover love, harmony, and happiness, providing that both partners are genuinely willing to make things work. Angels will restore joy, desire, and passion to the relationship. They will resolve conflicts and bring fulfillment to the couple. You will rediscover the desire to love, to give, and to share while staying what you are.

- *Ask yourself what you really want from the relationship.*

- *Be yourself around your lover.*

- *Establish an atmosphere of reciprocal trust.*

- *Talk about each other's desires and expectations.*

- *Preserve the secret garden of personal consciousness.*

- *Consider the relationship a source of fulfillment.*

- *Don't consider the relationship a source of constraint.*

- *Respect each other's freedom and do as you wish.*

- *Consider daily life the foundation for joy and surprises in the relationship.*

- *Avoid repetitive activities. Avoid fixed days or times for certain activities.*

- *Accept the idea of change: change of a location, of a house, of work, or of personal activities.*

- *Don't get lost in material concerns; always prioritize emotion, happiness, and the joy of being together.*

- *Daily life must be peppered with laughter, humor, and self-mockery.*

- *Don't take yourself seriously, but take your relationship seriously.*

- *Invoke the angels as soon as conflict erupts.*

- *In times of conflict, never attack your lover. Start by listening to them.*

- *Express your desires and unveil your dreams.*

- *Associate your lover with your desires and dreams.*

- *Don't base yourself in social or ideological molds. Angels recommend awakening your consciousness by letting your behavior and way of thinking evolve.*

- *Make progress through curiosity.*

- *Show interest in your lover and their life.*

- *Express your emotions through tender gestures, affection, and terms of endearment.*

- *Don't let the emotional attachment to your lover weaken.*

- *The true reason for living is to be loved.*

- *Open your heart to love.*

- *Accept angelic gifts and your partner's generosity.*

- *Give and receive.*

16 - Let Romance into Your Life

Happy couples don't let boring routines or rigorous habits invade their lives. Love is never fully acquired. Love is never an absolute certainty. Before adding romance to your life, know that love between two beings is a powerful and lively energy. Respect this energy as if it were a person.

LOVE IS A PERSON

You don't want to hurt the people you love. Don't hurt your relationship. Keep in mind that your partner deserves the best of you. Respect this person who makes you happy; they are worthy of your esteem. Never inflict upon them what you wouldn't want to experience yourself.

LOVE IS A FIRE

Love is burning, wonderful, and passionate, but it needs energy in order to grow. The more emotion you put into love, the more it will develop. A fire needs wood to remain ablaze, or else it goes out, just like love. When two people love each other, their love is a vibrant and active energy. Love is a flame that feeds off of energy, generous actions, and tender gestures. When we are in love, we show it, we say it, we express it. Tell the person you love how important they are to you. Tell them that you are by their side, that you will always support them. Reassure them by showing your love, and the sparkle of your sensibility and sensuality. Remember that a great blaze is preferred over a few embers dying out.

LOVE IS WATER

Love is a current that changes from one day to the next. This is why routine is not beneficial to love. Picture your love as a river. Do you want to throw trash in it and pollute it? Imagine swimming in this water every day; the more pure and transparent it becomes, the warmer it becomes, the more you want to swim in it. Don't pollute your water with negative thoughts, envy, jealousy, or intolerance. The more vinegar you put into your water, the harder it becomes to drink! Don't quench your thirst with dirty swamp water. Don't transform your love into a marsh. Don't let a situation or conflict rot. Deal with problems right away. Puncture the abscess. Know that in times of disagreement you must clean up whatever is wrong. Water is fragile. The dead leaves of your conflicts can muddy your relationship. Having a civil discussion will preserve the clarity and beauty of your love.

LOVE IS A BEAUTIFUL DWELLING PLACE

Love is not representative of danger, uncertainty, or abandonment. Love is wonderful. If you are in a beautiful relationship, you have nothing to fear. The only danger lies in thinking about danger. When you live in a beautiful house, you enjoy it with your friends and family. You aren't obsessed with the risk of a fire, flooding, or theft. Your beautiful interior and the pleasure you share in your house with the people you love is always greater than your fears. The same goes for love. Fears kill love and emotion. Put an end to your fears. Admire love. Enjoy the good times, and anything that brings pleasure, like when you make use of a beautiful house in the winter by sitting up close to the fireplace, or in the summer by sprawling out on a sun chair. Love is the beautiful dwelling place of your emotions.

LOVE IS AN ANGEL

The wonderful relationship you maintain with your partner resembles an angel. It gives you wings, stimulates your emotions, and fulfills you. Picture it resembling an angel. Would you hurt an angel? Would you disrespect an angel? Do you think an angel can hurt you? The suffering caused by love often comes from a lack of faith in love.

True love is a positive energy. And like all positive energy, it grows, it rises, it increases in beauty and happiness. Throw yourself into the reality of love by getting rid of your prejudice, your fear, and your past experiences. Don't taint an angel's wings with soot. Don't blacken an angel's purity.

Know that the wonderful love growing inside you is protected by angels. Open your arms and receive the love of your celestial companions.

17 - Always Romantic

Being romantic should not last for just a few days, a few weeks, or a few years. Romanticism is an emotional state of openness to the beauty of love.

Romantic people love softness, tenderness, and the most elegant manifestation of love. Romanticism comes from a current of thought at the beginning of the XIX century, when writers began praising the classic values of ancient civilizations. Painters went along with the literary movement, and became passionate about the melancholic beauty of ancient ruins. Ironically, this return to the past brought about a revolution to the traditional conception of society. The new cult of beauty transcended artists and writers. Romanticism became a new way of behaving in society. The romantics realized that beyond beauty lies moral, psychological, and emotional grandeur, and thus romanticism celebrates grandeur in all forms.

The quest for grandeur is a search for self-elevation through consciousness. It's also the emphasis of personal qualities, the improvement of physical traits, and the search for a beautiful kind of emotion. Romantic lovers look for the beautiful qualities of love and the most beautiful manifestations of this love in life.

Without romanticism, without a desire for grandeur and beauty, love remains at the same level of where it started. It doesn't grow: it stagnates. Remember that love is also water, and that stagnant water always goes bad. So don't let your love decompose; be romantic! Angels are romantic creatures. They express the beauty and grandeur of love. When you are in the angelic vibration, you shall receive the gifts of celestial love. You are open and desire elevation. In your eyes, the person you love is the most beautiful person in the world, and you feel the desire to make them even more wonderful through your emotions and acts of tenderness, which they will return to you. People with true and profound love get a fair exchange. Be a true romantic and you will see your love increase each day.

Don't forget that the angels will always support you when you experience love and let it grow.

Chapter 9

Enhance your Energy with the Angels

Working with angels brings comfort, the taste for life, and the energy to work, to be happy, and to make others happy. It will never be said enough how strong the power of love is.

1 - Raising the Vibratory Rate

The highest choirs of the celestial hierarchy are close enough to God to surround his throne and receive his light. The choirs of the intermediate hierarchy receive light from the angels closest to God, who teach the archangels and the angels. The structure and essence of the celestial hierarchy is divine love incarnate. Upon entering into divine consciousness, your prayers, rituals, and meditations will connect you to the angels. The energy of earth is beautiful, and necessary for equilibrium. But celestial energy encourages you to elevate your consciousness and spirit; it gives you wings that enable you to reach the angelic plane.

2 - How to Raise Your Vibratory Rate

Start by cleaning up the whole house. Give away the objects you no longer like or the ones that have been given to you by people you no longer see. An object carries the energy of the person who bought it or gave it away. Dust off the furniture. Fix any objects in bad condition, or simply get rid of them. Connecting to the angels is an opportunity to put your house back in order. Make sure you air out the rooms, and let a breeze circulate.

If the energies in your home have been blocked for a long time, and in spite of all the purifications, you still find the atmosphere heavy, you can cleanse it with sound; sound dissolves blocked energies. Use instruments that make pure sound to proceed with the sanitization. You can use Tibetan singing bowls, gongs, drums, small bells, or Tingsha.

Tingsha
These little Tibetan cymbals are particularly recommended for cleaning places with stagnant energy. Let them ring in all four corners of each room.

Tibetan Singing Bowls
The sound produced by these bowls and their wooden stick has the power to connect you to the celestial planes. They must be made according to the rules of Eastern tradition. They are composed of seven metals: gold, silver, iron, lead, tin, mercury, and copper.

Gongs
These much appreciated instruments of the East are good for chasing negative energies away from a place. The vibrations and resonance they emit can penetrate objects, walls, and the air. They are excellent purifiers of places that have been polluted with negative or stagnant energy.

Drums
Drums create the sound of the pulsating Earth connecting to the Universe. When you clean your house with the sound of a drum, you awaken dormant energies.

Musical instruments are an excellent way to purify space. Once you've finished cleaning your environment, proceed with personal purification. To do this, you must take a shower and get dressed in comfortable white clothes.

Incense

Burning incense in the room where you will perform the ritual is also recommended. Sanctuary incense are especially well adapted for the purification of a place. In addition, you can use gum Arabic or acacia, which chases away negative waves, and rose incense.

Candles

White candles are required for the purification of a place. Place a white candle in the room where you will perform your angelic rituals. Let it burn until the wick goes out. Don't blow it out. White candles cleanse a place of negative vibrations after they've burn out entirely. Remember to air out the room after burning the candle. Never leave an open flame unattended.

It's important not to blow out the flame of a candle, which establishes the connection between the terrestrial plane and the angelic plane. Using a snuffer is preferable for all rituals involving candles.

To raise the vibratory rate, begin by cleansing a place and then open up your spirit and availability, which will prevent the mind from preying upon you. Relaxation techniques will help you loosen your body, let go of your thoughts, and prepare yourself for angelic connection.

3 - Balancing Yin and Yang

Stress, anxiety, and the requirements of contemporary society often provoke inner imbalances between masculine and feminine polarities. The Chinese yin-yang symbol creates a universal and inseparable link between the two polarities; one cannot exist without the other and harmony is indispensable to them both. Yin is the black part, yang is the white part. The yin-yang figure symbolizes harmony between heaven and earth. The yin half has a yang circle, and the yang half has a yin circle. The complementarity and symmetry is perfect between these two opposites. The Chinese Tao interprets the yin-yang as an association between the world and the spirit. Men are yin and yang at the same time. In different moments of their existence, one or the other is predominant. Yin is the feminine side; it's dark, subconscious, and lunar. Yang is masculine; it represents day, light, and action. Yin and yang symbolize diversity and unity. Yin and yang manifest Jackson Neville's way of thinking: "From all things emanate a thousand things, and from a thousand things, there is but one." Yin and yang combine unity and totality in the most perfect complementarity. In yin and yang lies the microcosm and the macrocosm, and within it one can see the celestial plane where angels evolve and the terrestrial plane where men evolve. The Taoist symbol is the manifestation of perfection and harmony in the search for equilibrium between the masculine and the feminine.

In the Sefirot, the two angels with opposite polarities influence this effort to achieve inner balance and harmonization between the masculine and the feminine. Angel Metatron represents yin, the feminine, and angel Sandalphon represents yang, the masculine. In the Sefirotic tree, Sandalphon is associated with the Sefirah of Malkuth, the root, while Metatron is associated with the Sefirah of Keter, the crown and intersecting point between the terrestrial plane and the celestial plane.

The harmonization of polarities treatment should be done in a calm and quiet room. It's important that you aren't disturbed, because an intrusion will orient the energy toward the person who is entering into the room. It's necessary to work in a neutral energy.

4 - The Yin and Yang Balancing Treatment
(Approximately 15 minutes)
This treatment must be done in a dimly lit room that creates harmony between black and white, obscurity and day.

Material
- *A black candle.*

- *A white candle.*

- *A drawing or cut-out of the Chinese yin-yang symbol.*

• *A stick of lavender incense.*

Treatment

1. Light the candles, placing the white candle near the black side of the yin-yang symbol, and the black candle near the white side.

2. Burn the lavender incense for the purification and neutralization of the energies.

3. Sit down on a chair, with your eyes fixed upon the representation of the yin and yang. Make a right angle with your back and thighs. Place your hands on your thighs, with your palms facing the sky.

4. Breathe softly, and loosen your shoulders.

5. Stare at the yin and yang until your vision is blurred and you can't distinguish between the two opposites.

6. Breathe in angel Sandalphon's black energy, and the exhale slowly.

7. Breathe in angel Metatron's white energy, and then exhale slowly.

8. Breathe in and hold your breath to mix the energies for several seconds. Exhale.

9. Ask angel Sandalphon to anchor you into the earth.

10. Ask angel Metatron to open the gates of heaven.

11. Thank the angels.

12. Close your eyes. Open your eyes. Regain ordinary consciousness.

Effects of the Treatment

This treatment is for people who feel an imbalance of their masculine and feminine polarity.

It's recommended for men who have trouble manifesting their emotion or tenderness.

It's recommended for women who feel burdened by masculine responsibilities and who have trouble seducing and assuming their femininity or maternal instincts.

5 - *Thinking Positively with the Angels*

People who call upon the angels emit radiance and positive energy.

Their aura is luminous, their faces are young, their eyes glowing and effulgent. The presence of angels in your life transforms your way of thinking and increases your tolerance of others.

Angels are protectors, guides, advisors, or miracle-makers. Living in contact with angels requires not letting yourself being overrun by negative energies, pessimistic people, or sinister moods. It isn't always easy to escape negativity, but that is your mission with angels.

Hope, optimism, and faith in the power of angels will bring you what you want. This faith and trust you have in angels trigger more frequent angelic interventions, and miracles start to increase. A positive thought keeps you in touch with the angelic plane, and in some sort, you remain connected with the angels.

Angels help you overcome difficulties and lead you through hard times, so be grateful and thankful.

Angels are powerful, and this power is used on you. Strength and love are the main motors of the human soul (2 Timothy 1:7): "For God did not give us a spirit of fear and timidity, but a spirit of strength, love, and self-control."

Positive thoughts exalt the virtues of excellence. Working with angels will incite you to turn to situations and people that are favorable to you. Hope and desire inspired by angels will encourage you to do good in reality.

The duty of angels does not merely consist of elevating us to a vibratory plane; they also allow us to manage our lives better and offer us the kindness that we deserve. Positive thinking strengthens your energy and increases your capacity to receive angelic gifts.

The energy of angels must be used for good, and enable you to show joy and kindness to others.

6 – The Chakras of the Angels

The Chakras are energy points and psychic centers that circulate a vital force called "sukshma prana," subtle prana. The word "Chakra" is a

Sanskrit term evocative of a wheel, a circle, and movement.

The seven main Chakras turn based on our individual energy, and activate the desires linked to the particular function of each Chakra.

Each person has a predilection for a certain Chakra, which they feel more in harmony with depending on personal traits, emotions, and tastes.

The Chakras are not materialized in anatomy. They are subtle centers linked to the parasympathetic and sympathetic nervous systems. Their openness and proper functioning determines our general well-being. But it's not recommended to refer to the closest organs. These organs merely serve to situate the Chakras in specific parts of the body. They are independent of the Chakras. The Chakra meditations and angelic visualizations of these centers of energy don't reference an organ, but the corresponding Chakra, angel and colors.

The goal of working with the Chakras is to circulate an energy called "Kundalini." It's considered a vital force, the primordial energy of every human. The term "Kundalini" is often compared to a snake that is either resting or uncoiling.

In Asia, this original vital energy is considered to be a dimension of universal consciousness that each person possesses individually.

The Kundalini activates a force of action and movement that pushes people to act. While unconscious, the Kundalini is a dormant energy. Thus, it's necessary to activate it and to let it circulate in the Chakras to take full advantage of our energetic potential.

The contribution of angelic energy in the circulation of the Kundalini is essential. It amplifies the circulation of this energy, strengthens it, and increases its positive action on vitality and the love of life.

Figure 7: The Seven Chakras

7 – *The Seven Chakras and the Angels Associated with them*

First Chakra: Muladhara-Chakra – root Chakra

Position: pelvic plexus.
Color: red.
Angel: Chamuel.
Meaning of the Chakra's name: the base.
Symbolic representation: a lotus with four petals.

Locating the Root Chakra
The root Chakra is located in the pelvic plexus, between the anus and the genital organs. Red is its corresponding color.

The Angel's Power

Chamuel is one of the seven archangels of the dominations choir. He is the angel of force and energy. He contributes to anchoring people in reality, and helps them find their bearings when they are disoriented. Chamuel activates energy and vitality. He increases people's self-confidence and strengthens their will.

Meditation of the Root Chakra

(Approximately 15 minutes)

This meditation will allow you to anchor yourself in reality and face your everyday problems in life.

The meditation of the root Chakra also develops vitality, physical strength, and influences your love of life and desire to embark on new projects.

Material

- *A red candle.*

- *Caraway, carob, cardamom, or carrot incense sticks.*

Meditation

1. Light the red candle and the incense stick.
2. Sit down comfortably on a chair or a pillow, in the lotus position or cross-legged. The palms of your hands should be open on your thigh. Your thumb and index should be joined together softly.
3. Close your eyes.
4. Empty your spirit.
5. Invoke angel Chamuel.
6. Create a feeling of openness in the pelvic area.
7. Feel the warmth of the color red and the energy of the earth entering your body.
8. Let the energy act upon you.
9. Slowly regain ordinary consciousness.

Effects of the Meditation

This meditation is particularly useful for people with imbalances in their lives and who need to be anchored in reality.

It also brings strength, renewal, as well as vital and sexual energy.

Second Chakra: Svadisthana-chakra

Position: hypogastric plexus, genital organs.
Color: orange.
Angel: Jophiel.
Meaning of the Chakra's name: dwelling place of the self.
Symbolic representation: a lotus with six petals.

Locating the Second Chakra

The second Chakra is located under the belly-button, just above the sexual organs.

The Angel's Power

The name "Jophiel" means "beauty of God." This archangel is a prince of the law, and incarnates intelligence and teaching.

Visualization of the Second Chakra
    (Approximately 15 minutes)

This visualization will give you a lot of energy and enthusiasm. It awakens the passion for art, knowledge and all other fields of intelligence and creation.

Material
  • *Celtic music or sounds of water.*

  • *An orange candle.*

  • *A salt lamp.*

- *A meditation cushion.*

Visualization

1. Listen to the music.
2. Light the orange candle and the salt lamp.
3. Sit down comfortably on the meditation cushion.
4. Begin general relaxation. Breathe.
5. Calm your spirit.
6. Close your eyes.
7. Feel Jophiel's angelic vibration surrounding you in an orange aura.
8. Visualize an orange fluid penetrating through the Chakra, under the belly-button. Feel the warm energy of this fluid. Visualize this energy in your veins, in your arteries, in your capillary veins. This fluid is circulating throughout your whole body, bringing you a sensation of dynamic and energetic warmth.
9. Feel the new force in you. Allow this fluid to circulate; activate the Chakra by placing your hand under your belly-button in the area where it's located. Move your hand clockwise seven times in order to activate the fluid in your body.
10. Open your eyes and regain ordinary consciousness.

Effects of the Visualization

This visualization allows artists in need of inspiration to rediscover their imagination and intuition. This visualization is recommended for people who are pursuing studies and taking exams, intellectuals, or anyone whose job is related to the field of knowledge. Scientists, researchers, and teachers will experience intellectual renewal and psychological openness through this meditation.

Third Chakra: Manipura-chakra

Position: solar plexus, epigastric plexus.
Color: yellow.

Angel: Rhamiel.
Meaning of the Chakra's name: the city of jewels.
Symbolic representation: a lotus with ten petals.

Locating the Third Chakra
This Chakra is located in the solar plexus, close to the stomach.

The angel's Power
Rhamiel is Saint Francis of Assisi's angel. He is the angel of peace and mercy.

Meditation of the Third Chakra and of Angel Rhamiel
(Approximately 15 minutes)
The meditation of the third Chakra is a moment of relaxation and rest. The solar plexus is often considered the emotional brain of man. Moral anguish, sadness, separation and fear are stocked in the third Chakra. This meditation allows you to cleanse your plexus of emotional troubles and accumulated tensions.

Material
• *A yellow candle.*

• *A meditation cushion.*

Meditation
1. Light a yellow candle with a thick wick.
2. Sit down comfortably on a meditation cushion in the lotus position or cross-legged, with the palms of your hands open on your thighs.
3. Stare at the flame of the candle and repeat the following mantra:
   Angel Rhamiel,
   Soothe my heart and liberate my negative emotions.
   Angel Rhamiel,
   Soothe my heart and liberate my negative emotions.

Angel Rhamiel,
Soothe my heart and liberate my negative emotions.

4. Feel the energy of angel Rhamiel by placing your right hand on your solar plexus. Feel the warmth of the energy on the right side of your body.
5. Withdraw your right hand and place your left hand down in the same way so that you can feel the energy in the left side of your body.
6. Close your eyes.
7. Visualize a yellow vortex spinning and trying to enter the solar plexus. Feel the warmth and energy tingling in your plexus.
8. Open your eyes.
9. Take your time before regaining ordinary consciousness.

Effects of the Meditation
This meditation is for people who are stressed, or subject to emotional troubles, anxiety, or fear of abandonment.

Fourth Chakra: Anahata-chakra

Position: cardiac plexus.
Color: green.
Angel: Hagiel.
Meaning of the Chakra's name: unstruck (sound that cannot be heard).
Symbolic representation: a lotus with twelve petals.

Locating the Fourth Chakra
In the center of the chest, close to the heart.

The Angel's Power
Angel Hagiel is the angel of Venus. It's recommended that you do the meditation of the fourth Chakra on a Friday, the day of Venus. Angel

Hagiel aims to attract love and promote harmony in relationships.

Meditation of the Fourth Chakra
(Approximately 15 minutes)
This meditation establishes a connection with the Chakra of the heart. Emotions are no longer repressed, and the heart is open to love and harmony in relationships.

Material
- *A photo of a forest, garden, or park landscape.*

- *Rose incense sticks.*

- *Relaxing nature-themed music of the forest, birds...*

- *A meditation cushion.*

Meditation
1. Place the photo in front of you.
2. Burn the incense.
3. Play the music.
4. Sit down on the meditation cushion, with your palms joined in front of your heart.
5. Breathe. Relax.
6. Stare at the photo and picture yourself with angel Hagiel in the middle of the landscape.
7. Hagiel's wings spread out over you.
8. You feel safe. You are reassured. You are under the protection of Hagiel's wings and of all the angels. Let go of your emotions. You can feel the love.
9. Hagiel's energy illuminates your heart with green light. Embrace this reassuring and comforting sensation by placing your joined hands on your lips and then bring them back to your heart.
10. Thank Hagiel and slowly regain ordinary consciousness.

Effects of the Meditation

The meditation of the fourth Chakra is recommended for people who are looking for their soul mate or who wish to feel unconditional love for humanity. It's also recommended for anyone who wishes to have harmonious relationships with the people around them and their family.

Through this meditation, people who have trouble freeing their feelings will rediscover emotional sensations and the joys of love and sharing.

The fifth Chakra: Vishuddha-chakra
Position: carotidian plexus.
Color: light blue.
Angel: Uriel.
Meaning of the Chakra's name: pure.
Symbolic representation: a lotus with 16 petals.

Locating the Fifth Chakra
On the neck, by the throat and the trachea.

The Angel's Power

Angel Uriel is the messenger angel that God sent to Noah to warn him of the imminent flood. It is said that Uriel revealed to the alchemists the secrets of their science. He is the beneficent angel that keeps an eye on the communication between humans.

Meditation of the Fifth Chakra
  (Approximately 15 minutes)
This meditation brings self-confidence in human relations and facilitates communication with others.

Material
  • *A meditation rug*

Meditation

1. Lay down comfortably on your back, in a cool and calm room.

2. Soothe your mind and free yourself of parasitic thoughts. Close your eyes.

3. Visualize a clear blue sky without clouds.

4. Invoke angel Uriel. He will bring you toward a lake, an ocean, or a calm sea. He leaves you beside the water. You leave him to go swimming.

5. You're in the blue water, and its coolness relaxes you.

6. Feel this sensation of peace by taking in the immensity of the blue water.

7. Let this angelic treatment take effect. Inhale deeply and then exhale softly to release your negative energies. Do it again three times.

8. Relax.

9. Thank Uriel.

10. Slowly regain ordinary consciousness.

Effects of the Meditation

This meditation is for anyone who wishes to improve their communication in the private domain or at work. The inner peace caused by this meditation favors communication of all forms and increases self-confidence.

This meditation facilitates oral expression and is particularly well-suited for people who need to express themselves with ease.

Sixth Chakra: Ajna-Chakra – Chakra of the third eye

Position: pineal gland.
Color: indigo.
Angel: Raziel.
Meaning of the Chakra's name: authority, unlimited power.
Symbolic representation: a lotus with 96 petals.

Locating the Sixth Chakra

In the middle of your forehead, a dot between your eyebrows.

The Angel's Power

Angel Raziel is recognized in Rabbinic tradition as the angel that has all celestial and terrestrial knowledge. The Zohar mentions that the secret containing the 1500 keys of universal knowledge are revealed in the book known as the "Book of Angel Raziel."

Meditation of the Sixth Chakra
(Approximately 15 minutes)

This meditation is a spiritual awakening. It opens the third eye Chakra, thereby awakening consciousness and mediumship.

Material

- *Myrrh incense sticks*

- *A blue indigo candle*

- *A meditation cushion*

Meditation

1. Light the incense and the candle.
2. Sit down comfortably on the cushion in the lotus position or cross-legged.
3. Close your eyes. Breathe slowly.
4. Empty your spirit.
5. Picture a temple in the sky and the entrance door to the temple. Angel Raziel is waiting for you in front of the door. He opens it softly while you chant the Aum mantra three times.
6. Picture the door opening wide to an indigo sky.
7. Feel that you're soaring in the indigo sky. Feel a sensation of lightness and absolute well-being. You are light, free of all constraints and annoyances. The indigo sky puts you in a state of absolute consciousness.

8. You feel an opening pushing your eyebrows and eyes apart.

9. Raziel gives you his hand and leads you outside of the temple. He closes the door behind you.

10. Breathe slowly. Take a rest.

11. Slowly regain ordinary consciousness.

Effects of the Meditation

The meditation of the sixth Chakra is particularly recommended for people who wish to elevate their consciousness and be spiritually active. It's also recommended for anyone in search of universal love and the development of intuition and mediumship.

This meditation favors professional and artistic success because it awakens intuition.

Seventh Chakra: Sahasrara-chakra

Position: cerebral plexus.
Color: purple.
Angel: Seraphiel.
Meaning of the Chakra's name: 1000 petals.
Symbolic representation: a lotus with 1000 petals.

Locating the Seventh Chakra

At the top of your skull, in the center, by the fontanel.

The Angel's Power

Angel Seraphiel is the head of the Seraphim choir, the highest angels of the celestial hierarchy. They surround the throne of the Lord, and incarnate the divine virtues of love, light, and fire.

Meditation of the Seventh Chakra
    (Approximately one hour)
This meditation is a very special moment, which one must reflect

upon before beginning. The mediation of the crown Chakra with angel Seraphiel is one of the most important meditations, and requires a personal commitment of high spiritual value. Do it on a day when you are ready to live through a great experience that will bring you to the higher angelic vibration and will connect you to divine energy.

Do this meditation in the morning. It's imperative that you are alone and that you have chosen a pleasant room with light colors. Air out the room before starting the meditation. Then, close the windows and prepare yourself for personal purification.

Material
- *Comfortable clothes, preferably purple or white.*
- *A meditation cushion.*
- *Grain incense made of myrrh, benzoin or sandalwood.*
- *A perfume burner.*
- *Incense charcoal tablets.*
- *An amethyst.*

Meditation
1. Take a shower
2. Wear a purple or white outfit.
3. Purify the place of meditation by fumigating the room with incense.
4. Sit down comfortably on the meditation cushion in the lotus position or cross-legged.
5. Place the amethyst on your head where the Chakra is located.
6. Visualize the Chakra and angel Seraphiel, who is resting his hand on your head.
7. Remove the amethyst. You are under the impression that your skull is getting bigger and bigger.
8. A purple ray enters the Chakra's opening.
9. This purple ray from the higher angelic plane courses through your

body, descending down all the Chakras (third eye, throat, heart, plexus, second Chakra, root Chakra). The purple ray has exited through the root Chakra.

10. Thank angel Seraphiel for cleansing you with his divine light, his subtle and radiating essence.

11. You feel as though you are being bathed in purple light. You feel good.

12. Feel the connection to the divine plane.

13. Develop your feelings. Let your imagination work.

14. Your crown Chakra is opening even more. You are in the purple light. You are Seraphiel's purple light. Happiness bursts from your heart. You feel love, you have abandoned yourself to your emotions. Humbly receive this illumination with the joy of a child. Feel joy, love, goodness, and tenderness for all beings. You are connected to the higher vibration of divine love and the higher angelic plane of the Seraphim choir. You enter into the energy of the Lord.

15. Abandon yourself. Receive the divine gift and angelic presents. Be yourself, be all, be god and the angels in the beauty of illumination.

16. Following this ecstasy, empty yourself. Don't think of anything. Let yourself recover slowly.

17. Open your eyes.

18. Take your time to regain ordinary consciousness.

19. Put out the candles without blowing them out.

20. Rest for a moment before restarting your daily activities.

At the end of this meditation, you have transcended, transformed. You have reached an illumination that will change your existence and your way of feeling emotion. You are aware, you are free, you are in love.

This meditation is an important event in the existence of a person who wishes to attain spiritual elevation.

Effects of the Meditation

The ancient sages of India say that the crown Chakra grants access to immortality. The meditation of the seventh Chakra is for anyone who has experimented with the six other Chakras and who is connected to divine energy through the head of the Seraphim.

This meditation must be done while you are open and receptive to divine and angelic influences. It provides joy and unconditional love.

8 - *The Kundalini*

Meditation of the Kundalini

(Approximately one hour)

The Kundalini is a vital energy coiled up in an area located at the bottom of the spinal cord. This energy is often represented as a coiled snake stretching over the entire body, linking one Chakra to the other. The Kundalini isn't in one anatomic point of the body. It's an area of available energy that allows each person to transcend their energetic potential.

The meditation of the Kundalini activates this energy to establish a connection with the angelic plane and universal cosmic energy. The Kundalini unblocks energy channels and frees up vibratory flows. When the Chakra wheels are activated, the vibratory rate goes up, and energy increases. Cells regenerate more rapidly, physical strength increases, intellectual potential grows, and one regains physical strength, the love of life, and greater intellectual acuteness.

This meditation is energetic and therapeutic at the same time. It awakens dormant energies, and reinvigorates desires and the will to attain them.

The meditation of the Kundalini requires considerable preparation time and materials. Do this meditation on a day when you aren't pressed for time and when you're alone. You can make a recording of the relaxation if you have trouble visualizing your body at rest. You can also record the invocation. All that's left to do is to let yourself be guided and enjoy this exceptional meditation.

When you are particularly stressed or depressed, it's recommended that you do this meditation three times a week for three months. You mustn't stop doing this meditation abruptly; instead, phase it out slowly by doing it once a week during the fourth month, and then once every other week during the fifth month. Finally, do your last séance during the sixth month.

If you practice it diligently, this meditation has miraculous effects. You rediscover your love of life, you begin projects anew, and you find the resources to see them through to the end.

Material
- *Two colorless quartz crystals.*
- *An amethyst.*
- *A pink quartz.*
- *Grain myrrh incense.*
- *Grain benzoin incense.*
- *Grain olibanum incense.*
- *Place ¼ of each incense in the perfume burner.*
- *A perfume burner.*
- *Incense charcoal tablets.*
- *A meditation rug.*
- *A pillow.*
- *Soft music with angelic voices.*
- *A white rose.*
- *A recording of your voice saying the relaxation instructions.*

- *A white sheet of paper, cut into a square, on which you shall write the words of the angelic invocation (following page).*

- *A comfortable white outfit.*

Relaxation
Practice anatomic relaxation (see *Relaxation Techniques*, page 270).

- *You feel good. You are completely relaxed.*

- *Your body is heavy. Your body is sinking into the ground.*

- *It feels like you are sleeping, but you aren't sleeping.*

- *Read the invocation sheet now wholeheartedly.*

Invocation

> Holy archangel Seraphiel and related angels,
> I am invoking your love,
> I am invoking your beauty,
> I am invoking your light,
> I'm asking you to give me strength and willpower,
> I'm asking you to revive my desires.
> Holy archangel Seraphiel and related angels,
> I'm committing myself to using your energy,
> I'm making projects, I'm building my life,
> I love myself,
> I am me,
> I am happy,
> I am life and happiness,
> I am grateful,
> Let it be accomplished.

Meditation
1. Fumigate all four corners of the room with incense.
2. Air out the room before meditating.

3. Take a shower.

4. Wear something comfortable.

5. Place the pillow on the meditation rug.

6. Place the amethyst in the top right corner of the meditation rug, the pink quartz in the top left corner, and the two colorless quartz crystals in the bottom corners.

7. Pick up the rose and sit down on the rug. Remove its petals one by one and place them on the pillow.

8. Lay down.

9. Relax your body. Close your eyes.

10. Follow the different steps of relaxation.

11. Visualize a ball of white light at the bottom of your back. The light from this ball becomes bright white.

12. The light brings you warmth.

13. Feel this warmth at the bottom of your back.

14. Visualize the ball of light entering your flesh. It's shining in your spinal cord, filling your stomach with light.

15. Its light becomes brighter and brighter.

16. Your body is radiating from the inside because of this bright beam.

17. The light descends toward your root Chakra below the genital organs. The light enters the Chakra. The wheel of your root Chakra begins to turn.

18. Let yourself go. Let the light penetrate you. You feel its warmth and the good it does to your body. You are open to the light.

19. You feel the luminous ball rising in your stomach, penetrating the second Chakra between the pubic area and the belly button. The wheel of the Chakra starts to turn and the sphere of light rises toward the third Chakra in the solar plexus.

20. The light gets brighter and brighter, warmer and warmer. The wheel of the third Chakra starts to turn. You feel the sphere rising even further.

21. The light enters the fourth heart Chakra. You feel the warmth and brightness around your heart. The sphere rises even more.

22. You feel the light in your throat. The throat Chakra opens and begins

to turn. The sphere rises again.

23. The light inundates your third eye. You are blinded by its intensity. The wheel of the sixth Chakra starts to turn. The sphere rises again.

24. The seventh Chakra starts to turn at the top of your head. The sphere escapes from your skull through the Chakra's opening, which emits a powerful ray that crackles like fire.

25. Rest for a moment before opening your eyes.

26. Regain ordinary consciousness.

Effects of the Meditation

This meditation is for anyone who wishes to use their full potential in life. It increases energy, favors connection with the angelic plane, and opens your consciousness to freedom and emotional and spiritual fulfillment.

The meditation of the Kundalini is particularly recommended for people who are depressed, stressed, or overly anxious. It's also suggested for anyone having trouble envisioning their future, making projects, or for anyone who lacks self-confidence.

Chapter 10

Healing with Angels

Health is an important part of our lives. It allows our body to radiate and live in harmony with the spirit. Stress and other difficulties in our lives provoke physical problems, pain, and sicknesses that aren't always relieved with traditional care. Holistic medicine, which takes into account the global harmony of a person and the interaction between the spirit and the body, can sometimes better address the physiological and psychological needs of patients.

The spirit and the body function together. A great number of sicknesses are rooted in emotional disorders, childhood traumas, mourning, or sentimental breakups, abandonment, and other various causes of suffering. The spirit and the body combine to create a single personal energy, which is why it's important to monitor a patient's emotional and mental well-being. A blockage of energy can cause illness. Simply treating the sickness is not always enough to heal a sick person. Illnesses with psychic causes often become chronic or regressive. Chemical treatment only acts upon the symptoms without healing the cause of the pain. Stress and emotional suffering provoke energy blockages that lead to many kinds of cardio-vascular, neurological, intestinal, gynecological, and muscular diseases, as well as allergies, and skin and urinary problems.

Holistic treatment deals with the symptoms of the illness and treats its psychological or emotional causes. Whether you choose holistic or traditional medicine, there's always additional treatment to consider, such as psychotherapy, acupuncture, homeopathy, and energetic or angelic care.

When it comes to medical issues, it's wise to find out what heals. Traditional medicine speaks for itself, and one mustn't exclude it over other treatment options. Chinese medicine and Ayurvedic medicine can obtain excellent results as well, but it's important to consult renowned practitioners.

Taking the right therapeutic approach requires good judgment, and it's preferable to try various different treatments rather than resort to one healing method.

Illness is never a mere coincidence. For every sickness, it's important to ask yourself the right questions that allow you to know yourself and your body better. The subconscious communicates with the body, letting it know of the symptoms that the spirit must ask itself about and work on. Illness is a message from the subconscious that demands a change in behavior or way of thinking. It's a resounding alarm that must be listened to and taken into consideration. Becoming aware of the relationship between the body and the spirit is part of the angelic awakening. Angelic healing must take place while you are working on yourself so that you can make changes necessary to your personal evolution.

The help and support of angels allows a sick person to make space in their heart, their spirit, and their way of thinking in such a way that they gain access to the higher dimension of the angelic plane. This opens up every path to personal accomplishment and emotional balance, the essential elements of healing.

Angelic vibration and light are a wonderful source of healing power when they are supplemented with the treatment recommended by a doctor. Angelic energy is powerful. It brings about miracles. One of my friends, a fervent companion of the angels, was diagnosed with a brain tumor. During her second brain surgery, she fell into a coma and the doctor's prognosis was dim. All of her friends and family invoked the angels throughout the night following the operation, and in the morning, she miraculously awoke, to the surprise of the doctors. She has since returned to her normal life and has begun working again.

Angelic healing is possible when the angels are solicited with genuine faith and a strong will to obtain results.

1 - The Sacred Awakening of Consciousness and the Silver Ray

Angels bring about healing and self-understanding. They monitor our physical and psychological health. They guide our knowledge about the causes of disease, pain, and ailment. They facilitate communication between consciousness and the subconscious. They allow every individual to find their inner self and to access the sacred zone of their own personality. The angelic connection is a door to sacred consciousness. The simplest way of connecting to the angelic vibration is to picture the silver ray of an angel entering your heart.

Sacred consciousness means understanding the real self, the powerful and intuitive self, the self that knows best. This sacred self is constantly connected with the angels and receives their instructions through signs, clairvoyance, and repetitive thoughts, images or dreams. Awakening the sacred consciousness opens up the path to all healing and physical changes. Some people lose weight effortlessly; others miraculously recover from bad health. Depressed people rediscover their taste for life, and often find love.

The awakening of the sacred consciousness welcomes angelic energy into every domain of life and favors healing, self-questioning, self-transformation, and making positive choices.

Nonetheless, it's important to know that angelic aid changes the daily realities of connected people. These changes are caused by modifications in your state of consciousness. The sacred consciousness turns anxiety into confidence. Generally, you'll start to question your habits as well as your relationship with the people around you, your family, and friends. An angel's intervention can sometimes disturb those around you, but soon enough, positivity takes control and everyone realizes its advantage.

The awakening of sacred consciousness is an open door to the angelic plane, vibratory elevation, and a progression toward better health and increased tolerance and generosity. During this period of awakening, it's important not to yield to the influence of negative people. The willingness to undergo inner healing and transformation is the key to sacred communication with the celestial plane.

2 - Treatment to Awaken the Sacred Consciousness
(Approximately 30 minutes)

This treatment establishes connection with the sacred consciousness in each and every individual. The sacred consciousness welcomes angelic influence, favors behavioral transformation, and the evolution of personality. Do this treatment in the company of a healer who is already familiar with the angelic plane.

Precautions to Take Before the Session

For the Healer:
It's recommended that you wash your hands in cold water all the way up to your elbow. Wear comfortable white clothes made of natural fabric. Before the session, make sure you offer a blanket to the person lying on the treatment table. Before you start, rub your palms against one another very quickly, creating a circular movement of energy. Open your palms. Feel the energy weighing down your hands. As soon as you've cleared your mind and feel ready, begin the treatment by invoking angel Hodiel.

For the Person Following the Séance:
It's recommended that you don't eat for three hours before the treatment. Drink three glasses of water before and after to eliminate toxins. It's important to take off your watch, your jewels, and other metal objects to avoid energetic interferences. Don't cross your legs or arms or

you might block the flow of energy. Lay down on the treatment table on your back, with your legs spread a little, your arms along the side of your body, and your head on a pillow. Forget about your daily life by thinking of the angels. Close your eyes. Breathe slowly. Visualize a sphere of light entering through the top of your skull, descending through your body in a silver ray. This is angel Hodiel's ray, whose name means the "victory of God." Observe this ray as it courses through your body. You feel well. Relax.

Material
- *A transparent rock crystal that's been purified and devoted to angel Hodiel.*

- *A white candle kept lit throughout the entire séance.*

Treatment to Awaken the Healer
1. Charge the rock crystal by squeezing it in your palms and say the following words to yourself:

Angel Hodiel, I solicit your goodness and your love to open the sacred consciousness of (say the person's first name).

2. Place the rock crystal on the third eye Chakra of the person lying down.
3. Invoke angel Hodiel by tracing the body's outline with the open palms of your hands. Repeat to yourself:

Angel Hodiel, I solicit your goodness and your love to open the sacred consciousness of (say the first name of the person receiving the treatment).

4. If you feel negative energy from this person, immediately summon angel Michael to fight these polluting energetic influences that may disturb the séance.

5. Place your two palms flat against the heart of the person lying down, and invoke Hodiel once again, this time out loud and intelligibly:

Angel Hodiel, I solicit your goodness and your love to open the sacred consciousness of (say the person's first name).

6. Remove the rock crystal from the third eye Chakra, placing your hands over it, and repeat out loud:

Angel Hodiel, I solicit your goodness and your love to open the sacred consciousness of (repeat the first name).

7. Stay in this position for several minutes. The angel's work is achieved through the third eye Chakra.
8. Ask the person lying down to visualize a silver ray entering through the third eye. Remove your hands. Let the person feel the ray. The third eye opens up like a door, getting wider and wider. Ask the person to describe the opening of their Chakra and its expansion.
9. Listen to the person express their emotional feelings.
10. Thank angel Hodiel out loud:

Angel Hodiel, I thank you for opening the sacred consciousness of (say the first name).

11. Close the third eye Chakra by placing the palms of your hands over the Chakra. Turn the rock crystal counter-clockwise seven times, with the tip facing the Chakra, to close the Chakra entirely.
12. Let the person relax for a few more minutes.
13. Wash your hands.

Effects of the Treatment
This treatment is for people who wish to be cured of emotional pain, past suffering, or their inability to experience happiness. It's also for

people who get sick because of psychological or emotional problems.

3 - Inner Transformation with Angels

The angels are wonderful guides when we are preyed upon by recurrent anxiety or stress that makes life uncomfortable, and sometimes painful. You just have to identify what's making you suffer, and then ask for help. If, for example, you're impatient, inclined to control everything, or preyed upon by chronic anxiety, invoke angel Ariel (see *The Angel That You Need*, Chapter 23 page 553, for other questions).

Healing any malaise caused by fear or emotional anxiety is important. Without treatment, it may get worse and transform into a serious state of depression. The angels' powerful help allows for inner transformation that enables you to enjoy life, to laugh, or to perceive your existence in a lighter way.

Invocation

(Approximately 5 minutes)

Summon the angel for seven days in a row, after you wake up in the morning, or before you go to bed at night. Ask him to help you feel better and to remove the cause of your anxiety and emotional suffering.

Material
• *A silver candle*

Invocation

1. Stand up in front of the candle, with your palms against one another over your heart, and say the following words:

Holy angel (name the appropriate angel),
I'm asking you to make my anxiety disappear,
Give me joy and laughter,
Bring me help and assistance, always and in all places,
Let happiness enter my heart,

I shall be eternally grateful,
Amen.

Warning

During the seven days of the invocation, you'll notice a change that might be difficult to bear. Be attentive to your feelings, thoughts, and dreams. They are the manifestation of Ariel's work on the question you asked. If, for example, you're asking for financial relief, you'll experience renewed fear about not having enough money during the week that you're working with the angel. Being aware makes you react. Instead of reacting in a positive manner, you're letting all the fears eating you up burst from your subconscious. You may be angry at the angel's work, which proves more frustrating than you thought it would be. Whatever you do, don't stop the invocations. Be patient and wait until the end of the week. When you take medicine, you're usually prescribed a few days of treatment. The same goes for this angelic treatment. As the days go by, your subconscious opens up and you start to understand why you're scared or stressed. The angel may go back in time, to your childhood or a time in your life when you lost confidence in yourself. Understanding these events will be the key to your work with the angel.

Transformation

After you've finished the week's work, you'll have analyzed the fundamental questions and found the answers. Even if you still feel certain emotional trouble, the transformation will be complete. You reflect upon the past and the reasons for your psychological distress. You'll have opened the door, and cleansed yourself of negative energy. Emptying yourself will bring out the best in you.

Following the Transformation

Build a small angelic altar for the healing angel.

Angelic Altar

Following the week of invocation, this altar will keep you permanently connected with the angel. Every time you come back home, you'll simply need to light the candle for 10 minutes to have the angel monitor your progress and to support your evolution.

Material
- *A white tissue.*

- *A silver candle.*

- *A gemstone or crystal of your choice.*

- *A photo that makes you happy.*

Angelic Altar for Inner Transformation

1. Spread out the tissue.
2. Light the candle anytime you need the angel's support. Leave the candle lit for at least 10 minutes.
3. Choose a gemstone or crystal depending on how you feel.
4. Place the inspiring photo on the altar.
5. You can also add a drawing, a painting, an angel sculpture, or any other creation of your imagination. The homage will be appreciated by the invoked angel.

4 - The Etheric Body

The etheric body is an invisible energy layer that surrounds the physical body. This body is considered to be the energy double of the physical being. The interaction between these two bodies allows them to act upon one another in order to experience healing. The etheric body is the vibratory support of the physical body. Any manipulation or attack on the etheric will affect the physical body as well.

The etheric body was first discovered by the Kirlian couple in 1939. It's often called "aura." People accustomed to reading auras describe them as layers of color around the physical body.

The term "aura" is a Latin word that means "breeze." The origin of aura goes back to Antiquity. Aristotle called the etheric body the "vegetative soul." In Hinduism, the Pranamaya-kosha is an animated layer of vital breath. In the Upanishads, and Sankara Vedanta, Hindus distinguish the subtle body from the five layers of the body. In Taittiriya-Upanishad (VII century B.C.), it says: "In truth, there is another self made of breath and vital energy, different from the self made of the essence of food, though it is situated inside this one's sheath."

In Ancient Egypt, the ka is the energetic essence of the individual, the reservoir of vital energy. Egyptologist Serge Sauneron defines it as: "a manifestation of vital energies, as much in its creative function as its conservative function...A reservoir of vital forces from which all life springs, and thanks to which all life subsists, and toward which all life returns to after death, the ka is comparable, by its own nature, to vital force." This same vital force can be found in the African Bantu and Oule civilizations, who called it "muntu" and "Menehe," respectively.

Aristotle believed that the fifth element, after air, water, earth, and fire, was ether, the matter that composed the soul. This fifth element is heat, and the principal element of life. It's known in alchemy under the term quintessence, the fifth essence.

In his novel Seraphita, Balzac describes the aura and the etheric body as "an opal colored fog."

The aura is supposedly composed of seven bodily layers that correspond to the seven main Chakras. The aura changes according to the person's mood, emotional state, and thoughts, as well as the energies of their surrounding environment. It is said that tears in the aura or attacks against the etheric body are caused by illness, depression, stress, emotional imbalance, and the harmful influences of the people around you.

People with drug, tobacco, alcohol, or food addictions have a weakened etheric body.

5 - *The Seven Subtle Layers of the Aura*

The Etheric Body

The etheric body is closest to the physical body. It's generally a bluish color, and is located about an inch or two away from the physical body. It gathers the energies that ensure cohesion of the physical body. The subtle centers of the Chakras are located in the etheric body.

The Astral Aura

The aura's second body is in the shape of an oval that envelops the physical body and the etheric body. Its base is situated 2 to 4 inches underneath the feet, and its peak is about 8 to 12 inches above the head. At the level of the chest, the astral aura is at about 2 to 3 feet's distance. Its colors are always changing in relation to the nature of the person's emotions and feelings.

The Layer of the Aura

This third etheric body envelops the astral aura by only a few millimeters. Its function is to isolate the astral aura from attacks of negative energy. It is pale yellow.

The Mental Aura

The ovoid shape of this fourth layer of the aura is composed of every color of the rainbow. It reflects mental states, instincts, reflexes, and actions of intelligence.

The Mental Membrane

This fifth body protects the body of the mental aura.

The Layer of the Spirit

This body has an ovoid shape and is about one inch from the mental membrane. It holds the memory of a person's original knowledge, the memories of the Akashic records. It also shelters intuitive thoughts, mediumship, and divinatory abilities.

The Causal Aura

Its shape is spherical, and corresponds to a halo of bluish, silver, or golden light. The symbol of this causal aura is generally represented as a golden sphere (halo) around the face of saints in Christian iconography.

The causal aura contains a person's soul and the steps of their spiritual elevation.

6 - Visualization of the Seven Subtle Layers of the Aura

Energetic health is just as important as physical health. It interacts with the organs and systems of the physical body, and harmonizes the collective energies of a person. Doing this visualization exercise allows you to center your energies, to activate them, and to create harmony between the different subtle layers. This visualization must be done without being disturbed, in a calm dimly lit room.

Material
- *A salt lamp*
- *Four red candles*
- *Lavender essential oil*
- *Cotton*
- *A lavender incense stick*
- *A meditation rug*

Visualization
1. Place the four candles in the four corners of the meditation rug, about 8 inches apart.
2. Light the candles and the incense.

3. Pour three drops of lavender essential oil in the four corners of the room.

4. The salt lamp creates soft light.

5. Lay down, relaxing your body.

6. Close your eyes. Breathe slowly.

7. Begin general relaxation.

8. Start the visualization with the physical body. Feel your body getting heavy, surrounded in red light. Invoke angel Kamael. Kamael's red light brings you strength and beauty.

9. Visualize the first etheric body. It's surrounded by blue light. Invoke angel Haniel. Haniel's blue light brings your strength and beauty.

10. Visualize the second etheric body. This body is surrounded by radiant white light. Invoke angel Vehuiah. Vehuiah's white light brings you strength and beauty.

11. Visualize the third etheric body. This body is surrounded by yellow light. Invoke angel Raphael. Raphael's yellow light brings you strength and beauty.

12. Visualize the fourth etheric body. This body is surrounded by a rainbow-colored light. Invoke angel Gabriel. Gabriel's rainbow-colored light brings you strength and beauty.

13. Visualize the fifth etheric body. This body is surrounded by silver light. Invoke angel Uriel. Uriel's silver light brings you strength and beauty.

14. Visualize the sixth etheric body. This body is surrounded by a radiant white light. Invoke angel Metatron. Metatron's white light brings you strength and beauty.

15. Visualize the seventh etheric body. This body is surrounded by golden light. Invoke angel Zerachiel. Zerachiel's golden light brings you strength and beauty.

16. Now, visualize your physical body and your seven etheric bodies enveloped in a sphere of silver light. Its radiance is warm and pleasant. Abandon yourself to this silver light. Take a rest. The angels are watching over you and protecting you. Great, big wings stretch out over you. Feel

the safety. Enjoy this moment of beatitude with the angels.

17. Breathe slowly. Get back in touch with reality. Regain ordinary consciousness.

18. Thank the angels:

Holy angels Kamael, Haniel, Vehuiah, Gabriel, Uriel, Metatron, and Zerachiel,
I thank you,
Your light and your love bring me strength and beauty,
I shall be eternally grateful,
Amen.

Effects of the Visualization

This visualization is particularly recommended for people who suffer from asthenia, loss of energy, or a lack of enthusiasm and love of life.

7 - Stimulate your Chakras

When the energetic centers of your Chakras are blocked, energy has trouble circulating throughout the body. These blockages of energy can lead to a decrease in vitality, and provoke pain, muscular cramps, illness, and general bodily weakness. Energy blockages can also influence morale by diminishing the love of life. They provoke mood swings, stress, anxiety, and depression.

Being aware of the Chakras is the first step in stimulating the subtle centers of energy.

8 - Visualization of the Chakras Opening Up
(Approximately 15 minutes)

Opening up one's Chakras must precede the therapeutic visualization of the stimulation of the Chakras. It will allow you to become aware of the way the Chakras function. This work is done through angel Hasdiel.

It's recommended that you do this séance in a calm room where you're sure you won't be disturbed. It's best to do this visualization in the morning, at sunrise. Energies are dynamic at this time of day, and are particularly well-suited to awakening and stimulation.

Material
- *A silver candle*
- *Zen music*
- *A meditation rug*
- *A stick of jasmine incense*

Visualization
1. Light the candle.
2. Listen to the music.
3. Stretch out on the meditation rug.
4. Begin general relaxation.
5. Breathe slowly.
6. Invoke angel Hasdiel. Ask him to open up your Chakras.
7. Focus your attention on the root Chakra under your genital organs. Visualize a vortex of radiant green light entering your body through the root Chakra. Feel this spiral of spinning green light enter into the Chakra. Let the light pierce your stomach. Follow this vortex of light as it travels toward the Chakra below the belly button, the solar plexus Chakra, the heart Chakra, the throat Chakra, the third eye Chakra, and the crown Chakra, at the top of your head. When the vortex of green light exits through the crown Chakra, relax.
8. Thank Hasdiel and burn the incense as you say the angel's name seven times.

Effects of the Visualization
This visualization is for people who feel physical pain, depression,

fatigue, loss of professional motivation, emotional problems, and mood swings.

9 - Treatment to Energize the Chakras

The Chakras must be energized by a healer accustomed to healing with angels. There are two possible techniques. The easiest one consists of working with a transparent crystal rock pendulum, an amethyst pendulum, or a smoked crystal rock pendulum. The second technique is based on hand placement.

Treatment with a Pendulum
(Approximately 15 minutes)

The pendulum that you use to energize the Chakras should be about 2 inches long. Using a pendulum with a silver chain is recommended. Every person who has a pendulum uses the same method of communication for positive and negative answers. Generally, clockwise oscillation can be interpreted as a positive answer, while any counter-clockwise movement or swinging from left to right can be interpreted as a negative answer. It's important to start by cleaning off the crystal before using it therapeutically. Residues of negative energy can interfere with the treatment.

Material
- *A transparent, smoked, or amethyst crystal pendulum*
- *A silver chain*
- *A white candle*
- *A meditation rug or massage bed*

Treatment
1. Light the candle.
2. Invoke angel Raphael and start working on the root Chakra. Hold

the pendulum still over the pubic area of the person lying down. If the pendulum answers no, this mean it's necessary to purify the Chakra.

3. Do this to all seven Chakras: the second Chakra under the belly button, the third solar plexus Chakra, the fourth heart Chakra, the fifth throat Chakra, the sixth third eye Chakra, the seventh crown Chakra.

4. Once you have diagnosed the blockage in the Chakras, you can start treating the blocked or inactive Chakras.

5. Position the pendulum above the Chakra you wish to treat. Invoke angel Raphael. Visualize a yellowish-orange ray entering into the pendulum. Sometimes, the person lying down can see this ray.

6. Ask the person lying down to invoke angel Raphael quietly and to solicit the vitalization of their Chakras.

7. Concentrate on the blocked Chakra and push your pendulum so that it turns clockwise. Turn it seven times, repeating Raphael's name seven times.

8. Proceed in the same way for all the blocked Chakras.

9. Thank Raphael and let the person rest for a few moments before getting up.

Treatment Using Hand Placement
(Approximately 15 minutes)

The preparation of this treatment consists of feeling Raphael's energy in the palm of your hands before starting to work on the person. Rub your palms against each other energetically. They become warm and start to tingle. Open your palms toward the sky and invoke angel Raphael. When your hands warm up, you can begin the treatment.

The treatment should be done in the following way: when the Chakra is active, it lets off warmth. But when the Chakra is closed or inactive, you will feel a cold sensation. In this case, bring your hands closer, with your palms facing the Chakra, and turn them clockwise round and round over the Chakra seven times as you say Raphael's name seven times. The Chakra will open up under the influence of the healing angel's warmth. Move on to the next Chakra.

Material
- *A red candle*
- *A meditation rug or a massage bed*

Treatment
1. Light the candle.
2. Invoke angel Raphael.
3. Place your hands over the pubic area of the person lying down, without touching her. Do the diagnosis. When you feel a cold sensation, the Chakra is blocked.
4. Diagnose the six other Chakras, placing your hands on the Chakra near the belly button, on the solar plexus Chakra, on the heart Chakra, on the throat Chakra, on the third eye Chakra, and on the crown Chakra.
5. Start opening the Chakras that need treatment. Turn your hands clockwise round and round, with your palms open, side by side, around the blocked Chakra, repeating Raphael's name seven times.
6. When the treatment is over, thank angel Raphael.
7. Give the person lying down a few minutes to recover.
8. Wash your hands and lower arms in cold water.

10 – Treatment of the Etheric Body
(Approximately 30 minutes)

This treatment is particularly effective for physical or emotional imbalances. Working on rebalancing the etheric body can replenish losses of energy and cleanse energetic blockages. It also provides excellent angelic protection for the seven layers of the aura.

It's important to make the person who will receive the treatment drink two big glasses of water in order to facilitate the elimination of toxins. The therapist or healer must imperatively wash their hands and lower arms in cold water.

Material

- *A yellow candle*

- *A massage table or a meditation rug*

- *Zen music*

Treatment

1. Light the candle.
2. Stretch the person out carefully.
3. Have them begin general relaxation.
4. The person must take in a deep breath and then exhale entirely.
5. Make first contact by evaluating the person's etheric body. Place your hand about 8 inches from their physical body and feel the etheric body's energy, evaluating it by making supple hand movements from top to bottom. An etheric body with good energy should be about 2 inches away from the physical body, while a weakened etheric body is less than an inch away from the physical body.
6. Diagnose the weak zones of the etheric body, and try to detect losses of energy through a tingling feeling or a cold sensation in the palm of your hand.
7. Start working on the restoration of the etheric body by invoking Raphael, the healing angel.
8. For any area that's either weak or that has experienced a loss of energy, proceed in the following manner:
9. Invoke Raphael and his yellowish-orange ray. Picture a ray of sunlight nourishing the energy of the etheric body, and move the palm of your hand up and down seven times in order to thicken the etheric body or to fill the loss of energy.
10. Check the strength of the energy by sliding your open palm about 8 inches above the whole etheric body.
11. Make the person drink after the treatment.
12. Wash your hands and lower arms in cold water.

Effects of the Treatment

This treatment is for people who suffer from hypertension, stress, and physiological, emotional, hormonal, or sympathovagal imbalance. It should be used as a supplement to traditional medicine.

11 - Treatment to Eliminate Negative Energies

(Approximately 30 minutes)

This treatment should be done on a person suffering from migraines, stress, anxiety, or relationship and emotional problems.

Before the treatment, it's recommended that you skip a meal and drink two large glasses of water. The healer or therapist must wash his hands and lower arms in cold water.

Material
- *A massage table or meditation rug*
- *A yellow candle*
- *Zen music*

Treatment

1. Light the candle.
2. Stretch the person out.
3. Rub your palms against each other as you call upon angel Raphael.
4. Visualize a sphere of yellowish-orange light illuminating the entire room with warm and positive energy.
5. Ask the person to visualize a ray of sunlight entering through the third eye.
6. Start the treatment with the top of the person's skull. Place your hands about 2 inches away from the body, with your palms facing the top of the skull.
7. Without saying a word, ask Raphael to chase away the person's negative energies.

8. Start by treating the head, then stop at each Chakra. Make a downward spiraling movement with the palm of your hand on each Chakra as you visualize Raphael's golden ray penetrating the Chakra.

Effects of the Treatment

This treatment is for anyone who has undergone emotional suffering, painful situations, or professional stress.

12 - Healing Emotional Suffering

Emotional suffering is particularly hard to treat. This suffering often comes from emotional problems accumulated in the subconscious. Undoing old ways of thinking remains a difficult and delicate task. Emotions are often associated with weakness so many people refuse to express them, choosing instead to close themselves off, to isolate themselves, or to continue living in stressful situations.

To take hold of one's emotion, it's often necessary to cleanse yourself of suffering and to make referential transformations in the subconscious. Treatment with angels is remarkably effective when it comes to people who suffer emotionally. This treatment allows for the discovery or rediscovery of the pleasures of existence, the sensation of well-being, and enthusiasm. It opens up one's heart and facilitates having friendly relationships and finding genuine, long-lasting love.

Treatment
(Approximately one hour)

This work must be done alone, in a calm and quiet room. Solitude and silence are extremely important for this treatment, which calls upon the highest angels of the celestial hierarchy. You mustn't eat for three hours prior to the treatment. It's also recommended that you purify yourself by taking a shower or an angelic bath, and to fumigate the room where the healing will take place with incense.

Material
- *A white outfit.*
- *Zen music.*
- *Grain incense made of myrrh, Gum arabic, and olibanum.*
- *Charcoal.*
- *A perfume burner.*
- *A yellow or orange candle.*
- *A silver candle.*
- *A golden candle.*
- *A white candle.*
- *A meditation rug.*
- *A white chalice filled with cooking salt.*
- *A blanket.*

Angels to invoke: Raphael, Michael, Seraphiel, Gabriel.

Treatment
1. Start by fumigating the room with incense, and then air it out.
2. Put on the white outfit after your purification.
3. Play the music.
4. Position the candles into a square, with the chalice in the middle.
5. Light the candles.
6. Stretch out, cover yourself, and begin general relaxation.
7. Take in a deep breath and then exhale normally. Seven times.
8. Close your eyes.
9. Concentrate on your emotions. Observe your suffering. Think of them as if they do not belong to you. Observe again.

10. Invoke the four angels of emotion and ask them to heal you:

Holy angels Raphael, Michael, Seraphiel, and Gabriel,
Heal me of my suffering,
Heal my emotions,
Bring me peace and joy,
I shall be eternally grateful,
Amen.

11. Visualize Raphael's yellow ray entering through the top of your head. Then, let Gabriel's silver ray in, then Michael's golden ray, and finally Seraphiel's ray of pure radiating white light. Open yourself up to angelic energy.

12. The rays' warmth irradiates your body. You are hot and cold. Let the angelic rays warm you up entirely. Enter into the angels' radiance.

13. Negative emotions will exit through the crown Chakra. Picture black smoke rising out of the top of your head. This smoke continues to rise, until it becomes gray, and then transparent, and then stops altogether.

14. Breathe slowly, and open your eyes.

15. Thank the angels. Regain ordinary consciousness. Take your time before getting up.

Effects of the Treatment

This treatment is for people with relationship difficulties, people in search of a soul mate, people experiencing emotional conflict, or people who feel like victims of their past suffering.

13 – Meditation to Protect Yourself from Negative Energies
(Approximately 15 minutes)

At certain times in our lives, we are more vulnerable to negative energies. One's aura is sometimes weakened by stress, fatigue, or difficult personal situations. In this case, it may be urgent to protect yourself before treating the cause of your permeability to the lower energies.

Material
- *A meditation rug.*
- *A golden candle.*
- *Copal incense sticks.*
- *A yellow rose.*

Meditation
1. Purify yourself by taking a shower or an angelic bath.
2. Light the incense and the golden candle.
3. Pluck the petals off of the rose, placing them around your head on the meditation rug.
4. Lay down. Relax. Breathe slowly.
5. Close your eyes.
6. Invoke angel Michael. Visualize a golden dot. Increase the size of this dot until it becomes a golden sphere. This sphere gets even bigger, forming a large golden bubble, into which you enter entirely. This bubble envelops you in soft protective warmth.
7. Relax in this bubble. Let go of your tensions, your stress, your difficulties. Breathe slowly. Feel protected. Picture Michael's wings stretching out over you, enveloping you entirely. You feel infinitely well and safe. Michael's wings are warm and reassuring. Tell yourself they are always around you, in every situation of existence. They push away attacks and negativity. You are protected.
8. Breathe slowly. Open your eyes.
9. Thank Michael.
10. Regain ordinary consciousness.

Effects of the Meditation

The golden bubble you visualized remains around you after the meditation.

This meditation is for people who are tired, stressed, discouraged, or who wish to protect themselves urgently against the lower weakening and destabilizing energies.

14 - Harmonizing Relationships with Conflicts
(Approximately 15 minutes)

Angel Anael lights up one's heart and develops tenderness and forgiveness. He helps heal conflicted relationships and allows everyone to open themselves up to unconditional love, and the desire to give and share without expecting anything in return. Because disharmony is often associated with disappointed hopes and expectations, angel Anael opens up one's heart to compassion, understanding, tenderness, and emotion. Getting passed expectations and giving without asking for anything in return grants access to the higher angelic vibration. Divine light illuminates and transcends people who open up their heart to unconditional love. Their goodness and charisma radiate over others and quell conflict.

Anael is a powerful angel who opens up his heart to unconditional love, fixes broken relationships, and transforms lower energies into positive energies. His reassuring presence develops self-confidence, the love of life, well-being, and heals conflicts.

Material
- *A stick of jasmine incense*
- *A meditation rug*
- *A pink candle*
- *A pink quartz*
- *Angelic music*

Meditation

1. Light the incense and the candle.

2. Lie down on the meditation rug and relax to the sound of the angelic music.

3. Place the pink quartz on the heart Chakra.

4. Invoke Anael and visualize him in a pink aura filled with softness and love. Anael smiles at you. He rests a comforting hand on your heart. Feel his love and softness. Take the time to appreciate these sensations. Take the time to immerse yourself in the angel's love and peace.

5. Thank Anael and open your eyes. Regain ordinary consciousness.

Effects of the Meditation

This meditation is for people with conflicted relationships, and people who feel emotional frustration or who hold back their emotions.

15 - Distance Healing

Distance healings are reserved for people who communicate with the angels on a regular basis. It's an extraordinary experience to have with angel Raphael. Distance healings answer people's requests, or you can also decide to relieve someone that you know. No matter the origin of this kind of work, distance healings are very effective. Angel Raphael lends you his faultless support and gets to work with you. Distance healing energies are generous, and while you work to relieve another person, you open your heart to goodness and sharing.

Distance Healing Treatment

(Approximately 15 minutes)

This treatment is particularly effective with Raphael's help. The person healed from a distance feels the benefits of the treatment very quickly.

Material

None

You can do this treatment while traveling, at home, or in any calm and quiet place out in nature.

Treatment
1. Sit down comfortably, and if you're out in nature, lie down on a piece of clothing or a mat. Close your eyes and relax if you're in a vehicle or public place.
2. Think of the person who is receiving the healing. Picture their face.
3. Rub your palms against each other and open your hands toward the sky. (You can rest them on your thighs if you aren't alone.)
4. Invoke angel Raphael. Feel the energy in the palms of your hands through a sensation of warmth, tingling, or soft and malleable matter. Raphael is with you. He rests his hand on your right shoulder. Feel his presence. Raphael is transmitting the healing energy to you.
5. With your palms open and facing the sky, create an energy link with the person you are healing. Call out for this person. Picture their face again. Concentrate on their third eye and send out a golden ray of energy from your hands. The ray will cross the distance that separates you from this person. Visualize this golden ray penetrating the person's third eye. Your hands are lighter. You don't feel anything anymore.
6. Rub your hands, and then open and close your fist three times. And if possible, wash your hands in the cold water from a faucet, the sea, or a river. Avoid stagnant water.

Effects of the Treatment
This treatment is for people who wish to bring relief or to heal a person they know.

16 - Healing from Lack of Inspiration or Creativity

Artists, creators, researchers, inventors, and people who conceive new projects sometimes lack inspiration and creativity. The light and radiance of angel Zerachiel helps recover imagination and inspiration very quickly. This treatment should be done with a person who guides the angelic therapy. The healing acts directly upon the person experiencing it, without the intervention of the therapist or healer, who merely acts as a guide during the vibratory and energetic process.

Angel Zerachiel can also stimulate your memory and awaken your intellectual faculties while job hunting or taking a test. Zerachiel's solar energy is extremely powerful, and the healing is almost instantaneous. The person guiding the meditation must ask the person exactly what problem they wish to have treated. Targeting the treatment increases its effectiveness.

(Approximately 15 minutes)

Material
- *A red candle.*

- *Energizing music.*

Meditation

1. Sit the person down on a chair.
2. Play the music.
3. Invigorate the person sitting down with a neck massage. Ask them to straighten their back. The spine should be at a right angle in relation to their thighs. Their hands should lay flat on their thighs.
4. Invoke angel Zerachiel. Ask the person who is receiving the treatment to invoke Zerachiel as well.
5. Rest both of your hands on the top of the person's skull. Press down as hard as you can with both hands for 5 seconds, and ask the person to resist. Their back and neck must remain straight.
6. Ask the person to visualize angel Zerachiel's red light penetrating the crown Chakra in a vortex. In the meantime, facilitate the angelic light's entrance by tracing this vortex with your right hand, making seven clockwise spirals above the crown Chakra.
7. Let the person feel angel Zerachiel's red energy descending down their spinal cord and exiting through the root Chakra.

8. Place your hands on the person's shoulders and massage them softly.

9. Stop the music and let the person regain ordinary consciousness.

Effects of the Treatment

This treatment is for anyone lacking inspiration, imagination, or creativity. The results are a renewal of self-confidence and a return to success.

17 - *Healing of the Planet and Stimulation of the Universe's Energies*

Pollution and underground or underwater nuclear testing contribute to the destruction of the planet, soiling it with nuclear and toxic waste. Holes in the ozone layer provoke ecological disasters, melting glaciers, and a rise in the temperature of the sea and the air. It's urgent for every individual to act toward decreasing waste and energy consumption. It's also important to do this treatment, which transforms planetary energies and relies on the influxes of the Universe to heal a planet in distress.

Metatron will guide the treatment and contribute to the cleansing of lower energies. Metatron transcends the higher angelic vibrations to stimulate universal energy.

Treatment for the Planet and Universal Energies

(Approximately 15 minutes)

This treatment should be done in a group. The gathering of people comes together with the goal of healing the Earth and making the energies of the Universe interact with each other. The group creates an egregore of high vibratory range.

The participants should make a circle, and place a candle in front of each person.

One person directs the group's movements and guides the others.

Material
- *A white rose per person.*
- *A meditation cushion per person.*
- *A white candle per person.*
- *Relaxing music with the sounds of water or the sea.*

Treatment

1. Light the candles.

2. Sit down cross-legged on the meditation rug and sway to the sound of the water music.

3. Pluck the petals off of the white rose and make a carpet of petals in front of the meditation cushion.

4. Relax and breathe slowly, with your hands on your thighs, and your thumb and index barely touching. Inhale and exhale deeply seven times.

5. Raise your arms toward the sky altogether, with your palms open, and silently invoke angel Metratron.

6. Lower your arms and join your palms in front of your heart in a praying position. Silently invoke Metratron again.

7. The person leading the group will say these words:

Holy angel Metratron,
Let your healing act upon the Earth and the Universe,
Let your divine energy bring wisdom to men,
Raise awareness and respect for the planet,
Protect humanity,
Transcend the vibration of the Universe,
Make the hearts of each and every one us beat with pure emotion,
For the good of the Earth and humanity,
We will be eternally grateful,
Let it be accomplished.

8. The participants open their arms, with the palms of their hands turned toward the sky, offering Metatron's treatment to the Earth and to humanity.

9. The participants cross their arms over their chest and salute the angel by leaning over onto the ground.

10. The person guiding the group thanks the participants and ends the treatment by turning up the volume of the music.

18 - Healing from the Past

People who live in the past have difficulty finding inner peace. Looking back on negative events or painful situations slows down personal development. Perspectives of the future are marked by emotional states that prevent us from opening ourselves up to all possibilities. As the saying goes: "In order to obtain what we've never had, we must do what we've never done."

New opportunities arise after we've stopped thinking about bad memories, and put an end to nostalgia and regret, which prevent us from opening ourselves up to the future. People who experience sentimental failure, and remind themselves of it every day, will only reproduce the same psychological pattern during new encounters and become interested in people who are susceptible to put them through the same failure.

The past can condition our way of thinking and become our only frame of reference. A person mired in negativity, regret, and sadness, will be unable to see the sky above him and the new possibilities before him.

Cleansing oneself of the past represents liberation, newfound freedom, and a leap toward the future.

The treatment to heal from the past offers people going through a difficult situation, mourning, breakup, emotional loss, or material problems, to reconnect with the present and see the future as a trampoline and a possibility to live one's dreams.

Treatment to Heal from the Past
(Approximately 20 minutes)

By doing this treatment, you can look forward, you can change your way of living, you can say yes to the present and to the future.

Material
- *A yellowish-orange candle*
- *A white candle*
- *A chalice filled with cooking salt*
- *A stick of sage incense*
- *A meditation cushion*

Treatment

1. Light the candles and burn the incense.
2. Draw a diamond on the ground with cooking salt.
3. Sit down in the center of the diamond on your meditation cushion.
4. The part of the diamond behind you is the past. The part in front of you is the present.
5. Invoke the angels of the Sun to look toward the future and to chase away the shadow behind you. Summon Raphael and Uriel. Invoke their goodness, their light, their wisdom, and their strength. Picture the sun and its burning light inundating you like a sunbath. Feel the warmth. Feel the benefits of this light on you.
6. Feel Raphael's hand resting on your shoulder and Uriel's wings protecting you. Relax in the protection of the angels.
7. Turn toward the triangle of the past and sweep away this triangle's cooking salt. Close the base of the triangle of the future, with you on the inside. You turn back toward the triangle in front of you that indicates the elevated path of the future.
8. Ask the angels to open up the path of the future and to guide you

toward a better life. Say the following words:

Holy angel Raphael,
Holy angel Uriel,
Let your wisdom, your strength, and your love guide me toward the higher angelic vibration,
Let your wisdom, your strength, and your love shut the door of my past,
Let your wisdom, your strength, and your love guide me toward the future,
Let your wisdom, your strength, and your love offer me a happy fate,
I shall be eternally grateful,
Let it be so.

9. Meditate for a few more moments in silence in the triangle of the future before regaining ordinary consciousness.

Effects of the Treatment
This treatment is for people who are unable to look toward the future and who are conditioned by their past.

19 - Healing the Subconscious

It's often argued that some behavior is guided by the subconscious. But what do we really know about our subconscious? Through studies devoted to psychoanalysis, we have observed that emotion, certain events, joy, and suffering are recorded into the hidden memory of our subconscious. Throughout our existence, the subconscious fills itself up with new information. But the subconscious is not merely an archive or library of our life. It's also a driving force and source of inspiration. When we experience suffering, grief, mourning, or breakups, the subconscious sends us references that will influence our behavior. At certain points in our existence, when we are harassed by work or personal problems, we may no longer act according to our own will. We are teleguided by our subconscious and we obey the patterns of the past, often leading us to make mistakes.

To liberate yourself from these patterns, and the hold the subconscious has over you, the angels are of great help.

20 - Treatment to Cleanse the Subconscious and Thought Patterns

(Approximately 15 minutes)

This treatment will allow you to rid yourself of old thinking patterns that no longer apply to actual events. This treatment, done through the angelic vibration, raises our awareness about the infinite possibilities at our disposal and eliminates limited ways of thinking and restrictive patterns. It's a cleansing treatment that pushes back fear, limits, prohibitions, and frustrations.

It's recommended that you treat your subconscious under the guidance of angel Gabriel, on a Monday, day of the moon, at 10 o'clock at night, his specific hour of availability.

Material
- *A purple candle.*

- *An amethyst already purified and devoted for the treatment.*

- *Violet essential oil.*

- *Grain incense made of olibanum, mastic, and pontifical incense.*

- *A perfume burner.*

- *Incense charcoal tablets.*

- *A meditation rug.*

- *A photo or drawing of the moon.*

Treatment

1. Fumigate the meditation room with incense, and then air it out.

2. Light the purple candle.

3. Pour seven drops of violet essential oil onto the meditation rug.

4. Place the image of the moon under the rug, or under the pillow by your head.

5. Lay down and place the amethyst on the third eye Chakra.

6. Close your eyes.

7. Invoke angel Gabriel to cleanse your subconscious.

8. Take in a deep breath, imagining that you are inhaling a ray from the moon. Exhale slowly.

9. Inhale the ray of the moon seven more times and then exhale slowly.

10. Your body is bathing in a halo of lunar light. You are a bit cold.

11. Order your subconscious to fill itself up with angel Gabriel's lunar energy. It feels as though you've been cleaned and purified by angel Gabriel.

12. Picture the moon up high in the sky, radiating with silver light. Feel the general well-being of your body. Thank Gabriel.

13. Open your eyes. Regain ordinary consciousness.

14. Keep the amethyst that you used for the treatment for when you go to bed. Put it on your nightstand or under your pillow until the following Monday.

Effects of the Treatment

This treatment is for people who have decided to transform their negative subconscious patterns, and who wish to cast off their limits and fears so that they can lunge toward a better future. This treatment favors freedom of thought and the freedom to start anew.

21 - Healing Black Ideas

Most sensitive people, at one point or another in their lives, feel an influx of black, sad, or disturbing ideas. These black ideas come from unexpressed fears, frustrations, and unsatisfied dreams or unresolved situations with no means of escape.

During these times, the angels are of great help. They act very quickly, transforming anxiety and distress into active energy. With angels, black ideas are wiped out in favor of new vitality, and a desire to change and to rediscover enthusiasm and the taste of life.

22 - Treatment to Cleanse Black Ideas
(Approximately 15 minutes)

This treatment is useful during painful or stressful times, when your consciousness is overrun by emotions that prevent you from understanding problems and resolving them. This treatment is extremely effective. It must be done alone, in a well-lit room.

It's recommended that you don't eat for two hours before, but it's very important that you have a meal after the treatment and drink some tea or an energizing drink.

Material
- *A red candle*
- *A stick of patchouli incense*
- *A meditation rug*
- *Energetic music*

Treatment

1. Play the music. Light the candle, and burn the incense.
2. Sit down on the meditation cushion, keeping your spine and shoulders very straight.
3. Place your hands on your thighs, with your palms open.

4. Invoke angel Cerviel, the angel of strength and energy.

5. Close your eyes. Visualize a red flame entering through your root Chakra under your genital organs, and rising up your spinal cord. Feel the heat of this red energy flame coursing through your body, burning your shoulders, going up your neck toward the top of your skull. Feel the almost unbearable sensation of inner heat.

6. Think about the powerful, strong, and energetic angel Cerviel taking your hands and squeezing them tightly. The pressure of the angel's hands burns your fingers.

7. Work on your breathing by panting for a minute.

8. If your head turns, stop panting.

9. Breathe. Relax your back and shoulders. Open your eyes.

10. Thank angel Cerviel and lay down for a few moment before having a hearty meal.

Effects of the Treatment

This treatment is for people who wish to find the energy and strength to act by getting rid of their black ideas and inhibitions.

23 – Liberating Yourself from the Grasp of the Lower Spirits

It isn't uncommon to feel symptoms of depression, discouragement, asthenia, insomnia, and malnutrition. Sometimes, your mind may be troubled by recurring nightmares or anxiety attacks. You may also be the victim of mental confusion or permanent malaise, and experience loss of memory. Sometimes, feeling uneasy is a manifestation of tobacco, alcohol, or other harmful substance addiction.

Despite medical care or therapy, you feel no improvement and the treatments' failure only increases anxiety and uneasiness. A vicious circle begins, where the person feels unable to find a cure and incapable of quitting their addictions or getting out of their depressive state. In some cases, the depression gets worse, potentially leading to suicidal impulses. The absence of a solution to serious, recurring problems that neither a doctor nor psychiatrist is capable of treating can impact an entire family and circle of friends. It's a rare case, but it happens to people who are particularly sensitive or weakened by personal or family drama.

People attained by this malaise are preyed upon by lower energies that can come from anywhere. They may be spirits from the afterlife that weren't able to reach the light after their death. They may also be unbounded entities that evolve in the lower angelic planes. In the most serious cases, they're the spirits of people who killed themselves, victims of a violent death, or criminals wandering about the afterlife.

Being possessed under these circumstances is violent and extremely painful for the person overrun by negative energies. What's more, once an entity has taken possession of a person's energy, it can attract other like-minded entities.

Angels have the power to end astral possession. They are capable of recovering entities, or lower spirits, and driving them toward the celestial spheres of light and goodness. These entities, sometimes called "lost souls," will be guided by the angels toward peace and light.

Angel Michael will be the therapeutic angel throughout the treatment. Michael is the most powerful angel when it comes to galvanizing the forces of good against the forces of evil. He is the head of angelic army of light that fought against the forces of darkness. In the Bible (Revelations 12, 7-9), John says: "Then there was a war in heaven: Michael and his angels fighting against the dragon. And the dragon fought back, but he was not strong enough, and they lost their place in heaven. This great dragon was hurled down, that ancient serpent called the devil, or Satan, who leads the whole world astray. He was hurled to the earth and his angels with him."

According to tradition, Michael remains the most powerful angel of all, having slain the dragon and the dragon's angels. But he is also the angel of mercy; thus, he forgives those lost souls that have succumbed to the weakness of possession and drives them toward the kingdom of celestial light.

According to Christian tradition, Saint Michael is the angel of immortality, leading souls toward the eternal light. This is why he is the angel of astral purification. This purification is a delicate operation that must be prepared with the greatest care. During the operational or magical phase of the cleansing, the healer should invoke angel Michael under the secret name that gives him great occult power, "Sabbathiel."

Preparing for the cleansing of the contaminated person takes 24 hours.

24 – Treatment for the Liberation of the Lower Spirits
(Approximately 24 hours)

This treatment takes 24 hours of preparation and requires 3 purification sessions. After the purifications, the treatment must be done by a healer or someone accustomed to working with angels.

It's best to write each prayer on a white, square-shaped piece of paper and to burn it afterwards. (You can burn the paper in a casserole to avoid risk). It's recommended that you eat lightly and drink lots of water or green tea.

Material
- *A golden candle.*
- *Grain incense made of myrrh, mastic, and copal.*
- *About twenty fresh almonds or dried, unsalted almonds.*
- *A white chalice filled with cooking salt.*
- *A comfortable white outfit.*
- *A meditation rug.*
- *Five sheets of white non-lined paper, cut into a square.*
- *A pen (if possible with gold or black ink).*
- *A snuffer.*

Purifications

1. The first purification must take place on a Sunday, right after midnight. The person being treated must take a shower or an angelic bath.

After the shower, he must light the golden candle, invoke angel Michael, and then recite the first prayer:

Holy angel Michael,
I'm imploring you to liberate me from the lower spirits,
I'm imploring you to chase away negative energies,
I'm imploring you to keep astral entities away,
I shall be eternally grateful,
Amen.

Finish the first purification by eating five almonds and burning the first prayer sheet. Don't forget to extinguish the candle with a snuffer. Then, go to bed.

2. The second purification must take place on a Sunday, at eight o'clock in the morning. The person being treated must take a shower or an angelic bath. After the shower, re-light the golden candle and recite the second prayer:

Holy angel Michael
I'm imploring you to liberate me from all astral possession,
I'm imploring you to watch over me,
To protect me from lower energies,
And to liberate me once and for all,
I want it,
Amen.

Finish the second purification by eating five almonds and burning the second prayer sheet. Don't forget to extinguish the golden candle with a snuffer. Eat lightly throughout the day, drink lots of water or green tea, and take a rest.

3. The third purification should be done at 10 o'clock at night, on a Sunday. It must take place before the treatment. The person being treated should take a shower. Then, he should put on the white outfit, light the golden candle, and recite the third prayer:

Holy angel Michael,
I'm urging you to heal my soul, my body, my aura,
I'm urging you to nourish me with new energy,
Give me love, strength, and wisdom,
I shall be eternally grateful,
Amen.

After the third purification, the person should eat two almonds. Then, he should burn the prayer sheet and lie down on the meditation rug.

Treatment
1. The healer washes his hands in cold water.
2. The healer fumigates the area around the body of the person being treated with incense.
3. The healer guides the anatomic relaxation of the person lying down.
4. The healer rubs his hands against each other and places his palms on the crown Chakra of the person to heal. Then, he makes a counter-clockwise spiraling movement, in an outward direction in order to remove the negative energies and entities. He proceeds in the same way on the solar plexus Chakra, and then on the heart Chakra. In the meantime, the person lying down should picture angel Michael slaying the dragon.

5. The healer says the following exhortation:

> Lower spirits,
> Astral entities,
> Leave this body!
> Angel Michael, lead the lost souls
> Toward the eternal light.
> Let it be accomplished,
> Amen.

6. At the end of this prayer, the healer burns the paper.
7. The healer and the person being treated observe the flame of the golden candle rising, smoking, and twisting, indicating that the spirit has ascended toward the light.
8. The person being treated says the fifth prayer:

> Holy angel Michael
> I'm urging you to liberate me of the lower spirits once and for all,
> Give me happiness and freedom,
> Give me strength, love, and wisdom,
> I shall be eternally grateful,
> Amen.

9. The healer burns the prayer sheet.
10. The healer surrounds the meditation rug that the person is lying down on with cooking salt, thus creating a sacred space purified of all negative influence.
11. The person lying down breathes slowly and rests.
12. The healer washes his hands and lower arms in cold water.
13. The person lying down gets up and thanks the healer.
14. The healed person silently thanks angel Michael.

25 - Complementary Treatment for the Liberation of Lower Spirits

(Approximately five minutes)

The 24 hours of purification are emotionally and physically exhausting. This complementary treatment allows you to connect to the luminous vibration of angelic love. It allows a loving and nourishing energy from the celestial plane into your aura. This treatment is done with angel Kamael.

Material
- *A red candle*

- *A glass of red wine*

Treatment
1. Light the candle.
2. Invoke angel Kamael and ask him for energy and strength.
3. Join your palms together in front of your heart.
4. Inhale Kamael's energy, and then exhale slowly. Fill yourself up with the angel's energy.
5. Drink the wine.
6. Thank angel Kamael.

26 - Rediscover Self-Confidence

During certain times in our lives, we lose control of our actions and feel as though we're a victim. Stress, fear, and negative emotional states provoke physical uneasiness and a loss of self-confidence. This angelic treatment helps put an end to self-disparagement, self-pity, or the feeling that fate has blundered over you. A loss of confidence attracts catastrophe and disillusionment.

Stressful ways of living, profitability requirements, or psychological pressure that a great number of salaried employees go through contribute to a loss of self-confidence. Other people lose self-confidence after a sentimental breakup, a period of mourning, an accident, or failing a test. A loss of self-confidence is one of the factors of depression, isolation, or close-mindedness. These situations bring about a loss of sociability, and relationship and family problems.

Call upon Angel Seraphiel's powerful energy to rediscover self-confidence and the love of life. Seraphiel's energy, bright and pure white, irradiates love and strength. These two qualities of angel Seraphiel, the Prince of peace, allow people to understand that love is no synonym for weakness, but of strength, energy, and happiness.

27 - Treatment to Regain Self-Confidence
(Approximately 15 minutes)

This auto-healing treatment must be done in a calm room at a time when you won't be disturbed.

Material
- *A meditation rug*
- *A silver candle*

Treatment
1. Light the candle.
2. Relax on the meditation rug.
3. Begin general relaxation and breathe slowly.
4. Invoke angel Seraphiel.
5. Picture angel Seraphiel's face. Feel his hand resting on your heart Chakra, and his wings warming your shoulders. Feel Seraphiel's peace and love. Feel serenity and confidence coming back to you. Confidence is love. Feel this. Feel that Seraphiel loves you, and that this love is confidence.
6. Experience this pure love from the inside. See nothing but love. Feel nothing but love. The influx of emotion may bring tears to your eyes. Let yourself go. Cry if it makes you feel better. Let go of your emotions.
7. Relax. Thank Seraphiel. Be infinitely grateful of this love that has

entered you and that will support you at any moment in your life, more specifically when you feel low and without value. Seraphiel's love is unconditional and will carry you forever.

8. Rest for a few moments and then regain ordinary consciousness.

Effects of the Treatment

This treatment is for people who have lost self-confidence, who have lost confidence in life, and who think that fate is blundering over them.

28 - Rediscovering Joy

Difficulties sometimes alter our happiness, provoking a loss of desire and tarnishing our dreams. When all hope seems lost, and you feel alone, without anyone to lean on, summon Tsadkiel, the angel of mercy and benevolence. Tsadkiel will give you the taste for life, joy, and happiness again. When you are sad, you are no longer able to see love. You only see the negative side of things. Tsadkiel's unconditional love opens up your eyes to positivity, allowing you to see love and to feel joy again.

29 - Treatment to Rediscover Joy
(Approximately 15 minutes)

This auto-healing treatment should be done in a calm room where you won't be disturbed.

Material
- *Star anise to prepare an infusion.*
- *A blue candle.*
- *A meditation cushion.*

Treatment

1. Drink your star anise infusion.
2. Light the candle.
3. Sit down cross-legged or in the lotus position on the meditation

cushion, with your hands on your thighs, and your thumb and index barely touching.

4. Relax. Breathe slowly. Close your eyes.

5. Invoke angel Tsadkiel. Visualize a bubble of blue light.

6. You feel great happiness in this bubble of blue light. You feel good. You feel light. Your heart frees itself of emotional tension. You abandon yourself to the energy of the angel surrounding this bubble with his huge extended wings. You feel the angel's protection and softness.

7. Tsadkiel removes his wings. The blue bubble gets bigger, and you grow with it. You feel a pleasant sensation of expansion.

8. You rise toward heaven. You are in the clouds, and Tsadkiel watches you as he carries your bubble. You rise even higher. The bubble is refreshing. You feel light. You have abandoned all your worries and grief. Up high, in heaven with Tsadkiel, nothing bad can happen to you. You are happy. Tsadkiel brings you higher and higher. You are filled with happiness and joy. Enjoy this moment. Tsadkiel slowly brings you back to earth. The blue bubble breaks. You are no longer the same person. You are now a relaxed and happy person.

9. Thank Tsadkiel. Open your eyes.

10. Slowly regain ordinary consciousness.

Effects of the Treatment

This treatment is for people who have lost their love of life, their enthusiasm, and their desire to make projects for the future.

30 - Detoxifying the Body

Many people carry numerous responsibilities that exhaust the physical body. The result is an accumulation of nervous tension, muscular dystrophy or ligament problems, and energy blockages that provoke back and neck pain. These physical ailments increase stress and anxiety, which start a vicious cycle of pain and stress.

Detoxifying the body and clearing energetic blockages is possible with the help of angels.

31 - Treatment to Detoxify the Body
(Approximately 15 minutes)

This treatment is a remedy for physiological trouble caused by stress and anxiety. It's important to do it at night, after a hard day's work, when the body is tired and tense.

Material
* *A yellowish-orange candle*

* *A pink rose*

* *A stick of camphor incense*

* *A meditation rug*

Treatment
1. Light the candle and burn the incense.
2. Pluck the petals off of the rose and rub them with your hands.
3. Stretch out on the meditation rug.
4. Begin general relaxation.
5. Invoke angel Raphael to heal bodily tension.
6. Visualize a golden yellow light entering your solar plexus in the shape of a vortex. Raphael's cleansing light spreads throughout your body like liquid. Feel this golden yellow liquid in your body. In every painful spot, you feel a sensation of intense heat from the liquid. This sensation amplifies in the most painful spots, to the point of becoming unpleasant.
7. Let the liquid act until it reaches your head and the soles of your feet. It flows out of you through the extremities of your toes and the crown Chakra at the top of your skull.
8. Open your eyes. Thank Raphael.
9. Slowly regain ordinary consciousness.

Effects of the Treatment

This treatment is for stressed or anxious people, who feel muscular tensions, energetic blockages, dorsal or lower-back pain, and neuralgia.

32 – Asking for Psychological Help from Angels

Angels are the best confidants when you can't find someone who will listen to you amongst your family, friends, or work colleagues, and you don't want to undergo long and costly therapy.

Angels bring psychological help when you feel isolated and misunderstood. These critical times in your life aren't always understood by the people around you, who attribute this psychological weakness to temporary problems. Yet, it's essential to seek treatment for your troubles as they may lead to prolonged depression.

By connecting yourself to Raphael's angelic therapeutic vibration, you will recover from feelings of solitude and abandonment.

Before beginning the treatment, it's recommended that you take a linden or orange blossom infusion while you listen to Zen music, angelic music, or the sounds of water and the waves of the sea.

33 – Treatment for Psychological Help with the Angels
(Approximately 15 minutes)

This treatment will bring you the certainty of not being alone, of having someone who will listen to you, and the feeling of being understood by angels.

Material
- *A linden or orange blossom tea.*

- *Zen or angelic music, or music of water.*

- *Three blue candles.*

- *A white chalice filled with cooking salt.*

- *A meditation cushion.*

Treatment

1. Place the three blue candles into a triangle and light them.
2. Draw a circle around the meditation cushion with the cooking salt.
3. Sit down comfortably on the meditation cushion, inside the circle.
4. Relax while you listen to the music, and loosen your shoulders.
5. Breathe slowly. Close your eyes.
6. Invoke angel Haniel.
7. Haniel approaches you and sits down to listen to you. He extends his wings over your shoulders, isolating you from the world. Under Haniel's soft and loving protection, you can express all of your worries, your preoccupations, your pain. Haniel understands you and comforts you. You feel the warmth of his hand on your shoulder. Confide in him, anything you have on your mind. Cry if it makes you feel better. Haniel loves you and understands you.
8. Breathe slowly. Thank Haniel and open your eyes.
9. Rest for a few moments before regaining ordinary consciousness.

Effects of the Treatment

This treatment is for people who feel moral malaise, but can't confide in those around them.

It's for couples undergoing relationship difficulties, and people living through family dissension or troubled relations with their kids.

It's also well-suited for therapists and healers tired of their own treatments.

34 - Healing Your Heart

After going through a period of mourning, a sentimental breakup, or after getting fired, it's often necessary to recalibrate yourself and reconnect your heart. This treatment will help you rebuild yourself, allowing you to rediscover intimate and natural childhood sensations.

The guardian angels or birth angels assist with our arrival into the world. They know who we really are. They know the most intimate and pure secrets in our hearts. This angelic treatment allows you to reconnect to your essence and rediscover simple and beautiful emotions in life.

35 – Heart Healing Treatment
(Approximately 15 minutes)

This treatment connects you to the vibration of your birth angel, protects you from depression, anxiety, and stress provoked by painful situations.

Material
- *A meditation cushion*
- *A white candle*
- *A stick of jasmine incense*

Treatment

1. Light the candle and burn the incense.
2. Sit down comfortably on the meditation cushion and relax. Leave your palms open on your thighs.
3. Summon your birth angel by name and ask him to heal your heart. Visualize a ball of luminous pink energy entering your heart. The pink sphere inundates your heart with goodness and love. Enjoy this moment of healing. Feel the goodness and love. Feel the well-being, listen to the voice of your birth angel reassuring you and comforting you as though you were a child.
4. Rest in the purity of angelic love.
5. Slowly regain ordinary consciousness and thank your angel.

Effects of the Treatment

This treatment is for people who just went through a difficult or painful emotional time and who wish to rediscover joy.

36-Healing a Place Polluted with Negative Energies

Houses, and sometime apartments, are inhabited by people who die there under dramatic circumstances. They may also be located near a cemetery or a place where something tragic happened. The energy residue of the deceased, loaded with their suffering and torment, often pollutes these places, possessing the people who live there, and provoking illness and depression. This energetic vampirization manifests itself through inexplicable fatigue, headaches, vertigo, and depressive tendencies. Sometimes, couples and families will fight and argue for no apparent reason.

The angelic treatment allows you to get rid of pollutant energies and to help people who are suffering recover their health and sense of joy. The deceased will be led toward the light by angels.

37 - Purification Treatment of a Place Polluted by Negative Energies

(Approximately 10 minutes)

This treatment is particularly effective when it's done on a Saturday, at 10 o'clock at night. The treatment will be led by angel Cassiel, who reestablishes energy balance. Angel Johiel, the angel of Paradise, will be in charge of leading lost souls toward the eternal light.

Material
- *Gum arabic incense, grain angelus incense, and grain copal incense.*
- *A white chalice filled with cooking salt.*
- *A meditation cushion.*

Treatment

1. Fumigate every room in the house. After the fumigation, say the following words:

Holy angel Cassiel,

I'm imploring you to purify this place and let peace and love reign.
I shall be eternally grateful,
Amen.

2. Walk closely along the walls of the house carrying the chalice filled with cooking salt. Don't miss a room or even a closet.
3. Say the following words:

Holy angel Cassiel
This place is pure and you make peace and love reign,
Amen.

4. Dilute the polluted salt in boiling water. Run it under clear water until it disappears.
5. After treating the house, ask angel Johiel to lead the lost souls toward the eternal light. Sit down on the meditation cushion. Relax and invoke angel Johiel.

Holy angel Johiel,
Lead the lost souls to Paradise,
Lead them toward the eternal light,
Let it be accomplished,
Amen.

6. Thank angel Cassiel and angel Johiel.
7. Wash your hands in cold water. Air out all the rooms of the house.

Effects of the Treatment

This treatment is for people who wish to liberate their apartment, house, office, vacation home, or any other place where they feel languished, from negative influences.

38 - *Meditation to Chase Away Jealousy, Fear, and Guilt*
(Approximately 15 minutes)

This meditation can heal people who feel small, who lower themselves in relation to others, and feed on hate, resentment, and feelings of envy or guilt. Fear, which is most often the origin of emotional disorders, can also be treated with this meditation. This exercise must be done standing up, facing East, on a Sunday, at noon.

Material

- *A yellowish-orange candle, large and square.*

- *A green candle, large and square.*

- *A bag of dried verbena leaves.*

- *Grain incense made of olibanum, myrrh, and mastic.*

- *A snuffer.*

Meditation

1. Fumigate the meditation room with incense, and then air it out.
2. Place the green candle to the left of where you will stand. Place the yellowish-orange candle to the right.
3. Draw a circle on the ground with dried verbena leaves, but make sure you leave enough distance between them and the candles (at least 8 inches away) so that you don't start a fire.
4. Light the candles.
5. Enter the circle and stand up with your palms joined over your heart.
6. Concentrate on angel Raphael and angel Ariel. Invoke these two angels.
7. Close your eyes. Visualize a golden circle of light produced by the angels growing over the verbena leaves. This circle of light rises higher and higher, until it surpasses the height of your head. You are surrounded by a golden angelic light. You have nothing left to fear. The angels are protecting you. You are sheltered from negative energies, and the ones

already in you are chased away by the angelic light.

8. You feel great warmth, great protection, and an incredible sensation of well-being. You no longer need to feel jealous of anyone or be afraid.

9. The circle of light starts turning like a vortex and rises higher and higher toward heaven. You are seized by this vortex. You are spinning in the light. The bad energies, bad feelings, and negative emotions leave you. You are cleansed by this whirlpool of angelic light.

10. The whirlpool rises toward heaven, leaving the ground. It gets farther and farther from you.

11. Breathe. Loosen your hands and shoulders.

12. Sit down in the circle and put out the candles (with a snuffer). Take a rest.

13. Thank Raphael and Ariel for the healing.

14. Regain ordinary consciousness.

Effects of the Meditation

This meditation is for people suffering from personal disparagement. It's recommended for anyone who is preyed upon by negative energies or by pollutant emotions like jealousy, fear, and guilt.

39 - Meditation to Heal from Jealous Love

(Approximately 10 minutes)

Jealousy poisons relationships. Men or women who experience this feeling are fragile people who aren't self-confident; their fear of abandonment is manifested through jealousy. This meditation provides a remedy for this destructive feeling. Raguel's unconditional and luminous love heals this emotional frustration and opens up individuals to new emotional horizons filled with joy and sharing. Anytime you start to feel insecure, dive into Raguel's unconditional love, and negative feelings will soon disappear.

Material
- *A stick of copal incense*
- *A meditation cushion*
- *Angelic music*

Meditation

1. Burn the incense.

2. Sit down on the meditation cushion and listen to the angelic music.

3. Relax. Loosen your shoulders. Place your hands on your thighs, with your open palms facing the sky. Your thumb and index should barely be touching.

4. Take in a deep breath and then exhale.

5. Close your eyes.

6. Invoke Raguel and picture this wonderful angel coming towards you. Feel the beating of his wings. Observe his beauty, his perfect face, his smile. His presence proves that you will never be abandoned. Raguel is by your side. Raguel loves you. He proves it to you through his presence and unconditional love.

7. Raguel envelops you in his soft and warm wings. Feel the reassuring touch of his feathers and warmth. Let yourself go. If you suddenly feel a strong emotion that might bring you to tears, cry and relieve your emotional tension.

8. Enjoy this reassuring and relieving moment.

9. Thank Raguel.

10. Regain ordinary consciousness.

Effects of the Meditation

This meditation is for people who suffer from fear of abandonment, emotional anxiety, or a lack of self-confidence. It's also for people who feel the sting of emotional jealousy toward a spouse or partner.

Chapter 11

Call upon the Angels

*I*t is very rewarding to call upon angels. When you are in contact with angels, you always feel infused with a healing energy of love, compassion and help. You can never give up; you deal with your issues and hassles and open the gate of a promising future!

1 - Preparation of Meditations and Rituals

There are different kinds of angelic meditations. Depending on your needs and the importance of your request, your invocation ceremonies will not require the same preparation.

These meditations can be classified into different categories:

Meditations of Inner Transformation
These meditations are ceremonies of high magic. They concern:
- *The transformation of your subconscious.*
- *The search for your soul mate.*
- *Healing rituals for serious illnesses.*

For these meditations, it's highly recommended that you purify the house, the ceremony room, as well as your body, and make an angelic perfume. Having an empty stomach is important for these meditations, but it isn't necessary for you to fast for 24 hours or go without food during the day. You can, for example, call upon the angels at night before you go to bed, without having had dinner, or in the morning, when you first wake up. You can then have breakfast after your meditation.

Drinking alcohol, having sexual relations, or smoking the night before a ceremony is obviously forbidden. Access to the angelic plane is a highly magical procedure when you want it to transform your spirit or body, or if you wish to connect to your soul mate through the angels.

Invocation Meditations

These rituals concern:

- *Love encounters.*

- *Professional transformation.*

- *The healing of benign illnesses.*

- *Family harmony.*

- *Wealth and abundance.*

Practicing these rituals requires purifying the place, as well as incense and candles. The specific prescriptions for meditations of inner purification do not apply.

Meditations of Inspirations

These meditations are simpler than the preceding ones. They concern:

- *Creative help.*

- *Calling for a guide.*

- *A request for protection from a guardian angel.*

- *Advice when making a decision.*

- *General protection, concrete aid in the material and professional domain, or to obtain more money.*

- *The development of intuition.*

- *Buying material goods.*

- *The gratification of immediate desires.*

Practicing these meditations requires the usual material for angelic ceremonies: incense, candles, cooking salt, and a chalice filled with water.

Spontaneously Inspired Meditations

These meditations allow you to enter into vibratory communication with the angels. They concern:

- *The end of an argument with a friend.*

- *The return of joy.*

- *The end of your worries about the future.*

- *Requests for the distant future: moving, a trip, a change in your life...*

- *Healing a very benign wound or illness.*

- *A new life project.*

- *The protection of a loved one.*

These meditations require the use of incense, candles, Tingsha, or Tibetan singing bowls. Several words of prayer and a calm state of mind, free of mental strain, will establish contact with angels. These meditations establish immediate contact with the celestial plane.

Practicing these angelic rituals allows for a more and more direct contact with angels. You hear celestial voices, you see angels, you feel the air moving around you with the fluttering of wings, a hand rests on your shoulder. These sensations are exceptional. Know how to appreciate them. Make use of the meditations by following the advice that the angels offer, and transform your existence in positive way.

2 - Meditations

Meditating is the most common method to establish a connection with the angelic plane. You can do short meditations or meticulously prepared, hour-long meditations that will bring you to the heights of the celestial plane, amongst the highest-ranked angels of the angelic hierarchy.

The advantages of meditating are:
- *The quality of the physical relaxation.*

- *The distancing of negative energies.*

- *The visualization.*

- *The contact with angels close to God.*

- *The vibratory connection with the highest angelic plane.*

- *The long term effects.*

- *The increasingly facilitated contact with angels from one meditation to the next.*

- *Efficient therapy to treat personal problems and to experience angelic healings.*

Posture

1. The most common posture for meditating is sitting in an armchair, a chair, or on a meditation floor cushion or pouf.

People accustomed to meditating should sit on the cushion, with their legs in the lotus position. Sitting cross-legged is also recommended for meditating.

In any case, it's important to choose a position that maximizes personal comfort.

2. A lying position is recommended for long meditations and visualizations.

Relaxation

General relaxation takes place in a sitting position (see *Relaxation Techniques*, page 270).

Anatomic relaxation is mandatory for meditations of high vibratory elevation (see *Relaxation Techniques*, page 270), and is best practiced in a lying position.

Breathing

Inhaling and exhaling deeply is often recommended before meditation or relaxation. It helps to chase away negative energies and to center oneself before communicating with angels.

Material
- *Candles*
- *Incense*
- *Essential oils*
- *Gemstones or crystals*
- *Flowers*
- *Personal belongings*
- *Your own ritual materials*
- *Photos*
- *Angel statuettes*

3 - The Prayers

The light ritual of prayer should be done whenever you feel the need to. It requires no material, only an open psychic and vibratory disposition. Prayer can be useful for:

- *Making an immediate request.*

- *Resolving a material problem.*

- *Soothing daily worries.*

- *Finding a parking place.*

- *Being on time for a meeting.*

- *Seizing an opportunity.*

- *Finding the clothes that you want.*

- *Choosing the best day for a specific activity.*

- *Going to the right place to do research.*

- *Doing well on a test.*

- *Letting yourself be guided in a field in which you are hesitant.*

- *Making a choice at the last minute.*

- *Finding the right words to say to someone.*

- *Offering a gift to please someone.*

Angels offer an infinite source of inspiration, support, and protection. Never hesitate to summon them in any situation, even if you are scared to ask. Angels never discredit a request if it's right for you and the people around you. Angels aren't your judges, but your friends and confidants. Your requests are always taken into consideration as long as they aren't selfish or harmful to others, and your cause is good for you and doesn't hurt anyone else.

The few words and thoughts of a prayer are similar to a ritual in that you must devote all your energy to angelic contact. These prayers are most effective when you wake up in the morning, or at night before you go to bed, outside of the agitations of the day. Angels are especially reachable and effective minutes before you fall asleep. When you solicit them and pray in that specific moment, your modified state of consciousness increases your psychic receptiveness.

It's also possible to pray to angels in a variety of places by creating a mental void conducive to contact with the angelic plane. In public transportation, in your car, walking in the street, or while cooking, the public environment won't create a problem as long as you're capable of isolating yourself mentally and ignoring the energies around you. Focus on the question you wish to ask the angels, or on the advice you're waiting for. Recite prayers you have already learned by heart, or use your imagination, using words you feel comfortable with. Always ask with humility, faith, and trust.

If meditating doesn't give you a hint about which angel to consult, turn to the table of angels to choose an angel, a place of intervention, a day, a night, a month, an hour, a cardinal direction, a birth angel, and an angel for the field in which you wish to meditate.

There are several methods for summoning an angel, which differ according to the nature of the request. They are explained in detail for each subject, and there is an annex of these meditations on page 260.

A Quick Prayer

This method brings immediate results. You can recite your prayer wherever you wish, whenever you wish, and according to your needs. Yet, it's necessary to empty your spirit when you contact the angels. Focus on the solicitation. You need nothing other than your energy, your willingness, and sincerity to summon an angel.

Nevertheless, you must call upon an angel by name. It can be your guardian angel, your birth angel, an angel defending a particular cause, or a healing angel.

The advantages of a quick prayer are:
- *An immediate contact with a particular angel.*

- *Instant and efficient help.*

- *A rescue call heard immediately.*

- *Consolation.*

- *Help in any situation, in any place you may be, at any time.*

- *A connection to the angelic vibration.*

- *The presence of an invoked angel for several days.*

Posture
None

Relaxation
None

Breathing
None

Material
None

Create your Own Angelic Prayers
You can create your own prayers.

You can choose a prayer corresponding to the nature of the call you are addressing to the angels.

The advantages of prayer are:
- *The simplicity of communication with angels.*

- *The swift transmission of the message.*

- *The effectiveness of the written text and reciting it out loud.*

- *The possibility of repeating the same prayer several times to intensify the request.*

Posture

No specific posture recommended. You can pray for the angels at any given moment when you feel the need to.

Relaxation
Optional

Breathing
Optional

Material

- *You can invent your prayer spontaneously. In this case, you don't need any specific material.*

- *A sheet of paper.*

- *A pen.*

- *A prayer book.*

4 - Angelic Solicitation

Angelic solicitation is used for:

- *Getting an answer to a specific question.*

- *Asking for personal help.*

- *Soliciting personal healing.*

- *Soliciting healing for someone in your circle of friends.*

Its advantages are:

- *Solicitation is simpler and faster than meditation.*

- *You can obtain an immediate answer.*

- *The swift transmission of the message to the angelic plane.*

- *Help in case of emergency.*

Posture
Identical to the posture of meditation, sitting or in a lying position.

Relaxation
General relaxation recommended

Breathing
Recommended

Material
- *A notepad*
- *A pen*
- *Meditation accessories: gemstones, incense, candles, flowers…*
- *The text of a prayer*

5 - Angelic Visualization

Angelic visualizations are often associated with meditations or solicitations. Yet, they can be used spontaneously when you call upon angels during the day or at night before going to bed.

Its advantages are:
- *Immediate contact with the angels.*
- *No need for material.*
- *No mandatory postures required.*
- *Elevation of the vibratory plane.*
- *The joy of seeing angels.*
- *The joy of feeling the presence of angels.*

Posture
Sitting or in a lying position

Relaxation
General relaxation strongly recommended.
Anatomic relaxation is also an option provided that you have enough time.

Breathing
Recommended

Material
None

6 - Angelic Invocation

Angelic invocation is generally used within the framework of meditation or it can be accompanied by a visualization or prayer. You can also carry out an invocation by summoning the angels before going to bed or at any moment during the day when you feel the desire or need to.

Its advantages are:

- *A quick contact.*

- *A call for help.*

- *A request for angelic help for the short, medium, or long term.*

- *A request relating to another person.*

- *The optional use of materials.*

Posture
No mandatory posture required. You can invoke the angels in any position or at any time during the day.

Relaxation
Optional

Breathing
Recommended, but not mandatory.

Material
- *No material.*

- *Meditation materials when the invocation is made during meditation.*

7 - *Angelic Ceremony*

Angelic ceremonies are used for very particular cases: healing requests or existence-transforming requests. They require long preparation, but their effect is incredibly efficient and can produce genuine miracles!

The advantages are:
- *They keep negative energies away.*

- *Protection.*

- *Heightened elevation of the vibratory frequency.*

- *Miraculous results.*

- *Healings.*

- *Radical transformations of existence.*

- *Angelic visions and appearances.*

Posture
Sitting on a cushion in the lotus position or cross-legged.

Relaxation
General

Breathing
Seven long inhalation and exhalations.

Material
- *Cooking salt.*

- *Grain incense, myrrh, Storax and Galbanum.*

- *A white chalice filled with water.*

- *Four white pillar candles.*

- *A white or silver candlestick with a long, white candle.*

- *Comfortable, white clothes made of cotton or flax.*

8 - *Angelic Request*

An angelic request is written on a white sheet of paper that's been cut into a square.

The advantages are:
- *Efficiency.*

- *The energy of the written transmission does not change.*

- *The short-term effects.*

- *The amplification of energy achieved through great concentration in the writing of the request.*

Material
- *A pen.*

- *A white, non-lined sheet of paper, cut into a square.*

- *A gold or silver candle depending on the angel in question.*

- *A white, red or yellow rose, depending on the field of the intervention.*

- *A stick of myrrh.*

- *Dried verbena leaves.*

- *Vanilla powder.*

- *Cooking salt*

9 - Relaxation Techniques

You can relax in two different ways.

General Relaxation

You will put your whole body at ease.

Let your body go, loosen your shoulders, breathe softly. Let go of any tensions. Loosen your jaw.

This technique is quick and efficient, but is not ideal for long meditations with high vibratory levels.

General relaxation is well-adapted for meditations, quick prayers, solicitations, invocations, and angelic prayers.

Anatomic Relaxation

This relaxation serves to eliminate muscular tension and stress. It undoes energetic knots in the body and lets angelic fluids circulate.

Anatomic relaxation deals with the entire body from head to toe. It resembles the relaxation method of yoga.

The desired length is 20 to 30 minutes.

This type of relaxation allows the body to immerse itself in the effects of meditation and to integrate healing, psychological change, or emotional help.

You can record the steps of this relaxation in order to hear it during a meditation or visualization. A family member can also use the recording.

- *Stretch out on a meditation rug or a mattress, with your head on a pillow. Prepare a cover if you get cold easily.*

- *Relax your body.*

- *Chase away your thoughts, quiet your mind.*

- *Inhale deeply three times and then exhale deeply three times.*

Relaxation (you can record it)

You must concentrate all your attention on the part of your body that's in the process of relaxing.

- *I relax the toes on the right foot. My toes are at rest.*

- *I relax my heel, my heel is at rest.*

- *I relax my foot, my foot is at rest.*

- *I relax my ankle, my ankle is at rest.*

- *I relax my calf, my calf is at rest.*

- *I relax my knee, my knee is at rest.*

- *I relax my thigh, my thigh is at rest.*

- *Do the same for the left leg.*

- *I relax my pelvis, my pelvis is at rest.*

- *I relax my hips, my hips are at rest.*

- *I relax my chest, my chest is at rest.*

- *I relax my back, my back is at rest.*

- *I relax my breathing, I'm at rest.*

- *I relax my shoulders, my shoulders are at rest.*

- *I relax my neck, my neck is at rest.*

- *I relax my chin.*

- *I relax my cheeks.*

- *I relax my forehead.*

- *My eyelids are heavy, my eyelids are at rest.*

- *My head is heavy. My head is buried in the pillow.*

- *My body is heavy, it sinks into the ground.*

- *I am relaxed, at rest.*

- *I imagine a silver, fresh angelic fluid entering into my body through the top of my head. This fluid flows through my shoulders, my arms, my chest, my heart. I feel the freshness. It descends toward my hips, toward my legs. It courses down my legs. It is in my feet and leaves my body through a point in the center of the sole of my feet. My body empties itself of this fresh, silver liquid. I feel well. I feel light. I am getting lighter and lighter.*

You may begin your visualization or meditation. Your body has been cleansed by the angelic fluid. The tensions and stress are gone. Your thoughts are dormant. You are free, light, and ready to enter in communication with the angels.

10 – Dressing an Altar for the Angels

If possible, devote a space to the angels by dressing an altar for them. You can choose a small table, a part of your desk, or a small piece of furniture. This altar focuses angelic energies and favors communication with the celestial plane. The objects and images on your altar will help you visualize the angelic plane and open your higher vibratory channel, located in the crown Chakra above your head. This altar is effective when performing rituals, invocations, and prayers. Its presence in your home channels the angels' energies and raises the vibration of a place. An angelic altar creates harmony in your house and will inspire you to solicit the angels more often.

As you dress the altar for the angels, let your imagination run wild, and let the angels inspire you. Don't limit yourself to the recommendations of this book. The choice of objects, flowers, and images on the altar belongs to you as well as the angels. In this particular case, birth angels are powerful guides since they know what suits you best (see *Birth Angels*, page 403).

Let yourself be guided by your birth angel, and the other angels that you solicit. Feel free to cut out images of angels. Put down a white bowl filled with water every day: it will drive out negative energies. A white saucer filled with cooking salt will also do the trick. Pictures of your family are welcome on the altar of angels, especially ones that capture happy moments in your life. A white rose is a beautiful homage to angels.

The following ideas are merely suggestions. If you want, you can adorn your altar with rocks or seashells that you picked up along the shore, a white chalice filled with sand, incense sticks, a white candle, and gemstones or crystals that correspond to your angels (see *The Gemstones and Crystals of Angels*, p. 487). You can also put down statuettes, a vase with flowers that correspond to the color of your angel (see *The Colors of Angels*, p. 445), or some Mandalas you drew or colored-in using your inspiration and imagination (see *Meditation of the Mandala*, p. 287).

Angels like feathers, angel cards drawn every morning to determine the angelic vibration of the day, and books about angels you particularly like.

An essential oil diffuser chosen according to your angel (see *Essential Oils of Angels*, p. 431) will fill the atmosphere with a sanitizing perfume conducive to prayer and meditation. A Tibetan singing bowl should always be at your disposal to purify the room or to begin your invocations. When you have particular wishes or requests to address to the angels, objects symbolizing these wishes or requests can be placed on your altar. If you long for love, don't hesitate to find the object or image that represents love to you. If you wish to have abundance, do the same. Remember to wash any object that has circulated in other energies like coins or bills.

Don't be afraid to use symbols that speak to you, and that give you the desire to solicit the angels. The arrangement of your altar is in your hands, and the angels are always there to listen.

11 - Writing a Diary of Angels

Experiences with angels are always intense. During a meditation, you may see angels appear before you or hear them speaking to you. You may dream of angels. You may hear them giving you advice and recommendations. Sometimes, they manifest themselves physically, and you can feel their presence through the sound of a wing fluttering, a breath, an unknown scent, strange coincidences, feeling hot or cold, vivid emotions when you see an angel or hear them speaking, visions of their faces or a crowd of angels hovering around you.

The angelic plane holds incredible surprises in store. These events may seem wonderful as they're happening, but they're easy to forget once you become absorbed in your regular activities again. Writing a diary of angels is the best way to remember everything the angels have done and are continuously doing for you. This way, it's possible to thank them for their good and loyal service.

How you use this diary is up to you, but avoid lined paper because it limits your expression in a logic that doesn't belong to the angels. Your diary can be written with bubbles representing the speech of angels, words written vertically, poetic phrases, numbers, drawings, or symbols.

You will notice that throughout your intimate relationship with the angels in your diary, you will become connected with your celestial companions more and more every day.

12 - Collect Your Experiences

- *Begin by focusing on the precise memory that you wish to recount in your diary.*

- *Feel the emotions you first felt when the event took place.*

- *Let the images or sensations come to you.*

- *Write while your spirit is focused on the subject of angels. Don't let yourself get distracted by an outside event.*

- *Write down your dreams in case you forget them throughout the day.*

- *Be aware of the gift the angels are giving you through signs, information, advice, and miracles. Don't forget to say thank you at the end of each account you write in your diary.*

- *Say thank you: I thank you, holy angels, for you presence, for your help, for your support, and for your miracles. Amen.*

13 - Relating Your Experiences with Angels to Others

People who dare to talk about their experiences with angels and the miracles that have happened to them are rare. And yet, angels are grateful when we aren't scared to recognize their existence.

You mustn't proselytize or try to convince; simply talking about your experiences with the angels allows you to have a happy and peaceful connection to the angelic world.

Some people may ask you for advice when it comes to communicating with angels. Your collaboration with these people will elevate your relationship with the angelic plane even more.

14 - Trust and Faith

Angels constantly receive the thoughts, emotions, virtues, and justice of God. Therefore, the goodness, love, and light that radiates from an angel's heart cannot be put in doubt. Angels are the rays of the sun, the luminous emanations of the day's star. They accompany you and guide you no matter what your beliefs, religion, or way of thinking may be. But if you don't solicit them, they remain discreet, and won't influence your existence. Calling upon the angels brings miracles to your life. You awaken their desire to serve you, and to come to your aid. Between the angels and you, it's a true love story.

If you declare your faith to an angel, and open your heart to him, he will feel invested in you. The more you trust and believe in angels, the more they will come to your help.

In the beginning of your relationship with the angels, you start to receive recurring signs, images, and symbols. These angelic manifestations become more and more frequent when you are connected with angels.

Angels are beings of light and love; they always hurry toward you when you need them. When you are sick, you go to the doctor. Like the angels, the doctor will not come to you if you don't call upon him. Angels are not responsible for coming to help you if you have not asked for it. They respect your free will.

God offers simple assistance from the invisible plane to transform your existence. If that isn't your wish, the angels will stay in the background, ready to intervene only in extreme situations. In contrast, if you are connected, and have an open heart, the angels accompany you in your search for your ideals, and in the achievement of your dreams.

The amount of faith you have during the presence and help of angels is essential. It brings you confidence and the assurance of never being alone or abandoned when situations in life can be painful.

Having faith and trust in the angels is an indicator of your serenity and well-being. I've met many people who had faith in angels and saw their hopes and dreams come true beyond their wildest imagination. Angels don't always act in the way that you expect them to. You experience a love story with them. And true love is always surprising and astonishing. Angels feel for you the same love that God feels for them: eternal, infinite, and unconditional.

The effectiveness of the actions of angels is proportionate to your trust and faith in them. Those who only wish for small things will only get small things in return. People who think big receive miracles!

Angels are devoted to you. When you give them your faith and trust, they dedicate all their time and energy to you, and travel back and forth to the higher planes for you. Their teaching is an inexhaustible source of wealth.

15 - Living with Angels Everyday

The interventions of angels are not limited to the field of spirituality, love, money or material realities. Angels have absolute power in all spheres of existence.

You can solicit their support for various reasons: doing well on a test, finding a job, organizing a reception, finding a place to park, having a great trip, meeting loyal friends or people who will guide you throughout your personal or professional journey. Angels are omnipotent. Their power extends over all things.

Ask them to make flowers grow in your garden, to find another place for you to live, to find new interests that will replenish your love of life.

Don't hesitate to solicit them for creative stimulation in any field you wish. Reclaim their approval of your choices and decisions. The voices of angels manifest themselves as real voices that you can hear, or as a feeling in your heart. The voice of your heart is the voice of angels; it never deceives you. Lend your trust to angelic suggestion by excluding the mind and reason (see *The Angel That You Need*, p. 553).

The angels are in love with you. You interest them wholeheartedly. They don't pick which needs and desires of yours to fulfill. Call upon them under any circumstances. If you are lost on the road, you will meet someone who will show you the right way. If you are stuck in traffic and you are supposed to meet someone for an important meeting, angels will see to it that the person who would otherwise be waiting for you is delayed.

The help of angels is infinite. It comes wherever you want, whenever you want. You just need to ask, with faith and trust in them.

16 - Channeling

When you call upon angels, you can communicate with them in several different ways. Instead of rituals, prayers, and direct solicitations, some people are adept in channeling.

Channeling consists of establishing a connection between the material world and the invisible. This technique is often linked to the Eastern tradition of Spiritism and to communication with the dead.

Those adept in channeling communicate with the Other world through telepathy, automatic writing, or modified states of consciousness that allow for the direct reception of information from the angelic plane.

Some practice channeling through technical means:

• *Through the intermediary of a television that has been turned off, but still projects ethereal forms onscreen to transmit angelic messages.*

• *Through magnetic tape recordings on which the voice of angels can be heard.*

• *Automatic writing séances that transmit messages from the angelic plane.*

This method of angelic connection carries risks of energetic pollution. It's possible to receive authentic messages from the celestial plane, but the communication may be interrupted by negative entities. It's also possible that these entities will come to you instead of the angels you invoked, and deliver shocking or disturbing messages for the person doing the channeling.

Negative entities can be fallen angels or demons.

The person doing the consulting can generally discern loving messages from angels, but demons are sometimes subtle in their ways of luring sensitive or fragile people toward them.

17 - Sending Messages to the Angels

Written requests to angels are particularly effective. These requests are often addressed to the angels in times of disarray, sadness, anxiety, or deception, and garner a particular kind of attention from angels.

You can write to the angels if you're having trouble talking with the people around you after a period of mourning, a sentimental breakup, after being deceived by a friend, or for any other reason. Writing is a way of soothing tensions that have built up for too long, and sharing grief or pain with the angels who love you with all their heart.

The therapeutic advantage of writing and the action taken by angels to resolve problems you may be preoccupied with is absolutely extraordinary. Desperate people have regained their appetite for life; people who have been depressed for several years suddenly snap out of it.

Angels sometimes act in unexpected ways, but their interventions are particularly effective when dealing with people troubled with moral issues.

The angels' love for you is sincere and powerful, as the following verses demonstrate (Isaiah 63:9): "It was no delegate or messenger, but he himself who was their savior: in his love and in his compassion, it was he who redeemed them."

The messages you send angels should be written on white paper, preferably without lines. Make sure you write legibly, in black ink, out of respect for angels. Liberate yourself from the challenges weighing you down, from your anger, from your hatred, from your desire for revenge, and entrust the angels with the task of healing you. The angels are excellent therapists. Once your message is finished, add one of the following thank-you notes:

> Holy angels, thank you for healing me of...
> Holy angels, thank you for helping me forgive...
> Holy angels, thank you for liberating me from...

Choose the appropriate thank-you note and end your message with the following phrase:

> Holy angels, I thank you with all my heart,
> I wish to express my gratitude and thanks,
> Amen.

To send this message to the angels, fold your paper in four and burn it with the flame of a white or silver candle over a metal plate. Once your message has been sent, meditate for several minutes in the angelic energy.

18 - Reading Cards with Angels

People who read angel cards, tarot cards, or play divinatory games can ask the angels to develop their intuition and clairvoyance. Angels encourage people to interpret cards and create connections to the Akashic records, a source of universal knowledge. Angelic support in fortune-telling is extremely powerful. Professional or amateur fortune-tellers and tarot card readers who want to sharpen the visions or interpretation of their divinatory practice should call upon the angels. The invocation of an angel varies according to subject.

Health: invoke angel Raphael before drawing the cards.

Emotional, sentimental, or sexual domain: invoke angel Raziel before drawing the cards.

Money, financial questions, or the increase of wealth: invoke angel Tsadkiel before drawing the cards.

Social success or professional success: invoke angel Kamael before drawing the cards.

Knowledge, exams, science, or research: invoke angel Michael.

Work on the subconscious, psychoanalysis, renewal of structures, personal reflection, elevation of consciousness, or spiritual progression: invoke angel Gabriel.

Material organization, strategy, housing, request concerning the planet, or ecology: invoke angel Sandalphon before drawing the cards.

Past lives, or karmic influences: invoke angel Chamuel.

Material for Reading Cards with Angels
  • *A lit candle before the card draw.*

- *A rug on which to read the cards (preferably purple).*

- *An amethyst on the right side of the person reading the cards on the rug. (The amethyst develops faculties of mediumship and divination.)*

Additional Advice for Readings

Before reading cards, you should center your personal energies and meditate for a few minutes. The consultant and the person reading the cards should invoke the angel during this meditation.

It's very important to thank the angel at the end of the session.

There is a great variety of angel cards. These cards are often illustrated and pleasant to use. Their colorful and positive energy is effective for giving you information or transmitting angelic messages. Angels are sensitive to your energy, to the purity of your intentions, and to your gratitude when work with these cards.

Angel cards can be used in several different ways.

- *Start your day by pulling a card in the morning, in order to know the energy of that day.*

- *Ask a specific question as you choose three cards before making a choice or an important decision.*

- *Make sure that you are following your heart, and not just your mind, as well as the right reasons, which may not always be your own. Pull five cards and arrange them into a cross with one card in the middle. Read the cards, starting with the left one (the root of the question), then the bottom one (the answer you give to your question), then the top one (the advice of the angels), and finally the middle card (which gives you the solution and the best attitude to adopt).*

- *Sleep with an angel card on your nightstand or under your pillow. In your sleep, you will receive the energy of the angel of your choice.*

- *Wish for a good-luck charm, an occult protection. Define the area in which you wish to be protected. Mix your cards, and concentrate on summoning your angel (see The Angel That You Need, p. 553). Picture yourself in a bubble of blue light. Let the energy of the angel flow. And when you feel ready, choose your protective card. Observe it for a few moments. Fill yourself with its energy. Say thank you with the following prayer:*

Holy angels (say the name of your protective angel),
Thank you for protecting me, always and in all places,
Thank you for bringing me your help and support,
I will always be grateful,
Amen.

• *Slide this protective card in your wallet or purse and think of it regularly.*

• *This ritual is particularly effective when you wish to be protected financially, professionally, or in the field of love.*

Angel Readings

The Cross Shaped Reading with Five Cards
The left card represents the question's past. The top card represents the question's present. The right card is the question's future. The bottom card represents the energies dealing with the result of the question. The middle card is the answer to the question. When the energies are favorable and the answer is unfavorable, or the other way around, it means that it's not the most opportune moment to obtain results. It's recommended that you do another reading three days later, or three weeks later, depending on the question.

The Pyramid Shaped Reading
Five cards for the base (the question's root)

Then, three cards (the question's evolution)
Then, two cards (the question's energies)
Then, one card (the question's result)

The Great Annual Reading
    One card at the top
    Then, seven cards
    Then, two cards
    Then, two cards
    Then, one card at the base

This reading is in the shape of an angel with his wings outstretched. It's a general draw that looks ahead one year into the future. The card at the top represents the angels' advice for the following year. The other cards are read from left to right, starting with the month of January. The card at the base of the figure represents the month of December. It's the synthesis of the year gone by. You can pull two cards after the great draw to know the energy of the upcoming year as well as the general predictions for the year.

Metatron's Reading to Resolve a Problem
Three cards on the left (the problem's energies)
Three cards on the right (Metatron's advice)
Three cards at the base (the solution)

Start the draw by invoking angel Metatron. Write his name on a white non-lined piece of paper, cut into a square. Place this paper on the rug, on top of the draw.

After your readings, don't forget to thank the angels!

19 - How to Dress When Summoning Angels?

Angels are beings of exceptional purity. It's important to honor them by wearing appropriate clothing when performing rituals and invocations. Prayers can be recited at any moment in the day and don't require particular circumstances or specific clothes. Prayer is a verbal or mental exchange with the angels; it's simple and emotional. Your words and the angels' response circulate unrestrainedly between the angelic plane and the terrestrial plane.

Invocation rituals are intended to bring about real change in your life and your way of thinking. They act upon the evolution of your behavior with others, your work, your emotional relationships, and the person you love or desire. These rituals are considered functional magic. They must follow specific rules. It's important to undertake magical operations without reservations, and with faith and trust. The circulation of energies facilitates angelic connection. This is why it's important to choose a proper location, to purify it, and to wear comfortable clothes so as to avoid blocking the flow of energy.

Clothing and personal purification are the expression of your humility and desire to receive gifts and miracles from the angels. Naturally, the appropriate clothes for angelic celebrations are white, but sometimes purple. Preferably, you should choose clothes made of natural fabric, like flax or cotton; avoid anything synthetic. When you sit down to meditate, a white, silver, or golden pillow is preferable over other colors.

The purification of the body by taking a shower before any angelic ceremony encourages well-being and relaxation.

Remove any jewelry, rings, gemstones, or crystals you may be wearing. They can disturb the energy before and during communication. Also remove your watch and any belts with metal buckles. Be barefoot or in socks. Work in a well-lit room that has been aired out and make sure you are alone. Present yourself to the angels as you came into this world: natural, pure, and simple.

Angels are beings of light; avoid dark places and dark clothes. White is a must.

20 - *What Perfume to Choose for the Angels?*

Angels live and move about in the higher celestial plane where they are pure spirits. But when they take human form or if they establish a connection with humans, they become sensitive to beauty, refinement, and purity. Ancient traditions have always attributed particular importance to perfumes. In Greek, Roman, and Egyptian temples, the perfumes and scents of spiral incense pleased the Gods.

Angels like refined perfumes, essences, essential oils, and delicate fragrances.

When you purify yourself before an angelic ritual, the perfumes or essential oils you use give off even more scent. You can wear a perfume you like or feel comfortable with. Just make sure it goes with the incense and oils you will use for this angelic ritual. You can also make your own perfume.

Commercial perfumes should be avoided because they are transported all over the world and are worn by a great number of people. It's preferable to personalize your fragrance when you establish a connection with the celestial plane. The creation of an angelic perfume is a pleasant and refined activity that goes well with angelic rituals. You can also use essential oils, but using a perfume with your own personal touch is best for rituals involving inner transformation or invocations for love.

The usage of this perfume is personal. Don't let anyone else wear it. Throw away whatever remains in the bottle after the angelic ceremony. This perfume must be made the same day that it is used so that it isn't corrupted with time, but also because it corresponds to your state of mind regarding a particular request. Use your imagination to compose this perfume and follow your intuition.

Suggestion for Angelic Perfume

The choice of the angelic perfume's fragrance depends on your nature and tastes. Here are three perfumes that are easy to make.

Necessary Materials for the Fabrication of your Perfume
- *Spring water or rain water.*

- *The flower that determines the fragrance of your perfume.*

- *A small glass receptacle.*

- *A white cloth.*

The ingredients are the same for all three perfumes as is the method for making them. The three essences are composed of fresh flowers picked or bought the same day.

For rose perfume, you will choose an especially sweet-smelling white flower or a red rose with large petals. Avoid all other colors. This perfume is the easiest to make because the season doesn't matter. The two other flowers, jasmine and lily, are more sensitive to the climate and period.

Making the Perfume

When you have a fresh and sweet-smelling flower at your disposal, take off the petals one by one and place them gently on the white cloth. Then, softly crush each petal between your fingers. Let the drops of rose, jasmine or lily essence fall into the glass receptacle. Once the petals are completely crushed, mix them up with the residue you obtained using the stem of the flower. Then, add a bit of rain water or spring water, depending on how concentrated you want it to be.

Preferably, you shouldn't let more than an hour go by between the making of the perfume and performing the ritual. Perfume your body and hair.

21 - Visualizing Angels in Mandalas

Seeing angels is very common in your sleep, during meditation, in modified states of consciousness before sleeping, while taking a bath, and especially during rituals. But it's possible to see angels through a suggestion from our subconscious with help from the visual support of a Mandala.

Mandalas come from India. "Mandala" is the Sanskrit word for "circle." Symbolically, Mandalas are circles that create an environment around the gods. People who meditate with Mandalas are searching for the elevated state of consciousness of a bodhisattva, an Indian guru. The goal of these meditations is the elevation of the soul and ascension of the spirit toward the light.

You can make abstract Mandalas or ones that represent angels in order to establish contact with the angelic plane. It's also possible to get inspired from Indian Mandalas using motifs and colors that inspire you.

Suggestion of the Angelic Mandala

Make cut-outs of angels and organize them into a circle. If possible, reproduce the same angel many times around the circle. Diversity is distracting.

On the inside of the circle, draw some rays and color or paint the inside of these rays in a color evocative of an angel (see *The Colors of the Angels*, p 445). Then, place the Mandala's titular angel in the center of these rays, like a focal point. In this case, always invoke the angel in the center.

These angelic Mandalas are very useful during meditation and the visualization of angels. They focus your attention and quiet your thoughts. Meditation is simple. All it requires is a Mandala and a peaceful place where you won't be disturbed.

22 - *Meditation of the Mandala*
(Approximately 15 minutes)

This meditation aims to achieve physical and spiritual relaxation under the protection of an angel. It's not a meditation of invocation or request, but a soothing of physical and psychological tensions through the positive and loving energy of angels.

You'll be able to establish a particular kind of communication with the titular angel of your Mandala, who will bathe you in his soft vibration, creating a sensation of well-being and rest.

Material
- *A Mandala*
- *A white candle*
- *Lavender incense sticks.*

Meditation
1. Burn the incense and light the candle.
2. Sit down comfortably on a chair or a meditation cushion. Relax. Breathe softly.
3. Look at the Mandala in front of you. Let yourself be hypnotized by the image and colors. After a certain amount of time, the image and colors blend together into a single shape. Fill yourself with the energy of this shape. Feel the release of your tensions.
4. Let the softness of angelic vibration bring you peace. Abandon your thoughts and your preoccupations and concentrate entirely on the shape and colors.
5. Close your eyes. Appreciate this moment of well-being. Let yourself go.
6. Open your eyes. Slowly regain ordinary consciousness.

Effects of the Meditation
This meditation allows you to connect to the angelic plane, to detach yourself from the mind, your thoughts, and agitated or nervous states of consciousness. It's specifically recommended for people who are anxious, stressed, or who cannot detach themselves from the material plane. This meditation connects the spirit and conscience to the higher planes. It brings lightheartedness and the love of life.

23 - Taking a Bath with the Angels

In a bath, the body can relax and rest. You can take an "angelic bath" by preparing for a specific ritual that attracts angels. After the ritual of the bath, you will be in a state of deep relaxation, and open to a more involved form of communication with angels. It's preferable to do a ceremony, ritual, meditation, or directly go to bed so that the angels can send you advice and ideas during the night.

You can also do a meditation after an angelic bath.

This bath is a soft and pleasant step. Angels are always in favor of your physical relaxation. Don't hesitate to take angelic baths regularly: you will feel great well-being and a relaxation of the spirit.

Material
- *A yellow rose.*

- *Heena incense (oriental incense), or sandalwood or lavender incense.*

- *Don't use foaming gel or bath salts. The water must be pure and clear.*

- *A white or golden candle.*

The Bath
1. Burn the incense. Light the candle.
2. Pluck the petals off of the rose and throw them into the bath.
3. Slowly enter the water, thinking about the angel you wish to invoke.
4. Relax.
5. Close your eyes. Imagine yourself being plunged into a golden bubble. Say these words:

Holy angels, I'm abandoning myself to your soothing energy.
Holy angels, I am happy and relaxed.
Let it always be so.

6. Open your eyes. Regain ordinary consciousness. You can stay in the water for as long you like.

Effects of the Bath

The angelic bath has soothing powers. It facilitates the vibratory opening between planes through the water, which is a conductor of energy.

All meditation, prayer, or invocation that follows an angelic bath will be all the more effective since you have gotten rid of bodily tensions and relaxed your muscles.

This bath is recommended for anyone who is stressed or anxious. It's also advisable that you do it before a meditation or angelic ceremony.

24 - Massage with the Angels

A massage is particularly recommended for stressed or anxious people. A massage in the company of angels is a step toward self-esteem and confidence in life. A body that has been left in the hands of a masseuse leaves itself open to angelic receptiveness. You can quiet your mind and thoughts. You enter the vibration of angels.

The massage room must only be lit with candles. The masseuse should use a variety of oils, and massage you for at least an hour. Massages that are too short don't allow the body enough time to relax.

Base Oils That Can Be Mixed with Essential Oils

- *Soft and balmy almond oil, adapted for all kinds of skin.*

- *Argan oil, very nourishing.*

- *Avocado oil, recommended for dry skin.*

- *Bourrache oil.*

- *Cottonseed oil.*

- *Wheat germ oil*

- *Jojoba oil, recommended for dry and fragile skin.*

- *Macadamia oil, very nourishing.*

- *Apricot kernel oil, recommended for very dry skin.*

- *Olive oil.*

- *Sesame oil.*

- *Onagra oil.*

- *Hazelnut oil.*

- *Sunflower oil.*

Mix two drops of essential oil for every tablespoon of massage oil.

The perfume must be light. It's advisable that you do a preliminary tolerance test. Test the perfumed oil on the finest skin of your forearm. Do this test at least two days before using it.

Material
- *Essential oils that perfume the massage oil according to the angel you wish you to invoke. If you need several essential oils, mix them together before integrating them with the massage oils (see Essential Oils of the Angels, p. 431).*

- *Massage oil.*

- *Three golden candles and a white candle.*

- *Relaxing music, if possible without a vocal track.*

Massage

1. The room must be calm and very dimly lit. The music mustn't be too loud.
2. The three golden candles should be positioned in a row. Place the white candle in front of the golden candle in the center.
3. During the massage, enter the inner silence. While your body loosens up, liberate your spirit of stress and worrisome thoughts. Empty yourself by thinking of the angel that you're calling upon for protection.
4. Feel the presence of the angel through an influx of well-being, the

sensation of a light breeze, a wing brushing up against your shoulder. The presence of the masseuse does not interfere with the arrival of the angel.

Effects of the Massage

An angelic massage is a moment of physical harmony that opens the Chakras, allowing you to receive the energy of the angels. Relaxation provides a feeling of well-being conducive to opening yourself up and discovering the angelic plane. This massage is recommended for anyone who wishes to get in touch with angels through the association of bodily and spiritual relaxation.

25 – The Yoga of Angels

Health is a precious asset that must be treated and maintained every day. The body, the muscles, the nervous system, and general balance are preserved through regular physical exercise adapted to each person's age, gender, and personal training.

Yoga is recommended for people of all ages. It reestablishes equilibrium, harmonizes energies, strengthens the body, and develops body tone.

After yoga séances, relaxing allows the body and spirit to be rest. No matter what kind of yoga you practice, it's best to associate each séance with the angel of the day, of the hour, or to a birth angel.

Before the séance, invoke the angel whose protection you want, and during the séance, wear a small red jasper gemstone that you have devoted to angel Kamael.

Red jasper stimulates action, energizes the Chakras, and warms up the muscles.

Devoting the Red Jasper to Angel Kamael

1. Clean off the red jasper with clear water and soap.

2. Recharge the gemstone on the eve of a full moon.

3. Put the gemstone on a white non-lined sheet of paper, cut into a square, and then place your palm on the gemstone as you say the following words:

Holy angel Kamael,
Devote this gemstone for my yoga,
Give me strength and energy,
Preserve my health and youth,
I thank you,
Amen.

Chapter 12

The Miracles of Angels

According to tradition, angels are beneficent and protective creatures that support and comfort humans. The religions of the Bible assign them the role of divine messengers, and servants of God responsible for carrying out divine orders.

Through individual and planetary awakening of consciousness, the number of people who have witnessed angelic miracles is growing larger and larger. The presence of angels is an active and constantly evolving reality.

It's necessary to call upon the angels to obtain an answer to a specific question or to benefit from their direct intervention. Despite their multiple functions, the angels do their best to carry out requests as quickly as possible. Urgent calls always have priority.

Miracles occur in very different domains: in the material plane just as much as in the spiritual plane. The angels can be solicited to obtain financial wealth or to acquire real estate. The angels are ready and willing to assist humans in every sphere of existence as long as the request is sincere and unprejudiced, but they are wary of requests that don't come from the heart or that are motivated by negative sentiments. The intentions of the person who is soliciting help from the angels must be pure and honest. If this is the case, the angels will do everything they can, allowing for incredible events to take place. A new encounter alters a person's life; joy enters a household; families find harmony and couples find happiness; a student aces a test; professional success, financial wealth and material abundance come within reach. These angelic miracles in the field of love or the material domain are always followed by an incredible spiritual elevation. Every person that experiences angelic miracles gives thanks, and recognizes the goodness and generosity of angels. This new consciousness raises the vibratory rate, facilitates communication with angels, and elevates the consciousness of the planet. This is why you shouldn't hesitate to solicit angels, to ask them to do what's good for you. What's good for an individual is universally good.

Never forget to thank the angels after they've granted you a miracle. Never forget to share your material gifts, and to give back to others the love you've received.

1 - Meeting Your Soul Mate

The angels are responsible for the spiritual evolution of men. Their mission is to help humanity progress toward heightened consciousness and love.

The angels' love toward humans is unconditional, pure, and infinite. The angels know that they evolve on a high spiritual level since some of them are by God's side and receive their orders directly from the Lord. The angels orchestrate the process of human spiritual elevation, and in the delicate domain of finding a soul mate, they must display sharp intuition and an abundance of love. Of all the human feelings, love between two souls represents the highest possible degree of elevation in the material plane. Soul mates create an egregore of love, goodness, and reciprocal admiration.

Contrary to popular belief, soul mates don't necessarily have material affinities, a common passion, or emotional resemblance. They may very well be different by nature, and have different religions, cultures, or come from different social backgrounds. There are no barriers or limits when it comes to two soul mates meeting. A soul's only guide toward it's other half is the absolute love that unites them for all eternity. The attraction between two soul mates is an allurement that cannot be explained. Awakened people who are ready to meet their soul mate open themselves up completely, without judging, criticizing, or comparing. Your soul mate may not be like you, and may even have no relation to you. Many people never meet their soul mates for lack of openness and lack of faith in the reality of soul mates. Often, the idea of a soul mate reminds people of painful emotional experiences. But it's important to know that a soul mate does no harm. A soul mate is a person with the same emotional nature as you, even if it's difficult to understand their behavior, their actions, and their way of life or way of thinking. The main challenge in finding a soul mate is being able to recognize them for what they are in spite of often misleading appearances.

The texts of the Bible evoke love in a poetic and eternal way. Love cannot be ugly, painful, or sad, which is why the angels are ready to lead us toward our soul mate. This love is pure, and it participates in the elevation of the vibratory rate of humanity.

In the Old Testament, the Prophets (Jeremy 31:3), it says: "From afar, the LORD appeared to me: I love you with an everlasting love; I have drawn you with loving friendship."

In the New Testament, Epistles of Paul (Galatians 5:22), it says: "But the fruit of the Spirit is love, joy, peace, patience, goodness, kindness, faithfulness, softness, self-control..."

The beauty of love, as described in the Bible, corresponds to the love between two souls that recognize each other as two halves that form a whole, and that share the same goal and the same desire to elevate their hearts. The angels are particularly active in this mission of elevation and love, and will help us find our soul mate if we ask them to.

2 - Meditation to Meet Your Soul Mate

(Approximately 45 minutes)

Everyone has a soul mate that shares the same emotions and emotional desires. Most people think that a soul mate is a person that shares the same passions, interests, or way of perceiving the world, which often leads them to making mistakes about the people they end up choosing. The reality of the soul mate is located on a higher vibratory plane of emotion and love. When a soul mate establishes an energetic connection with its other half, this connection is so strong that the beauty and quality of the universal love uniting them trivializes any differences of opinion or ways of living.

Asking an angel to help you find your soul mate takes great responsibility. You must be prepared to make this encounter, you must believe in infinite and eternal love, and you must be willing to raise your vibratory rate in order to experience the soul's most heightened feelings.

Material
- *A meditation rug*

- *A white candle*

- *A white rose*

- *Rose essential oil*

- *A stick of rose incense*

- *Angelic music*

- *Pink quartz*

Meditation
1. Burn the incense and listen to the angelic music.
2. Pour seven drops of rose essential oil on your hands and rub them together energetically. Then, wash your hands in cold water.
3. Pluck seven petals off of the rose and make a circle with these petals. Place the white candle in the center. Light the candle.
4. Stretch out on the meditation rug. Place the pink quartz over the heart Chakra.
5. Begin anatomic relaxation (see *Relaxation Techniques*, p. 270).

6. Breathe slowly. Close your eyes.

7. Invoke Anael, the angel of love.

8. Chant the AUM mantra seven times. Feel it resonate in your body.

9. Visualize pink light enveloping the outline of your body perfectly. Anael's energy is warming up this second body of light.

10. Remove the quartz from your Chakra and say the following words:

> Holy angel Anael,
> Open my heart and my soul mate's heart to infinite love,
> Let our souls be reunited for all eternity,
> In fidelity, goodness, beauty, peace, and tenderness,
> Let it be so.

11. A golden ray illuminates your heart Chakra. This ray comes from your soul mate. At the same time, your soul mate receives your pink ray.

12. Open up your heart Chakra. Feel its expansion. Your chest is bathing in the pleasant and luminous warmth of your soul mate's golden ray, giving you an impression of safety, well-being, and softness. Make use of this golden ray and visualize your pink ray illuminating your soul mate's chest.

13. Thank Anael.

14. Enjoy this moment of relaxation. Picture Anael uniting your hand with your soul mate's hand.

15. Open your eyes. Take your time to regain ordinary consciousness.

Effects of the Meditation

This meditation is for people who truly wish to meet their soul mates and give up on superficial romantic conquests. This meditation should only be done with the certainty of wanting to commit yourself to a long lasting relationship of high quality vibration and energy.

3 – Developing Your Intuition

The development of intuition is an important asset when it comes to managing your life, without controlling actual events. Control is the manifestation of fear. Asking the angels to guide you in the development of intuition will allow you to stop being preyed upon by fear. It opens up a new perspective, the field of possibility, and favors making new encounters. If you use your intuition during work, when you socialize with other people, or in everyday life, you follow your inner guide and are no longer held hostage by the fear that leads you to make mistakes. Intuition is a wonderful guide that develops self-confidence and removes limitations. The angels can help us develop intuition; all we need to do is ask.

4 – Meditation to Develop Your Intuition
(Approximately 15 minutes)

This meditation offers great angelic protection and establishes a permanent connection with angel Vehuiah.

Material
- *A stick of rose incense*
- *A meditation cushion*
- *A silver candle*

Meditation

1. Light the candle and burn the incense.
2. Sit down on a meditation cushion and loosen your shoulders. Place your open palms on your thighs. Your thumb and index should barely be touching.
3. Close your eyes. Take in a deep breath and then exhale.
4. Concentrate on the third eye Chakra and feel the expansion of the Chakra. The Chakra opens as it receives Vehuiah's angelic vibration in the form a blinding white light irradiating with love. Your eyelids close

because you are overwhelmed by the white light. The light bathes your Chakra, which expands more and more.

5. The Chakra is open wide enough that you can see angel Vehuiah smiling at you and looking at you with love. Your heart beats faster and faster, and energy courses through your body. You feel a tingling sensation, like a small electrical current.

6. The blinding light softens. The feelings fade.

7. Thank Vehuiah.

8. Regain ordinary consciousness.

Effects of the Meditation

This meditation is for people who try to control their existence and limit their actions. The development of intuition allows them to develop their discernment, to trust themselves completely, and to live openly.

5 - *Feeling Compassion*

Compassion is a great human feeling that excludes judgment or criticism. Learning how to feel compassion for others is one of the great human steps that will also allow you to feel compassion for yourself. People who pass judgment or criticize others are often self-deprecating people who disparage themselves by constantly comparing themselves to others. Self-love is the first step toward compassion. Not judging yourself and accepting who you are allows you to feel complete and sincere compassion for others.

Asking the angels to help you feel compassion should be done in two steps. The first step consists of developing love for yourself, and the second will allow you to feel compassion for others.

6 – Meditation for Self-Love
(Approximately 15 minutes)

This meditation is very effective. Angel Rahmiel is one of the angels of mercy and love.

Material
- *A pink rose*
- *A pink candle*
- *A stick of jasmine incense*
- *A meditation cushion*

Meditation

1. Light the candle and burn the incense.

2. Pluck the petals off of the rose and rub your hands with them.

3. Sit down on the meditation cushion. Your hands are on your thighs. Your thumb and index are barely touching. Relax. Breathe slowly. Close your eyes.

4. Invoke angel Rahmiel. The angel envelops you in his affectionate wings. You no longer feel alone. Rahmiel's presence is reassuring, soft, and tender.

5. Concentrate on your solar plexus Chakra. Inhale, and then repeat the AUM mantra as you exhale slowly. Do this several times. The mantra's vibration opens up your solar plexus. Feel the Chakra's expansion.

6. Rahmiel rests his hand on your solar plexus. Repeat the AUM mantra. The mantra's vibration connects you to Rahmiel's love. Feel the love and openness. Enjoy this emotional communion with Rahmiel. Say thank you.

7. Open your eyes.

8. Regain ordinary consciousness.

Effects of the Meditation

This meditation is for people without self-esteem or self-love, and who compare themselves to others. This meditation creates the desire to make projects, and allows you to look upon the future with serenity and optimism.

7 - *Meditation of Compassion*
(Approximately 20 minutes)

This meditation follows the meditation for self-love. It's best to do it three days after. It must be done in a calm, dimly lit room.

Material
- *A blue candle*
- *A stick of jasmine incense*
- *A meditation cushion*

Meditation

1. Light the candle and burn the incense.

2. Sit down on the meditation cushion, your hands on your thighs with your palms open, ready to receive angelic energy.

3. Close your eyes. Invoke angel Haniel.

4. Picture the starry sky of a summer night. The stars represent the souls of the people who receive your compassion. Haniel helps you find your star amongst all the others. Accept the star with your hand and watch it shine in your fingers.

5. Now, with Haniel's help, pick another star, one that belongs to a person who feels your compassion. The star is shining in your left hand. You feel a tingling sensation in your hands from the radiance of the stars. Let these stars enter your heart Chakra. Close one palm over the other on your heart. The stars are inside you.

6. Breathe the light of the stars inside you and feel compassion for yourself and for the people in your heart.

7. Thank Haniel. Open your eyes and regain ordinary consciousness.

8 – Letting the Angels into Your Life

The angels are the messengers of God, and God is love. In the Old Testament, the Poetic Books (Proverbs 21:21), it says: "He who pursues righteousness and love finds life, justice, and honor." The angels are infallible companions that guide us toward personal accomplishment.

When you summon the angels for help in a particular situation, they will rescue you and open up new paths in your personal and professional life. The angels aren't content with merely helping. When you call upon them, they change your energy. Invoking the angels elevates consciousness, increases the vibratory rate, and awakens joy.

People who summon angels free themselves of negative karma and past lives loaded with painful memories. Angels clean up the negative layers of your subconscious. They transform your life by creating openings and new possibilities. The experiences of the many people who call upon the angels demonstrate that miracles frequently occur in the angelic vibration. Angels have real power over matter. Their interventions appear genuinely miraculous when someone finds work after an extended period of unemployment or when a large sum of money suddenly lands in the bank account of someone who truly needs it. Miraculous job opportunities present themselves unexpectedly; miraculous encounters between two soul mates occur. The angels encourage people who wish to transform their existence by encouraging great personal, professional, or family changes. You can summon the angels when you want to change the country where you live or change environments. But no matter what the domain of the angelic intervention, the angels' actions are uncontrollable and unpredictable. Angels belong to a celestial plane that doesn't abide by the terrestrial plane's rules of logic. The best results are obtained when you detach yourself from the outcome and cease to control the events in your life. Asking the angels for miracles requires complete trust in their influence over the result. Make your request and let the angels do the rest. Miracles generally happen when you least expect them to.

9 - The Angelic Agreement

The angelic agreement is something you must negotiate with the angels. You agree to confide in them about your past, present, and future so that they can bring out the best in you. You sign a moral commitment with a pen dipped in trust and faith.

10 - Visualization

(Approximately 15 minutes)

This visualization is extremely useful if you feel the slightest doubt regarding the actions of angels and the miracles they bring about in your life. Concentrating is easier if you work in an isolated place where you're sure you won't be disturbed. Before the visualization, make sure you air out the room for at least 20 minutes.

Material
- *A blue candle*
- *A green candle*
- *A yellowish-orange candle*
- *A purple candle*
- *A white candle*
- *A black candle*
- *A golden candle*
- *A silver candle*

Visualization

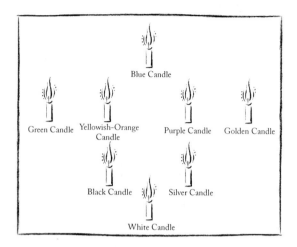

1. Position the candles in the following way to form the figure below. Figure 8

2. Light the candles.

3. Empty your mind. Concentrate on the figure. Let the shape and colors enter in you. Imagine that you are a bird with colorful feathers. You fly away, across the blue sky, and then through the clouds. You rise higher. You are in a soft fog. You fly without difficulty. Suddenly, the angels appear before you. They are wonderful. There are many of them flying in front of you. Some are smiling at you, others are looking at you with love and goodness. They fly with you, embracing you in their wings. You feel amazingly good.

4. It's time to return to earth. You go through the clouds and the blue sky again. You open your eyes. Relax. Breathe slowly.

5. Regain ordinary consciousness.

11 - Seeing the Angels' Signs

When you're accustomed to doing angelic meditations, or if you celebrate the presence of angels in your everyday life by meditating with angels, reading books about angels, keeping statuettes of angels in your home, or in any other way you please, you are in angelic agreement. The angels accompany you in your activities, protect you, and guide you when you ask them to.

Living with angels helps your everyday life incredibly. Their support and advice helps you to never feel alone, and to be aware that someone who loves you will always do their best to show you the way when you feel in need of guidance.

Angels often manifest themselves in unpredictable and surprising ways. When you ask for their assistance, they bring about coincidences, incredible encounters, improbable situations, or news from people you haven't heard from in 20 years. Be open when ask for help from the angels. Be attentive to the slightest sign that may indicate their presence around you. When you find a white feather, the angels are there. When you see angels in commercials or on television, they are there with you.

The angels can also communicate with you through telepathy, and thus manifest themselves through ideas that come to you. You seek solutions you had never thought of before. You celebrate change, or a new project. The angels transform your psychological approach to situations. They make you want to speed ahead when you were once reticent, or they make you want to slow down when you were once overly enthusiastic. You must listen to your inner feelings. The angels guide you through your emotions, so you must be attentive to them.

The angels may also speak to you in your dreams, or reveal new information to you through a sudden feeling of intuition that overwhelms your spirit.

12 - Finding an Immediate Solution

In certain situations in life, it's necessary to give an immediate response, to make an urgent choice, or to take an instant decision. If you need assistance right away, ask the angels. Don't be afraid to solicit them. Don't forget that angels are messengers of God, and that God strives for the elevation of human consciousness and values. In the Bible,

Old Testament, the Poetic Books (Proverbs 28: 12), it says: "When the righteous triumph, there is great glory."

Angels want humans to be happy. When we connect ourselves to angels and ask for support and assistance in order to make progress and increase the well-being of those around us, the angels' help is miraculous.

13 – Meditation to Find an Immediate Solution
(Approximately five minutes)

This meditation is quick and requires no material. It can be done anytime you feel the sudden need for help in making a decision.

Material
None

Meditation
1. No matter where you are, fixate your eyes on an object, a wall, a door, or anything else around you. Concentrate on the object until it becomes blurry.
2. Connect yourself to the angels. Transform the blurry object into an angelic apparition. Feel the angelic energy. Feel the infinite love surrounding you and ask your question to yourself.
3. Regain ordinary consciousness.
4. A few minutes later, you will receive the answer through an immediate reversal of the situation, a suggestion, or a surprising idea. If it doesn't come to you, it's because you've asked a useless question or for something that isn't beneficial to you.

Effects of the Meditation
This meditation is for people who wish to obtain advice, a solution, or an immediate answer to a question.

14 - Understanding Others

The angels are your guides and personal allies. They also help you develop relationships with the people around you, your friends, acquaintances, and work colleagues.

At certain times in your life, it's more difficult to relate with others, either because of a lack of receptiveness, or because you're going through a hard time.

During these periods of inner and outer conflict, simply ask for the angels to help facilitate harmonious relationships, the recognition of work, or the desire to make new projects. Harmony with others begins by accepting who you are. This is why you must start the mediation of others by working a little on yourself.

15 - Meditation for Self-Acceptance

(Approximately 10 minutes)

This meditation must be done in a calm room where you won't be disturbed.

Material
- *A white candle*
- *Jasmine incense*

Meditation

1. Light the candle and burn the incense.
2. Stand up, with your legs spread 12 inches apart, your arms open, forming a cross with your body, and your palms facing the sky.
3. In this position, feel the angelic white light radiating and entering your crown Chakra through the top of your head.
4. Feel this light going through the third eye Chakra, then down into the throat Chakra, the heart Chakra, the solar plexus Chakra, and the second Chakra under the belly button. Your Chakras are illuminated and warm. You feel alive and reinvigorated. The white energy exits your

body through the root Chakra. Lower your arms, letting them dangle at your side. Loosen your shoulders.

5. Feel the expansion of your root Chakra. Squeeze your buttocks and stiffen your legs to anchor yourself in the ground. The angelic energy that went through your body stabilizes you between heaven and earth. Picture this energy as a white stem passing through your body, linking you to heaven and earth.

6. Slowly regain ordinary consciousness.

Effects of the Meditation

This meditation is for anyone who wants to accept who they are and balance their energies.

16 - Meditation to Understand Others

(Approximately 10 minutes)

This meditation allows you to better situate yourself in relation to others. If you are shy, worried, or insecure during social interaction, others feel your weakness and often react to it in a way that destabilizes you or provokes aggressive behavior. This mediation allows you to accept who you are while being tolerant of others.

Having harmonious relationships reestablishes personal and emotional balance. It's best to do the meditation for self-acceptance before doing this meditation. The effects will be anchored into the subconscious in a more durable way. It's recommended that you space out these two meditations by at least a few hours, but ideally by three days.

You can do this meditation after every new encounter or when you doubt the sincerity of a person. Raphael will make appropriate suggestions about the situation.

Material
- *A yellowish-orange candle*

- *A meditation cushion*

- *A yellowish-orange rose*

Meditation

1. Light the candle and sit down on the meditation cushion.

2. Pluck the petals off of the rose and rub your hands in them as you invoke angel Raphael. While smelling the rose's perfume, quietly ask Raphael to help you reestablish harmonious relationship with others.

3. Place your hands flat on your thighs, with your palms facing the sky.

4. Close your eyes.

5. Picture yourself shaking hands with someone you don't know. Observe this stranger's face smiling at you. Look at his teeth and his mouth. See the joy on his face.

6. Raphael protects your new friendship. He envelops both of you in his big, safe wings. From now on, entrust your relationships to Raphael's protection.

7. Open your eyes. Thank Raphael and slowly regain ordinary consciousness.

Effect of the Meditation

This meditation is for anyone who wishes to reestablish communication or trust in their relations with others.

17 - Having Great Ideas

Angels will always offer support and encouragement to people who invoke them to make advances for humanity. They suggest great ideas to inventors, scientists, researchers, or doctors participating in projects that lead to the progress of human history.

The more they are solicited, the more active the angels become. If you are destined to make advances for humanity, if your mission on Earth is to heal, innovate, discover, facilitate everyday tasks, embellish life, or elevate artistic or literary consciousness, then don't hesitate to ask for great ideas from the angels. You will always be heard and your request will always be fulfilled.

18 - Meditation to Have Great Ideas
(Approximately 10 minutes)

Material
- *A meditation cushion.*

- *A stick of amber incense.*

- *Small gemstones of your choice (transparent, rutile, or smoked quartz, amethyst, pink quartz, ruby, sunstone…).*

- *A piece of smooth fabric.*

- *A cord (string, ribbon, cotton, yarn…)*

Meditation

1. Light the incense.

2. Sit down on the meditation cushion and relax. Think of the request before formulating it.

3. Summon angel Teiaiel and ask him to fulfill your wish by sending you great ideas that you need for your evolution and the evolution of humanity.

4. Make a wish pouch with the piece of smooth fabric sprawled out in front of you. Choose the most appropriate gemstone for the domain in which you wish to have a great idea. Place the gemstones on the piece of fabric and close it up with a piece of string, making it into a pouch.

5. Devote your wish pouch to angel Teiaiel.

Holy angel Teiaiel,
Inspire me with the great idea that I need to evolve,
Give me the strength and energy to make it happen,
Open me up to infinite knowledge,
Let my wish be fulfilled,
Let it be accomplished,
Amen.

6.Place the pouch on your heart. Close your eyes and thank angel Teiaiel.

7.Regain ordinary consciousness.

Effects of the Meditation

This meditation is for people who wish to receive great ideas from angels that will transform their existence and the existence of those around them as well as other people who will profit through spiritual and material elevation.

When the wish or wishes are fulfilled, open up the pouch and recover the stones, which must be cleaned, purified, and recharged in the moonlight before being used again.

19 - Attracting Success

The angels intervene to help and serve us in any domain, including in the material plane, so that we can achieve financial, professional, or artistic success. This meditation brings substantial help to people in the process of acquiring a diploma, or taking any other step necessary for their professional evolution.

When we ask for it, angels make miracles happen in the material domain. They can help you find a new job, get a better position at the company you work for, or provoke real artistic and creative success. It will never be said enough, the angels achieve genuine miracles!

20 - Meditation to Attract Success

(Approximately 15 minutes)

This meditation brings success to artists, people who want their talent recognized, people who wish to climb the career ladder, or anyone passing an important exam.

Material
• *A red candle.*

- *Music with the sounds of the forest or nature.*

- *A piece of red non-lined paper, cut into a square.*

- *A white chalice filled with cooking salt.*

- *Dried verbena leaves.*

- *A red ribbon.*

- *A pen.*

Meditation

1. Light the candle.
2. Listen to the music.
3. Write your desires for success on the square piece of red paper. No more than three requests at a time. Be concise and specific.
4. Add some verbena leaves and roll up the square piece of paper. Seal the scroll with hot wax from the red candle. Concentrate on your requests. Invoke angel Kamael. Tie up the scroll with the red ribbon.
5. Draw a circle of cooking salt on the ground, in which you will do your meditation.
6. Stand up, with your legs spread 12 inches apart. Grab the scroll with your right hand. Place it over your heart, and close your eyes.
7. Concentrate on angel Kamael, who enters the room beating his wings.
8. Visualize the angel getting closer to you. Smell his perfume. Extend your right hand toward him, and offer him the scroll.
9. Visualize the angel's hand touching the scroll in order to know your requests.
10. Thank Kamael and ask him to fulfill your wishes.
11. Open your eyes and regain ordinary consciousness.
12. Keep the scroll in your nightstand or under your pillow until the wishes have been fulfilled.

Effects of the Meditation

This meditation is for people who wish to attract success in every professional field, artistic domain, or to do well on exams.

21 - Attracting Money

This invocation brings fresh money in an unexpected way to people who wish to increase their revenue, who want to improve their financial situation, or who need a certain amount to achieve a project. It also allows you to solicit new job opportunities with higher pay. Angels favor material comfort as long as it doesn't engender domination, pride, hoarding or accumulating wealth. Angels respond to material requests when the money is circulated and shared with others.

Clement of Alexandria (150-220 A.D., Father of the Church), says: "He then is truly and rightly rich who is rich in virtue, and is capable of making a holy and faithful use of any fortune; while he is spuriously rich who is rich, according to the flesh, and turns life into outward possession, which is transitory and perishing, and now belongs to one, now to another, and in the end to nobody at all."

When it comes to money, the angels' interventions are miraculous. In the Bible, Old Testament, the Pentateuch (Deuteronomy 14:26), it says: "Use the money to buy whatever you like: cattle, sheep, wine or other fermented drink, or anything you wish. Then you and your household shall eat there in the presence of the LORD your God and rejoice." Money acquired through the miracles of angels must be used for terrestrial good, the well-being of those around you, and anything that brings about joy or happiness.

The angels in the Bible favor wealth and abundance. In the Old Testament, the Prophets (Zachariah 3:4-5), it says: "The angel said to those who were standing before him, 'Take off his filthy clothes.' Then he said to Joshua, 'See, I have taken away your sin, and I will put rich garments on you.' Then he said, 'Put a clean turban on his head.' They put a clean turban on his head and clothed him. And the angel of the

LORD stood by."

God favors abundance and power. In the Bible, Old Testament, the Pentateuch (Genesis 24:35), he says: "The LORD has blessed my master, who has become a great person. He has given him sheep and cattle, silver and gold, menservants and maidservants, and camels and donkeys."

When the angels are generous, they create the energy of generosity through their gifts. The angels' goodness comes from God, who gave them his love and his desire to bestow well-being upon men. In the Bible, New Testament, the Epistles of Paul (2 Corinthians 9:8), it says: "God is able to make all grace abound to you, so that in all things at all times, having all that you need, you will have an abundance for every good work."

22 - Invocation to Attract Money
(Approximately 10 minutes)
This invocation must be done in a calm room where you're sure you won't be disturbed.

Material
- *A blue candle.*
- *A stick of cinnamon incense.*
- *Music of the sea, of moving water, of a spring or waterfall.*
- *A silver coin.*
- *A chalice filled with cooking salt.*
- *Ten dried star anise leaves.*

Invocation
1. Light the candle and burn the incense.
2. Listen to the music and relax.
3. On the ground, draw a circle around the silver coin with the cooking

salt, and surround this circle with the dried anise leaves.

4. Concentrate on the specific request you wish to formulate.

5. Invoke angel Tsadkiel and say the following words:

Holy angel Tsadkiel,
I'm imploring you fulfill my essential needs,
Bring me wealth, abundance, and success.
Holy angel Tsadkiel,
I'm committing myself to living in goodness, generosity, and sharing,
I shall be eternally grateful,
Let it be so.

6. Walk clockwise around the circle containing the silver coin seven times.

7. Stand up, facing east, with your arms open to form a cross with your body and your palms turned toward the sky, and say the following words:

Holy angel Tsadkiel,
Cover me with your wealth and abundance,
Let it be so.

8. Cross your arms over your chest and say the following words:

Holy angel Tsadkiel,
I shall be eternally grateful,
Amen.

9. End the prayer by closing your eyes for a few moments and filling yourself up with Tsadkiel's energy.

10. Regain ordinary consciousness.

Effects of the Invocation

This invocation is for people who want to increase their revenue. It's also for people who need money to achieve a project dear to their heart, or for anyone whose material needs haven't been satisfied.

23 – Radiating with the Angels

A person's radiance is the reflection of their inner strength. The Sun shines because its inner light is phenomenal. Lamps give light because the light bulb makes them shine from the inside. Radiance requires no outer influence. It's autonomous and independent. The Moon doesn't radiate, it refracts the Sun's light.

A person's radiance comes from their positive energy, their vitality, and their way of considering existence a passionate and enriching experience. Radiant beings grow old peacefully and in serenity. Joy and inner harmony dwells in them, often spreading to the people around them. A radiant being is tolerant, joyful, and funny. He charms others no matter what his age is, and brings happiness to everyone he meets.

When a person wants to be more radiant and asks the angels for help, they will bring about power, strength, and the energy to move forward in life without fear or insecurity. The prayer to radiate with the angels is done with the energy of Seraphiel, rector of the Seraphim choir. This angelic choir is the highest in the celestial hierarchy. The Seraphim are enthroned above the throne of God and constantly receive his light and love. They guide people who want to radiate with increased confidence, strength, goodness, and success.

24 – Prayer to Radiate with the Angels

(Approximately 10 minutes)

It's recommended that you do this prayer in a calm room with pleasant lighting.

Material

- *Four white or silver candles.*

- *A white rose.*

- *Angelic music.*

- *Comfortable white clothes.*

- *A white braid placed on your head like a crown. It should be made in the following way: cut a piece of white fabric into three pieces, each about three feet in length. Braid the three pieces, and then tie them under your neck.*

Prayer

1. Wear white and place the braid on your head.
2. Play the music and relax.
3. Make a triangle with the three candles, and place the remaining candle in the middle of this triangle. Light the candles.
4. Pluck the petals off of the rose and rub your fingers in them.
5. Stand up, facing north, with your palms against each other in a praying position over your heart, and say the following words:

Holy angel Seraphiel,
Let God's light radiate in my heart.
Holy angel Seraphiel,
Grant me the peace, love, and goodness,
To increase my inner radiance.
Holy angel Seraphiel,
I shall be eternally grateful,
Amen.

6. Close your eyes and visualize angel Seraphiel's radiance. Fill yourself up with his radiance.
7. Open your eyes and give thanks.

8. Regain ordinary consciousness.

Effects of the Prayer
This prayer is for anyone who wishes to overcome shyness, inhibition, or lack of self-confidence, and let their inner beauty radiate.

25 - Being Happy Thanks to the Angels

Happiness is never by coincidence. The first condition of finding happiness is to live openly. Happiness can be achieved if you want to be happy, and don't live in fear or in constant control over events. People who map out their existence, or who try to yield influence over others cannot attain happiness. Happiness comes from surprises in life, and unexpected events. But, above all, it comes from inside. Happiness is the ability to astonish yourself, to become enthusiastic, and to savor love, tenderness, friendship, and the joys of sharing.

Angels are glad to contribute to our happiness. They love to open up our spirit, while emptying it of judgment and criticism, thereby creating a positive state of mind that leads to our personal happiness.

Angels liberate us from the control, certainties, and fears that create obstacles to our happiness.

26 - Visualization of Happiness
(Approximately 15 minutes)

This visualization should be done in a calm room where you're sure you won't be disturbed.

Material
- *A white candle*
- *A stick of myrrh incense*
- *A meditation rug*

Visualization

1. Light the white candle and burn the incense.

2. Sit down on the meditation cushion.

3. Begin general relaxation. Breathe slowly.

4. Close your eyes and invoke angel Metatron.

5. Visualize a crystal temple illuminated from the inside. You are attracted to this wonderful building. Metatron invites you in. The angel is in front of the door. He gives you his hand. You enter the temple, and soon enough, you feel an ineffable inner joy and absolute happiness.

6. The temple's inner light has entered in you. You feel bright and radiant. Metatron smiles at you. Your heart is flooded with happiness. Let yourself go, cry if your emotion is strong enough.

7. Experience sensations. Enjoy this wonderful moment.

8. The temple becomes less bright, less luminous. The light dims. Metatron takes your hand and accompanies you back to reality.

9. Breathe slowly. Open your eyes.

10. Rest for a few moments and then regain ordinary consciousness.

Effects of the Visualization

This visualization is for people who can't stop from judging and criticizing others, or comparing themselves to others. It's also for people who live with excessive control and fear of the future. It's particularly recommended for people who can't feel emotion and can't reap the benefits of happiness.

27 – Becoming Clairvoyant with the Angels

The angels are our inner guides. They favor the development of personal intuition and prescience. If you've had a gift for clairvoyance since you were a child but are afraid of using it, ask the angels to advise you on the right path to follow.

If you have no mediumistic predisposition, you can ask the angels to open up your third eye Chakra and increase your receptiveness to images and information about the future.

Fortune-telling is not reserved for professionals. A great number of people have a talent for clairvoyance, clairaudience, or precognition. Angels guide this talent so that these people can better direct their own lives and help others see more clearly.

28 – Visualization of Clairvoyance with the Angels
(Approximately one hour)

This visualization should take place in a dimly lit room. It's important that you aren't disturbed.

Material
- *A stick of amber incense*
- *A purple candle*
- *Two amethysts*
- *A meditation rug*

Visualization

1. Light the candle and burn the incense.
2. Lay down on the meditation rug.
3. Place an amethyst on each side of your head by your temples.
4. Close your eyes.
5. Begin general relaxation. Breathe slowly.
6. Visualize Och, the governing angel of the Sun. Och comes looking for you and gives you his hand. You squeeze your hand in his, and he brings you up to heaven. You are flying with Och. You feel light, and sprightly. Feel the softness of the air around you.
7. You notice the door to a temple. Och brings you inside. He leads you toward a place of universal knowledge, where all of the past, present, and future knowledge of humanity is stored. He brings you into the library of the Akashic records.
8. Och opens the double doors. You enter. Standing before you is a

huge transparent crystal obelisk containing the universal records. Och signals you to move forward. He grabs your hand and puts it down on the smooth, transparent surface. The surface is so hot, it burns your hand. But Och keeps your hand on the crystal, and its touch becomes more and more pleasant. You feel a great sensation of peace. Your spirit becomes clearer. Your third eye opens more and more. Its expansion almost gives you a headache. You breathe in deeply. You breathe in the knowledge. You keep your hand on the crystal for a long time to fill yourself with knowledge.

9. Och will now lead you outside of the temple. You follow him. He brings you across heaven and back to your body.

10. Rest. Slowly let the third eye Chakra close until you don't feel it anymore and it returns to its regular level of openness.

11. Open your eyes. Regain ordinary consciousness.

29 - Being Open and Experiencing Angelic Miracles

Angelic miracles occur when people open themselves up. Simply believing in angels, praying to them, or invoking them isn't enough to experience an angelic miracle. Being ready to receive the best, without trying to guess exactly what you will receive, is important.

Angels have important powers in the material world. They are always ready to help humans unconditionally. Yet, the nature of their intervention and the power of their actions depend upon no one except yourself.

People who limit themselves, who create material impossibilities, or who exercise constant control over their existence will have trouble imagining that life sometimes keeps pleasant surprises and angelic miracles in store. Openness is a state of psychological tolerance toward yourself and toward others. It implicates a desire for progress and change. Be open, and ready to receive the angels' gifts, and you shall not be disappointed!

If you respect the following pieces of advice, angels will bring about miracles in your life.

Advice to Help You Experience Angelic Miracles

- *Notice the angels' signs.*

- *Be open to new experiences.*

- *Don't be afraid of change.*

- *Analyze the fears paralyzing you.*

- *Understand why you're limiting yourself.*

- *Don't let yourself be influenced by negative people.*

- *Escape negative environments.*

- *Be tolerant of yourself as well as others.*

- *Be compassionate for yourself and others.*

- *Enjoy yourself.*

- *Don't judge yourself or others.*

- *Don't feel guilty.*

- *Forgive yourself and forgive others.*

- *Don't complain about the past.*

- *Look toward the future.*

- *Have ambition.*

- *Help others realize who they are.*

- *Believe that the best can happen.*

- *Express your emotions.*

- *Open yourself up to love.*

- *Give compliments.*

- *Encourage deserving and courageous people.*

- *Share and circulate money.*

- *Act with discernment.*

- *Accept yourself.*

- *Live passionately.*

- *Be yourself.*

- *Create objects, and make projects.*

- *Always have hope.*

- *Love life and relish the pleasures of Earth.*

- *Love yourself.*

- *Give love and affection.*

- *Offer happiness to loved ones.*

- *Share the best of yourself and offer the best to others.*

- *Live life righteously.*

Angels will always encourage you toward the path of progress and change. Trust them. Open your heart to the angels, and they will bring about miracles.

30 - Strange Phenomenon

Throughout all of human history, there have been testimonies of angelic interventions. Among the most well-known angelic interventions, the following stand out: Jacob' dream, Gabriel's annunciation to Mary, Tobias and angel Raphael, Michael's fight with the dragon, the angels of Christ's Resurrection…

Numerous testimonies attest to the authenticity of these angelic interventions.

31 - The Angels of Mons

The famous apparition of the angels of Mons took place in Belgium during World War I, on the 22nd and 23rd of August 1914. It has yet to be proven a real angelic apparition, but the episode is so strange and stunning that it still fosters debate.

On the 22nd of August, the British Expeditionary Force was engaged in the battle of Mons. Though outnumbered by German forces, the British successfully inflicted great losses upon the Germans. And the next day, to everyone's surprise, the Germans retreated.

The testimony of British soldiers supports the theory that angels intervened on their part. Some claimed that they saw ghost cavalry and archers during the enemy's retreat while others said they saw the angels of Saint George intervening to change the course of the battle. Some even declared that they saw Michael at the head of an angelic army. Others swear that a cloud of light enveloped the British troops.

Whatever the origin of these angelic apparitions, whether they were real or just visions of exhausted men seeking comfort, they seemed to have helped the British get out of a desperate situation.

32 - Padre Pio (1887-1968)

Padre Pio, a priest of the Catholic Church who was canonized in 2002, was a man who not only believed in guardian angels but talked with his angels. One day, after a religious man asked him about an important spiritual case, Padre Pio paused before answering: "Can't you see all these angels around me? The guardian angels of my spiritual sons came to deliver their messages. And I had to answer."

The famous priest claimed with conviction: "If you invoke your guardian angel, he will light the way and guide you. The Lord made him your neighbor for that reason. Make use of him."

33 - Angelic Apparitions

People who have the chance to see angels are usually experienced with angelic communication. But sometimes, people who want to see angels more than anything in the world are granted that opportunity after their first request. These apparitions generally coincide with painful experiences where angels are in charge of saving or protecting that person.

When coming out of a coma, many people claim that angels had explained that their path in life had not reached its end, and that they needed to regain consciousness.

People who live to talk about their near-death experiences following an accident, an illness, or a surgical operation often claim to have witnessed the apparition of celestial beings. Some say they were accompanied by angels during the voyage through the tunnel of light that precedes death, but angelic voices, and other angels, compelled them to return to Earth and reintegrate their body.

During nocturnal visions, dreamers can also see angels, who give them advice, information, directions to follow, as well as answers to their questions.

Children see angels more easily than adults. Their candor and absence of judgment often allow them to see angels at the foot of their bed. The celestial messengers are surrounded in white light filled with love and goodness. Many children claim to have seen angels during the death of a parent, a brother or sister, or during surgery.

In any case, angelic apparitions transform the existence of those who experience them. Witnesses don't hesitate to discuss what they saw with heartfelt sincerity and emotion. They live in hope of one day finding the angels that came to help them, and no longer fear death.

Some terminally ill patients tell their families that they aren't alone and that the angels are assisting them in their last moments of life. Meanwhile, the families that witness the death of a loved one claim that they passed away in peace. This angelic presence reassures the sick and comforts families in mourning.

Chapter 13

The Most Well-Known Angels

There are so many angels that it's impossible to name, identify, or list them all. Kabbalah's precious reference list names 72 angels that are also birth angels. Yet, the 10 Sefirotic archangels or the seven angels spoken of in the Book of Revelation – Orifiel, Anael, Zachariel, Raphael, Samael, Michael, and Gabriel – aren't among these angels.

The angelic world is a complex universe given that canonical and non-canonical sources differ depending on the author, interpretation, and translation of ancient texts. Thus, discussing knowledge of the celestial world calls for great humility, and one must resort to intuition and personal feeling. Contemporary authors often disagree on the attributes and functions of angels. Ancient authors also disagree depending on the era and civilization they come from. But despite these disagreements on terminology or the functions of lesser known angels, celebrity angels unite every author and every source. The four most well-known, and most solicited angels since the dawn of time, are Raphael, Gabriel, Michael, and Uriel. Seraphiel is a higher angel more recently invoked. These five archangels belong to the higher choirs of the celestial hierarchy.

Note that the term archangel refers to any angel located above the angels in the third choir of the last angelic hierarchy, the closest one to the terrestrial plane.

Raphael, Gabriel, Michael, Uriel, and Seraphiel are archangels of high spiritual elevation. Their power is in the service of humanity.

1 - Uriel

The name "Uriel" means "Light of God." This great archangel is considered a Seraph, a Cherub, or the angel of Presence.

When Uriel makes himself visible to humans, his size and physical strength is impressive. It is said that he predicts catastrophes. Apparently, it was Uriel who warned Noah of the imminent flood. This great archangel is haloed in radiating white light that recalls his name, "Light of God." Uriel imposes himself as an angel with the presence of God, the power of God, and immanent justice. Uriel is the enemy of iniquity. He fights injustice against the weak and oppressed. He can be frightening when he gets mad. He unleashes destructive storms, tears open the sky with terrifying lightning, and rains down floods. It's recommended that you don't upset his temper or provoke his wrath. When you invoke him, be in moral agreement with the request you're making and respect your commitments.

Uriel specifically encourages goodness, equity, charity, and generosity. Uriel carries the light and divine love. Open up your heart to him with sincerity and he will grant you a multitude of miracles.

Temporal function: Uriel governs the month of September.

Magical function: It is said that Uriel revealed the secrets of alchemy to the wizards, and that he revealed the Kabbalah to believers.

Uriel's symbol: An open hand holding a flame.

Astrological sign: Uriel is the head of the Libra sign.

Planet: Uriel governs Uranus.

You can invoke Uriel in the following cases:

- *To find inspiration.*

- *For writing and creation.*

- *For anything related to beauty or art.*

- *To aid justice or law professions.*

- *To command great ideas.*

- *For the practice of alchemy or ceremonial magic.*

2 - *Mediation of Archangel Uriel*
(Approximately 15 minutes)

It's recommended that you do the meditation of archangel Uriel in a calm, dimly lit room, where you won't be disturbed.

Material
- *A light blue candle.*

- *Grain incense made of benzoin, incense of Nazareth, mastic incense.*

- *A perfume burner.*

- *Incense charcoal tablets.*

- *A meditation cushion.*

Meditation
1. Fumigate the room before the meditation, and then air it out.
2. Light the candle.
3. Sit down on the meditation cushion.
4. Relax. Breathe slowly.
5. Invoke archangel Uriel by saying the request to yourself.
6. Raise your arms toward the sky as high as you can, with your palms flat facing the sky.
7. You feel a tingling in the palms of your hands, and then, a slight burning sensation.
8. Uriel transmits his flame and strength to you.
9. Lower your arms, bringing your two palms together in front of your heart Chakra as if to pray.
10. Close your eyes. A radiant white light envelops you. This light is hot and strong. Uriel is with you.

11. Thank the archangel for the achievement you are committing yourself to accomplish.

12. Open your eyes. Regain ordinary consciousness.

13. Stay in the dimly lit room for several moments, meditating about the commitment you made to Uriel.

Effects of the Meditation

This meditation is for people who wish to become lawyers, or men of law who act against injustice.

It's also for artists, and more specifically, writers and journalists.

It's recommended for painters, composers, architects, and people who work in high fashion.

It's recommended for people who wish to increase their knowledge of alchemy and for wizards that practice white magic for the good of those around them.

3 - Raphael

Archangel Raphael's name means "healed God." He is a very ancient angel of the Chaldean tradition. Archangel Raphael belongs to the Seraphim, Cherubim, Dominations, and Powers choirs of the celestial hierarchy. It is said that he is one of the seven angels from the Book of Revelation. He is also in the Hod Sefirah in the Sefirotic tree.

Archangel Raphael is referenced for the first time in the Book of Tobit (12:15): "For I am Raphael, one of the seven, who stand before the Lord." The Book of Tobit is considered an apocryphal work by Protestants, but canonical by Catholics. In this text, Raphael is already a healer, Book of Tobit (3:25): "The holy angel of the Lord, Raphael, was sent to heal Tobias and Sara, whose prayers were said at the said time in the presence of the Lord." In this text, Raphael takes human form and appears to young Tobias (Tobit's son). He guides him from Nineveh (Assyria) toward his exiled community in Ecbatana (Persia) where Tobias must marry Sara. But the demon Asmodeus killed Sara's seven husbands during the night of their honeymoon. Raphael allows Tobias to marry Sara. He chases Asmodeus away, and the two young people's love triumphs. Because of Raphael, Tobit, Tobias' blind father, regains his sight.

In Book I of Enoch, Raphael appears as an angel that heals sicknesses and wounds. The Zohar I defines him as the angel "in charge of healing the earth" and the angel who saves humans since he relieves "the man he has also healed of illness."

Raphael's role as a healer needs no further explanation. His function as the angel of love, though, is often cast aside in favor of other angels. And yet, it was Raphael who allowed Tobias to marry Sara, letting love, beauty, youth, and good triumph over evil. Therefore, it's recommended that you invoke Raphael for any questions pertaining to long lasting love, or to favor marriage, and the healing of negative emotions in a relationship.

Temporal function: Raphael is more active on Wednesdays.

Magical function: Raphael contributes his love and goodness in rituals for long lasting love and marriage.

Warning: Be careful not to do magical love or marriage rituals that go against one of the two people's will. In this case, the solicited angel's energy will turn against the person making the request, who could become enslaved by this love, thereby losing all energy and hope.

Raphael's symbols: His beauty, and the angelic purity of his traits. His majestic and triumphant flight. A fish. The caduceus.

Astrological Signs: Gemini and Virgo.

Planet: Raphael governs Mercury.

You can invoke Raphael in the following cases:
- *For physical healing.*

- *For healing mental illness.*

- *For marriage.*

- *For a long lasting romantic relationship.*

- *To receive the angelic light.*

- *To support scientific research.*

- *To favor knowledge and discovery.*

- *To guide particular research.*

- *For protection during a trip.*

4 - Meditation of Archangel Raphael and the Gold Star
(Approximately 20 minutes)

This meditation should be done in a calm room with a salt lamp turned on. It's particularly recommended that you work on a Wednesday at 10 o'clock at night.

Material
- *A yellowish-orange candle.*

- *A salt lamp.*

- *A stick of lavender incense.*

- *A yellowish-orange rose for the healing, or all other requests.*

- *A red rose for love.*

- *A meditation cushion.*

Meditation
1. Light the salt lamp and the candle, and burn the incense.
2. Pluck the petals off of the rose, and place the petals around your meditation cushion.
3. Sit down on your cushion and place your hands on your thighs, with your palms open. Your thumb and index should barely be touching. Close your eyes.

4. Invoke angel Raphael. Give him a few minutes to come to you.

5. Visualize a star with golden light shining in front of your eyes. The star shines more and more. It transforms into a gold star. Open your third eye Chakra. Feel the expansion of your Chakra. Let Raphael's gold star enter into your third eye. Feel the gold star's benefits inundating your head with Raphael's light of love and goodness. Let the star descend into your throat, into your chest, and into your heart.

6. Picture Raphael. He may appear as a huge angel with great big wings extended into the air, or simply as an astonishingly beautiful face. Ask Raphael for what you want.

7. Empty your spirit. Look at Raphael. Allow enough time for the archangel's answer to come.

8. Open your eyes. Thank Raphael.

9. Take your time before regaining ordinary consciousness.

Effects of the Meditation

This meditation is recommended for people who wish to experience great love. It assists people who want to obtain healing.

It brings precious help to travelers, people who want advice from Raphael regarding their personal life, to do research, or people who simply want to receive Raphael's goodness and love.

The archangel's angelic light creates a soothing vibration that increases inner peace.

5 - Seraphiel

Archangel Seraphiel is the head of the Seraphim choir, the angelic choir closest to God. The Seraphim chant the Trisagion, in praise of the Lord. They receive love, goodness, and divine light. The Seraphim are endowed with four faces and six wings. Seraphiel is a huge angel, with great presence, and whose light is so pure that it's difficult for human eyes to see. Generally, only his silvery luminous aura can be perceived. Invoking Seraphiel is an exceptional privilege. It's advised not to disturb this archangel for material matters or questions that other angels can answer. Seraphiel is the archangel of delicate questions, of love, and of goodness.

Temporal function: Tuesday.
Magical function: Seraphiel is invoked for rituals that unite soul mates or help them recognize each other.
Seraphiel's symbol: The diamond.
Astrological sign: Leo.
Planet: Seraphiel governs Mercury.

You can invoke Seraphiel in the following cases:
- *To experience great love.*

- *To awaken your consciousness.*

- *To evolve with goodness and charity.*

- *To resolve serious personal problems.*

- *To transform your existence.*

6 - Meditation of Archangel Seraphiel
(Approximately 30 minutes)

It's strongly recommended that you invoke Seraphiel on a Tuesday. Before the meditation, fumigate the room with incense, and then air it out.

Material
- *A white rose.*

- *Grain incense made of olibanum, myrrh, or pontifical incense.*

- *A perfume burner.*

- *Charcoal.*

- *A white chalice filled with cooking salt.*

- *Transparent quartz or a rough diamond.*

- *A meditation rug.*

Meditation

1. After fumigating the room with incense, and airing it out, surround the meditation rug with cooking salt.

2. Pluck the petals off of the rose and rub your hands in them.

3. Place the quartz or rough diamond above your head on the meditation rug.

4. Stretch out on the rug and begin general relaxation. Close your eyes.

5. Empty your mind and concentrate on angel Seraphiel. Visualize the archangel's apparition; you see nothing but an aura of sparkling light. You feel his energy pierce your etheric body. You feel great warmth, a sensation of being bathed in the purest and most beautiful form of love, the greatest love you have ever imagined.

6. Enjoy this sensation. Marvel in it. Feel the immensity of angelic love, and let an image, a form, or a symbol come to you, bringing you the answer to your question or wish.

7. Rest while Seraphiel's light slowly dissipates. Thank the archangel.

8. Open your eyes and regain ordinary consciousness.

Effects of the Meditation

This meditation should be done in a solitary and contemplative mood. If you relive this experience regularly, your life will be transformed by Seraphiel's energy of love and goodness.

This meditation is for people who wish to find solutions to all of their problems.

It's also for people who wish to experience greater love, to meet their soul mate, or for people in the midst of spiritual evolution.

7 - Gabriel

Archangels Gabriel, Raphael, and Michael are three angels mentioned in Biblical writings. Gabriel is referenced in the Old Testament, the Prophets (Daniel 9:21): "As I was praying, Gabriel, whom I had seen in the earlier vision, came swiftly to me at the time of the evening sacrifice."

Raphael is mentioned in the Book of Tobit, and Michael (Michel) appears in the New Testament. These three angels are the pillars of the angelic world, and tradition rests upon them.

The name "Gabriel" means "God is my strength." Gabriel is an angel of the Judeo-Christian tradition. He is called "Djibril" in Islam.

Gabriel is the angel of the Annunciation who tells Mary she is pregnant with Jesus. In the Gospels (Luke 1:19), it says: "The angel answered, 'I am Gabriel, who stands before God. I have been sent to speak to you and to tell you this good news.'"

He is the angel who announces to Zachariah that his wife will give birth to John the Baptist. One of Gabriel's most important functions is to be close to women. This is why he is often represented as a woman in iconography. As the angel of the Annunciation, he is painted or drawn as a woman, the protective angel of women who give birth. And it's for this reason that Gabriel is the angel of the Moon, of Monday, and of the Cancer sign. Ruzbihan Baqli (1128-1209), Sufi poet and mystic, recounts a visionary experience: "In the first row, I saw Gabriel, who looked like a young girl, or like the moon amongst the stars."

But Gabriel has other more masculine functions. He is the angel who blows one of the trumpets in the Book of Revelation. It is also said that he sits to the left of God. In this function, Gabriel cannot be a feminine angel. In ancient texts, there is no precedent showing feminine angels close to God.

According to Jewish legend, Gabriel is the angel of vengeance, carrying out death and destruction in Sodom and Gomorrah.

The Kabbalists describe Gabriel as "the man dressed in linen."

Gabriel is also a teaching angel. It was Gabriel who appeared to Muhammad in an aura of light to dictate the Koran to him. He was also Joseph's tutor.

In Milton's Paradise Lost, Gabriel is the head of the angels of Paradise, and in this role, he cannot present himself as a woman. Thus, Gabriel has multiple functions, as an angel of teaching, as an angel of annunciation, or as an angel of authority and vengeance. He can be invoked for various reasons. People who wish to pursue their studies, elevate their spirituality, or do research in the service of humanity, can call out for Gabriel's help and support.

Gabriel's greatest quality toward humans is his generosity.

Temporal function: Monday.

Magical function: Gabriel can be invoked for any rituals related to fecundity, sterility issues, or requests to have children. He can also be invoked in case of injustice, and make divine justice reign.

Astrological sign: Cancer.

Star: Gabriel is the angel of the Moon.

You can invoke Gabriel in the following cases:

- *For fecundity.*

- *To become pregnant.*

- *To protect yourself during pregnancy.*

- *To make justice reign.*

- *To reestablish order in times of social or family conflict.*

- *To accompany the deceased to paradise.*

- *For teaching and research.*

8 - *Fertility Prayer to Angel Gabriel*

It's particularly recommended that you invoke Gabriel on a Monday, during a waxing moon, at 10 o'clock at night.

Material
- *A silver candle.*

- *A moonstone.*

Prayer

1. Light the candle.

2. Grab the moonstone in your right hand after having already purified and devoted it. Place the moonstone on your bellybutton and say the following words:

Very holy angel Gabriel,
I'm imploring you to give me the grace of being with child,
I'm imploring you to make me fertile,
I'm imploring you to protect my child,
Now, and forever.
Very holy angel Gabriel,
I shall be eternally grateful,
Let it be so.

Effects of the Prayer

This prayer is for anyone who wishes to have a child and be protected during pregnancy.

9 - *Prayer for Justice to Angel Gabriel*

This prayer should be done on a Monday, during a waxing moon, at three o'clock in the morning.

Material
- *A white candle*

- *A red candle*

- *A stick of olibanum incense*

- *A white chalice filled with cooking salt*

Prayer

1. Light the white candle on the left, and the red candle on the right. Place the chalice filled with cooking salt in the center.

2. Burn the incense. Concentrate on your request and say the following words:

Very holy angel Gabriel,
I'm imploring you to do justice,
I'm imploring you to spare the innocent and to punish the guilty.
Very holy angel Gabriel,
I shall be eternally grateful,
Amen.

Effects of the Prayer

This prayer is for people who have suffered injustice and who want to solicit divine vengeance. It's important to address your request to Gabriel, and ask for him to right true moral or physical injustice that has not been punished by human justice. Taking revenge for personal or financial gain is discouraged, except for particularly serious cases.

10 - Michael

Archangel Michael is without a doubt the most well-known angel of all. His excellent reputation as the head of the celestial armies comes from his victory against Satan, the dragon in the Book of Revelation. The New Testament, the Book of Revelation (Revelation 12:7) says: "And there was war in heaven: Michael and his angels fought against the dragon."

Michael is the head of the Virtues choir in the angelic hierarchy. He is also the head of the archangels.

Michael is the angel of the forces of good that destroy the forces of evil. His hand held back Abraham to avoid the sacrifice of his son Isaac.

He appeared to Moses as the fire in the burning bush.

Christianity renamed archangel Michael Saint Michael.

Micheal has other functions that go beyond his role as the head of the armies of good. He is a psychopompic angel that leads souls toward the eternal light. In the Hereafter, he participates in the judgment of souls in order to find the just ones that will go to Paradise.

In the Qumran manuscripts (the Dead Sea Scrolls), Michael is called the "Prince of Light" to counter the forces of darkness, and more specifically, Satan or "the Prince of this world."

Apparently, it was Michael who encouraged Joan of Arc to lead the French army.

In 1950, the Pope named Saint Michael the patron of policemen.

Temporal function: Sunday.

Magical function: In magic rituals, Michael is invoked under the name of "Sabbathiel." He can be invoked with this term to increase physical strength or to transform your life.

Gabriel's symbol: A sword.

Astrological sign: Leo.

Star: Michael is the archangel of the Sun.

You can invoke Michael in the following cases:
- *To awaken consciousness.*

- *To go on a spiritual journey.*

- *To find new direction in life.*

- *To accomplish something that requires courage and willpower.*

- *To help humanity.*

- *To defend just causes.*

- *To ask for willpower, courage, and motivation.*

- *To invoke his protection under any circumstances.*

11 - *Visualization of Michael*

(Approximately 15 minutes)

The visualization of archangel Michael will allow you to regain energy and physical strength. It offers anyone who practices it regularly the possibility of taking control of their life, of doing things they're passionate about, of evolving spiritually, of finding courage and willpower. It's recommended that you do this visualization on a Sunday, at eight o'clock in the morning.

Material
- *A golden candle*

- *A sunstone*

- *A meditation rug*

- *A stick of amber incense*

Visualization
1. Light the candle and burn the incense.
2. Lay down on the meditation rug.
3. Place the already purified and devoted sunstone on your solar plexus.
4. Breathe slowly. Begin global relaxation. Close your eyes.
5. Visualize a dot of golden light. This dot gets bigger and bigger until it becomes a sphere of light. In the middle of this sphere, you detect the sparkling of a sword. Then, you see a hand holding the sword, and

then, you see the arm. Finally, you see Michael's hardened body and face. This apparition immerses you in a feeling of security and strength. Nothing bad can happen to you. Michael will fight to defend you under any circumstances.

6. Enjoy these feelings and Michael's presence.

7. As soon as the apparition dissipates, say thank you. You now know that, no matter what happens, Michael will support you and defend you so that you can accomplish anything.

8. Open your eyes and regain ordinary consciousness.

Effects of the Visualization

This visualization is for people in need of urgent help or protection. It's also for people who want to transform their existence, help humanity, start doing sports, or who wish to find the willpower and energy to move, to change their personal life, to travel, or to go off on an adventure.

Chapter 14

Meditations and Rituals to Change your Life and the Energy of the Planet

The following meditations will allow you to undertake important changes in your life. They connect you to the angelic plane and open up new perspectives on your own future, as well as the future of those around you and the future of the planet.

1 – The Archangel's Ritual

(Approximately 10-15 minutes)

Choose the name of the archangel you wish to invoke. Report to specialized angels or choose an archangel by intuition. In any case, invoke him by his name and never forget to thank him at the end of any angelic request.

The archangel's meditation is particularly effective. The archangels' superior energy is powerful and their vibrations come from the highest planes of the hierarchy. The love and light of archangels illuminates the heart, bringing joy and happiness.

Material
- *Myrrh incense sticks*
- *A white candle or a silver candle*
- *A meditation rug*

Meditation
1. Light the incense and the candle.
2. Stretch out on the meditation rug. Relax. Close your eyes. Lay your arms out by your side. Practice general relaxation. Empty your spirit.
3. Concentrate on the archangel and speak his name three times.
4. Picture his face in an aura of the archangel's color or in a bubble of radiating white light.
5. Imagine that the archangel is enveloping you entirely in his safe, warm wings. Enjoy this exceptional moment of angelic vibration and make the request you wish the archangel to address.
6. Thank the archangel and regain ordinary consciousness.

The Effect of the Meditation
The archangel will intercede to God for you.

This meditation is recommended for anyone who really wishes to transform their existence, live happily in the presence of loved ones, and feel joy on a daily basis.

2 - Cleansing of the Past and Karmic Residue
(Approximately 30 minutes)

When energies from the past block our progression, we feel frustrations, fears, and anxieties that prevent us from advancing, making projects, and quite simply from being happy.

The best results of this visualization will be obtained after several séances. It's recommended that you carry out this visualization on Tuesday, the day named after the planet Mars, when energies are particularly stimulating.

Material
• *Cotton dipped in Juniper essential oil.*

• *A white chalice filled with cooking salt.*

• *A meditation rug.*

- *A purple candle.*

- *An orange candle.*

- *A green candle.*

Visualization

1. Place the candles in front of the meditation rug in the following order: on the left, the orange candle; in the center, the green candle; on the right, the purple candle. Place the white chalice filled with cooking salt in front of the three aligned candles. This will absorb the negative energies. It must be dissolved in hot water after the visualization.

2. The cotton dipped in essential oils shall be placed in the entrance of the room.

3. Lay down. Relax. Begin general relaxation.

4. Invoke your guardian angel or the angel of your choice.

5. Visualize a sphere of green light above the crown Chakra in the center of your skull. The light enters your head and descends down your neck, through your spine and into your pelvis, and then divides into two at your legs. You feel a tingling, sometimes burning, sensation.

6. Take a rest.

7. Now visualize two spheres of purple light entering your body through the soles of each of your feet. This light moves up through your legs, crosses your pelvis, and ascends your spine and neck, finally leaving your body through the crown Chakra at the top of your head. This light's exit is sometimes painful when the karmic residue is very old and deep.

8. Take a rest. Breathe softly. Thank your angel. Regain ordinary consciousness.

Effects of the Visualization

The effects of this visualization are very effective. Doing this visualization at least three Tuesdays in a row is highly recommended. The cleansing of the past liberates the etheric body from concentrations of negative energies, and undoes muscular knots and tensions in the physical body. If you leave the past behind, confidence will return and you can overcome fears caused by painful karmic experiences.

This visualization works best for those who feel stagnant in their lives and who aren't finishing their projects, or for people who are losing hope in the future.

3 - Prayer of the Golden Ray for Success and Prosperity
(Approximately three minutes)

If you want personal fulfillment, or wish to be at the peak of your professional life and experience financial success, recite the prayer of the golden ray. It will bring light and grandeur into your existence. It's recommended that you do this prayer in the morning, at sunrise. Its effectiveness increases by reciting it regularly, each morning, for seven weeks.

Material
- *A gold candle*

- *Pine incense*

Prayer
Light the gold candle. Burn the incense.
Invoke angel Cherubiel, Gabriel, Sandalphon, or an angel of abundance and success:

Holy angel (call him by his name),
Give me abundance, wealth, and power,
Send your golden ray upon my life,
Open the path of success for me,
Give me your benefits,
I pledge to use them with goodness and generosity,
I shall be eternally grateful,
Amen.

Before extinguishing the candle and finishing your prayer, cross your arms over your chest and say:

Let it be so.

Effects of the Prayer of the Golden Ray
This prayer is for those who desire personal and material fulfillment. The prayer of golden light brings abundance and professional success.

4 - Meditation of the Stars for Deceased Beings
(Approximately 20 minutes)
This meditation sends light and love toward deceased people.

Material
- *A gray or silver candle*
- *A meditation rug*
- *Thyme essential oil*
- *A perfume diffuser*
- *A tea candle*

Meditation
1. Light the candle.
2. Heat up nine drops of pine oil.
3. Lay down on the rug and close your eyes.
4. Begin general relaxation and breathe softly.
5. Invoke the birth angel of the deceased person (see *Birth Angels*, page 403).
6. Close your eyes and picture the starry sky. Pick a star and think of it as the deceased person. Concentrate on this star as its radiance and light increase. The more you concentrate, the more the star radiates. Its light illuminates the meditation room. You receive its light.

7. Address yourself to the deceased person. Tell them how much you love them. Let this love enter into the light. Illuminate the room, illuminate the star, illuminate the sky.

8. Breathe softly. Place your two open palms on your heart. Thank the angel. The light goes out softly. The sky resembles every star-filled summer sky, with stars gleaming in the distance.

9. Open your eyes. Regain ordinary consciousness.

Effects of the Meditation

This meditation of the stars is for those who wish to get in touch with a deceased person in order to send them love and show them that they have not been forgotten.

5 – The Sun Meditation for Pregnant Women
(Approximately 15 minutes)

The sun meditation allows pregnant women to share angelic energy with the child they are carrying. The child benefits from the peace and love of the angels, which encourages a harmonious and balanced pregnancy.

If you're toward the end of your pregnancy, sitting or lying down on your side is recommended.

Material

- *A sunstone.*

- *An orange candle.*

- *A picture of the sun or an object representing the sun.*

- *A perfume burner with a tablet of incense charcoal.*

- *Grain incense made of incense from Lourdes or Bethlehem, of myrrh, or frankincense.*

- *A meditation rug.*

Meditation

1. Burn the incense before starting the meditation and air out the room.

2. Light the orange candle in front of the photo or object representing the sun.

3. Lay down and relax. Begin general relaxation. Breathe softly, laying the palm of your right hand on your belly. Close your eyes.

4. Invoke angel Raphael during the first two trimesters of your pregnancy, and angel Gabriel for the last trimester.

5. Visualize a ten-foot-tall angel extending its wings. Where its heart should be, a sun burns with the force of a thousand fires, sending you its golden rays. Feel these rays enter your body through the solar plexus.

6. The golden rays irradiate your solar plexus and bathe your child in angelic light.

7. Enjoy this moment, let yourself be taken in by a feeling of well-being, and breathe softly.

8. Thank the angel and regain ordinary consciousness.

Effects of the Meditation

This meditation encourages contact with the child yet to be born. It's particularly recommended for pregnant women throughout the course of their pregnancy. It's recommended to do the sun meditation every Sunday, preferably in the early morning when the sun is rising, and from the beginning until the end of the pregnancy.

6 - Preparing your Future with the Angels

(Approximately 15 minutes)

This exceptional connection to the angelic plane will bring answers to questions you may be asking yourself about your future.

Material
• *A note-pad.*

- *A pen.*

- *An incense stick corresponding to the subject of your request (see The Incense of Angels, page 475).*

- *A white candle.*

- *A pink candle.*

- *A meditation cushion.*

Solicitation

1. Choose a calm room where you will not be disturbed.
2. Light the candle and burn your incense stick.
3. Pluck the petals off the white rose and rub your palms with three petals.
4. Sit down on the cushion in the lotus position or cross-legged, with your pen and note-pad.
5. Inhale deeply and then exhale. Repeat this breathing pattern three times.
6. Relax. Empty your spirit.
7. Think of the question you wish to ask. Think of nothing else.
8. Recite this invocation:

Holy Gabriel,
I'm directing this humble solicitation to you,
Let your love, your beauty, and your goodness illuminate my spirit.
Holy Gabriel,
Help me lift the veil of my mind,
Help me lift the veil of my doubts,
Help me lift the veil of my fears.
Holy Gabriel,
Open my spirit,
Unleash my power,
Give me consciousness and knowledge,

Reveal the secrets of the future and of my life to me,
I shall be eternally grateful,
Amen.

9. Once you have finished your prayer, grab your pen and begin to write. If the answer to your question does not come to you immediately, let the angelic energy rise. Wait a few moments. With a little patience, you will always obtain an answer. All you must do is let yourself go and trust the angels.

Effects of the Solicitation

This angelic solicitation will enlighten you about your future and will allow you to obtain specific answers on the direction you can take. It is for those who feel like they're stagnating in their existence and who wish to learn about all the new possibilities open to them.

7 - *Visualization of the Diamond Body*

The angels are always ready to visit us, help us, or bring us support and comfort. When we feel a little depressed or discouraged by the uncertainties of existence, when our family relations are strained, when our romantic relationships aren't always harmonious, it's comforting to perform the visualization of the diamond body.

Material
Rose essential oil

Visualization
(Approximately 15 minutes)
1. Perform this visualization at night, before going to bed.
2. Place three drops of rose essential oil on your pillow.
3. Lay down in your bed, and begin general relaxation.
4. Become aware of your breathing, and the beating of your heart.

5. Let your thoughts wander.

6. Inhale deeply three times and then exhale softly.

7. Once you are relaxed, relieved, and your mind is at rest, close your eyes.

8. Picture your body surrounded in a radiant white light sent to you by the angels.

9. The angelic light surrounding your body gets brighter and brighter.

10. Your whole body is beaming in this light.

11. You feel unconditional love.

12. You feel the love brought to you by the angels.

13. Concentrate on your heart. Visualize it as a diamond shining with the force of a thousand fires.

14. You receive the radiance and love of the angels.

15. Inhale deeply and relax.

16. Thank the angels.

17. Keep your eyes closed and wait for sleep. Your night will be protected by the angels. You will wake up feeling well.

18. You can redo this visualization as many times as you wish. Practicing it brings inner peace and great serenity. When you perform it regularly, you will rediscover your vitality and love of life.

Effects of the Visualization

This visualization is recommended for discouraged people, whose aura has weakened, and whose vibratory rate has decreased.

It connects you to the angelic plane and activates vital energy, desires, and the will to improve one's life and harmonize one's relationships.

8 - Visualization of the Angelic Plane's High Sphere
(Approximately 45 minutes)

Visualizing the angelic plane's high sphere is an important moment that requires psychological preparation. It should imperatively be done in the morning, at dawn, and never at night. It demands great concentration and absolute faith in the connection with the angels.

This visualization is voyage to the celestial world. You will meet angels, and you will receive information pertaining to your life and your destiny.

Material
- *A seraphinite (see The Gemstones and Crystals of Angels, page 487).*
- *An outfit made of natural white or purple fabric*
- *A meditation rug*
- *A blanket*

Visualization
1. Start by taking a shower.
2. Get dressed in the visualization outfit.
3. Lay down.
4. Cover yourself if you are cold.
5. Place the seraphinite in the center of your chest.
6. Begin anatomic relaxation.
7. Breathe softly.
8. Focus on a ray of white light entering your body through the top of your skull.
9. Call upon archangel Seraphiel.
10. Ask that his ray of holy light inundates you with divine love.
11. You are absorbed by the light, you become the light.
12. Your body of light rises toward the sky. You pass through the blue sky and the white clouds.
13. You rise very high. You leave the Earth.
14. Seraphiel comes to meet you. He leads the way by elevating toward a radiating world of light where thousands of angels fly around you.
15. Seraphiel brings you even higher toward a light so white and so bright that you are blinded.
16. You feel unconditional love.

17. You feel like you know everything. The answer to your question appears obvious. You know what you must make of your life.

18. You feel an infinite happiness.

19. Seraphiel smiles upon you and brings you back down to Earth, toward your body, toward yourself.

20. You reenter your body. You're shaking, which signals that you are there.

21. Feel the tangible touch of the rug against your body. Open your eyes.

22. Thank Seraphiel.

23. Take the time to return to reality.

Effects of the visualization

The visualization of the angelic plane's high sphere is recommended for people who are looking to bring meaning to their lives, who wish to discover new passions, transform their existence, or undergo a radical change in the organization of their lives.

9 - Visualization to Summon Your Guardian Angel
(Approximately 20 minutes)

This visualization brings great serenity. Your guardian angel came to welcome you the moment you were born and will accompany until your death. He's a good, protective angel that brings you peace and comfort.

In the Bible, New Testament, the Gospels (Matthew 4:6), it says: "He will order his angels for your sake and they will hold you up with their hands so you won't hurt your foot on a stone."

Guardian angels are protectors; they steer danger away and protect your health. This particular angel is dedicated to serving you. It's important to solicit him regularly, even when you feel good. Be grateful toward your angel for the pleasant situation you are in. Your guardian angel is an eternal friend, an entity that follows you from your first incarnation until the eternal light. Know that you can solicit him as soon as you feel an inner imbalance. He will relieve it very quickly.

If you've never been in touch with your guardian angel and if you don't know his name, performing the meditation of the guardian angel will encourage him to appear to you in your dreams or when you are awake and asking to meet him. One day, he will introduce himself to you, of that you can be certain.

Guardian angels are always among us. They answer every call. You can ask your guardian angel for help anytime you feel the need to.

Material
- *A white candle*
- *A stick of myrrh incense*

Visualization
1. Light the candle and burn the incense.
2. Concentrate on your guardian angel. Ask him his name.
3. Visualize your angel. Let the images flow.
4. Say the following words in your head:

Holy guardian angel, I'm calling out for your help. Amen.

5. You feel the presence of your guardian angel by a brush against your shoulder, by a sensation of well-being and joy, and warmth in the center of your solar plexus.
6. Visualize your angel. The first time that you carry out the visualization, you see its winged body or its face, but rarely both. Persevere. Renew the visualization. You shall see your angel in its unity and luminous beauty.
7. Ask for help.
8. Thank your angel.
9. Take a rest and slowly regain ordinary consciousness.

Effects of the Visualization

This visualization is for all of those who wish to get in touch with their guardian angel in order to ask for help and assistance. This visualization can be repeated as many times as necessary.

10 – Universal Prayer for the Future of the Planet and Environmental Awareness

(Approximately five minutes)

The future of the planet is in danger. Pollution is destroying the ozone layer, and global warming is causing natural catastrophes. The angels are the best advisors when it comes to the protection of the environment. Their support pushes us to act for the good of the planet and to feel concerned about the protection of nature and the ecosystem.

In the New Testament (Revelation 7:1), it says: "After this, I saw four angels standing at the four corners of the earth, holding back the four winds of the earth to prevent any wind from blowing on the land, or on the sea, or on any tree."

Protecting the planet has always been a major preoccupation of the angels. Each and every one of us can solicit the angels' assistance and participate in safeguarding the planet.

Universal prayer for the future of the planet calls for the healing talents and generosity of archangel Raphael.

Material
• *A stick of sandalwood incense.*

Prayer
Holy Raphael,
Protect our Earth, her oceans and her mountains,
Raise awareness for the safeguarding of the planet,
Encourage people already acting for the good of the environment,
Act in favor of the fertility of nature,
Protect the purity of water and air,

Let the planet's heart palpitate,

Keep negative energies away,

Encourage environmental awareness,

Holy Raphael,

I shall be eternally grateful,

Amen.

Effects of the Prayer

This prayer is for anyone who wishes to join the angels in their fight for environmental and ecological causes.

11 - Shamanic Meditation of the Earth and the Sky
(Approximately 30 minutes)

This meditation of the earth and the sky establishes a connection between celestial energies, and allows you to embed yourself in the energies of mother Earth. It also rebalances bodily and spiritual energies through traditional shamanic methods.

Material
- *A meditation rug*

- *Sweet grass (sacred grass or the hair of mother Earth)*

- *A dish with a piece of charcoal*

- *Shamanic drum music*

- *A black tourmaline*

Meditation

1. Play the shamanic drum music.

2. Burn some sweet grass in the dish and fumigate the area around the meditation rug.

3. Lay down. Relax.

4. Place the tourmaline over your heart. This stone facilitates embedding

yourself in the earth.

5. Close your eyes, breathe softly.

6. Invoke the angel Melahel. Ask him to connect you to the earth and the sky.

7. Let the energy of the sky enter your body through the crown Chakra at the top of your skull.

8. Open the root Chakra between your legs and let the energy of the earth enter your body.

9. The energies of the earth and the sky are mixing in your body. You are hot and cold.

10. Breathe softly. Vibrate to the sound of the drums, which seals in you the unity of the earth and the sun.

11. Feel the harmony of the terrestrial, celestial and angelic energies.

12. Thank angel Melahel.

13. Open your eyes and slowly regain ordinary consciousness.

Effects of the Meditation

This meditation is for anyone looking to find inner balance, harmony, and serenity. It's also for people who are developing aggressive tendencies or anyone with a sad or melancholic temperament. This meditation can be practiced very regularly. Its effectiveness will be stronger.

12 - Angelic Ceremony of Universal Love
(Approximately one hour)

Meditating about universal love opens up the universal dimension of existence. This meditation helps fight against prejudice and preconceived ideas, against passing judgment on others, and against controlling the people around us. It opens up the spirit to the universality of emotion, to sharing with people of all races and origins. Angels consider humans free and equal in their rights. They bring help and assistance to everyone, with no regard to their origin, race, ideas, or creed.

This ceremony will connect you to the unconditional and universal love of the angels. It elevates the energies of the person who practices it regularly. It goes beyond all social, political, or religious conditioning. It elevates consciousness toward universality and brings about the freedom to act entirely independently.

It's recommended to do this ceremony on a Friday, the day of Venus, at twilight, when the energies of night and day cross.

Material
- *Pontifical grain incense*
- *A perfume burner*
- *Incense charcoal tablets*
- *White clothes*
- *A white rose*
- *Rose essential oil*
- *A white tablecloth*
- *A white chalice filled with cooking salt*
- *A meditation rug*
- *Six silver candles*
- *A white candle*

Ceremony
1. Begin with personal purification by taking a shower.
2. Get dressed in comfortable white clothes made of natural fabric.
3. Purify the room by fumigating it with pontifical incense.
4. Perfume the white tablecloth with seven drop of rose essential oil.
5. Surround the meditation rug with a circle of cooking salt, leaving an open space. You will close it when you are on the rug.
6. Keep the chalice of salt in the circle.
7. Outside of the circle, light the silver candles after they've been arranged

into a diamond shape. Three candles in the upper triangle, and three in the lower triangle.

8. On the right of the diamond, light the white candle.

9. Pluck the petals off of the rose and place them around the head of the meditation rug.

10. Sit down on the meditation rug. Close the circle of salt.

11. Close your eyes.

12. Begin anatomic relaxation (see *Relaxation Techniques*, p. 270).

13. Inhale deeply three times and then exhale.

14. Your body is very heavy. It's sinking into the rug.

15. Your head is heavy.

16. Visualize a procession of angels approaching you. The angels envelop you in a soft and warm silver bubble.

17. This bubble awakens your love as if you were a blooming flower. Your heart opens up. Your spirit opens up. Your Chakras open up.

18. You are in the love, you inhale love, you exhale love. All that is in you is love.

19. You feel happy and free.

20. The silver bubble slowly clears like a fog.

21. You feel beautiful and pure.

22. Thank the procession of angels.

23. Open your eyes. Slowly regain ordinary consciousness.

Effects of the Ceremony

This ceremony is recommended for anyone who wishes to rise toward angelic vibration, toward generosity and goodness. It brings about tolerance and opens up your heart. Practicing it regularly will allow you to live in universal love and self-fulfillment while respecting the liberty of others.

The spiritual scope of this ceremony is very high. Its effects are durable and help determine the future of humanity, since it opens one up to divine consciousness, to angelic light, and to unconditional love.

13 - Meditation of the Sacred Tree for the Preservation of the Earth

(Approximately 30 minutes)

Ecological disasters have been recurring for several decades. The time has come to summon the angels to save the planet. This meditation is specifically addressed to archangel Raphael; it asks him to help change people's thinking and behavior in light of environmental threats. Under Raphael's influence, it's recommended to do this meditation on a Wednesday, the day of Mercury, the archangel's planet of influence.

Material

- *Four green candles*

- *A stick of sage incense*

- *A stick of myrrh incense*

- *A meditation rug*

- *A white tissue*

- *Seven drops of Valerian essential oil*

Meditation

1. Let the myrrh incense burn entirely in the meditation room.
2. Air out the room.
3. Burn the sage incense.
4. Pour seven drops of Valerian essential oil on the white tissue
5. Place a candle in each cardinal direction of the room.
6. Stretch out on the meditation rug.
7. Close your eyes.
8. Begin general relaxation (see *Relaxation Techniques*, p. 270).
9. Picture a small, twenty inch tree in front of you. Its branches are not yet developed. It just started growing.
10. Call upon angel Raphael.
11. The angel appears, extending his wings above the tree. A green aura

envelops the tree.

12. You look at this little tree encircled in a green bubble. It begins to grow. It starts to rise toward the sky. The bubble grows with it.

13. It's a huge tree growing before your very eyes. It doesn't cease to grow. It towers over all trees. It is so big, it towers over the mountains.

14. You feel deeply happy. You trust Raphael to heal the planet's trees.

15. The sacred green tree dissipates as if behind a fog. You breathe softly.

16. Open your eyes. Regain ordinary consciousness.

17. Thank Raphael with these words:

Holy Raphael,
I thank you for saving the trees, the earth and nature,
Holy Raphael,
I shall be eternally grateful,
Amen.

Effects of the Meditation

This meditation is for anyone who wishes to activate angelic energy in order to establish respect for nature and the preservation of ecosystems. Anyone who practices it on a regular basis will be convinced that angelic action unleashes positive energies in the terrestrial plane. Every time you do this meditation, you will become aware of new efforts to protect nature and the environment.

14 - Angelic Requests

(Approximately 10 minutes)

Since the dawn of time, men have prayed and pleaded to God and the angels. These prayers are greatly effective. God and his celestial messengers always respond to sincere and justified requests.

In the Bible, New Testament, the Historical Books (1 Kings 8, 54-56), it says: "Now as Solomon finished offering all this prayer and plea to the LORD, he arose from before the altar of the LORD, where he had knelt with hands outstretched toward heaven. And he stood, and blessed all the assembly of Israel with a loud voice, saying, "Blessed be the LORD who has given rest to his people Israel, according to all that he promised. Not one word has failed of all his good promise, which he spoke by Moses his servant."

Requests addressed to the messengers of the Lord obtain very quick answers in professional and financial areas.

When the request solicits angelic intervention in the field of emotion or sentimentality, responses sometimes require a longer amount of time. The reason for this is that people's emotional reactivation time is slower.

Angels always bring help and support when you solicit them. But you must let them act. Don't get impatient and don't try to influence their actions. Learn to let go of your influence over the results and stop trying to stay in control. You will be surprised by what means the angels use. Miracles can often occur beyond the range of your imagination. Don't expect anything and let the angels do their work!

Choose a specialized angel according to the field in which you wish to make your request (see *The Angel That You Need*, p. 553).

You can make these requests in the following emotional fields:

- *Finding your soul mate.*

- *Harmonizing your romantic relationships.*

- *Harmonizing your family relationships.*

- *Getting along with your children and step-children.*

- *Getting along with your parents.*

- *Making new friends.*

- *Getting along with colleagues at work.*

- *Being appreciated in society.*

- *Learning to give and share.*

- *Detaching yourself from materialism, avarice, and greed.*

You can make these requests in the following material domains:
- *Your profession.*

- *The increase of your revenue.*

- *Moving homes.*

- *The buying of real-estate.*

- *The selling of real-estate.*

- *Finding lost objects.*

- *Offering a gift.*

- *Buying an object you hold dear to your heart.*

- *Going away on a trip.*

You can also make requests for:
- *Artistic creativity.*

- *Inspiration and imagination.*

- *The fulfillment of your greatest dream.*

- *Finding a good teacher in the field of your choice.*

- *Finding training adapted to your needs.*

- *Buying a car.*

- *Practicing a sport.*

Written requests to angels must always be made according to a particular ritual and kind of concentration. Doing them in a calm room where no one will disturb you is highly recommended.

Avoid music and street noise. Soften the light by closing the curtains or the shutters. Turn on a low intensity lamp and a salt lamp.

Material
- *A pen or a white quill dipped in ink.*
- *A white, non-lined sheet of paper, cut into a square.*
- *A gold, silver, yellow, pink, or green candle.*
- *A stick of myrrh incense.*
- *Dried verbena leaves.*
- *Vanilla powder.*
- *Gray cooking salt.*
- *A white or silver ribbon.*

Request
1. Light the candle.
2. Burn the incense.
3. Concentrate on your request.
4. Write your request on the square of white paper to the targeted angel.

Holy angel (write his name),
I thank you for hearing my request,
I thank you for (write what you wish)
I shall be eternally grateful.

5. Drop a pinch of salt, some verbena leaves, and a pinch of vanilla powder onto the paper. Concentrate and say:

Holy angel (call him by name),
Grant me your grace and goodness,

Grant me happiness and prosperity,
I shall be eternally grateful.

6. Roll up the square of paper with the verbena, the salt, and the vanilla.

7. Seal the scroll with several drops of wax from the candle.

8. Tie the ribbon around the scroll.

9. Keep this scroll in your nightstand, in the drawer of your dresser, or in a drawer of your desk that no one can access. Once your wish is granted, burn this scroll in the fireplace, a casserole, or a stew-pot, and then say your thanks by uttering these words:

Holy angel (call him by name),
I thank you,
Amen.

15 – Angelic Ceremony of Past Lives
(Approximately one hour)

This ceremony is reserved for people who have already worked with angels and whose path must be enlightened by the understanding of past lives. Access to the Akashic Records requires the utmost respect to specific rules. Access to records of the past, present, and future allow us to better understand where we come from and what path will lead us to happiness and serenity. It's important to understand the past in order to build a better future. Opening the Akashic Records enables us to see the past and the great lines of the future. This ceremony brings concrete answers to metaphysical and spiritual questions.

This ceremony can yield excellent results after a certain amount of practice, as long as the precise rules of the ritual are respected.

Material
• *A comfortable white outfit.*

- *A meditation cushion.*

- *Four white candles, preferably large and square.*

- *A silver candlestick with a long silver candle.*

- *A white chalice filled with cooking salt.*

- *A white chalice filled with water.*

- *A rock crystal of whatever size in the form of an obelisk.*

- *A small amethyst.*

- *Pontifical grain incense.*

- *A perfume burner.*

- *Incense charcoal tablets.*

Ceremony

1. Begin with personal purification by taking a shower.
2. Put on the white clothes.
3. Fumigate the room where the ceremony will take place with incense.
4. Air the room out.
5. Trace a circle of cooking salt in which you will place the meditation cushion. Leave an opening, so that you can close the circle once you are inside.
6. Outside of the circle, place the four white candles in the four cardinal directions. Light them.
7. Place the candle in the candlestick in front of you, facing north. This is the angelic candle. You won't light it until the circle of salt is closed.
8. Place the chalice filled with water inside the circle, facing north. Keep the chalice filled with salt inside the circle so that you can close it once you are ready.
9. Enter the circle with the amethyst and the crystal. Close the circle. Light the angelic candle. Place the amethyst to the north, inside the circle.

10. Sit down cross-legged or in the lotus position.

11. Hold the crystal in your closed hands.

12. Begin general relaxation.

13. Concentrate on your breathing. Slow down your breathing and then stop inhaling for three seconds, and stop exhaling for seven seconds.

14. Call upon archangel Metatron. Ask him to read your past lives to you. Ask him to reveal your objectives in life.

15. Feel the presence of Metatron. A breath, the sound of rustling clothes, a hand on your shoulder, the sound of wings fluttering...

16. Open up your spirit. Open up your heart. Open up your soul. Be ready to receive. Open your hands, with your palms facing up toward the sky.

17. Ask Metatron to reveal your past lives to you.

18. Visualize the temporary connection like a vortex of golden light that is enveloping you and spinning around you. It's rising and descending in an uninterrupted turning movement.

19. Receive the information about the past. Let the vortex reduce its speed.

20. Ask to see the future if you wish.

21. The vortex starts spinning again. It's spinning around you at full speed. It feels like you're losing your balance. Don't worry. You are travelling in time.

22. Receive the information about the future.

23. The vortex slows down and dissipates.

24. Take the time to remember all the information that you have received.

25. Thank archangel Metatron. Slowly regain ordinary consciousness.

Effects of the Ceremony

This ceremony is for people who have already experimented with angelic contact, and who wish to understand their past lives so that they can transform their existence and reach new objectives in life.

16 - Pentacle of the Five-Pointed Star

Figure 9

17-The Ceremony of the Pentacle

Traditions that refer to angels showcase their power in the pentagram, a star with five points enclosed in a circle. The pentagram has always been a symbol of perfection, harmony, and chance. It also symbolizes the microcosm of man made in the image of the macrocosm of God. Let us remember that the Bible says (Genesis 1:27): "God created man in his own image, in the image of God he created him; male and female he created them."

According to tradition, God asks archangel Raphael to offer King Solomon a ring in order to assist him with the construction of the Temple of Jerusalem. Gemstones encircled the ring and a star with five points was carved into the center.

The Sumerians used the pentagram to represent the five cardinal directions of the Earth with the heavens hanging over it.

The five points of the pentagram are symbolic of the five senses, and the unity of the body encircled by the spirit. The pentagram is used in Western magic as a cure against negative energies, and to invoke angels. The following ritual can be used to summon the protective energies of the four main archangels: Michael, Raphael, Gabriel, and Uriel.

Ceremony
(Approximately 45 minutes)
The ceremony of the pentacle is the most universal and traditional angelic ritual. The archangels are extremely powerful; you will channel their energy through the pentacle, allowing it to engulf you.

Perform the ceremony in a calm and quiet place where you will not be disturbed.

Material
- *A comfortable white outfit made of natural fabric.*

- *Cooking salt.*

- *Four white or silver candles.*

- *A golden candle.*

- *A photocopy or drawing of the pentacle.*

- *A white pillow.*

Ceremony
1. Begin by taking an angelic bath or a shower in order to purify yourself. Put on the white clothes. Archangels particularly appreciate white, especially when you invoke them all together.
2. Draw a circle with the cooking salt, about three feet in diameter, and place the reproduction of the pentacle in the center. (You are creating the universe through which the angels will enter.)
3. Place a white candle, corresponding to each of the four horizontal triangles of the pentacle, in the four cardinal directions of this circle.

Place the golden candle in the center of the star formed by the white candles. Place a white cup filled with water at the top of the star. This will absorb the negative energies that could disturb your ritual. Place the drawing or photocopy of the pentacle under the pentacle made of candles.

4. When your ritual is in place, you can light the candles and sit down cross-legged, or in any position you like, on the white pillow, outside the circle. Breathe slowly. Relax. Stare at the pentacle made of candles or the drawing of the pentacle (whichever one speaks to you) until it enters into you. You will feel a tingling sensation.

5. Visualize the pentacle being set ablaze with white light. This pure white light forms an aura around your body. Let the light feed you, warm you. You are hot. You feel as though you are being bathed in the warmth of the sun. Let this feeling develop.

6. Repeat the following invocation prayer to the archangels three times:

Archangels Michael, Gabriel, Raphael, and Uriel,
Through this sacred pentacle,
Open my heart to divine energy,
Open my heart to the sacred star of the pentacle,
Amen.

7. Visualize white light coming from the five points of the star and unite these five beams into one ray of light. Focus all your attention on this ray and direct it toward your heart. The feeling is extraordinary. You feel love, generosity, beauty, and goodness. Repeat the following words three times:

Holy archangels Michael, Gabriel, Raphael, and Uriel,
I thank you.
Amen.

8. Rest in the energy of the archangels. Open your eyes.

9. Regain ordinary consciousness.

Effects of the Ceremony

This ritual of the pentacle is very effective. You summon the archangels, great celestial powers who make themselves accessible to men, through prayer and invocations. Don't hesitate to perform this ritual of the pentacle when you feel lost, bitter, hateful, angry, self-contemptuous, or guilty. The archangels will bring you self-respect, tranquility of the spirit, and the desire to be good and generous. The archangels are masters of self-love, which radiates toward others.

18 - The Subconscious

In everyday life, we are conscious of what we do, but we are sometimes submerged in negative emotions, anxieties, or stress.

The work we do for ourselves is not enough to find peace and inner harmony. If we call the angels to our rescue through the intermediary of our subconscious, they do wonderful work. They transform the subconscious programming of our negative thoughts into positive energies and actions.

Results can be obtained after several weeks. A readjustment period is necessary for the subconscious to change its way of functioning. The subconscious doesn't know negativity. When you feel negative emotions, the subconscious transforms them into an objective reality. Thus, it's necessary to deprogram and then reprogram the subconscious by formulating positive statements. This transformation will provoke a great change in you. You will feel the desire to be happy and give yourself the means of achieving it. Your health will get better. The way you look at people and things will be more positive and enthusiastic. You will no longer use negative terms to characterize the people around you and you will rediscover self-respect.

Using the language of the subconscious is one of the most challenging methods of calling upon the angels, but also one of the most useful for durable personal change. It's important to start by eliminating any words from your vocabulary that demean you. Words carry an energy that always finds a target. When you shoot an arrow, it always lands somewhere. The same goes for words. Be aware of this, and know that negative speech hurts anything around you; most of all, it hurts you since you emit this negative energy.

19 - Meditation to Cleanse the Subconscious

(Approximately 40 minutes)

Reflect upon this verse from the Bible, Epistles of Paul (Galatians 5:22): "But the fruit of the Spirit is love, joy, peace, patience, goodness, kindness, faithfulness, softness, self-control..." This text is profoundly inspiring. Copy it, and read it before meditating.

While reading these words, visualize a golden light around the letters as if they were radiating.

This meditation is a cleansing of your subconscious that will change your negative thoughts into positive ones. In the long term, the meditation to cleanse the subconscious produces extraordinary effects. It brings you health and joy, and changes the course of your existence because you yourself change.

During this meditation, you will summon archangel Gabriel who governs the Moon and acts upon the subconscious. He is represented by three silver candles. The white candles represent the angels of creation. The red candle symbolizes the divine fire above the celestial world.

Archangel Gabriel will assist you in the deprogramming and reprogramming of your subconscious. It's recommended that you do this meditation on a Monday, the day of the moon and the day of archangel Gabriel. It's also recommended that you repeat this meditation during three lunar cycles. Its effects will be all the more active on your subconscious.

Before beginning the meditation, say this prayer:

I ask archangel Gabriel,

To come assist me in the transformation of my energies,

In the transformation of my subconscious,

In the transformation of my life,

In the transformation of my emotions,

In the transformation of my relationships,

Let it be so.

Material

- *A white pillow.*

- *Three white candles.*

- *Three silver candles.*

- *A red candle.*

- *A white chalice filled with cooking salt.*

- *Grain incense made of camphor, benzoin, and myrrh.*

- *Incense charcoal tablets.*

- *A perfume burner.*

Meditation

1. Fumigate the room with incense.

2. Air out the room before beginning the meditation.

3. Light the candles in a diamond shape, with a white triangle (made of the three white candles pointing upward) above the silver triangle (made of the three silver candles pointing downward). The red candle will be placed above the diamond. Put the chalice filled with cooking salt under the diamond. While you're meditating, the cooking salt will absorb the negative energies.

4. Sit down on the pillow, cross-legged or in the lotus position. Relax. Breathe.

5. Concentrate on the geometric shape of the candles. Let your sensations

and emotions flow. Let your subconscious send you images of what it wants cleansed. (If this meditation brings back unpleasant memories, painful feelings, or tears, don't prevent the emotion from overwhelming you.)

6. Inhale deeply three times, and then exhale softly. Close your eyes.

7. Call upon archangel Gabriel. Enter into his energy. Gabriel envelops you in his wings. Abandon yourself to his reassuring and protective warmth.

8. Visualize angel Gabriel saying to you:

"Your spirit is free,
Your subconscious is free,
Receive joy."

9. Meditate for a moment in the energy of angel Gabriel.

10. Open your eyes. Regain ordinary consciousness.

After doing the meditation to cleanse the subconscious, you can continue to reinforce the effects of your work by saying prayers with positive statements.

Prayer with Positive Statements

Purification Prayer

Archangel Gabriel and all the angels,
I ask you to purify my subconscious,
Please chase away negative energies, negative memories, negative emotions.
Close your eyes and let the angels do their work while you remain silent and in peace for several minutes.

Then, say this prayer:

Archangel Gabriel and all the angels, I ask you to bring positive energies, positive thoughts and positive emotions into my subconscious.

Close your eyes and let the angels do their work again while you keep quiet for several moments.

Open your eyes. Breathe softly. A new sense of well-being invades you. You feel lighter.
Say thank-you:

Archangel Gabriel and all the angels, thank you.
Amen.

Effects of the Meditation

This meditation eliminates negative programming in the subconscious. It's desirable to do it on a Monday, the day when archangel Gabriel is most present. This ritual awakens emotions buried in your spirit and brings them back to the surface of consciousness in order to cleanse the negative energies. Like an alchemist, archangel Gabriel transforms bad energies into positive ones. This meditation is recommended for everyone who wishes to transform the conditioning of the past, to forget suffering and open themselves up to more fulfilling relationships. This meditation also allows you to abandon old thinking patterns to live a freer, more tolerant, and more fulfilling life.

20 - The Rainbow of Angels

The human eye's perception of color is determined by the frequency of visible light waves that it captures. Our eyes can capture wavelengths ranging from 400 nanometers to 780 nanometers. Thus, it is scientifically proven that colors are a perception of wavelengths. Color perception is the reception of low frequency electromagnetic radiation. In contrast to sound, color wavelengths don't need to be disseminated through physical matter like air or water.

In the domain of angels, color wavelengths are particularly important for communication with the celestial planes. Perfumes, essential oils, and incense emit symbolic prayers from the terrestrial plane to the angels and to God. In the Bible (Revelation 8:4), John says: "The smoke of incense, together with the prayer of the saints, rose before God." Fragrant essences represent rising prayers, and the rising energy of humans toward the higher plane. The exchanges between the angels and Earth differ according to the various incense, oils, and colors that we use.

Colors are waves that come from electromagnetic radiation that we capture. Therefore, color is the reception of energy, in contrast to perfumed essences, fragrant smoke, or candle flames, which are emissions of energy.

The radiating energy of angelic colors allows us to receive the vibrations of the celestial plane.

The Bible depicts angels as radiant beings of divine light. In the Acts of the Apostles (Act 12:7), it says: "But, all of a sudden, the angel of the Lord stood by him, and the prison was flooded with light."

The angels carry the light of God, Old Testament, Prophets (Habakkuk 3:4): "His brightness was like the light. Rays flashed from his hand: and there he veiled his power."

God transmits his light to his servants, who are responsible for passing it on to humans. Each angel emits his own radiance, with a frequency that corresponds to a color. This is why it's possible to communicate with angels based on the color they emit and intend for us.

The rainbow is nature's most beautiful representation of the colors. For people working with angels, the seven colors of the rainbow are extraordinary symbols of angelic radiance. This symbolism appears in the Bible (Ezekiel 1:28): "Like the appearance of a rainbow in the clouds on a rainy day, so was the radiance around him. This was the appearance of the likeness of the glory of the LORD."

The rainbow is the symbol of the effulgence and beauty of divine light, which makes its way to humans through the intermediary of angels. The word of the Lord in the Bible confirms it (Genesis 9:13): "I have set my rainbow in the clouds to be a sign of the covenant between me and the earth."

In a great number of mythologies, the bridge between heaven and earth is depicted as a rainbow; it can be crossed by the gods, as well as celestial and terrestrial creatures, in order to move from one plane to the other.

Nordic mythology defines the rainbow as the "floating bridge of the heavens" that brings the kingdom of the gods within reach.

In India, Shiva resembles a rainbow, and Buddha descends from the heavens after his illumination via the "stairway of seven colors."

In reality, the seven colors of the rainbow correspond to the 700 hues that men are capable of perceiving. The rainbow is not only a symbol, and a chromatic reality, but also a beam of numerous rays that correspond to angelic vibrations.

When you are lucky enough to see a rainbow, you can connect to the angelic plane by staring at its colors until they slowly disappear in the sky. While you're staring at the colors, let the vibration of the angels enter in you. The night after you see the rainbow, you may have angelic dreams, or receive precious information about the direction of your existence, or answers to questions you've been asking yourself.

You can also meditate by picturing a rainbow, thereby entering in direct contact with the angelic plane to ask for advice or a piece of information that you need in order to make progress on a project or for personal perspective.

21 - Meditation of the Rainbow

(Approximately 20 minutes)

This meditation should be done in a calm and quiet place. It brings great well-being and favors high quality communication with angels. This meditation calls upon a great number of angels. Do it when you need an answer regarding your sentimental, professional, or family life.

It will bring you concrete answers through the intermediary of dreams, visions, or obvious decisions.

This meditation must not be done too often because it solicits a great number of angels and calls for a high concentration of angelic energy.

Do this meditation to ask the angels an important question. Don't disturb them for minor concerns. Reserve this meditation to figure out your greatest directions in life.

The meditation of the rainbow puts you directly in touch with the energy of angels. While you are meditating, remember this verse from the Bible (Genesis 9:16): "When I see the rainbow in the clouds, I will remember the eternal covenant between God and every living creature on earth."

It's preferable to lie down because the meditation of the rainbow demands great concentration.

Material
- *A red candle.*

- *A blue candle.*

- *A meditation rug.*

- *A Tibetan bowl, or Tingsha, or a gong.*

Meditation
1. Light the candles.
2. Sound the tingsha, or the gong, or make the Tibetan bowl sing.
3. Lay down. Close your eyes. Breathe slowly.
4. Evacuate your parasitic thoughts. Don't contain them. Liberate your spirit. Wait until you've gone over anything you may be preoccupied with. Empty your spirit.
5. Imagine a landscape with a rainbow just after rainfall.
6. Picture the rainbow.
7. Concentrate on the rainbow.
8. Enter into the energy of the colors and observe the angels presenting

themselves before you. Remain in this energy for a moment. Feel the color that touches you most and imagine a liquid of the same color circulating through your body. Feel the well-being and warmth that this liquid brings you.

9. Ask the angels your question and wait for an answer. If it doesn't come to you instantly, it will soon enough in the form of an idea, intuition, or dream.

10. Let the energy of angels flow in the quiet and relaxed surroundings.

11. Open your eyes.

12. End the meditation with the same sound that you began it with.

13. Say thank you.

Suggestion on how to say thank you:

Holy angels of the rainbow,

And all the angels of heaven,

I thank you for answering my question and supporting all of my projects in life,

Amen.

Effects of the Meditation

The meditation of the rainbow is for anyone who wishes to establish a high-quality vibratory connection with the angelic plane. It allows you to answer the great questions of life regarding the direction of your life and making emotional, professional or personal choices.

22 - Meditation of the Guardian Angel

(Approximately 15 minutes)

This meditation is more effective if you do it often. Establishing contact with your guardian angel will allow you to get to know him quickly and will create a comforting relationship that makes you feel supported at every moment of your existence. This meditation must always be done with myrrh incense the first time, but you can use different incense and essential oils afterwards.

Material
- *A white candle.*

- *A stick of myrrh, jasmine, pine, rose, Japanese, Tibetan, or Indian incense. It's imperative that these incense are made with natural products.*

- *A meditation cushion.*

Meditation
1. Light the white candle and burn the incense.
2. Sit down comfortably on the meditation cushion and relax.
3. Breathe in deeply several times and then exhale.
4. Empty yourself. Let go of your thoughts and preoccupations. Rediscover yourself. Connect yourself to your breathing.
5. Place your right hand over your heart. Feel it beating. Feel the life of it. Be happy you are alive.
6. Relax and close your eyes.
7. Visualize the silhouette of your guardian angel in a purple light, far away, in heaven. Little by little, he comes closer toward you to bring you his purple light. You recognize him. Even if you've never seen him before, it's him. He gives you his hand and smiles. He may reveal his name to you so that you can invoke him personally.
8. Enjoy his presence. Feel his goodness and love.
9. Open your eyes. You feel relaxed and happy. Enjoy this sensation for a few more moments, and then regain ordinary consciousness.

After the meditation, you can say this prayer to your angel:
Holy guardian angel,
Your light illuminates me,
I want you to accompany me,

To support me,
And comfort me,
Be with me, forever,
Amen.

Effects of the Meditation

This meditation is for people who feel psychological or moral discomfort, who wish to find peace and to live in the safety and comfort of their guardian angel.

23 – Prayer to the Archangels and to the Choirs of the First Hierarchy

I'm asking the divine connection to reveal to me the beauty of heaven.

Holy angels, I am humble and I come to you with open arms,

I'm asking for love and grace from you,

I'm asking for tolerance and generosity,

I am poor in pride and rich in goodness,

I will be what you are,

I promise. I promise. I promise.

Let it be so.

Chapter 15

The celestial messengers influence every domain of existence. You can ask for a specific intervention from the angels, who oversee the astrology of the cardinal directions, the astrology of the zodiac, horary astrology, and the astrology of the planets.

1 – Astrology of the Cardinal Directions

Angel of the North: Uriel

According to tradition, Uriel is the angel that governs the North. He incarnates the qualities of the cardinal direction characterized by shadows, the subconscious, occult forces, mediumship, science, and the secrets of life and death.

Uriel is the angel of earth and winter. He reigns over the world of knowledge and initiatory wisdom.

In the meditations and rituals of the North, Uriel must be invoked with a transparent rock crystal.

2 – Invocation of Uriel, Governor of the North
(Approximately 10 minutes)

We invoke Uriel, governor of the North, to obtain revelations about the mysteries of our existence and our mission on Earth. We will also solicit him to achieve our projects and greatest dreams. Make sure you wear warm and comfortable clothes for this invocation.

Material
- *A transparent rock crystal.*
- *Heena grain incense or a stick of benzoin incense.*
- *A meditation cushion.*
- *A white or silver candle.*
- *A blanket.*

Invocation

1. Place the candle in the northern direction of the room where you will do the invocation. Light this candle and burn the incense.
2. Sit down comfortably on the meditation cushion or on a chair facing north.
3. Hold the crystal in your right hand and draw a symbolic aura around yourself, with the tip of the crystal facing downward. Put the crystal down near you.
4. Take in a deep breath and then exhale slowly.
5. Close your eyes.
6. Visualize the aura that you have drawn around yourself. It envelops you in white light. Inside this aura, let your imagination take you to a cold landscape. You can see stretches of Arctic glaciers, snowy forests, sleds, skiers, or any other image that inspires you. You feel cold. This cold is more and more piercing. Warm yourself up with the blanket.
7. Invoke Uriel:

Very holy angel Uriel,
Reveal the secrets of my existence to me,
Make my dreams come true and help me achieve my projects,
Deliver the secrets of my terrestrial mission to me,

Very holy angel Uriel, guide me toward success,
I thank you for your help,
I shall be eternally grateful,
Let it be so.

8. Open your eyes. Breathe slowly. Regain ordinary consciousness.

Effects of the Invocation

This invocation is particularly for people who are looking for a job or a new direction in life that corresponds to their personal aspirations or passions.

This invocation is especially recommended for people who wish to achieve an important project or accomplish their dreams.

Angel of the South: Michael

Archangel Michael's name means "the one that is like God." Michael is the powerful carrier of light who fights the forces of darkness. When he governs the South, Michael radiates his warm rays universally. He is divine energy incarnate, and the angel of fire and summer.

Michael is also a psychopomp. He leads souls toward the eternal light.

3 - Visualization of Michael, Governor of the South
(Approximately 10 minutes)

Michael brings light, intelligence, and knowledge. He allows everyone to experience existence with a sense of discernment, wisdom, and intuition.

Material
- *Cinnamon essential oil.*

- *A stick of cinnamon incense.*

- *A piece of white or yellow fabric.*

- *A piece of amber or a honey calcite gemstone.*

- *Five unsalted dried almonds.*

- *Cinnamon tea.*

- *A meditation cushion.*

Visualization

1. Wet the fabric with five drops of cinnamon essential oil and put it down in front of you.

2. Burn the cinnamon incense.

3. Sit down facing south.

4. Eat the five dried almonds as you concentrate on the energy of the South. Drink the cinnamon tea. Take your time to relax.

5. Begin the visualization by inhaling deeply.

6. Using your right hand, place the calcite or piece of amber on your solar plexus.

7. Close your eyes.

8. Picture yourself on a sandy white beach. The sun is intense. Angel Michael lands on the sand and opens his wings in front of you, obscuring the sun. His light and warmth are even more intense than that of the sun. You're sweating. You're in the angelic light. You're in the energy of angel Michael. Enjoy this extraordinary moment.

9. Say thank you:

Holy angel Michael, I thank you for your goodness, your warmth,
And your light,
I'm opening up my heart to you,
Amen.

10. Take in a deep breath, and then slowly exhale the warmth in you.

11. Open your eyes. Regain ordinary consciousness.

Effects of the Visualization

This visualization is for anyone who wishes to increase their intellectual potential, to expand their knowledge, to find a source of information, or to develop their discernment, wisdom, and intuition.

Angel of the East: Raphael

We invoke angel Raphael to obtain inspiration for artistic creation, to develop new professional projects, or to start a new activity. Angel Raphael governs the East in relation to spring, the germination of the spirit, and emotions. He is the angel of air, the lightweight energy of the first impulse that creates movement.

4 - Prayer to Raphael, Governor of the East
(Approximately five minutes)

This prayer will allow you to enter into the energy of angel Raphael and to place yourself in the active vibration of the first energy that commands over all others.

Material
- *A stick of caraway or anise incense.*
- *A meditation cushion.*

Prayer
1. Burn the incense.
2. Sit down facing east.
3. Relax before beginning the prayer, and then say the following words:

Very holy angel Raphael,
You who governs the East,
Open up my heart to divine creation,
Open up my heart to divine energy,
Give me vitality,
Give me willpower,

Open up the doors of excellence and beauty for me,

Open up the doors of grandeur and intelligence for me,

Open up the doors of goodness, which presides over all other qualities,

I shall be eternally grateful,

Amen.

4. Take in a deep breath and exhale all at once.

5. Open your arms. Turn the palms of your hands toward the sky and say the following words:

Holy angel Raphael,

Your wishes have been fulfilled,

I am the one that is,

I am the one that knows,

I am the one that creates,

Amen.

Effects of the Prayer

This prayer is for people who want to stimulate their professional activity, or for people who wish to bring new impulses to their existence. This prayer is recommended for artists, creators, and researchers who wish to develop their imagination and breathe new life into their creativity.

Angel of the West: Gabriel

Angel Gabriel, governor of the West, acts upon the element of water, and his action is even more effective when he is called upon in the fall.

Gabriel influences emotions, the subconscious, and the questioning of unsatisfactory situations. He allows for better knowledge of oneself, as well as progress in relation to others.

5 - *Visualization of Gabriel, Governor of the West*
(Approximately 10 minutes)

The name Gabriel means "God is my fortune." This visualization will allow you to connect to Gabriel's energy and transform negative energies into happiness. It will open you up to love, goodness, and self-knowledge.

Material
- *A white candle.*

- *A stick of ylang-ylang or jasmine incense.*

- *A white chalice filled with water.*

- *A meditation cushion.*

Visualization

1. Light the candle and burn the incense facing westward.
2. Place the chalice filled with water facing east in front of the incense and the candle.
3. Sit down on the cushion facing west. Close your eyes.
4. Picture the sun setting over the sea. Take in the smell of the sea and admire the golden rays diluting into the water.
5. Angel Gabriel appears on the horizon, haloed with light. You distinguish a huge silhouette. You perceive the astonishing beauty of his face. His smile illuminates you with his goodness and love.
6. You bathe in his energy. You feel so good that you don't wish to interrupt this moment.
7. The angel rises toward heaven while the sun disappears into the sea.
8. The lighting is dim. You feel good.
9. Open your eyes. Slowly regain ordinary consciousness.

Effects of the Visualization

This visualization is for people who want to open up their heart to emotion or who wish to question themselves in order to make progress in their sentimental life. It's also for people who wish to be happier and more balanced in their personal lives.

6 - *Astrology of the Zodiac*

The angels of the zodiac are responsible for presiding over the 12 astrological signs and for influencing the lives of people who consult them. When you wish to obtain the protection of an angel of the zodiac, it's preferable to work with the angel of your sign; invoke him at the same time as you invoke the angel of the day and time of your birth. If you don't know the time of your birth, you can work with the angel corresponding to the cardinal direction of the place where you were born. In this case, face this cardinal direction as you work and turn your angelic altar in this direction.

7 - *Angelic Altar of the Zodiac for Gathering Yourself and for Saying Requests*

(Approximately 15 minutes)

Create your angelic altar on a small table, part of a dresser, a console or chair.

Material
- *A white tablecloth.*

- *Cut-outs or drawings of the astrological signs, with the name of the angel written over it.*

- *The name of the angel for the birth day and hour of birth, or the angel of the cardinal direction, written in blue letters on a white, non-lined sheet of paper, cut into a square.*

- *Objects of your choice corresponding to the three angels you invoke.*

- *A candle for each angel you invoke.*

- *A stick of myrrh incense.*

- *A photo of yourself.*

Altar and Prayer

After you've built your altar, light the candles and incense. Invite the angels by saying this invocation:

Very holy angel of the zodiac (say the astrological sign)
Very holy angel of the day of my birth (say his name)
Very holy angel of the hour of my birth (say his name), or very holy cardinal angel (say his name),
I devote this altar to you as a way of soliciting your help,
Grant me protection,
Grant me joy, success, and happiness,
I am infinitely grateful,
Amen.

Effects of these Requests

This altar is built so that you can pray or gather yourself in front of the symbols that you've devoted to the angels.

It's recommended for all prayers and requests dealing with protection, keeping negative energies away, personal success, financial abundance, or professional and artistic success.

This altar can stay in place permanently so long as no one besides you touches the objects devoted to the angels.

It's of great use because it allows you to connect with the angels anytime, and to recite prayers in case you need to call for help or make an urgent request. The answers are quick and its effects are long-lasting.

8 - Horary Astrology

The angels of day and night are available at specific intervention times. It's imperative that you invoke them at the time when they are active. They should be solicited for very urgent questions, a birth, an accident, or for any urgent matter.

Urgent Prayer

These prayers are addressed to the angels of the hours when a request is urgent or when you wish to obtain an immediate answer.

You don't need any material. You can invoke an angel of the hour when you feel anxious, worried about someone else, or if you want a quick answer to a question. The angels of the hour will act as soon as the request is received. You can say this prayer silently to them, anywhere and anytime you feel the need to. You must simply be concentrated and motivated as you make this request.

9 - Astrology of the Planets

There are seven angels that govern the planets. Some astrologers still consider Pluto a planet, but the field of astronomy has relegated the dwarf planet Pluto, which no longer belongs to the planets of the solar system. We will not consider Pluto a planet. Angel Azrael, who was attributed with governing the dwarf planet, will continue being the angel of death, according to Hebrew and Islamic tradition. In this role, Azrael watches over the separation of the soul from the body just after death. His role is essential since he helps souls follow the path of their lives after their physical death.

The history of the planetary angels is founded in a tradition that goes back to the Spanish occultists and mystics of the XII century. In this time period, the blend of Christian, Arab, and Jewish cultures allowed the great currents of occultist thought to flourish. The texts of Arab alchemists were translated into Latin and spread throughout the West. At the same time, the dissemination of the Zohar (The Book of Splendor), traditional initiatory text, revealed the secrets of Jewish thought.

The angels that govern the planets have a historical, mystical, and initiatory legitimacy. Their power is indisputable.

Invoking the angels of the planets is extremely efficient when you wish to obtain results in the domain of each angel and its corresponding planet.

It's also possible to work with the angels of the stars, who are often mistakenly confused with the angels of the planets. We can invoke Gabriel, the angel of the moon, and Michael, the angel of the Sun.

10 - Praying For and Invoking the Angels of the Planets, the Sun, and the Moon

Angel of the Sun: Michael

The angel of the Sun is archangel Michael. You can invoke him or pray to him in order to obtain wealth, material abundance, and spiritual elevation. If you wish to be joyful and illuminated, pray to archangel Michael. The best day for prayer or invocation is on Sunday, day of the sun, when the sun is at its highest in the sky.

Angel of the Moon: Gabriel

Angel Gabriel, governor of the moon, helps develop intuition, mediumship, and introspection. He opens up one's heart to emotion and love. It's best to summon or invoke him on a Monday.

Gabriel's presence is particularly recommended during angelic ceremonies, sessions of psychotherapy, astral projections, mediumistic séances, or before sleep.

Angels of the Lunar Cycle

A different angel presides over each day of the lunar cycle. You can summon an angel of a day of the lunar cycle if you have a specific request, whether it relates to finances, or professional or family questions. This angel will make himself available as soon as you get in touch with him. He will answer within three days, or within the number of days that remain until the next lunar cycle.

Depending on the nature of your request, you should work with a waning moon if you want results that take away, diminish, lessen, or create a break or end. You should work with a new moon, or waxing moon, when your request deals with growth, an increase, or an improvement.

Full Moon or New Moon

Magicians and theurgists recommend performing magic rituals and angelic ceremonies during a full moon or new moon. Tibetan Buddhists celebrate these days by doing meditations and silent prayers.

During a full moon or new moon, invoke the angels of the lunar cycle for matters dealing with fecundity, treatment against sterility, feminine issues, genital problems, or hormonal imbalance.

Waxing Moon

During the first fifteen days of the waxing moon, invoke the angels of the lunar cycle. This phase of the moon favors all requests concerning an increase of revenue, material growth, a better harvest, fecundity, as well as anything that demands growth or improvement.

Waning Moon

During this time, the angels will be particularly useful for people who wish to decrease their spending, slow certain events down, break up with someone, or quit a job. The waning moon helps keep negative energies away and encourages the end of harmful situations. This phase of the moon can help to quit smoking or other addictions, and end unhealthy attachments and meditative isolation. It's also the period for diets.

11 - Angels of the Planets

Angel of Venus: Hagiel

It's recommended that you invoke and pray to Hagiel on a Friday, the day of Venus. The influence of this angel is extremely favorable for all requests related to love.

Hagiel helps attract love, and encourages people to maintain healthy relationships with loved ones and feel unconditional love for humanity.

Hagiel can also help people fix frayed relationships or rediscover their joyful childhood emotions.

This angel encourages lonely people to find their soul mate.

Angel of Mercury: Raphael

The day to invoke Raphael is Wednesday, the day of Mercury. As the planetary governor of Mercury, Raphael lends his support for any action dealing with communication, meditations, intermediaries, or intercessors. Raphael also supports writers, poets, journalists, and anyone whose job is related to writing.

Angel of Mars: Kamael

Kamael's name means "the one that sees God." He governs the planet Mars and can be invoked for all requests concerning a decision to make, a difficult choice, a sentimental breakup, a divorce, or a separation. Angel Kamael helps people make the right decisions, or to choose between two options when a situation seems blocked.

It's preferable to invoke or pray to him on a Tuesday, the day of Mars.

Angel of Jupiter: Tsadkiel

It's recommended that you solicit Tsadkiel on a Thursday, the day of Jupiter. His help and advice will be particularly useful in the domain of power, inner strength, intelligence, efficiency, and material success.

Tsadkiel's influence brings real tangible benefits. The results are quick, and changes occur almost immediately.

Angel of Uranus: Uriel

According to legend, angel Uriel revealed alchemy to men. It was Uriel too who dictated the texts of the Kabbalah to them.

Uriel is the governing angel of Uranus, the planet of change and the bursting of structure.

It's recommended to invoke and pray to Uriel as a means of changing one's existence or to transform situations that are no longer satisfying.

This archangel acts very quickly; this is why it's important to know exactly what you want changed or transformed before you call upon Uriel. The request must be precise and explicit.

The best time to invoke Uriel is just before nightfall, when the energies of the day and the night come together before the transformation.

Angels of Saturn: Zaphiel or Orifiel
The governing angels of Saturn should be invoked on a Saturday. They influence all aspects of the structure of personality, and working on oneself. The invocations and prayers to the angels Zaphiel and Orifiel benefit people who are sincere about wanting to change negative aspects of their personality in order to highlight their moral and emotional qualities. Zaphiel and Orifiel are particularly good at drawing people out of depression, helping them bounce back after a breakup, guiding them through a period of mourning, or helping them rediscover their taste for life.

12 - Request to Make Your Dreams Come True
(Approximately 15 minutes)

By making this request, expect to experience a genuine miracle! But only under certain conditions. This request is exclusively reserved for people whose vibratory rate is already elevated, and who have already become aware of the reality of angels. It's absolutely necessary to believe in the infinite possibilities that the angels offer if you wish to receive wonderful angelic gifts.

People who don't believe in the transformation of reality mustn't make this request, or they might experience psychological troubles or emotional imbalance.

This angelic connection yields the best results when your dreams aren't coming true and you are no longer able to control your life.

The results obtained are really extraordinary, but you mustn't try to influence the angels' work under any circumstances.

Material

- *Three silver candles.*

- *Three purple candles.*

- *A long candle on a white or silver candlestick.*

- *A stick of incense. The kind of incense depends on the domain of the request.*

- *For a request dealing with emotion or love: jasmine, rose, cinnamon, apple blossoms, patchouli, dragon's blood.*

- *For a request dealing with health: lavender, camphor, myrrh, pine sage (rejuvenating).*

- *For a request dealing with work: benzoin, olibanum, linden.*

- *For a request dealing with money: star anise, benzoin, cedar, pine.*

- *For a request dealing with spiritual elevation: nag champa, copal.*

- *A white rose.*

- *A chalice filled with cooking salt.*

- *A purple ribbon.*

- *A white, non-lined square piece of paper or, if possible, a square piece of parchment.*

- *A pen with black or silver ink.*

Solicited Angels

Metatron, Raphael, Seraphiel, Cherubiel, Michael, and Uriel.

Request

1. The request should be made in a calm room where you know you won't be disturbed. Light the incense.

Figure 10

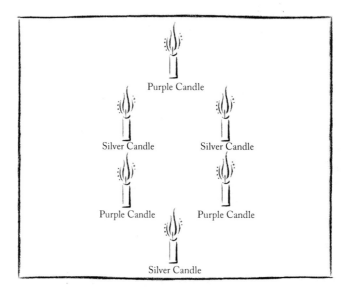

Purple Candle

Silver Candle   Silver Candle

Purple Candle   Purple Candle

Silver Candle

2. Organize the candles in a way that resembles the figure above. Form a square with two purple candles on the bottom and two silver candles on top. Place a purple candle above the square, and a silver candle under the square.

3. Draw a circle with cooking salt around the figure you made with the candles. Place the candle into the candlestick in the circle, facing west.

4. Write your request on the square piece of paper or parchment.

5. An example of a written request:

Very holy angels Metatron, Raphael, Seraphiel,
Cherubiel, Michael, and Uriel,
I ask that you make my greatest dream come true:

(Explain your dream in a short sentence)
I'm committing myself to goodness, generosity, and compassion,
Keep bad feelings and negative energies away
from me forever,
I shall be eternally grateful,
Let it be accomplished.

6. After the ink has dried, throw a pinch of salt over the words you've written. Add five rose petals onto the paper or parchment.
7. Say: Let it be so as you roll up the parchment or paper.
8. Wrap the scroll with the purple ribbon and put it away in the drawer of your nightstand, the drawer of your desk, or somewhere in the house where no one will find it.
9. As soon as the dream comes true, burn the parchment or paper with its ribbon (in a pot or fireplace) and thank the angels.

Effects of the Request

This request is for people who have experimented with the angelic connection, who have raised their awareness, and who wish to accomplish their objectives, their mission on Earth, and their dreams!

Chapter 16

Principal Angels to Invoke

"We are like children, who stand in need of masters to enlighten us and direct us; God has provided for this, by appointing his angels to be our teachers and guides."

-Thomas Aquinas ("Summa Theologica")

1 – Birth Angels

Hermetic texts evoke 72 geniuses, or messengers of God. In Kabbalistic tradition, the 72 messengers of God make up the 9 choirs of the angelic hierarchy with 8 angels in each choir.

Birth angels are recognized in Christian tradition. In the New Testament (Matthew 18:10), the word of Jesus is quoted in the following way: "Beware of looking down on any of these little ones, for, I tell you, that in heaven their angels are always in the presence of my Father in heaven."

Birth angels preside over the day that we arrive into the world. They are our protectors throughout our entire lives, and accompany us on the day of our death toward the change in planes.

Name of the Angel	People Born on the Dates Below
Vehuiah	March 21 – 25
Jeliel	March 26 – 30
Sitael	March 31 – April 4
Elemiah	April 5 – 9
Mahasiah	April 10 – 14
Lelahel	April 15 – 20
Achaiah	April 21 – 25
Cahetel	April 26 – 30
Haziel	May 1 – 5
Aladiah	May 6 – 10
Lauviah	May 11 – 15
Hahaiah	May 16 – 20
Yezalel	May 21 – 25
Mebahel	May 26 – 31
Hariel	June 1 – 5
Heckamiah	June 6 – 10
Lauviah	June 11 – 15
Caliel	June 16 – 21
Leuviah	June 22 – 26
Pahaliah	June 27 – July 1
Nelchael	July 2 – 6
Yeyayel	July 7 – 11
Melahel	July 12 – 16
Haheuiah	July 17 – 22
Nith-Haiah	July 23 – 27
Haaiah	July 28 – August 1
Yerathel	August 2 – 6
Seheiah	August 7 – 12
Reyiel	August 13 – 17
Omael	August 18 – 22

Lecabel	August 23 – 28
Vasariah	August 29 – September 2
Yehuhiah	September 3 – 7
Lehahiah	September 8 – 12
Chavakiah	September 13 – 17
Menadel	September 18 – 23
Aniel	September 24 – 28
Haamiah	September 29 – October 3
Rehael	October 4 – 8
Yeiazel	October 9 – 13
Hahahel	October 14 – 18
Mikael	October 19 – 23
Veuliah	October 24 – 28
Yelahiah	October 29 – November 2
Sealiah	November 3 – 7
Ariel	November 8 – 12
Asaliah	November 13 – 17
Mihael	November 18 – 22
Vehuel	November 23 – 27
Daniel	November 28 – December 2
Hahasiah	December 3 – 7
Imamiah	December 8 – 12
Nanael	December 13 – 16
Nithael	December 17 – 21
Mebahiah	December 22 – 26
Poyel	December 27 – 31
Nemamiah	January 1 – 5
Yeialel	January 6 – 10
Harael	January 11 – 15
Mitzrael	January 16 – 20
Umabel	January 21 – 25
Iah-Hel	January 26 – 30
Anauel	January 31 – February 4

Mehiel	February 5 – 9
Damabiah	February 10 – 14
Manakel	February 15 – 19
Ayael	February 20 – 24
Habuhiah	February 25 – 28/29
Rochel	March 1 – 5
Yabamiah	March 6 – 10
Haiaiel	March 11 – 15
Mumiah	March 16 – 20

2 - The Archangels of the Sefirot and their Domains of Intervention

Metatron	New existence, Wish fulfillment
Raziel	Love, Intuition, Joy
Tsaphkiel	Fecundity, Inspiration, Spiritual elevation
Tsadkiel	Prosperity, Money, Discernment
Kamael	Success, Exploits, Courage
Michael	Lost causes, Pushes away negativity and obstacles
Haniel	Communication, Love, the Couple, Emotion
Raphael	Healing, Transformation, Personal success
Gabriel	Happiness, Change, Consciousness
Sandalphon	Knowledge, Profession, Professional success

3 - The Principal Angels of the Angelic Hierarchy

The same angels sometimes work in different planes of the angelic hierarchy.

First Angelic Hierarchy

First Choir: the Seraphim and the Fallen Angels
  • *Seraphiel*

- *Jehoel*

- *Metatron*

- *Michael*

- *Uriel*

- *Nathanael*

- *Kemuel*

- *Satan before his fall*

Second Choir: the Cherubim
- *Gabriel*

- *Cherubiel*

- *Ophaniel*

- *Uriel*

- *Zophiel*

- *Raphael*

Third Choir: the Throne Angels
- *Zaphkiel*

- *Oriphiel*

- *Zabkiel*

- *Jophiel*

- *Raziel*

Second Angelic Hierarchy

First Choir: the Domination Angels
- *Zacharael*

- *Hashmal*

- *Tsadkiel*

- *Muriel*

Second Choir: the Virtue Angels
- *Michael*

- *Uriel*

- *Peliel*

- *Uzziel*

- *Gabriel*

- *Sabriel*

- *Haniel*

- *Hamaliel*

- *Tashish*

Third Choir: the Powers Angels
- *Verchiel*

- *Kamael*

- *Ertrosi*

Third Angelic Hierarchy

First Choir: the Principalities Angels
- *Requel*

- *Haniel*

- *Cerviel*

- *Amael*

- *Suroth*

Second Choir: the Archangels

- *Sandalphon*

- *Metatron*

- *Gabriel*

- *Raphael*

- *Haniel*

- *Michael*

- *Kamael*

- *Tsadkiel*

- *Tsaphkiel*

- *Raziel*

- *Uriel*

- *Seraqael*

- *Raguel*

- *Barachiel*

- *Jehudiel*

- *Samuel*

- *Oriphiel*

- *Azrael*

- *Samael*

- *Jeremiel*

- *Camuel*

- *Zachariel*

- *Sammael*

- *Zachiel*

- *Cassiel*

- *Hagiel*

Third Choir: the Angels
The 72 birth angels and a great number of other angels listed in the traditions of the ancient Near-East.

4 – The Angels of the Planets

Sun: Michael
Mercury: Raphael
Venus: Hagiel
Moon: Gabriel
Mars: Kamael
Jupiter: Tsadkiel
Saturn: Zaphiel or Orifiel
Uranus: Uriel
Neptune: Azrael

5 – The Angels of the Zodiac

Some angels govern multiple signs.

Aries: Kamael
Taurus: Hagiel
Gemini: Raphael
Cancer: Gabriel
Leo: Michael
Virgo: Raphael
Libra: Hagiel

Scorpio: Kamael
Sagittarius: Tsadkiel
Capricorn: Zophiel
Aquarius: Uriel
Pisces: Tsadkiel

6 - The Angels of the Days of the Week

Sunday: Michael
Monday: Gabriel
Tuesday: Kamael
Wednesday: Raphael
Thursday: Tsadkiel
Friday: Hagiel
Saturday: Zaphiel or Orifiel

7 - The Angels of the Seasons

Spring: Raphael
Summer: Michael
Fall: Gabriel
Winter: Uriel

8 - The Angels of the Months of the Year

January: Gabriel
February: Barchiel
March: Malahidael
April: Asmodel
May: Ambiel
June: Muriel
July: Verchiel
August: Hamaliel
September: Uriel
October: Barbiel

November: Adnachiel

December: Anael

9 - The Angels of the Moon

Lunar cycles last 28 days, and each day of the cycle corresponds to an angel.

1st day of the cycle: Geniel

2nd day of the cycle: Enediel

3rd day of the cycle: Anixiel

4th day of the cycle: Azariel

5th day of the cycle: Gabriel

6th day of the cycle: Dirachiel

7th day of the cycle: Scheliel

8th day of the cycle: Amnediel

9th day of the cycle: Barbiel

10th day of the cycle: Ardifiel

11th day of the cycle: Neciel

12th day of the cycle: Abdizuel

13th day of the cycle: Jazeriel

14th day of the cycle: Ergediel

15th day of the cycle: Atliel

16th day of the cycle: Azeruel

17th day of the cycle: Adriel

18th day of the cycle: Agibiel

19th day of the cycle: Amutiel

20th day of the cycle: Kyriel

21st day of the cycle: Bethnael

22nd day of the cycle: Geliel

23rd day of the cycle: Requiel

24th day of the cycle: Abrinael

25th day of the cycle: Aziel

26th day of the cycle: Tagriel

27th day of the cycle: Atheniel

28th day of the cycle: Amnixiel

10 - Angels of the Hours of the Day and the Night

Sunday

The Hours of Sunday Governed by an Angel

DAY	NIGHT
Michael (7 am - 7 pm)	Sachiel (7 pm - 7 am)
Anael	Samael
Raphael	Michael
Gabriel	Anael
Cassiel	Raphael
Sachiel	Gabriel
Samael	Cassiel
Michael	Sachiel
Anael	Samael
Raphael	Michael
Gabriel	Anael
Cassiel	Raphiel

Monday

The Hours of Monday Governed by an Angel

DAY	NIGHT
Gabriel (7 am - 7 pm)	Anael (7 pm - 7 am)
Cassiel	Rapahel
Sachiel	Gabriel
Samael	Cassiel
Michael	Sachiel

Anael	Samael
Raphael	Michael
Gabriel	Anael
Cassiel	Raphael
Sachiel	Gabriel
Samael	Cassiel
Michael	Sachiel

Tuesday
The Hours of Tuesday Governed by an Angel

DAY	NIGHT
Samael (7 am - 7 pm)	Cassiel (7 pm - 7 am)
Michael	Sachiel
Anael	Samael
Raphael	Michael
Gabriel	Anael
Cassiel	Raphael
Sachiel	Gabriel
Samael	Cassiel
Michael	Sachiel
Anael	Samael
Raphael	Michael
Gabriel	Anael

Wednesday
The Hours of Wednesday Governed by an Angel

DAY	NIGHT
Raphael (7 am - 7 pm)	Michael (7 pm - 7 am)
Gabriel	Anael
Cassiel	Raphael
Sachiel	Gabriel

Samael	Cassiel
Michael	Sachiel
Anael	Samael
Raphael	Michael
Gabriel	Anael
Cassiel	Raphael
Sachiel	Gabriel
Samael	Cassiel

Thursday
The Hours of Thursday Governed by an Angel

DAY	NIGHT
Sachiel (7 am - 7 pm)	Gabriel (7 pm - 7 am)
Samael	Cassiel
Michael	Sachiel
Anael	Samael
Raphael	Michael
Gabriel	Anael
Cassiel	Raphael
Sachiel	Gabriel
Cassiel	Cassiel
Michael	Sachiel
Anael	Samael
Raphael	Michael

Friday
The Hours of Friday Governed by an Angel

DAY	NIGHT
Anael (7 am - 7 pm)	Samael (7 pm - 7 am)
Raphael	Michael
Gabriel	Anael

Cassiel	Raphael
Sachiel	Gabriel
Samael	Cassiel
Michael	Sachiel
Anael	Samael
Raphael	Michael
Gabriel	Anael
Cassiel	Raphael
Sachiel	Gabriel

Saturday
The Hours of Saturday Governed by an Angel

DAY	NIGHT
Cassiel (7 am - 7 pm)	Raphael (7 pm - 7 am)
Sachiel	Gabriel
Samael	Cassiel
Michael	Sachiel
Anael	Samael
Raphael	Michael
Gabriel	Anael
Cassiel	Raphael
Sachiel	Gabriel
Samael	Cassiel
Michael	Sachiel
Anael	Samael

11 – Angels of the Cardinal Directions

Angel of the North: Uriel
Angel of the South: Michael
Angel of the East: Raphael
Angel of the West: Gabriel

Chapter 17

❦ Angelic Candles ❦

C andles are an indispensable tool for inviting angels into our lives.

Their symbolism is related to the symbolism of the flame, and unites all four elements. The fire and air of the flame complements the earth represented by the wax, and the water represented by the hot wax.

Flames express the verticality of the four elements. This verticality is a symbolic ladder between the terrestrial plane and the angelic plane.

Candles symbolize the anchoring of the earth (the wax) as well as the connection to heaven (the flame). For this reason, blowing out a candle breaks this connection and the energies are abruptly interrupted. It's always better to use a snuffer.

The candle's flame elevates terrestrial vibration toward heaven. It represents the liberation from material constraints and brings light downward into matter from the angelic plane.

Candles are also a symbol of the divine light that is manifested through air, breath, and "prana" (the Sanskrit word for "breath"), in other words, the energy of life.

On numerous occasions, the Bible evokes the lamps that shine light before the Lord, New Testament, Pentateuch (Leviticus 24:4): "The lamps on the pure gold lampstand before the LORD shall be tended to continually."

Light is the manifestation of God, Old Testament, the Poetic Books

(Psalm 4:7): "Let the light of your face shine on us, O LORD!"

When you light a candle during an angelic ritual, think of it as a way of connecting yourself to the celestial plane and entering a vibration where beauty, light, and love shine brightly.

Respect your candles: put them out softly, take care of the wicks and remove the wax that has dripped down.

It's recommended that you invoke the angels on your birthday, choosing candles according to the angel that you wish to invoke for the new year (see *The Colors of the Angels*, p. 445, and *The Birth Angels*, p. 403).

The shape and color of the candle that you choose is important. Large square or round shaped candles should be reserved for angelic altars, meditations, and visualizations. They delineate an area for the angels. Long and thin candles symbolize the presence of angels in all your work.

You can also use the wax from thin candles to seal written requests that you send to angels.

1 - Written Requests Addressed to Angels

You can address a written request to angels when you are at an emotional impasse, if you wish to act upon your professional future, if you need simple practical advice, or if you need to take a new direction in life.

Material
- *A candle that corresponds to the color of the angel you are invoking.*

- *A white sheet of paper, non-lined, cut into a square.*

- *A pen with blue ink.*

- *A white rose.*

- *A piece of white string.*

Ritual of the Written Request

1. Meditate for a few moments while you concentrate on the request you are addressing to the angels.

2. Write your request by invoking the appropriate angel.

3. Remove the rose's petals and place them on the sheet of paper while you say these words: Holy angel (call him by name), I thank you for fulfilling my request.

4. Roll up the sheet of paper with the petals inside and wrap it with the white string.

5. Seal the scroll with the hot wax of the candle.

6. Thank the angel.

Effects of the Request

These written requests have great energetic power when they are addressed to angels, who are happy to provide you with the information that you need.

The answers will come to you through intuition, through people who are talking to you, through a TV show on the same subject, or in a dream. Sometimes, you will receive an immediate answer as soon as you finish writing the request.

2 - The Angels and Their Associated Candle Colors

Black Candles

Black candles are used in rituals to increase physical strength, as well as to hold power over matter, ideas, and inspiration. Black represents the uterus and the symbolic matrix where life, energy, and artistic creation are conceived.

Black eliminates negative energies from your ritual. It also allows for a change in personal behavior and the elevation of consciousness.

3 - Angels That Correspond to Black Candles

- *Archangel Tsaphkiel, Udriel, angel Unael, angel Cophi, angel Gazriel, angel Armisael.*

- *Maternity angels.*

- *Birth angels.*

- *Angels of fecundity.*

- *Angels of project achievement.*

- *Angels of intelligence.*

- *Angels of travel.*

- *Angels of creativity.*

- *Angels of inspiration.*

- *Personal growth angels.*

Brown Candles

Brown represents the anchoring into matter, strength, and the terrestrial energy that rises toward the celestial plane. Brown is reassuring; it's the gestation of matter and incarnates realization.

4 - Angels That Correspond to Brown Candles

- *Archangel Sandalphon, angel Geburathiel, angel Jerazol, angel Anael.*

- *Angels of knowledge.*

- *Angels of science.*

- *Angels of learning and apprenticeship.*

- *Angels of personal success.*

- *Angels of prosperity.*

- *Angels of organization and logic.*

- *Angels of wisdom.*

- *Angels of efficiency and moral strength.*

Gray Candles

Gray is the link between celestial energy and terrestrial energy. It represents the door to the angelic plane and the harmonization of opposites. It influences mediumship and favors intuition. Gray helps put an end to conflict. It protects human relationships and favors love.

5 - Angels That Correspond to Gray Candles

- *Archangel Raziel, angel Anahel, angel Ieiaiel, angel Urzla, angel Melioth.*

- *Angels of love.*

- *Angels of luck.*

- *Angels of responsibility.*

- *Divination angels.*

- *Mediumship angels.*

Blue Candles

As a symbol of the infinite, blue is a color frequently used in rituals involving requests. Blue develops all potential since it opens up the humane to the infinite and the eternal. Blue is the color of requests regarding the future, perspectives, prosperity, abundance, and the achievement of dreams.

6 - Angels That Correspond to Blue Candles

- *Archangel Tsadkiel, angel Pastor, angel Sywaro, angel Esabiel, angel*

Menadel, angel Yeyayel.

- *Angels of wealth.*

- *Angels of material objects.*

- *Angels of luck.*

- *Angels of work.*

- *Protective angels.*

- *Angels of generosity.*

- *Angels of charity.*

- *Angels of the imagination.*

Green Candles

Green candles are useful for requests regarding renewal, communication, awakening, growth, and progression. Green favors expressing and liberating emotion.

7 - Angels That Correspond to Green Candles

- *Archangel Haniel, angel Itqal, angel Uzziel, angel Nith-Haiah, angel Yezalel, angel Coreh.*

- *Angels of communication.*

- *Angels of relationship harmony.*

- *Family angels.*

- *Angels of friendship.*

- *Angels of emotion.*

- *Angels of children.*

- *Angels of couples.*

- *Protective angels.*

- *Guardian angels.*

- *Angels of projects.*

Angels of the future.

Yellow Candles

In this vibration, yellow is a sublime ray that cleanses one of negative energies, relieves physical pain, favors success as well as physical, moral, mental and spiritual transformation. The radiance of yellow candles illuminates your work and has a rejuvenation effect in your body and in your life. Yellow is the color of solar energy and radiance.

8 - Angels That Correspond to Yellow Candles

- *Archangel Raphael, angel Esabiel, angel Hamaya, angel Rehael, angel Vehuiah, angel Zerachiel, angel Lelahel, angel Seheiah.*

- *Healing angels.*

- *Meditation angels.*

- *Angels of inner transformation.*

- *Rejuvenation angels.*

- *Angels of cellular regeneration.*

- *Protective angels.*

- *Guardian angels.*

- *Angels of work.*

- *Manifestation angels.*

- *Angels of success.*

Purple Candles

Spirituality is represented by the color purple. Angelic requests made with purple candles will bring you happiness, and make your dreams come true. Purple opens the door to your subconscious and allows for the awakening of consciousness.

Purple is the most effective color for people who want to transform their existence to experience love and happiness.

9 - Angels That Correspond to Purple Candles

- *Archangel Seraphiel, archangel Gabriel, archangel Cherubiel, angel Lauviah, angel Hahaiah, angel Haziel, angel Sidqiel.*

- *Guardian angels.*

- *Protective angels.*

- *Angels of happiness.*

- *Angels of prosperity.*

- *Angels of sleep.*

- *Angels of energy and strength.*

- *Angels of inner transformation.*

- *Angels of hidden things yet to be revealed.*

- *Angels of luck.*

White Candles

White is a synthesis of all the colors. White is the symbol of purity, new beginnings, beauty in all its forms, virtue, and angelic manifestation in all domains of existence.

10 - Angels That Correspond to White Candles

- *Archangel Metatron, archangel Seraphiel, archangel Cherubiel, angel Vehuiah, angel Aniel, angel Yeiazel.*

- *Angels of wish fulfillment.*

- *Angels of personal transformation.*

- *Protective angels of nature.*

- *Angels of art.*

- *Angels of beauty.*

- *Angels of the deceased and resurrection.*

- *Angels of creativity.*

- *Angels of goodness and brotherhood.*

- *Protective angels.*

- *Guardian angels.*

Orange Candles

Orange is a provider of positive energy. It ensures great vitality and boosts self-confidence. Requests made with orange candles increase physical and mental energetic potential.

11 - Angels That Correspond to Orange Candles

- *Archangel Michael, angel Noriel.*

- *Protective angels of humanity.*

- *Angels that protect against accidents.*

- *Angels fighting against negative energies.*

- *Guardian angels.*

- *Angels of courage.*

- *Healing angels.*

- *Angels that protect the home.*

- *Angels of athletes.*

- *The whole angelic plane, with archangel Michael acting as the head of the angels.*

Red Candles

Energy and passion are represented by the color red. Because of their strong energetic potential, red candles aren't recommended for angelic altars. Their use should be reserved to requests regarding an increase in energy, vitality, and emotion in every domain of existence.

12 – Angels That Correspond to Red Candles

- *Archangel Kamael, angel Arkhas.*

- *Angels of athletic exploits.*

- *Angels of romantic passion.*

- *Angels of positive energy.*

- *Angels of courage.*

- *Angel of professional or artistic success.*

- *Angels of sexuality.*

- *Angels of Feng shui.*

Gold Candles

Gold is the color of divine protection, celestial guidance, and revelation. Gold brings material and spiritual wealth. The alchemists' sought to transform lead into gold. This color incarnates power, magnificence, and grandeur. Gold is the color of celebration in the Bible, Old Testament, the Pentateuch (Exodus 40:5): "Place the gold altar of incense in front of the Ark of the Covenant and put the curtain at the entrance of the tabernacle."

13 - Angels That Correspond to Gold Candles

• *Seraphiel, Cherubiel, Raphael, Gabriel, Ophaniel, Rikbiel, Zophiel, angel Seratiel, angel Nuriel, angel Temmael, angel Shimshael, angel Hardaniel, angel Sarmiel.*

• *Angels of power.*

• *Angels of beauty.*

• *Angels of artists.*

• *Angels of wealth.*

• *Angels of luck.*

• *Angels of moral and spiritual grandeur.*

• *Angels of discovery and science.*

• *Angels of rituals.*

• *Angels of meditation.*

Silver Candles

The light, love, and beauty of the angels are symbolized by the color silver. For written requests, silver candles are recommended alongside a candle of another color. They are ideal for angelic altars, meditations, and visualizations.

In the Bible, gold and silver are the most beautiful offerings to God, Old Testament, the Pentateuch (Exodus 35:5): "Take from among you a contribution to the LORD. Whoever is of a generous heart, let him bring the LORD's contribution: gold, silver, and bronze…"

14 – Angels That Correspond to Silver Candles

- *Archangel Seraphiel, archangel Cherubiel, archangel Metatron, angel Jehoel, archangel Michael, angel Boel, angel Kabshiel, angel Phuel, angel Shetel, angel Yekahel.*

- *Angels of light.*

- *Guardian angels.*

- *Protective angels.*

- *Angels of love.*

- *Angels of friendship.*

- *Angels of reconciliation.*

- *Angels of mercy.*

- *Angels of goodness.*

- *Angels of generosity and charity.*

- *Angels of loyalty.*

Chapter 18

The Essential Oils of Angels

Vegetal essence and essential oils are concentrated extracts obtained from the aromatic compounds of a plant through distillation. Essential oils can last a long time if they are kept in a sealed vial, away from light. They are soluble in oil and alcohol, but not water.

Essential oils contain active properties and can cause allergies or skin irritations. It's important to take several basic precautionary measures.

- *Avoid directly inhaling the essential oils in the vial.*

- *Don't apply essential oils to a mucosa and keep them away from the eyes.*

- *Don't ingest essential oils.*

- *Avoid using essential oils on children or animals.*

- *Use essential oils in a room that has been aired out.*

- *Mix the essential oils with alcohol and oil. Never use pure essential oil on the skin. An ideal dilution is 5% essential oil in an alcohol or oil base.*

- *Only use pure oils on inorganic material (cloth, diffuser...).*

- *Never expose yourself to sunlight after using massage oil containing essential oils or after perfuming yourself with aqueous solutions containing essential oils.*

1 - Using Essential Oils

For massages, dilute two drops of essential oil in a spoonful of moisturizing oil.

Don't use essential oils during baths because they aren't water-soluble. They will stay at the surface of the water, and you risk experiencing skin or mucosal irritations.

Pure essential oils can be used in various ways:

2 - Diffusers

The heat from a diffuser emits fragrances and chemical molecules that react with the angelic vibratory plane. It's recommended that you choose essential oils in relation to the angel you wish to invoke (see *The Angel That You Need*, p. 553). Never forget to air out the room.

3 - Lamp Rings

Pour three or five drops of essential oil into a lamp ring made of white ceramic. The perfume and molecules will be diffused by the heat from the electric bulb. Make sure you don't leave the room without airing it out.

4 - Candle Wax

After burning an unscented candle for a little while, put it out. Then, pour three drops of essential oil into the hot wax. Relight the candle. Make sure you never leave the candle unattended. Using essential oils in this way is well suited for invocation rituals or specific requests.

5 - Dried Flowers or Flowers Made of Fabric

Pour three drops of essential oil into the heart of one of the flowers of the bouquet. This is perfect for dried flowers adorning angelic altars.

6 - Cloth

You can pour five to seven drops of essential oil onto the duvet cover at the foot of your bed, a cotton ball in your bathroom, on your pillows, or more specifically the cushion used for your angelic meditations. Avoid using essential oils on handkerchiefs or any other fabric in close proximity to your mucosa, such as bath towels or wash cloths. Perfume your home by pouring seven drops of essential oil on a rug, a couch, or the hem of your curtains. Make sure you take the precaution of dabbing the oil in places that aren't visible so as to avoid stains.

7 - Salt Lamps

Pour three drops of essential oil onto your salt lamp, and the perfume will spread out when you light the lamp.

8 - Oils in Tradition

Essential oils and perfumes have been used for ages in various religions, cults, and magic rituals. Egyptian priests used balms and scented ointments while women placed cones of solidified oil on their hair. The extraction of lily essence is depicted on an Egyptian bas-relief of a tomb from the Late Period.

Perfume has always been considered an olfactory subtlety, and an homage to the gods.

In the Old Testament, Pentateuch (Exodus 25:6), it says: "oil for the light, spices for the anointing oil and for the fragrant incense."

The Bible is filled with passages evoking perfumes and incense as an homage to the Lord. It's forbidden to use these perfumes, essences, and incense to worship idols. Perfumes must be used to honor the All-Mighty, Pentateuch (Exodus 30:35): "make a fragrant blend of incense – the work of a perfumer – salted, pure, and sacred."

Perfumes, ointments, and various floral essences are used today according to ancient traditions. The renewal of interest in perfumes and natural essences is no trend, but a traditional source of high spiritual value and great vibratory effectiveness. In the Book of Revelation (8:3-4), it says: "Another angel, who had a golden incense burner, came and stood at the altar. He was given much incense to offer, with the prayers of all the saints, on the golden altar before the throne. The smoke of the incense, together with the prayers of the saints, went up before God from the angel's hand."

Angels are particularly sensitive to perfumes, and using essential oils facilitates contact with them.

9 – The Nature of Essential Oils

Essential oils are extracted from plants, roots, wood, rhizomes, and flowers with diverse fragrances like benzoin of Laos, tea tree, star anise, rosewood, rose, cade oil, juniper, pine, chamomile, cinnamon, cedar, lemon, Cyprus, curcuma, eucalyptus, geranium, ginger rhizomes, laurel, lavender, St. John's wort, marjoram, myrtle, rhizomes of Himalayan nardostachys jamandi from which nard oil is extracted, orange, oregano, patchouli, rosemary, sandalwood, sage, ylang-ylang, vanilla…

10 – The Properties of Essential Oils

• *Angelic: Has curative qualities and heals contagious diseases. It's called "Medicine of the Holy Spirit."*

• *Star anise: Stimulates and sanitizes.*

• *Wormwood: Fosters fecundity.*

• *Tea tree: Sanitizes, purifies, and cleanses places where negative energies reign.*

• *Bergamot: Heals imbalances in the neurovegetative system.*

• *Yellow birch: Called "the tree of wisdom." Fosters discernment, accurate judgment, contemplation, and meditation.*

• *Chamomille: Improves quality of sleep and meditation.*

- *Cinnamon: Stimulates intelligence, and improves concentration.*

- *Carrot: Powerful cleanser of places and negative energies.*

- *Cedar: Used during funeral rites, for the elevation and grandeur of the soul.*

- *Lemon: Relieves anxiety.*

- *Geranium: Fosters inner balance.*

- *Juniper: Keeps negative energies and past traumatisms at bay.*

- *Clove: Stimulant of the spirit and the body. Relieves moral pain and grief.*

- *Jasmine: Develops well-being and peace. A very pleasant fragrance.*

- *Laurel: Stimulates. Fosters the development of energy, combativeness, and lucidity.*

- *Lavender: Purifies. Keeps negative energies at bay.*

- *Marjoram: Keeps fear away and opens up the heart to emotion.*

- *Peppermint: Stimulates and purifies.*

- *Myrrh: Purifies personal energies and places of ritual.*

- *Myrtle: Brings about abundance, and encourages brave people with a fighting spirit.*

- *Neroli (orange blossom): Diminishes anxiety, negative energies, and improves quality of sleep.*

- *Sandalwood: Encourages communication between the different planes and spiritual elevation.*

- *Clary sage: Encourages meditation.*

- *Thyme: Helps the souls of the deceased leave the terrestrial world.*

- *Vanilla: Facilitates the expression of emotion, softness, and tenderness.*

- *Vetiver: Purifies and cleanses oneself of negative energies.*

- *Ylang-ylang: Favors spiritual elevation, and relieves stress and anxiety. A delicate fragrance.*

The essential oils you choose must correspond to the angel you wish to communicate with or whom you want protection from. When you perfume the inside of your home, choose the essential oil of a protective angel, an angel of wisdom, or an angel that chases away negative energies. The angel will vary depending on the room you perfume and the angelic energy that you wish to bring to the place. For meditations, massages, or rituals, you can determine which angel to contact by yourself (see *The Angels That You Need*, p. 553). All of the main angels have corresponding essential oils. For angels not included in the following explanation, rely on intuition and let yourself be guided by angelic energies.

11 - Angels and Their Corresponding Essential Oils

Below is a list of the archangels and their related angels, organized by field of intervention, with the appropriate essential oils that you can use.

12 - Archangel Metatron

Archangel Metatron is the archangel of the crown Sefirah. Metatron signals the beginning, the starting point of a new existence, wish fulfillment, self-realization, the development of power, and inner strength.

Angels Related to Archangel Metatron
- *Angels of wish fulfillment*

- *Angels of personal transformation*

- *Protective angels of nature*

- *Angels of personal achievement*

- *Angels of the deceased*

- *Angels of goodness and brotherhood*

Archangel Metatron's Essential Oils

Angelic, benzoin, cardamom, cinnamon, cedar, Cyprus, juniper, geranium, lavender, laurel, peppermint, white sandalwood, thyme, valerian, ylang-ylang.

13 - Archangel Raziel

Archangel Raziel is the archangel of love, times of happiness, and every kind of luck. He represents the masculinity, and helps develop intuition.

Angels Related to Archangel Raziel
- *Angels of love*

- *Angels of luck*

- *Angels of responsibility*

- *Divination angels*

- *Angels of mediumship*

Archangel Raziel's Essential Oils

Yarrow, benzoin, chamomile, jasmine, myrtle, geranium, ginger, marjoram, myrrh, sandalwood, clary sage, vanilla, ylang-ylang.

14 - Archangel Tsaphkiel

Archangel Tsaphkiel represents femininity, fecundity, understanding, the world of thought and great ideas, inspiration, travel, the achievement of projects, meditation, psychotherapy, self-questioning, and spiritual elevation.

Angels Related to Archangel Tsaphkiel

- *Angels of maternity*

- *Birth angels*

- *Angels of fecundity*

- *Angels of project realization*

- *Angels of intelligence*

- *Angels of travel*

- *Angels of creativity*

- *Angels of inspiration*

- *Angels of personal growth*

Archangel Tsaphkiel's Essential Oils

Dill, angelic, wormwood, benzoin, incense, geranium, jasmine, sweet orange, vanilla, ylang-ylang.

15 - *Archangel Tsadkiel*

Archangel Tsadkiel is the archangel of prosperity, abundance, material wealth, acquisitions, rewards, loan reimbursement, loans, and any kind of gain. The archangel encourages discernment and judicious choices.

Angels Related to Archangel Tsadkiel

- *Angels of wealth*

- *Angels of material wealth*

- *Angels of luck*

- *Angels of work*

- *Protective angels*

- *Angels of generosity*

- *Angels of charity*

Tsadkiel's Essential Oils

Star anise, wormwood, yellow birch, carrot, incense, geranium, lavender, laurel, peppermint, myrtle, sandalwood, vetiver.

16 - *Archangel Kamael*

Archangel Kamael encourages the accomplishment of our mission on Earth, the harmonization of our desires, success, exploits, will, results obtained through personal effort, strength, rigor, and courage.

Angels Related to Archangel Kamael
- *Angels of the mission on Earth.*

- *Angels of will.*

- *Angels of athletic exploits.*

- *Angels of positive energy.*

- *Angels of courage.*

- *Angels of professional and artistic success.*

Kamael's Essential Oils

Benzoin, bergamot, cinnamon, lemon, cumin, clove, laurel, red mandarin, peppermint, myrtle, oregano, Scots pine.

17 - *Archangel Michael*

Archangel Michael is the defender of humanity, the protector of lost causes and victims. He is responsible for the survival of people in danger. He pushes negative energies and obstacles away.

Angels Related to Archangel Michael
- *Protective angels of humanity.*

- *Protective angels against accidents.*

- *Protective angels against negative energies.*

- *Guardian angels.*

- *Angels of courage.*

- *Healing angels.*

- *Angels of health.*

- *Protective angels of the home.*

- *Angels of athletes.*

- *The whole angelic plane, with archangel Michael acting as the head of the angels.*

Archangel Michael's Essential Oils

Yarrow, star anise, camphor, chamomile, cumin, galbanum, geranium, ginger, eucalyptus, lavender, mandarin, marjoram, mimosa, carnation, rosemary, rose, sandalwood, vanilla, ylang-ylang.

18 – Archangel Haniel

Archangel Haniel is the archangel of communication, conviviality, relationship harmony, love expressed with sincerity, and emotional links between beings.

Angels Related to Archangel Haniel
- *Angels of communication*

- *Angels of relationship harmony*

- *Family angels*

- *Angels of children*

- *Angels of couples*

- *Protective angels*

- *Guardian angels*

Haniel's essential oils

Chamomile, bergamot, yellow birch, jasmine, geranium, mandarin, marjoram, neroli, sweet orange, rose, linden, vanilla, ylang-ylang.

19 - *Archangel Raphael*

Archangel Raphael is the healing archangel, who relieves physical and emotional pain. He brings about healing, well-being, transformation, sociability, and success through hard work and courage. He favors personal success and helps realize any kind of project.

Angels Related to Archangel Raphael
- *Healing angels*

- *Angels of meditation*

- *Angels of inner transformation*

- *Rejuvenation angels*

- *Angels of cellular regeneration*

- *Protective angels*

- *Guardian angels*

- *Angels of work*

- *Manifestation angels*

- *Angels of success*

Raphael's Essential Oils

Angelic, archangelic (called "angel herb"), Artemisia, bergamot, chamomile, Ceylon cinnamon, lemon, rose essence, ginger, hyssop, jasmine, lavender, green mint, neroli, bitter orange, salvia officinalis, wild thyme (called "tree of life"), eucalyptus, sandalwood, garden savory.

20 - Archangel Gabriel

Archangel Gabriel is the archangel that dominates our subconscious, and regenerates our strength and energy while we are asleep. He symbolizes the transmutation of existence through the awakening of consciousness. He brings out the best in us so that we can attain happiness.

Angels Related to Archangel Gabriel
- *Guardian angels*

- *Protective angels*

- *Angels of happiness*

- *Angels of prosperity*

- *Angels of sleep*

- *Angels of energy and strength*

- *Angels of inner transformation*

- *Angels of hidden things yet to be revealed*

Gabriel's essential oils

Dill, angelic, benzoin, cinnamon, Atlas cedar, lemon, coriander, estragon, juniper, laurel, vervain.

21 - Archangel Sandalphon

Archangel Sandalphon governs over matter, logic, wisdom, science, knowledge, individual fulfillment through self-realization, and professional success, all of which must be organized and structured.

Angels Related to Archangel Sandalphon
- *Angels of knowledge*

- *Angels of science*

- *Angels of learning and apprenticeship*

- *Angels of professional success*

- *Angels of prosperity*

- *Angels of organization and logic*

- *Angels of wisdom*

- *Angels of efficiency and moral strength*

Archangel Sandalphon's Essential Oils

Star anise, yellow birch, cinnamon, ginger, laurel, peppermint, myrtle, nutmeg, wild thyme, Palmarosa, Ravintsara.

Chapter 19

The Colors of the Angels

Each angel has a corresponding color. Performing rituals with colors allows you to establish a spiritual link with the celestial plane to receive angelic energy.

The color rituals are performed to solicit an angelic response. Be receptive and open.

The language of color is universal. The traditions of the whole world and of all eras have used colors to express emotion, desire, states of being, particular thoughts, meditative states and action. When you get dressed in the morning, the colors you choose to wear are never random. They reflect your mood for the day. Colors are symbols. They represent the spirit of the person who wears them or who chooses them for a meditation. If you want to receive an angelic ray of light through the intermediary of a color, you should determine which angel corresponds to your request.

Figure 11: The Tree of Colors with Angels related

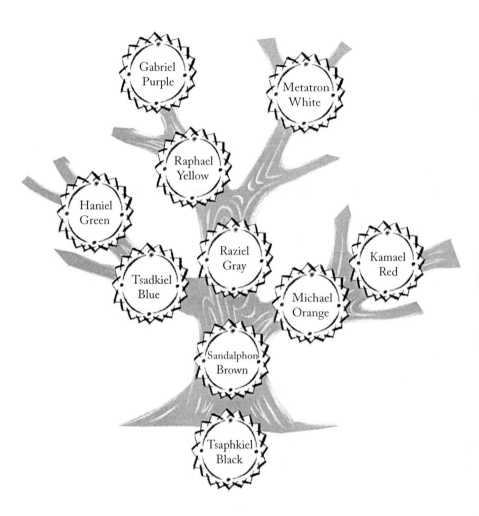

1 - The Tree of Colors

The colors that are attributed to the archangels vary depending on the author. The most reliable and uncontested historical source is the Kabbalist tradition and the 10 Sefirot. The tree of colors establishes a connection between the colors of the archangels and the Sefirot.

The tree's roots: black (Tsaphkiel).

The trunk: brown (Sandalphon), gray (Raziel).

The first branch: blue (Tsadkiel), green (Haniel).

The second branch: yellow (Raphael), purple (Gabriel).

The third branch (the highest of the four): white (Metatron).

The fourth branch: orange (Michael), red (Kamael).

2 - Black – Archangel Tsaphkiel

Archangel Tsaphkiel represents femininity, fecundity, understanding, the world of thought and great ideas, inspiration, travel, the achievement of projects, meditation, psychotherapy, self-questioning, and spiritual elevation.

Angels Related to Archangel Tsaphkiel
- *Angels of maternity*

- *Birth angels*

- *Angels of fecundity*

- *Angels of project realization*

- *Angels of intelligence*

- *Angels of travel*

- *Angels of creativity*

- *Angels of inspiration*

- *Angels of personal growth*

Black – The Roots of the Tree of Colors

Archangel Tsaphkiel and Related Angels

Black is the counter-color of every other color. It symbolizes the interior of the matrix, fecundity, and self-birth. It is said that the skin lets light pass into the body. Thoughts that develop within the brain come from the blackness of the cranium. The gestation of all things takes place in the color black.

Black is also the Sun disappearing behind the Earth in the night, which is called the "black sun." It governs the subconscious, great ideas, inspiration, and creativity.

The great goddesses of fertility in ancient civilizations are black mother goddesses. The black virgin is a depiction of Isis, the veiled goddess that sees beyond appearances. Black represents the deepness of the soul and the subconscious. Black is the feminine yin, the universal matrix from which creativity was born. Black is pre-Big Bang, the original situation preceding the Universe. In the Bible (Genesis 1:5), it says: "God called the light "day," and the darkness he called "night." And there was evening, and there was morning: the first day."

3 – Meditation of the Color Black with Archangel Tsaphkiel and Related Angels

(Approximately 20 minutes)

Meditating about black is very enriching. The subconscious opens up and liberates its inhibitions.

With the meditation of the color black, archangel Tsaphkiel and his related angels help women become pregnant, inspire artists who are beginning a new creation, and fertilize the soil of the earth or a garden.

Material
  • *A square of thick black paper or cardboard. Make sure you measure the square, which must be 8 inches by 8 inches. Put this square up on the wall, and sit down about three feet away.*

  • *A black candle.*

  • *A meditation cushion.*

Meditation

1. Light the candle.

2. Sit down comfortably on the cushion.

3. Breathe slowly. Relax.

4. Concentrate on the black square. Let the color penetrate you. Abandon yourself to the black energy.

5. Close your eyes.

6. Visualize yourself in complete blackness. You are in the matrix of creation. Feel the humidity and warm liquid that you're bathing in. You are in the original creation. You are ready to create anything you wish.

7. Feel the pleasant sensations of the matrix. Feel the comforting presence of archangel Tsaphkiel.

8. Take in a deep breath, and aspirate the blackness.

9. Exhale the blackness slowly.

10. Inhale deeply three times and then exhale the blackness.

11. Breathe regularly again.

12. Relax.

13. Open your eyes. Take your time before regaining ordinary consciousness.

Effects of the Meditation

Black opens up the door to the subconscious and liberates creative energies. Do this meditation when you wish to become pregnant, when you lack inspiration, or before you start a new job. The meditation of the color black is also very useful for people who need to anchor themselves to the Earth.

4 - Brown – Archangel Sandalphon

Archangel Sandalphon governs over matter, logic, wisdom, science, knowledge, individual fulfillment through self-realization and professional success, all of which must be organized and structured.

Angels Related to Archangel Sandalphon
- *Angels of knowledge*

- *Angels of science*

- *Angels of learning and apprenticeship*

- *Angels of professional success*

- *Angels of prosperity*

- *Angels of organization and logic*

- *Angels of wisdom*

- *Angels of efficiency and moral strength*

Brown – The Trunk of the Tree of Colors

Archangel Sandalphon and Related Angels

The tree of color's trunk is brown. The trunk symbolizes strength, gestating energy, and the ascent toward light. It also links the terrestrial with the celestial. The brown of archangel Sandalphon represents the anchoring in matter and the tangible reality of existence. Brown incarnates the manifestation of matter in all its strength and vigor. Brown is the potential of black, which starts to manifest itself in matter.

5 - The Prayer of the Color Brown with Archangel Sandalphon and Related Angels

Brown connects you to terrestrial reality. Archangel Sandalphon creates harmony with the material plane. He creates an anchoring that allows you to obtain material success.

Material
- *Pick up a piece of clay, a brown rock, or a clump of earth. The shade of brown is of no importance.*

- *A brown candle.*

- *A stick of birch or fennel incense, or frankincense.*

Prayer
1. Sit down comfortably.
2. Light the candle.
3. Burn the incense stick.
4. Pick up the rock, the clump of earth, or the clay and hold it in the pit of your hand like an offering.
5. Relax. Breathe slowly.
6. Turn toward the flame of the candle or incense.
7. Present your offering by saying:

Archangel Sandalphon and all the angels governed
by your power
Grant me knowledge and success,
Grant me strength and prosperity,
Connect me to the energy of the earth,
Give me energy and power,
Amen.

Effects of the Prayer
Meditate on the color brown when you are in need of intellectual knowledge, reflection, balance, or professional success. Solicit archangel Sandalphon for all of your professional projects and to ask for prosperity or material abundance.

6 - Gray – Archangel Raziel

Archangel Raziel is the archangel of love, times of happiness, and every kind of luck. He is the angel of efficiency and awareness. He helps develop intuition.

Angels Related to Archangel Raziel
- *Angels of love*

- *Angels of luck*

- *Angels of responsibility*

- *Divination angels*

- *Angels of mediumship*

Gray – The Trunk of the Tree of Colors

Archangel Raziel and Related Angels

Gray is composed of an identical amount of black and white. It's located on the top of the tree of colors' trunk and symbolizes the exchange between matter and thought, between the soul and the body, between men and angels. Clouds are gray. Clouds hide the infinite reality of heaven from humans. Piercing through the grayness allows one to lift the veil over all things and to see reality in all its splendor and richness. To cross the frontier between matter and the angelic world where divine light shines, one must pierce through the grayness. Gray incarnates softness, harmonizing the opposing forces of black and white. It's an active principal, tearing down the veil of hidden things. It's the color of love in all its softness and tenderness. Most of all, gray is the color of intuition, mediumship, and clairvoyance.

7 - The Visualization of the Color Gray with Archangel Raziel and Related Angels

(Approximately one hour including the composition)
This visualization opens the door to the future through mediumship. It also brings luck and good news.

Material
- *Black and white clothes or gray clothes.*

- *A white candle.*

- *A black candle.*

- *A photo of a cloud.*

- *A meditation cushion.*

- *Cut out a photo of a cloud or take a photo of the cloudy sky yourself, one that matches your sensibility or mood.*

- *A gray frame.*

- *Glue the photo to the gray frame or to some other kind of support that you have already colored or painted gray.*

- *A piece of transparent netting or cloth.*

- *Add this piece of netting over the frame, like a curtain. Create a harmonious composition, letting yourself be guided by your imagination.*

- *A gray rock.*

- *Place the gray rock, which you picked up in your garden or along the shore, in front of the composition that you just made and that will serve as the inspiration for your meditation.*

- *A gray feather.*

- *Add the gray feather to your composition.*

- *Optional: gray seashells, silver coins, or silver statuettes representing angels.*

Take your time to prepare your composition, and enjoy this moment to relax and be creative.

Visualization

1. Light the white candle and the black candle on each side of your composition. Make sure you allow about eight inches of space between

the candles and the composition to prevent them from burning the netting.

2. Wear gray, or white and black.

3. Sit down on the cushion in front of the composition you just made. Observe your work. Look at every detail, and every element that may inspire you.

4. Relax. Loosen your arms and shoulders. Breathe slowly, with your eyes fixed upon your composition.

5. Take in a deep breath and let the gray energy circulate in you. Exhale.

6. Close your eyes. Visualize archangel Raziel covering you with his wings. Feel the warmth of his thick gray feathers covering your shoulders. Feel his softness, his tenderness. Feel the angels around him who are sending you soft, harmonious, gray light.

7. Visualize a veil lifting before you. What do you see? Enter into the energy of what is appearing before you.

8. Breathe slowly.

9. Open your eyes.

10. Observe your composition.

11. Be yourself again. Slowly regain ordinary consciousness.

Effects of the Visualization

Anyone in search of mediumship, an awakening of their consciousness, or the gift of clairvoyance and divination, will find a way of crossing into the angelic plane, where the mysteries of the future are unveiled, in the meditation of the color gray. People in need of luck for gambling or professional opportunities should also meditate on the color gray, archangel Raziel, and his related angels.

8 - Blue – Archangel Tsadkiel

Blue is the most immaterial color, the symbolic manifestation of the infinite. Blue represents water and its transparency, the ocean, and purity. Blue is a cold color that erases the shape of something and dissolves it in the infinite. The spiritual dimension of blue is purity, and the dematerialization of matter and its shapes.

In Tibetan Buddhism, blue is the color of potential. The apparent contradiction between the color blue and the skills of archangel Tsadkiel stems from the common confusion between the infinite, the immaterial, and the idea that the immaterial is nothing but emptiness. Through his energy, archangel Tsadkiel brings abundance to anyone who knows how to empty themselves and whose existence isn't driven by money. He offers wealth and abundance when these benefits are used for the greater good. Tsadkiel is the archangel of infinite and dematerialized abundance. His vibration is negative for greedy people who transform abundance into an act of deprivation and accumulation. The beauty of Tsadkiel lies in his infinite gift, which must be used in an unlimited way.

Any wealth obtained from Tsadkiel's good grace is infinite; it's used to help generous people. Before invoking Tsadkiel, it's important to reassess your perception of money and what it brings you. You must empty yourself in order to see and to know how you can use the archangel's substantial aid. The Bible associates beauty and wealth with the color blue (Esther 1:6): "The garden had hangings of white and blue linen, fastened with cords of white linen and purple material to silver rings on marble pillars. There were couches of gold and silver on a mosaic pavement of porphyry, marble, mother-of-pearl and other costly gemstones."

Archangel Tsadkiel
Archangel Tsadkiel is the archangel of prosperity, abundance, material wealth, acquisitions, rewards, loan reimbursement, loans, and any kind of gain. The archangel encourages discernment and judicious choices.

Angels related to archangel Tsadkiel
- *Angels of wealth*
- *Angels of material wealth*

- *Angels of luck*

- *Angels of work*

- *Protective angels*

- *Angels of generosity*

- *Angels of charity*

Blue – The First Branch of the Tree of Colors

Archangel Tsadkiel and Related Angels

Archangel Tsadkiel is infinitely good and generous, and invoking him is an important act. It's necessary to consider all the different uses of the material wealth that this archangel can offer you. Archangel Tsadkiel is a very powerful archangel since he unites the material with the spiritual. Entering into his vibration is an important step in self-development. Tsadkiel brings you into a demanding angelic energy. Infinite wealth and abundance is within reach for anyone who opens up their heart to goodness.

9 – Invocation of the Color Blue with Archangel Tsadkiel and Related Angels

(Approximately 20 minutes including the preparation of the angelic altar)

This invocation brings abundance and wealth, as well as success. It's essential that you do it with the intention of spreading, consuming, and sharing what you have obtained through this invocation.

Material

- *An angelic altar (table, the top of a dresser, chair...)*

- *A blue cloth.*

- *Blue clothes (of any shade, navy blue or light blue).*

- *Three blue candles.*

- *A photo of the blue sky or the sea.*

- *A fresh or dried blue flower.*

- *Optional: blue gemstones, a blue cloth dipped in an aquamarine fragrance.*

Invocation

1. Cover the piece of furniture you will use as an angelic altar in a light blue cloth.

2. Put on some blue clothes.

3. Position the three candles in a triangle and light them.

4. Place the photo of the sky or the sea, along with the flower and the gemstones, onto your angelic altar. You can also use a white cloth or a cotton ball dipped in an aquamarine fragrance.

5. Prepare yourself for the invocation, and stand up in front of the altar.

6. Breathe slowly. Relax. Let your arms hang loose along the side of your body.

7. Emptying your spirit and mind is an essential part of this invocation. Archangel Tsadkiel fills up what is empty, and brings infinite wealth.

8. Concentrate on the following words and say them with sincerity, your arms loose at your sides, and your palms facing the altar. Lift the sole of your foot to form a triangle with your heels. This invocation requires physical openness and a loosening of the spirit. Now, say the following words as you lift your arms toward the sky, with your palms open in a position of offering:

Holy archangel Tsadkiel and related angels,
I'm soliciting your blessing and support.
Let wealth rain down upon me,
Let abundance fill my home,
Let joy inundate my spirit,

Let generosity open up my heart.
I thank you for your generosity and goodness,
Amen.

Effects of the Invocation
Blue is the color of infinity. Soliciting material aid from Tsadkiel is
an act of elevated consciousness that brings money, material wealth, and
security, on the condition that you accept it with the intent of sharing
and being generous.

10 - Green – Archangel Haniel

Archangel Haniel is the archangel of communication, conviviality,
relationship harmony, love expressed with sincerity, and emotional links
between beings.

Angels Related to Archangel Haniel
- *Angels of communication*
- *Angels of relationship harmony*
- *Family angels*
- *Angels of children*
- *Angels of couples*
- *Protective angels*
- *Guardian angels*

Green – The First Branch of the Tree of Colors

Archangel Haniel and Related Angels
Green incarnates spring and renewal. It's the alliance between yellow
and blue, the link between hot and cold, the bright and the mundane,
the feminine and the masculine. Green is the color of alliance, harmony,

and balance. In Islam, green is the symbol of the one sent from God, whose coat was green. Green incarnates life, transformation, and hope. It carries every quality of harmonious relationships between beings, between the yellow of life and the blue of infinity. In the Bible, green incarnates foliage, protection, and blessing (Chronicles 28:4): "He offered sacrifices and burned incense at the high places, on the hilltops and under every green tree."

Alchemists call gold the "blood of the green lion."

Osiris, the Egyptian god, is transformed into the vegetative Osiris (with his body covered in green dust), after his trip to the silt of the Nile. He incarnates resurrection, rebirth, and the triumph of life over death.

In the Bible (Revelation 4:3), John says: "and he who sat there had the appearance of jasper and carnelian, and around the throne was a glow that had the appearance of an emerald."

Archangel Haniel incarnates the power of green, the power of life, the relationships between humans, and communication.

11 - The Prayer of the Color Green with Archangel Haniel and Related Angels

(Approximately five minutes)

The prayer of the color green brings great comfort and can mend broken relationships. It encourages all forms of communication, and brings renewal in existence.

Material
None

Prayer
1. Sit down comfortably.
2. Close your eyes.
3. Breathe slowly, let peace enter into you.
4. Visualize a green bubble enveloping you. Feel the good it does to you.

Feel its freshness. Open your eyes.

5. Repeat this prayer three times:

Holy Archangel Haniel and all related angels,
Soothe my heart,
Improve my relationship with the person I love,
Protect my relationships with my family and friends,
Help me see clearly into my heart,
Teach me tolerance and goodness,
Bring renewal into my existence,
Amen.

Effects of the Prayer

The prayer of the color green is extremely useful for people with relationship problems. This prayer transforms broken family or romantic relationships. It facilitates communication and is particularly recommended for shy or introverted people. It brings great renewal to people who wish to experience important transformations in their existence.

12 - Yellow – Archangel Raphael

Archangel Raphael is the healing archangel, who relieves physical and emotional pain. He brings about healing, well-being, transformation, sociability, and success through hard work and courage. He favors personal success and helps realize any kind of project.

Angels Related to Archangel Raphael
- *Healing angels*

- *Angels of meditation*

- *Angels of inner transformation*

- *Rejuvenation angels*

- *Angels of cellular regeneration*

- *Protective angels*

- *Guardian angels*

- *Angels of work*

- *Manifestation angels*

- *Angels of success*

Yellow – The Second Branch of the Tree of Colors

Archangel Raphael and Related Angels

Yellow is the quintessential hot color. It incarnates strength, energy of life, and radiance.

The Indian god Vishnu wears yellow clothes.

Yellow is often associated with gold, the color of beauty and wealth; it's the color of the gods. Yellow is assimilated by light and the sun. Kings have used yellow and gold to highlight their power.

The saints' halos are golden.

Gold and yellow are the manifestations of perfect and immortal divinity on earth. Yellow is the light of the divine ray, the aura that surrounds saints and sacred things. Tabernacles are gilded or made of gold.

In China, yellow was the color of the emperor, the sun in the center of the Universe. Louis XIV called himself the "sun king."

The yellow of the sun is a symbol of celestial power. Yellow brings life, energy, and radiance.

13 – *Archangel Raphael's Prayer of the Color Yellow*
(Approximately 15 minutes)

Archangel Raphael's prayer of the color yellow has a healing energy for physical and psychic pain. Archangel Raphael's energy is extremely powerful. Don't hesitate to call upon this archangel, who is especially available. This prayer also brings about material abundance, which relieves anxieties and favors flourishing health.

Material
- *A place of prayer (a table, a dresser, a chair…).*
- *A yellow tablecloth.*
- *Four yellow candles.*
- *A photo of yourself.*
- *Angelic music.*
- *A yellow flower, a yellow gemstone, a golden angel, or any other golden object that inspires you.*

Prayer

1. Adorn your place of prayer in honor of archangel Raphael. You can do prayers and invocations here regularly.

2. Cover this spot with a yellow tablecloth.

3. Position the four candles in a square, and on the inside, draw a five pointed star facing upward. Light the candles. The five pointed star represents the human body. This layout is useful as a way of depicting yourself physically and to activate the healing process. You can also put down a photo between the candles.

4. Adorn the altar with a yellow flower, a yellow gemstone, a golden angel, or any other yellow or golden object you wish to dedicate to the archangel.

5. Listen to some soft music. Archangel Raphael is particularly sensitive to the atmosphere you create when you invoke him. Do this prayer on a Wednesday, the day of Mercury, archangel Raphael's dominant planet.

6. Recite this prayer four times:

Holy archangel Raphael and related angels,

Grant me healing and joy,
Open the door to my heart,
Give me happiness and health,
Grant me your benefits, abundance and wealth,
I am opening my arms to receive them,
I shall be eternally grateful,
Amen.

Effects of the Prayer

This prayer is particularly recommended for people who wish to be healed of physical illness, or anyone suffering from bereavement, separation, or a break-up. This meditation is also for people who wish to rediscover their love of life, grow younger, go on a diet, be athletic, or get back in shape. Archangel Raphael and the color yellow promise depressed or demoralized people a return to success and abundance.

14 - Purple – Archangel Gabriel

Archangel Gabriel is the archangel that dominates the subconscious, and regenerates strength and energy during sleep. He symbolizes the transmutation of existence through the awakening of consciousness. He brings out the best in people in order to give meaning to their lives.

Angels Related to Archangel Gabriel
* *Guardian angels.*

* *Protective angels.*

* *Angels of happiness.*

* *Angels of prosperity.*

* *Angels of sleep.*

* *Angels of energy and strength.*

* *Angels of inner transformation.*

- *Angels of hidden things yet to be revealed.*

Purple – The Second Branch of the Tree of Colors

Archangel Gabriel and Related Angels

Purple is the first color on the inside of the rainbow. It blends equal portions of the color red (symbol of the earth) and the color blue (celestial symbol). Purple paves the road between the terrestrial world and the angelic plane, a road that everyone can take. Medieval paintings sometimes depict Christ wearing a purple robe during the Passion, the moment he will die and then resurrect, provoking the reunion of terrestrial and celestial energies.

Purple is the symbolic color of spirituality because it represents the union of matter and the spirit. Purple appears on the fourteenth card of the Tarot of Marseille, Temperance. An angel pours water from a red vase into a blue vase, thereby transferring the energies of the heavens toward the earth, and then back. This symbolic transfer of energy demonstrates the power of the color purple, which contains terrestrial strength as well as celestial power. Purple is the color of meditation, contemplation, and spiritual peace.

15 – Meditation of the Color Purple with Archangel Gabriel
(Approximately 10 minutes)
This meditation brings peace, serenity, and spiritual elevation.

Material
- *A meditation rug.*

- *A purple cloth.*

- *Four purple candles.*

- *A white cloth.*

- *Violet perfume.*

- *Zen music.*

- *An amethyst.*

Meditation

1. Stretch out the purple cloth over a meditation rug.
2. Put down a purple candle in the four corners of this rug (keeping a distance of at least 12 inches).
3. Dip a white cotton ball or a white piece of cloth in violet perfume.
4. Play the Zen music.
5. Light the candles.
6. Stretch out slowly, without making any abrupt movements.
7. Place a small amethyst between your eyebrows on the sixth Chakra of the third eye.
8. Close your eyes. Smell the violet perfume. Relax.
9. Visualize archangel Gabriel in a purple aura and quiet your thoughts. Receive his love and goodness.
10. Stay for a moment in this state of well-being and relaxation.
11. Come back to reality. Open your eyes.
12. Take your time before regaining ordinary consciousness.

Effects of the Meditation

The invocation of the color purple is recommended for people in the process of elevating their consciousness, and who wish to take the path of spirituality and psychic equilibrium. People who want to acquire serenity can call upon archangel Gabriel with this invocation.

This meditation is recommended for anyone who works for the good of others and for personal balance.

16 - White – Archangel Metatron

Metatron signals the beginning, the starting point of a new existence, wish fulfillment, self-realization, the development of power, and inner strength.

Angels Related to Archangel Metatron
- *Angels of wish fulfillment*

- *Angels of a change in direction*

- *Angels of personal achievment*

- *Angels of the deceased*

- *Angels of goodness and brotherhood*

White – The Third Branch of the Tree of Colors

Archangel Metatron and Related Angels

White is the synthesis of all colors, or the absence of colors.

In the rituals of ancient mystery religions, the recipient of a title, diploma, or special authority was dressed in white in order to unite all the colors and to present himself as pure before the divinity.

White incarnates silence and meditation.

Angels are most often depicted wearing white tunics. During their solemn or first communion, Catholics wear a white cassock, which means that they have vowed to be pure before communing with the divine.

Dawn is white. It introduces the day, which then becomes colorful with the first rays of sunlight. White is the threshold between black and color. Most rites of passage are done with white clothing. In initiatory rites, wearing white clothing is a way for people to enter the invisible, the infinite, and the eternal.

Celtic druids wore white.

White signals the dawn of realization, the starting point and annunciation of life, as well as the color of passage toward death. White represents a transitory state or change.

The Sufis (mystics of Islam) associate white with the virtue of wisdom.

In the New Testament, Gospels (Marc 9:2-3), the transfiguration of Jesus is symbolized by the color white: "After six days Jesus took Peter,

James and John with him and led them up a high mountain, where they were all alone. There he was transfigured before them. His clothes became dazzling white, whiter than anyone in the world could bleach them."

Whiteness is virginal, pure, and stainless. It symbolizes the light of God, his radiance and love. Love is associated with white through the purity of sentiment. This is why angels are the white and luminous messengers of the Lord. Terrestrial love is also pure white, lending it a divine quality, Old Testament, The Poetic Books (Canticles 5:10): "My beloved is white and ruddy, the chiefest among ten thousand."

17 - Invocation of the Color White and of Archangel Metatron

(Approximately 15 minutes)

The invocation of archangel Metatron is a magical procedure that requires personal purification. The results are exceptional. We invoke Metatron to obtain power in our work, in the achievement of our projects, or for self-fulfillment. We also invoke archangel Metatron to satisfy desires. If you wish to help the soul of a parent or friend who has left the terrestrial plane through meditation, place a photo of the deceased next to a feather, which symbolizes archangel Metatron, and at the end of the meditation, say the following words:

Holy archangel Metatron and all other related holy angels,
Watch over the soul of (say the person's first name),
Lead him (or her) toward the eternal light and love of God,
Amen.

Material
- *Six white candles*
- *A white feather*
- *A white meditation cushion*

- *Comfortable white clothes*

Invocation

1. Begin this invocation with personal purification (a shower or a swim in the sea).

2. Pick a calm and quiet place. Silence is essential for this white meditation. It's more symbolic if you do it at daybreak.

3. Wear a white outfit.

4. Position the six white candles into a diamond and light them.

5. Place the white feather, which symbolizes archangel Metatron, in the center of this diamond.

6. Sit down on the cushion.

7. Close your eyes.

8. Evacuate all your parasitic thoughts.

9. Let the dim light and silence fill your spirit.

10. Picture archangel Metatron extending his wings. His white radiating light penetrates the crown Chakra on top of your head.

11. Feel the light of Metatron coursing through your body, giving you a tingling sensation. Your body is warm and emits warmth.

12. Breathe in the archangel's light and exhale everything cluttering your life.

13. Let Metatron's divine energy react in the emptiness and silence.

14. Accelerate your breathing to return to reality.

15. Open your eyes.

16. End this meditation with these words:

Holy Archangel Metatron and all other related holy angels,
I am pure and stainless,
I am filled with your light and love,
I thank you,
Amen.

18 - Orange – *Archangel Michael*

Archangel Michael

Archangel Michael is the defender of humanity, the protector of lost causes and victims. He is responsible for the survival of people in danger. He pushes negative energies and obstacles away.

Angels Related to Archangel Michael

- *Protective angels of humanity.*

- *Protective angels against accidents.*

- *Protective angels against negative energies.*

- *Guardian angels.*

- *Angels of courage.*

- *Healing angels.*

- *Angels of health.*

- *Protective angels of the home.*

- *Angels of athletes.*

- *The whole angelic plane, with archangel Michael acting as the head of the angels.*

Orange – The Fourth Branch of the Tree of Colors

Archangel Michael

The light from the color orange pushes negative energies away.

The saffron robes of Buddhist monks symbolize the revelation of illumination. Orange also represents the balance between the spirit and the flesh.

In ancient Greece, Apollo's Muses wore orange tunics to celebrate the glory and beauty of their god.

The sun is the star of the color orange. Its radiance and warmth guarantee life.

Orange protects life, creates equilibrium, heats up the home, and provides energy and strength.

It's also one of the colors of the universal force that illuminates, supports, and encourages each individual. Orange is an active and positive force.

19 - Prayer of the Color Orange with Archangel Michael

The prayer of the color orange brings abundance, strength, energy, and vitality. It's also a protective prayer against negative energies.

(Approximately 15 minutes including preparation time for the place of prayer)

Material
- *A white sheet or tablecloth*
- *An orange*
- *A salt lamp*
- *A photo of sunrise*
- *A stick of orange blossom incense*

Prayer

1. Prepare a place of prayer with a white tablecloth, an orange, a lit salt lamp, orange blossom incense, a photo of sunrise, and any other object of your choice.

2. Relax, breathe slowly. Enter into archangel Michael's energy.

3. Recite the following prayer:

Holy archangel Michael and related angels,
I thank you for watching over me,
For keeping negative people and energies away from me,
In order to protect me and my family

and the people that I love.

I'm asking for new strength and flourishing health.

I thank you and I open my heart to you,

Amen.

Effects of the Prayer

People who pray to archangel Michael and the color orange ask him to help them build strength, and to protect their home and their vital energy. This prayer is particularly well-suited after reciting Archangel Raphael's prayer to accelerate healing and to encourage the return of an invigorative personal energy.

It's also recommended for anyone who wants charisma, or to shine in society.

20 - Red – Archangel Kamael

Archangel Kamael encourages the accomplishment of our mission on Earth, the harmonization of our desires, success, exploits, will, results obtained through personal effort, strength, rigor, and courage.

Angels Related to Archangel Kamael

- *Angels of the mission on Earth.*

- *Angels of will.*

- *Angels of athletic exploits.*

- *Angels of romantic love.*

- *Angels of positive energy.*

- *Angels of courage.*

- *Angels of professional and artistic success.*

Red – The Fourth Branch of the Tree of Colors

Archangel Kamael

Red is the outer color of the rainbow. It expresses vitality, strength, and energy.

In Irish tradition, it represents the warrior's fervor. Irish Celts celebrate the beauty of a young man or woman by calling them red.

Red is fire and blood: vital energy.

In the Far East, red is a symbol of passion, fire, and life. The union between two people is represented by red string interlaced with destiny.

In Japan, dyeing rice red is a way to wish for happiness.

In the East, red is also representative of fiery passion and love. Red roses are offered to loved ones.

21 - Visualization of the Color Red and of Archangel Kamael

Material
None

Visualization
1. Begin by sitting down comfortably, with your palms open on your thighs.
2. Visualize a red light.
3. Invoke archangel Kamael and the angels associated with him.
4. Let the red light into your heart and then place your hand over your heart to keep it in.
5. Inhale deeply in order to let archangel Kamael's energy circulate throughout your whole body.
6. Exhale as you remove your hand from your heart. You have recharged your body with strength and positive energy.
7. Open your eyes.
8. Say thank you.
9. Regain ordinary consciousness.

Effects of the Visualization

The visualization of the color red is recommended for people who wish to rediscover the energy and vitality of their youth. It's particularly well-suited for athletes preparing themselves for an athletic event, or for people who wish to recover their sexual fervor, romantic passion, or artistic and professional success. It's recommended for people who are going through professional challenges or situations that require a fighting spirit and courage.

This visualization is not recommended for people with high blood pressure.

Chapter 20

The Incense of Angels

Burning incense facilitates contact with the angelic plane.

Since the dawn of time, incense has been used for religious practices as well as consecration and worship rituals. In the Bible (Leviticus 2:15-16), incense is an offering to God: "Put oil and incense on it; it is a grain offering. The priest shall burn the memorial portion of the crushed grain and the oil, together with all the incense, as an offering made to the LORD by fire."

The Egyptians used incense to purify sacred places, for rituals practiced by priests, and for the composition of perfumes. Incense is the main ingredient of Kyphi, a solid perfume that was burned in honor of the god Ra. Kyphi is composed of cinnamon, myrrh, and sandalwood incense. The Kyphi recipe was found on the walls of the Egyptian temples of Edfu and Dendera, along with the elements used for its composition and its production technique.

The Nabataeans of Arabia developed the incense trade. They lined the Incense Road with a perfected irrigation system. This road extended from Egypt and Arabia all the way to India. In turn, the Romans used the resources of incense.

The Assyrians celebrated the cult of god Ba'al by offering him burning incense.

The Old Testament recounts the composition of incense (Exodus 30:34): "The LORD said to Moses, 'Take fragrant essences: Storax, amber, galbanum, and pure frankincense, all in equal amounts."

Other forms of incense are also referenced in the Bible: Spikenard, saffron, Calamus, cinnamon, myrrh, and aloe.

In Hinduism, priests burn camphor and other types of incense in honor of god Krishna.

In India, incense is used in temples. People who come to offer incense elevate their souls toward their god and amplify their prayer.

The New Testament (Matthew 2:11) recounts how the three kings came to baby Jesus: "They entered the house and saw the child with his mother, Mary, and they bowed down and worshiped him. Then they opened their treasure chests and gave him gifts of gold, frankincense, and myrrh."

Frankincense is produced by harvesting the resin of the Boswellia sacra tree. It can be found in Oman, Somalia, Yemen, and India, where the Boswellia serrata tree provides olibanum.

Burning incense diffuses wonderful fragrances, and elevates energies through the intermediary of smoke clouds. Incense allows for communication between the visible and invisible worlds.

The use of incense isn't without risks because they contain harmful particles. It's recommended that you use no more than one incense stick per day, and that you air out the room after using it.

Incense have a soothing and relaxing quality. Which incense you choose will depend on how they will be used. Meditation incense are soft and promote well-being. Prayer or angelic invocation incense are more powerful and stronger smelling. A ritual's incense is chosen according to the nature of the invocation.

1 - The Main Incense

• *Amber: Pleases the gods who receive them as offerings. Favors meditation.*

• *Star anise: Increases luck, abundance, and the acuteness of conscience.*

- *Wormwood: Increases discernment and lucidity. Favorable for making choices.*

- *Benzoin: Used for all purifications, and can be mixed with other incense.*

- *Bergamot: Attracts abundance.*

- *Sandalwood: Opens up the Chakras. Used for offerings and invocation rituals.*

- *Camphor: Purifies places and people. Contributes to the increase of energy and the elevation of vibrations.*

- *Cinnamon: Favors abundance, the influx of money, and anything related to the field of finance and luck. Elevates spiritual consciousness.*

- *Cedar: Balances yin and yang. Brings about peace, and allows for stressed people to rediscover calm and serenity.*

- *Nag Champa: Favors meditation and the elevation of consciousness.*

- *Copal (Mayan incense): Purifies people and objects. Pushes negative energies away.*

- *Incense of Arabia: Favors invocation and prayer.*

- *Incense of Bethlehem: Favors feminine invocations.*

- *Heena incense: Favors meditation.*

- *Incense of Jerusalem: Keeps negative energies away. Purifies.*

- *Incense of Lourdes: Amplifies invocations made by women.*

- *Incense of Nazareth: Favors professional and career development.*

- *Apple Blossoms: Favors healing and longevity.*

- *Jupier: Purifies places. Pushes negative energies away.*

- *Clove: Attracts money, and material wealth. Acts like a magnet.*

- *Gum arabic: Chases negative energies away from a place.*

- *Hyssop: Purifies.*

- *Jasmine: Favors love, new encounters, and relationship harmony. The incense of the heart Chakra.*

- *Lavender: Develops mediumship, intuition, and clairvoyance.*

- *St. John's wort: Develops mediumship.*

- *Myrrh: Purifies and heals. Favors emotions, spiritual elevation, meditation, and prayer. The incense of invocation rituals.*

- *Olibanum: Keeps negative energies away, purifies, develops mediumship, and elevates consciousness and intuition.*

- *Patchouli: Favors abundance. Attracts money and material wealth. Favors love and harmonious sexual relations.*

- *Pine: Purifies. Favors fertility. The incense of energy and virile strength.*

- *Peony: Maintains love and preserves relationship harmony.*

- *Rose: Encourages the love of life and preserves happiness. The incense of love.*

- *Dragon's blood: Favors love and desire.*

- *Sage: Purifies, and cleanses the negative energies of a place.*

- *Sesame: Favors prosperity and business.*

- *Tea: Favors luck and the influx of money.*

- *Linden: Keeps away negative people and their influence.*

- *Valerian: Purifies.*

- *Violet: Favors love and seduction.*

2 - Angels and their Corresponding Incense

3 - Archangel Metatron

Metatron signals the beginning, the starting point of a new existence, wish fulfillment, self-realization, and inner strength.

Angels Related to Archangel Metatron
- *Angels of wish fulfillment*

- *Angels of personal transformation*

- *Angels of personal achievement*

- *Angels of goodness and brotherhood*

- *Angels of success and all achievements*

The Incense of Archangel Metatron and Related Angels
Sandalwood, Camphor, Cinnamon, Gum arabic, Jasmine, Lavender, St. John's wort, Myrrh, Olibanum, Patchouli, Pine, Peony, Rose, Dragon's blood, Violet.

4 - Archangel Tsaphkiel

Archangel Tsaphkiel represents femininity, fecundity, understanding, the world of thought and great ideas, inspiration, travel, the achievement of projects, meditation, psychotherapy, self-questioning, and spiritual elevation.

Angels Related to Archangel Tsaphkiel
- *Angels of maternity*

- *Birth angels*

- *Angels of fecundity*

- *Angels of project realization*

- *Angels of intelligence*

- *Angels of travel*

- *Angels of creativity*

- *Angels of inspiration*

- *Angels of personal growth*

The Incense of Archangel Tsaphkiel

Wormwood, Benzoin, Camphor, Cedar, Nag Champa, Incense of Bethlehem, Incense of Lourdes, Jasmine, Myrrh, Pine, Valerian.

5 - *Archangel Tsadkiel*

Archangel Tsadkiel is the archangel of prosperity, abundance, material wealth, acquisitions, rewards, loan reimbursement, loans, and any kind of gain. The archangel encourages discernment and judicious choices.

Angels Related to Archangel Tsadkiel
- *Angels of wealth*

- *Angels of material wealth*

- *Angels of luck*

- *Angels of work*

- *Protective angels*

- *Angels of generosity*

- *Angels of charity*

The Incense of Archangel Tsadkiel and Related Angels

Star anise, Bergamot, Cinnamon, Incense of Nazareth, Clove, Olibanum, Patchouli, Sesame, Tea.

6 - Archangel Kamael

Archangel Kamael encourages the accomplishment of our mission on Earth, the harmonization of our desires, success, exploits, will, results obtained through personal effort, strength, rigor, and courage.

Angels Related to Archangel Kamael
- *Angels of the mission on Earth.*

- *Angels of will.*

- *Angels of athletic exploits.*

- *Angels of positive energy.*

- *Angels of courage.*

- *Angels of professional and artistic success.*

The Incense of Archangel Kamael and Related Angels
Star anise, Wormwood, Benzoin, Cinnamon, Incense of Nazareth, Clove, Pine, Sesame, Linden.

7 - Archangel Michael

Archangel Michael is the defender of humanity, the protector of lost causes and victims. He is responsible for the survival of people in danger. He pushes negative energies and obstacles away.

Angels Related to Archangel Michael
- *Protective angels of humanity.*

- *Protective angels against accidents.*

- *Protective angels against negative energies.*

- *Guardian angels.*

- *Angels of courage.*

- *Healing angels.*

- *Angels of health.*

- *Protective angels of the home.*

- *Angels of athletes.*

- *The whole angelic plane, with archangel Michael acting as the head of the angels.*

The Incense of Archangel Michael and Related Angels
Amber, Benzoin, Camphor, Copal, Incense of Jerusalem, Juniper, Gum arabic, Hyssop, Olibanum, Pine, Sage, Linden, Valerian.

8 - *Archangel Haniel*

Archangel Haniel is the archangel of communication, conviviality, relationship harmony, love expressed with sincerity, and emotional links between beings.

Angels Related to Archangel Haniel
- *Angels of communication*

- *Angels of relationship harmony*

- *Family angels*

- *Angels of children*

- *Angels of couples*

- *Protective angels*

- *Guardian angels*

The Incense of Archangel Haniel and Related Angels
Benzoin, Sandalwood, Cedar, Copal, Jasmine, Patchouli, Peony,

Rose, Violet.

9 - Archangel Raphael

Archangel Raphael is the healing archangel, who relieves physical and emotional pain. He brings about healing, well-being, transformation, sociability, and success through hard work and courage. He favors personal success and helps realize any kind of project.

Angels Related to Archangel Raphael
- *Healing angels*
- *Angels of meditation*
- *Angels of inner transformation*
- *Rejuvenation angels*
- *Angels of cellular regeneration*
- *Protective angels*
- *Guardian angels*
- *Angels of work*
- *Manifestation angels*
- *Angels of success*

The Incense of Archangel Raphael and Related Angels
Amber, Benzoin, Sandalwood, Camphor, Nag Champa, Incense of Arabia, Heena Incense, Apple Blossoms, Juniper, Gum arabic, Myrrh, Sage.

10 - Archangel Gabriel

Archangel Gabriel is the archangel that dominates our subconscious, and regenerates our strength and energy while we are asleep. He symbolizes the transmutation of existence through the awakening of consciousness. He brings out the best in us so that we can attain happiness.

Angels Related to Archangel Gabriel
- *Guardian angels*

- *Protective angels*

- *Angels of happiness*

- *Angels of prosperity*

- *Angels of sleep*

- *Angels of energy and strength*

- *Angels of inner transformation*

- *Angels of hidden things yet to be revealed*

The Incense of Archangel Gabriel and Related Angels
Wormwood, Benzoin, Bergamot, Cinnamon, Cedar, Jasmine, Lavender, Olibanum, Rose, Sesame, Violet.

11 - *Archangel Sandalphon*

Archangel Sandalphon governs over matter, logic, wisdom, science, knowledge, individual fulfillment through self-realization, and professional success, all of which must be organized and structured.

Angels Related to Archangel Sandalphon
- *Angels of knowledge*

- *Angels of science*

- *Angels of learning and apprenticeship*

- *Angels of professional success*

- *Angels of prosperity*

- *Angels of organization and logic*

- *Angels of wisdom*

- *Angels of efficiency and moral strength*

The Incense of Archangel Sandalphon and Related Angels

Amber, Star anise, Bergamot, Cinnamon, Clove, Olibanum, Sesame, Tea, Linden, Valerian.

Chapter 21

The Gemstones and Crystals of the Angels

Since Antiquity, men have used gemstones and crystals for symbolic and magical ceremonies, traditional rites, and to celebrate decorative beauty on ornaments and jewels.

The ancient Egyptians left behind magnificent golden jewels adorned with amethysts, blue turquoise, malachite, emeralds, and jaspers. The jewels of Tutankhamun, and queen Tausert, as well as the ones discovered in royal tombs, are astonishingly beautiful and rich.

In China, jade is used in the field of medicine.

In India, young Brahmans are initiated with gemstones and learn the symbolism of minerals.

In Zen philosophy, the Japanese see the stimulation of ideas and the association of colors in rocks.

Oceanian, American-Indian, African, and Australian shamans use gemstones symbolically to heal or harmonize the sky and the earth, the body and the spirit.

In Mesopatamia, the Nippur tablets mention the usage of minerals and plants for therapeutic reasons.

For Hebrews, gemstones have symbolic value. The Bible often mentions gemstones.

In the Old Testament, the Historical Books (2 Chronicles 9:9), Queen Saba: "gave the king one hundred and twenty talents of gold and a very great amount of spices and precious stones."

According to Ezekiel (28:13), the Garden of Eden, the garden of

God, was: "surrounded by walls made of gemstones: sardonyx, topaz and jasper, chrysolite, beryl and onyx, lazuli, carbuncle, and emerald…"

The Book of Revelation (21:10-11) describes the celestial city as transparent as a crystal: "He carried me away in the Spirit to a mountain great and high, and showed me the Holy City, Jerusalem, coming down out of heaven from God. Its brilliance was like that of a very precious jewel, like a jasper, clear as crystal."

In the Middle-Ages, alchemists did research on gemstones and their symbolic value.

The high-rank angels of the celestial hierarchy live among gemstones. In Ezekiel (28: 14), it says: "You were anointed as a guardian cherub, for so I ordained you. You were on the holy mount of God; you walked among the fiery stones."

Gemstones are crystallizations or stable states of organized matter emanating from the earth. The use of clay as a bandage, poultice, or cast is recognized in classical medicine and dermatology as a skin purifier.

Crystals and gemstones have a great variety of colors and chemical compositions as well as degrees of hardness and transparency, lending them specific qualities. Their refraction and absorption of light influences their use in lithotherapy and angelic magic.

The word "lithotherapy" comes from the Greek "lithos," meaning "stone," and "therapeia," meaning "care." Lithotherapy has been practiced for several years as an alternative medicine, but should not, under any circumstances, substitute a medical consultation. Lithotherapy uses four fundamental qualities of gemstones and crystals:

1. Chromotherapy, therapy through the colors of the gemstones.
2. Oligotherapy, the use of oligo elements and minerals contained in gemstones.
3. The energy of gemstones.
4. The absorption and refraction of light.

Other than the use of crystals and gemstones in solid form, some lithotherapists work with stone elixirs composed of a solution of purified water or spring water in which a stone or crystal has been immersed.

In association with angelic work on Chakras and aura, here is a list of what lithotherapy is useful for.

- *Connecting to the angelic plane.*

- *Using the healing power of angels.*

- *Reinforcing positive energies.*

- *Chasing away negative energies.*

- *Protecting oneself from negative planetary influences.*

- *Acting upon the nervous system and the lymphatic system.*

- *Clarifying one's aura.*

The geometric shape of gemstones and crystals determines their usage and effectiveness. Large, rough gemstones are recommended for cleansing a room or living space from negative waves.

Rough gemstones channel energy better than refined gemstones. They are highly recommended for meditation, visualization, and angelic ceremonies.

Refined gemstones act upon specific domains in function to their geometric shape. Their usage depends on their beauty and shininess. They are recommended for the decoration of angelic altars and to attract positive energy. When gemstones are devoted to angels, it's advisable to place them in the different rooms of your home.

On your desk, a black tourmaline stone is most appropriate, especially if you work with a computer. A Tiger's eye will give you a feeling of confidence and serenity. Onyx will help you concentrate better.

An amethyst on your nightstand will lull you to sleep.

In the entrance of your home, agate, citrine, or even black tourmaline devoted to angel Haheuiah is an excellent protection against negative energies that could otherwise come in.

Some gemstones, like amethysts, are particularly effective for spiritual elevation. Blue turquoise is a great protective stone.

1 - Jewels Devoted to Angels

You can wear crystal jewels on pendants, bracelets, necklaces, earrings, or rings. These jewels devoted to angels will carry the energy of your angel and will give you energy or protect you all throughout your day.

The energy of these jewels will be even stronger if you wear them on your skin.

To devote a jewel made of crystal to an angel, see *The Angel That You Need*, p. 553.

2 - Massages

You can do massages with massage oils (see *Massage with the Angels*, p. 290), leaving out a crystal or a gemstone devoted to an angel. Massages done with oils will be reinforced by the angelic energy of the devoted crystal (see *Devoting a Gemstone to an Angel*, p. 491).

3 - Making a Gemstone Elixir

Fill up half of a vial or transparent receptacle with distilled water. Place the crystal of your choice, previously cleaned and devoted to an angel, into the vial or receptacle. Let the vial sit in the sun for three or four hours. Under the heat and light of the sun, the water will charge itself with the crystal's vibratory energy. Then, fill the other half of the vial with alcohol.

For elixirs devoted to angels of the evening or night, it's recommended that you place the vial or receptacle under the moonlight for at least three hours.

Seven drops of this angelic elixir carrying mineral vibrations will be used to heal the energies of the aura.

Never drink this elixir.

4 - Choosing a Crystal or Gemstone

There's a great variety of crystals and gemstones of different sizes and colors. The difference in color, from lightest to darkest, can change your impression of one gemstone or another. In any case, trust your intuition to make the choice. Choose gemstones and crystals that you're drawn to. Then, place the open palm of your left hand over each gemstone or crystal. If you feel warmth or tingling, this gemstone or crystal suits your energy.

5 - Cleaning the Crystals

Before each use, it's important to clean the crystals in order to eliminate the residue of negative energies.

Wash your crystals with clear water and soap. Then, let them soak for three minutes in water with a half-teaspoon of cooking salt for every liter. Rinse off your crystals with clear water.

6 - Recharging and Purifying Crystals

The purification of crystals should be done once a month, on the eve of a full-moon. Leave your crystals out overnight on your balcony, windowsill, or garden. The moon purifies your gemstones and reactivates their energy.

7 - Personal Use of Crystals

Your gemstones soak up the vibrations of the people who touch them. If you wish to preserve the positive energy of your crystals, don't let anyone handle them, touch them, or move them.

Crystals don't all have the same hardness. Don't knock them against things, they may crack or get scratched. Be careful not to expose them to different vibrations. And above all, trust your intuition and gut feeling.

8 - Devoting a Gemstone to an Angel

1. Start by choosing a crystal based on the angel of your domain (see *The*

Angels That You Need, p. 553).

2. Then, clean the crystal.

3. Say the consecration prayer while holding the crystal in your left hand, and placing your hand over your heart. Say the following words:

> Holy angel (say his name),
> I thank you for protecting this crystal and giving it all your energy,
> Your love, your power, and your light.
> Amen.

4. Place your crystal on a white non-lined sheet of paper, where you have written the name of the angel of your choice. Draw a circle in black ink around the name of the angel and place the crystal on the inside of this circle. Join your hands together over the crystal. Concentrate. Stay in this position for one minute. The crystal soaks up your energy and the angelic vibration. From this moment on, no one must touch your gemstone.

9 - The Geometric Shapes of Crystals

10 - Crystal Balls

Sphere-shaped crystals are generally expensive, but they are very interesting as work tools and protection tools. Crystal balls 1 to 3 inches in diameter are effective enough, but larger sized spheres, 4 to 5 inches in diameter, concentrate even more energy.

Crystal balls are particularly interesting for meditation.

11 - Meditation of the Crystal Ball
(Approximately 20 minutes)

Material
- *A sphere-shaped, transparent quartz crystal, or a sphere-shaped*

amethyst.

Meditation

1. Pick up a small crystal ball devoted to an angel.

2. Lay down and breathe slowly.

3. Hold the crystal ball in the pit of your hands, joined together above your eyes, in front of the third eye Chakra.

4. Enter into the vibration of the crystal ball.

5. Bring the crystal ball toward the heart Chakra.

6. Feel the angelic vibration.

7. Bring the crystal ball toward the solar plexus.

8. Feel the angelic vibration.

9. Continue doing this movement, alternating between the 3 Chakras, for 20 minutes.

10. Regain ordinary consciousness.

Effects of the Meditation

This meditation connects you to the angel associated with the crystal ball and opens up the superior Chakras. The meditation of the crystal ball concentrates energy, develops intellectual faculties, the ability to work, and intuition.

12 - Crystal Eggs

The egg's energy is mostly distributed through the tip. The energy field of an ovoid shape is directional. Eggs are best for angelic visualization.

13 - Visualization of the Crystal Egg
(Approximately 10 minutes)

Material

• *A crystal egg made of transparent rock (including a white veil), that you've previously cleaned and devoted to an angel.*

Visualization

1. Sit down comfortably on a chair and breathe slowly. Let your mind wander.

2. Hold the egg between your eyebrows near the third eye Chakra. Point the tip toward the Chakra and close your eyes.

3. After a few minutes, you will see the angel that you devoted the crystal to and you will make a request.

4. Thank the angel and slowly regain ordinary consciousness.

Effects of the Visualization

The shape of the egg guides the angelic energy directly toward the Ajna Chakra of the third eye. This visualization is recommended when you wish to ask a practical question to an angel. The answer will come to you through a thought or idea that you will have several hours after the visualization. If you do the visualization in the evening or at night, the answer or idea will come the next day, upon awakening.

14 - The Crystal Pyramid

A crystal pyramid can be placed next to your workspace, on your desk or near your computer. Its shape attracts light and concentrates energy into the tip.

A pyramid devoted to an angel is particularly appropriate for angelic altars because it channels angelic energies, conserving them in its base.

Pyramids are not recommended for meditation or visualization because of its tip, a powerful receiver of energy, and its vibratory intensity.

15 - The Crystal Obelisk

Obelisks devoted to angels are powerful receivers of negative energy, and very effective for the protection of your house or office.

When you place an obelisk devoted to an angel on an angelic altar, it will concentrate all angelic energy. It captures negativity, and all of its harmful effects are annihilated by angelic vibration.

It's important to clean obelisks regularly and to devote them to an angel after each cleaning.

16 – Icosahedrons

Icosahedrons are complex geometric shapes made up of 20 equilateral triangles. This geometric shape has remarkable properties for meditation, visualization, and prayer. Placing an icosahedron on an angelic altar is not advisable. It's a very active stone that should be used in an operational manner.

Its many facets and its refraction of light make it a wonderful tool for condensing angelic vibration.

Before working with icosahedrons, make sure you purify it before each use and devote it to the appropriate angel.

17 – Angelic Solicitation with an Icosahedron
(Approximately 10 minutes)

Material
- *A transparent quartz icosahedron.*

Solicitation
1. Sit down on a chair, with your back straight, but not tense. Loosen your shoulders. Breathe slowly.
2. In your right hand, you are holding an icosahedron devoted to the angel of your choice.
3. Close your eyes. Place the icosahedron near the crown Chakra above your head. Breathe deeply. Feel the luminous energy of the icosahedron entering the superior Chakra. You feel a tingling sensation near the Chakra. It feels as though your skull is opening up.
4. Ask a question about your profession and ask for support from the devoted angel of the icosahedron.
5. Remove the icosahedrons and keep it in the closed palm of your left hand for several minutes.

6. Breathe slowly, and open your eyes. Regain ordinary consciousness.

Effects of the Solicitation

The icosahedron absorbs angelic energy, which then penetrates into the crown Chakra from every facet of the crystal figure.

This solicitation brings answers and solutions to your professional life. This figure is particularly active for job hunting and career development.

18 - The Crystal Companion

You can choose a polished or refined gemstone as your crystal companion. This crystal will accompany you in your purse or jacket pocket. It's preferable if you keep it in a small pouch made of polished fabric or velvet. It's your daytime angelic companion. It must be cleaned and devoted to an angel once a week. Don't use it for meditations or other rituals with angels.

19 - The Chakras' Gemstones and Crystals

First Chakra: Root Chakra (Muladhara-Chakra)
Color: red
Angel: Chamuel
Gemstones and crystals: ruby, onyx, garnet, black tourmaline

Second Chakra: Svasdisthana-chakra
Color: orange
Angel: Jophiel
Gemstones and crystals: citrine, carnelian, agate, sunstone
Music: forest sounds

Third Chakra: Manipura-chakra
Color: yellow
Angel: Rhamiel

Gemstones and crystals: smoky quartz, yellow tourmaline, topaz, honey calcite
Music: classical music

Fourth Chakra: Anahata-chakra
Color: green
Angel: Hagiel
Gemstones and crystals: emerald, malachite, jade, amazonite, labradorite, green apatite, moldavite, seraphinite
Music: singing birds

Fifth Chakra: Vishuddha-chakra
Color: light blue
Angel: Uriel
Gemstones and crystals: blue turquoise, blue topaz, chrysoprase, aquamarine, celestite, angelite
Music: sounds of water and waterfalls, Zen music

Sixth Chakra: Ajna-chakra
Color: indigo
Angel: Raziel
Gemstones and Crystals: sapphire, lapis lazuli, blue fluorite, blue tourmaline, tanzanite, indigo iolite
Music: sounds of waves and the sea, Zen music, relaxation music

Seventh Chakra: Sahasrate-chakra
Color: purple
Angel: Seraphiel
Gemstones and Crystals: opal, amethyst, purple tourmaline, quartz, diamond
Music: angelic music, experimental music

Working on the Chakras is good for personal development. It opens up energetic centers with angelic energy. These exercises should always be done in a calm and quiet place.

20 - Visualization of the Seven Chakras
(Approximately 45 minutes)

This visualization circulates the Kundalini in all seven Chakras. The body is in harmony, and energies are balanced. Individual potential is developed.

Material
- *A red candle*
- *An orange candle*
- *A yellow candle*
- *A green candle*
- *A light blue candle*
- *An indigo blue candle*
- *A purple candle*
- *A red gemstone*
- *An orange gemstone*
- *A yellow gemstone*
- *A green gemstone*
- *A light blue gemstone*
- *A purple gemstone*
- *A meditation rug*

Visualization

1. Place the candles corresponding to the Chakras in the order of their bodily placement. Light these candles.

2. Stretch out, placing the gemstone corresponding to each Chakra on your body. For the root Chakra, place the gemstone on your pubic area. For the crown Chakra, place the gemstone on the highest point of your forehead, on your hairline. Close your eyes.

3. Relax. Feel the energy of the gemstone in your root Chakra by invoking angel Chamuel. Visualize the color red.

4. Let the energy rise to the second Chakra by invoking angel Jophiel. Visualize the color orange.

5. The energy rises into the third Chakra. Invoke angel Rhamiel. Visualize the color yellow.

6. The energy makes its way to the fourth Chakra. Invoke angel Hagiel. Visualize the color green.

7. The energy rises to the fifth Chakra. Invoke angel Uriel. Visualize the color light blue.

8. In the sixth Chakra, invoke angel Raziel. Visualize the color indigo.

9. In the seventh Chakra, your body feels heavy and is sinking into the rug. You feel a tingling sensation. Let the energy out through the crown Chakra, in the middle of your skull, by invoking Seraphiel

10. Take a rest. Regain ordinary consciousness.

Effects of the Visualization

This visualization of the seven Chakras is for people who wish to cleanse their energy and develop their potential in all domains of life. It raises the angelic vibration, bringing about a return of self-confidence, esteem, and success. Its effects are long-lasting.

It's recommended that you practice this visualization regularly in times of great difficulty, stress, or anxiety.

21 - Gemstones and Crystals to Devote to an Angel

General List

- *Aquamarine*

- *Amazonite*

- *Amethyst*

- *Angelite*

- *Honey calcite*

- *Celestite*

- *Diamond*

- *Emerald*

- *Blue Fluorite (or fluorine)*

- *Garnet*

- *Indigo iolite (cordierite or water-sapphire)*

- *Green jade (jadeite)*

- *Labradorite*

- *Lapid lazuli*

- *Malachite*

- *Onyx – Tiger's eye*

- *Opal*

- *Moonstone*

- *Sunstone*

- *Quartz – rock crystal*

- *Pink quartz*

- *Ruby*

- *Seraphinite*

- *Blue topaz*

- *Black tourmaline*

- *Blue turquoise*

22 - *Aquamarine*

Color: a more or less intense blue, bluish-green
Nature: beryl, group of silicate minerals
Hardness: 7 ½ - 8
Angels: Uriel and related angels

Power over the Body
- *Unblocks energies.*

- *Stimulates the throat Chakra.*

- *Keeps negative energies away.*

Power over the Spirit and the Mind
- *Favors communication with the angelic plane.*

- *Favors communication and human relationships.*

- *Develops lucidity and discernment.*

- *Relieves anxiety.*

- *Calms the mind.*

- *Stimulates courage.*

Power over the Etheric Body
It separates the etheric body from the physical body in order to give

the energies space.

Chakra
Fifth Chakra – throat Chakra

Related Astrological Signs
Aquarius, Pisces, Libra, Gemini

23 - Amazonite

Color: Bluish-green
Nature: feldspar microcline, potassium aluminum silicate
Hardness: 6 – 6 ½
Angel Hagiel and related angels

Power over the Body
- *Helps absorb calcium.*

- *Acts on bones.*

- *Keeps negative energies away.*

Power over the Spirit and the Mind
- *Soothes emotions.*

- *Calms overly nervous people.*

- *Favors the expression of love, tenderness, and affection.*

Power over the Etheric Body
Amazonite is a very good gemstone for charging the etheric body with positive energy. It opens up the spirit to the beauty of emotions.

Chakra
Fifth Chakra – throat Chakra.

Related Astrological Signs
Virgo, Pisces

24 - *Amethyst*

Color: mauve to violet
Nature: violet quartz
Hardness: 7
Angels: Seraphiel and related angels

Power over the Body

- *Brings serenity.*

- *Purifies energies.*

- *Aids sleep.*

- *Relieves anxiety.*

- *Relieves migraines.*

Power over the Spirit and the Mind

- *Favors meditative states.*

- *Favors visualizations.*

- *Develops intuition.*

- *Favors vibratory elevation.*

- *Favors artistic inspiration (the amethyst is the writer's crystal).*

- *Activates the crown Chakra.*

Power over the Etheric Body
An amethyst devoted to an angel captures angelic light and illuminates the etheric body, which becomes more radiant.

The etheric body's radiance gives energy, the love of life, and the elevation of consciousness.

Chakra
Seventh Chakra – crown Chakra.

Related Astrological Signs
Sagittarius, Pisces, Virgo, Aquarius, Capricorn.

25 - Angelite

Color: light blue
Nature: anhydrite (Greek word meaning "without water")
Hardness: 3 – 3 ½
Angels: Uriel and related angels

Power over the Body
* *Relieves tensions.*

* *Neutralizes violent impulses.*

* *Relieves sunburns.*

* *Unblocks bodily energetic knots.*

Power over the Spirit and the Mind
* *Favors the connection with the celestial plane.*

* *Establishes communication with angel Uriel and related angels.*

* *Activates celestial energies during angelic ceremonies and meditations.*

* *Soothes the mind.*

* *Balances the equilibrium between the body and the spirit.*

Power over the Etheric Body
Angelite soothes etheric bodies filled with energetic tensions and favors the penetration of angelic vibrations.

Chakra
Fifth Chakra – throat Chakra.

Related Astrological Sign
Gemini, Libra.

26 - Honey Calcite

Color: yellowish orange, transparent yellow
Nature: calcium carbonate
Hardness: 3
Angels: Rhamiel and related angels

Power over the Body
- *Contributes to feeling well-balanced.*

- *Harmonizes the bodily energies.*

- *Stimulates convalescent people*

Power over the Spirit and the Mind
- *Sharpens intelligence and memory.*

- *Brings stability.*

- *Stimulates concentration during meditations and visualizations.*

- *Encourages out of body experiences.*

Power over the Etheric Body
In the form of a ball, honey calcite is an excellent provider of energy to the aura. It vitalizes the etheric body.

Chakra – solar plexus Chakra

Related Astrological Signs
Scorpio, Leo, Sagittarius.

27 - Celestite

Color: light blue, bluish with mauve nuances.
Nature: strontium sulfate
Hardness 3 – 3 ½
Angels: Uriel and related angels

Power over the Body
- *Brings peace and inner harmony.*

- *Encourages good moods.*

- *Brings happiness and playfulness.*

- *Relieves stress.*

- *Relieves digestive pains linked to stress and anxiety.*

Power over the Spirit and the Mind
- *Establishes a connection with the angelic plane.*

- *Encourages exchanges between planes.*

- *Calms violent emotions.*

- *Develops creativity.*

- *Develops inner resources.*

- *Encourages spiritual research.*

- *Cleans emotional influxes.*

Power over the Etheric Body
Celestite makes the etheric body react slowly to stress, allowing for good psychic balance.

Chakra
Fifth Chakra – the throat Chakra.

Related Astrological Signs
Pisces, Gemini, Cancer

28 - Diamonds

Color: white, yellow, blue, pink, brown or beige, black
Nature: pure crystallized carbon
Hardness: 10 (diamonds are the hardest gemstones of all)
Angels: Metatron and related angels

Power over the Body
- *Reinforces vital energy.*

- *Acts upon cellular regeneration.*

- *Amplifies the actions of other gemstones.*

Power over the Spirit and the Mind
- *Opens up the crown Chakra, making it receptive to angelic energy.*

- *Establishes a connection with the higher angelic plane.*

- *Awakens cosmic consciousness.*

- *Opens oneself up to universal wisdom.*

- *Permits readings of Akashic records.*

- *Develops the conscience of universality.*

- *Liberates the conscience of the being's unity.*

Power over the Etheric Body
Diamonds concentrate angelic energy in the etheric body.
It crystallizes angelic light on the etheric body and gives it radiance, which activates the Chakras.

Chakra
Seventh Chakra – crown Chakra

Related Astrological Signs

Leo, Cancer, Libra

Warning: People whose energy isn't positive mustn't use a diamond because it would soak up their negative energy. Diamonds are prescribed for depressed people.

29 - Emeralds

Colors: green

Nature: beryllium aluminum silicate

Hardness: 7 ½ - 8

Angels: Hagiel and related angels

Power over the Body

- *Helps the sick.*

- *Tones the body.*

- *Gives a renewal of energy.*

Power over the Spirit and the Mind

- *Improves intellectual power.*

- *Helps reasoning.*

- *Allows one to adapt to new situations and life changes.*

- *Brings inner peace.*

- *Facilitates harmony between the physical, emotional and mental planes.*

- *Favors unconditional love.*

- *The emerald is the gemstone of Venus. Lovers like to offer emeralds.*

- *Emerald Tablet, by Hermes Trismegistus, contains the wisdom of the initiated and the alchemists.*

Power over the Etheric Body

In the Bible (Revelation 4:3), John says: "Around the throne was a glow that had the appearance of an emerald."

The emerald's effects on the etheric body are powerful. With an emerald, the etheric body is charged with the angelic energy of Hagiel and related angels. This energy develops physical, emotional, and intellectual potential.

Chakra
Fourth Chakra – heart Chakra.

Related Astrological Signs
Taurus, Cancer, Libra, Capricorn.

Warning: Emeralds shouldn't be worn continuously or it may provoke negative energies. It should be worn as a jewel only occasionally, or to do energetic work.

Emeralds should not be associated with crystals or gemstones other than diamonds.

30 - Blue Fluorite (or Fluorine)

Color: blue, bluish green
Nature: calcium fluoride
Hardness: 4
Angel: Tophiel

Power over the Body
- *Relieves.*

- *Helps regulate the digestive system.*

- *Encourages muscle tone.*

Power over the Spirit and the Mind
- *Provides serenity.*

- *Helps during reflection and concentration.*

- *Structures the imagination.*

- *Stimulates creativity in an office or research laboratory.*

Power over the Etheric Body
Fluorite harmonizes an etheric body with excessive energy in the head, and not enough in the legs.

Chakra
Fifth Chakra – throat Chakra.

Related Astrological Signs
Aquarius, Pisces.

31 - Garnet

Color: red (there are garnets of all colors, except for blue)
Nature: silicate (aluminum, calcium, manganese, chrome, magnesium), depending on the group
Hardness: 6 ½ to 7 ½
Angel: Caliel

Power over the Body
- *Helps competitive athletes.*

- *Gives courage and physical energy.*

Power over the Spirit and the Mind
- *Helps fight against adversity.*

- *Increases self-confidence.*

- *Gives self-assurance.*

- *Comforts in times of success and professional ascension.*

- *Increases the desire to surpass oneself.*

- *Stimulates mental energy.*

Power over the Etheric Body
Garnet strengthens the etheric body and increases its density.

Chakra
First Chakra – root Chakra

Related Astrological Signs
Sagittarius, Aries.
Warning: Wearing garnet is discouraged for nervous, agitated, or hypertensive people.

32 - Indigo Iolite (Cordierite or Water-sapphire)

Color: indigo
Nature: magnesium aluminum silicate
Hardness: 7 – 7 ½
Angels: Raziel and related angels

Power over the Body
- *Helps calm anxious people.*

- *Encourages the assimilation of aliments.*

- *Accompanies people overcoming addiction.*

Power over the Spirit and the Mind
- *Transforms negativity into optimism.*

- *Accompanies one during out of body experiences.*

- *Aids meditation.*

- *Aids intuition and clairvoyance.*

- *Develops mediumship.*

- *Assists fortune-tellers and tarot card readers.*

Power over the Etheric Body
Iolite is a highly spiritual gemstone that makes the etheric body permeable to the angelic energy of angel Raziel and related angels.

Chakra
Sixth Chakra – third eye Chakra.

Related Astrological Signs
Cancer, Pisces.

33 - Green Jade (Jadeite)

Color: green
Nature: sodium aluminum silicate
Hardness: 6 ½ – 7
Angels: Hagiel and related angels

Power over the Body
- *Builds strength.*

- *Encourages longevity (according to tradition).*

- *Represents the yang energy (the masculine principal)*

Power over the Spirit and Mind
- *Links spiritual and terrestrial powers.*

- *Develops the faculty for using fair judgment.*

- *Helps during negotiation and mediation.*

- *Increases tolerance and improves listening.*

Power over the Etheric Body

Green jade (jadeite) stabilizes the etheric body around the body and creates balance between the physical energies and the angelic energies.

Chakra
Fourth Chakra – heart Chakra.

Related Astrological Signs
Libra, Gemini, Aquarius.

34 - Labradorite

Color: bluish-green, golden, red, gray
Nature: feldspar, calcium alumniosilicate
Hardness: 6 – 6 ½
Angels: Hagiel and related angels

Power over the Body

- *Encourages rest after great physical exertion or intellectual ordeals.*

- *Regenerates physical energy.*

- *Increases intellectual power.*

- *Helps people who work a lot and who are in contact with a great number of people.*

Power over the Spirit and the Mind

- *Improves the quality of communication with the angelic plane.*

- *Supports morality and stimulates desires.*

- *Encourages friendship and human relationships.*

- *Protects against negative energies and people.*

Power over the Etheric Body
Labradorite reflects light wonderfully. This refraction of light allows

it to push negative energies away.

Labrodorite purifies and regenerates the etheric body.

Chakra
Fourth Chakra – heart Chakra.

Related Astrological Signs
Sagittarius, Cancer, Pisces, Gemini.

35 – Lapis Lazuli

Color: opaque blue, often including golden pyrite.
Nature: aluminum sodium sulfur silicate
Hardness: 5 – 6
Angels: Raziel and related angels

Power over the Body
- *Unblocks the throat Chakra.*

- *Relieves respiratory problems.*

- *Relieves headaches.*

Power over the Spirit and the Mind
- *Absorbs negative energies.*

- *Protects against bad luck and curses.*

- *Encourages decision making.*

- *Stimulates the imagination.*

- *Elevates consciousness.*

Power over the Etheric Body
The lapis lazuli lets angelic vibration enter into the etheric body. This angelic vibration energizes the etheric body and influences the physical body's well-being.

Chakra
Sixth Chakra – third eye Chakra

Related Astrological Signs
Pisces, Aquarius.

36 - Malachite

Color: all shades of green
Nature: basic copper carbonate
Hardness: 3 ½ – 4
Angels: Hagiel and related angels, Anafiel

Power over the Body
- *Absorbs the negative energies of bodily pain.*

- *Reduces articular inflammation.*

- *Rebalances one's organism.*

Power over the Spirit and the Mind
- *Keeps harmful spirits away.*

- *Protects against negative energies.*

- *Attracts love.*

- *Favors abundance, money, and business.*

Power over the Etheric Body
Malachite absorbs negative energies and purifies the etheric body.

Chakra
Fourth Chakra – heart Chakra.

Related Astrological Signs
Libra, Scorpio, Capricorn.

37 - Onyx – Tiger's Eye

Color: brown, yellow, golden, brown.
Nature: calcium dioxide
Hardness: 7
Angels: Chamuel and related angels, Azariel

Power over the Body
- *Sends negative energies back to their emitters.*
- *Protects against evil spells.*
- *Protects the home.*

Power over the Spirit and the Mind
- *Influences self-esteem.*
- *Protects against anxieties.*
- *Provides energy and drive.*

Power over the Etheric Body
Onyx acts as a refractor of negative energies that attack the etheric body.

Chakra
First Chakra – root Chakra.

Related Astrological Signs
Leo, Virgo, Gemini.

38 - Opal

Color: opaque white, iridescent
Nature: hydrated silicon dioxide
Hardness: 5 ½ - 6 ½
Angels: Cherubiel, Zotiel

Power over the Body

- *Undoes energetic knots.*

- *Favors physical strength.*

- *Increases confidence in personal beauty.*

Power over the Spirit and Mind

- *Helps achieve one's desires.*

- *Helps one to be conscientious.*

- *Stimulates intuition and mediumship.*

- *Amplifies the imagination.*

- *Stimulates creativity.*

- *Helps open up the crown Chakra.*

Power over the Etheric Body
Opal crystallizes the angelic light in the etheric body. This inner radiance of the etheric body amplifies physical beauty.

Chakra
Seventh Chakra – crown Chakra

Related Astrological Signs
Pisces, Aquarius, Cancer, Libra, Gemini

39 - Moonstone

Color: white, cream-colored
Nature: potassium aluminosilicate
Hardness: 6 – 6 ½
Angels: Naromiel, Neriel, Aub, Gabriel

Power over the Body

- *Influences menstrual cycles.*

- *Relieves premenstrual syndromes.*

- *Tempers stressed and anxious people.*

Power over the Spirit and the Mind
- *Soothes emotions.*

- *Develops mediumship and intuition.*

- *Grants access to the subconscious.*

- *Favors clairvoyance.*

- *Develops magnetism.*

- *Stimulates the imagination of poets.*

- *Favors premonitory dreams.*

Power over the Etheric Body
Before using a moonstone to treat the etheric body, it's necessary to charge it by leaving it out in the moonlight on the eve of a full moon. Expose it to the moonlight of the full moon every lunar cycle.

The moonstone brings the celestial angelic energy of the higher plane. People who are treated with it are more intuitive, more clairvoyant, and rediscover inner harmony.

Chakra
Sixth Chakra – third eye Chakra.

Related Astrological Signs
Cancer, Pisces, Scorpio.

40 - Sunstone

Color: red, orange, includes goethite and hematite
Nature: sodium calcium aluminosilicate

Hardness: 6 – 6 ½

Angels: Jophiel and related angels, angel Zerachiel, angel Atuniel, angel Michael

Power over the Body
- *Revitalizes masculine and feminine sexual energy.*

- *Purifies bodily fluids.*

- *Diffuses vitality and tone.*

- *Warms up the organism.*

- *Facilitates corporal expression.*

Power over the Spirit and the Mind
- *Amplifies telepathic abilities.*

- *Increases happiness and joy.*

- *Stimulates lazy or nonchalant people.*

- *Encourages friendships and new encounters.*

Power over the Etheric Body

The sunstone brings the radiance of the sun to the etheric body. It's necessary to recharge the sunstone every month by exposing it to sunlight for three hours.

The sunstone diffuses angelic energy throughout the etheric body and brings it warmth and celestial love.

Chakra
Second Chakra – Chakra under the bellybutton

Related Astrological Signs
Leo, Aries.

41 - Quartz – Rock Crystal

Color: colorless, transparent.

Nature: silicon oxide

Hardness: 7

Angels: rock crystals allow you to work with all the angels

Power over the Body

- *Amplifies the power of other gemstones.*

- *Calms one's emotions.*

- *Calms agitated or stressed people.*

- *Dissolves energetic blockages.*

Power over the Spirit and the Mind

- *Amplifies the power of other gemstones.*

- *Favors travelling to past lives.*

- *Channels energies.*

- *Establishes a connection to the angelic plane.*

Power over the Etheric Body

Rock crystal purifies and cleanses the etheric body of negative energies. It aids vibratory exchanges between the terrestrial and angelic plane.

Chakra

Rock crystal associates itself with the Chakras' gemstones in order to circulate the Kundalini and to unblock energy clogs.

Related Astrological Signs

All the signs can work with rock crystal.

42 - Pink Quartz

Color: transparent pink
Nature: silicon oxide
Hardness: 7
Angels: Anael, Jelial, Teriapel, Theliel, Thiel, Gadamel, Habbiel

Power over the Body

- *Normalizes your heartbeat.*

- *Relieves stress.*

- *Materializes softness and tenderness (crystal recommended to children).*

Power over the Spirit and the Mind

- *Supports lonely people in search of their soul mates.*

- *Helps the healing process after a relationship breakup.*

- *Prevents the accumulation of negative energies.*

- *Opens up the heart Chakra.*

- *Comforts one during periods of mourning.*

- *Develops the joy of love.*

- *Opens up one's heart to love.*

Power over the Etheric Body
Pink quartz envelops the etheric body with angelic softness and tenderness.

Chakra
Fourth Chakra – heart Chakra in association with the Chakra's green gemstone.

Related Astrological Signs
Taurus, Cancer, Virgo, Libra, Scorpio.

43 - Ruby

Color: red
Nature: red corundum, aluminum oxide
Hardness: 9
Angels: Chamuel, Gaviel

Power over the Body
- *Helps physically anchor oneself into the earth.*

- *Increases energy and physical strength.*

- *Crushes energy knots.*

- *Activates the Chakras.*

Power over the Spirit and the Mind
- *Helps anchor oneself into mother Earth.*

- *Allows you to impose yourself in society.*

- *Favors stability.*

- *Develops willpower and courage.*

- *Increases one's fighting spirit.*

- *Improves concentration.*

- *Removes fear and develops courage.*

- *Lends new taste to life.*

- *Favors strength and material power.*

Power over the Etheric Body
Ruby strengthens the etheric body and helps anchor oneself in reality.

Chakra
First Chakra – root Chakra.

Related Astrological Signs
Capricorn, Leo, Taurus, Aries.

44 - Seraphinite

Color: green with white veins
Nature: clinochlore
Hardness: 8 ½
Angels: Hagiel and related angels

Power over the Body
- *Alleviates pain.*

- *Relaxes stressed or nervous people.*

Power over the Spirit and the Mind
- *Facilitates communication with the angelic plane.*

- *Purifies the Chakras.*

- *Creates balance between material and spiritual energies.*

- *Encourages discernment.*

- *Allows you to take a step back from your existence.*

- *Develops compassion and universal love.*

- *Participates in spiritual elevation.*

Power over the Etheric Body
Seraphinite relaxes the etheric body by giving it angelic flexibility and softness.

Chakra
Fourth Chakra – heart Chakra.

Related Astrological Signs
Aquarius, Gemini, Libra, Scorpio.

45 – Blue Topaz

Color: blue
Nature: aluminum fluosilicate
Hardness: 8
Angels: Uriel and related angels

Power over the Body
- *Soothes sore throats.*

- *Calms nervous people.*

Power over the Spirit and the Mind
- *Evacuates emotional tension.*

- *Encourages emotional balance.*

- *Develops the expression of desires and will.*

- *Allows you to stand up to verbal aggression with rational and efficient communication.*

- *Dissipates mental confusion.*

- *Helps during conversation and oral expression.*

- *Encourages friendship and human relationships.*

Power over the Etheric Body
Blue Topaz harmonizes the energies of the physical body with the etheric body.

Chakra
Fifth Chakra – throat Chakra.

Related Astrological Signs
Sagittarius, Gemini, Aquarius, Pisces.

46 – Black Tourmaline

Color: black
Nature: borosilicate rich in sodium and iron
Hardness: 7 – 7 ½
Angels: Chamuel and related angels, Raguel

Power over the Body

- *Protects against negative energies and people.*

- *Protects against electromagnetic radiation and pollutant waves (place tourmaline near computers, telephones, televisions…)*

- *Helps to find nervous equilibrium by rooting oneself to earth.*

Power over the Spirit and the Mind

- *Encourages meditation.*

- *Helps anchor oneself into mother Earth.*

- *Allows for knowledge of karma and the visualization of past lives.*

- *Pushes negative energies away.*

- *Opens up the crown Chakra.*

- *Encourages the first awakening of consciousness.*

Power over the Etheric Body
Black tourmaline balances terrestrial and angelic energies in the etheric body.

Chakra
First Chakra – root Chakra.

Related Astrological Signs
Capricorn, Sagittarius, Virgo, Taurus.

47 - Blue Turquoise

Color: sky blue, green, bluish green, with brown, ocher, and black veins
Nature: hydrated copper aluminum phosphate
Hardness: 5 – 6
Angels: Uriel and related angels

Power over the Body
- *Encourages circulation of vital fluids.*

- *Protects against the negative waves of people.*

- *Acts against physical aggression.*

- *Protects from wounds.*

Power over the Spirit and the Mind
- *Keeps evil and bad luck away.*

- *Represents a good luck charm.*

- *Develops a taste for beauty and aestheticism in art.*

- *Favors communication.*

- *Helps to develop optimism and to practice positive thinking.*

Power over the Etheric Body
Blue turquoise protects the etheric body. It uses the angelic vibration as a shield against negative energies.

Chakra

Fifth Chakra – throat Chakra, and the seven protected Chakras.

Related Astrological Signs

Aquarius, Pisces, Cancer, Libra, Scorpio.

And all other signs for protection.

48 - The Chakra Angelic Solicitation to Obtain an Immediate Answer

(Approximately 15 minutes)

This solicitation allows you to ask a precise question to the angels, and garners a very quick answer.

Material

- *Grain incense made of myrrh, olibanum, or Pontifical incense.*

- *A perfume burner or a censer.*

- *Incense charcoal tablets.*

- *A white sheet.*

- *A red candle and a purple candle.*

- *A gemstone or crystal corresponding to each of the Chakras.*

Solicitation

1. Place the gemstones and crystals onto a white sheet, forming a row of stones and crystals that correspond to the color of the Chakras. Red for the root Chakra, orange for the second Chakra, yellow for the solar plexus Chakra, green for the heart Chakra, sky blue for the throat Chakra, indigo for the third eye Chakra, and purple for the crown Chakra.

2. Burn the incense.

3. Light the candles and place the red candle under the red gemstone, and the purple candle over the purple gemstone.

4. Concentrate on your solicitation. Say what you wish and summon

your angel out loud (see *The Angel That You Need*, p. 553).

5. Say the following words:

> Holy angel (call him by name)
> I solicit your benevolence and your love,
> Devote these gemstones and crystals in order to
> Open up my Chakras,
> Let the divine energy wash over me,
> So that you can answer my solicitation of
> (repeat your request)
> I shall be eternally grateful,
> Amen.

6. Close your eyes. Let your angel act. Wait for the answer. It will come to you right away or within 24 hours of the solicitation.

7. Regain ordinary consciousness.

Effects of the Solicitation

This solicitation is for anyone who wishes to obtain a quick answer to a specific question, no matter what the domain may be. This solicitation is appropriate for an urgent request.

Chapter 22

The Angels' Great Secrets

Your numerous experiences with angels have transformed your life. You've done meditations and obtained extraordinary results. Angels bring you comfort, help, and support. You can now take the next step in your work with the angels. This step is reserved for people who have an established connection with angels, and who get in touch with them regularly.

Angels are the alchemists of the spirit and the subconscious. They hold the secrets of God, God's light and God's love. As messengers of the divine order, they know the mysteries of the human soul, as well as the secrets of life and the transmutation of the soul after death. The origins of alchemy must be briefly summarized to better know and benefit from their teaching.

1 - Alchemy

The word "alchemy" has several roots: the Arabic term "al-Kimiya" comes from the Egyptian word "Km.t," which was a common designation for the country of Egypt.

The origins of alchemy go back to the I and II century B.C. Alchemy is related to hermetic philosophy, which proposes to establish communication between the top (the celestial plane) and the bottom (the material plane). This communication between the celestial and terrestrial planes creates a connection between the microcosm and the macrocosm.

In Alexandrian Egypt, the first alchemists were already trying to make gold through the transformation of certain metals.

In the VI century, an Arabic author proposes to do the first Arabic translation of The Emerald Tablet, a text establishing the philosophical foundation for alchemy. The following famous philosophical and alchemistic quote begins to circulate amongst Arab thinkers, philosophers, and alchemists: "The highest comes from the lowest, and the lowest from the highest."

Alchemy is mostly developed in the XI and XII century, greatly influencing the thinking of the time. The alchemists research the transmutation of metals in order to change their inner structure. But they also adapt this idea to the transmutation of matter and of the spirit, and continue to do research on their greatest piece of work: the creation of a philosopher's stone that, much like the Akashic records, contains universal science and knowledge. At the same time, they work on creating the Panacea, also called the "elixir of immortality." Research on this universal drug contributed greatly to all of the progress made in the world of Arab medicine.

The alchemic quest can be classified into the following essential categories:

- *The creation of a universal drug.*

- *The composition of the elixir of immortality.*

- *Universal knowledge.*

- *The transmutation of metals to obtain material abundance.*

- *The transformation of man into a transcendent, immortal, rich and powerful being.*

This alchemic quest was long considered to be a product of pride and human vanity, and yet it was the cause for considerable progress in the field of medicine, science, physics, and especially chemistry. It also laid the foundation for a new existential philosophy where man finds unity and happiness in his quest for power.

When the alchemists struggled to transmute metals, they considered it possible to modify the inner structure of matter, and so they thought they could also alter the inner structure of the spirit.

In his alchemic quest, philosopher and psychoanalyst C. G. Jung considers it possible to transmute the interior structure of the human spirit through the layers of the subconscious. "Matter and psyche are two aspects of the same phenomenon," he claims.

Some alchemists have worked on personal transmutation, attempting various alchemic operations in order to transform themselves into supermen with infinite and unlimited powers. Most alchemists also tried to interrupt the aging process of matter and the spirit's corruption process by social and environmental influences. Their studies were based on the research of materia prima, primary matter, primordial, original, and pure nature. This is where alchemistic angels intervene, implicating themselves equally for transmutation of the spirit and transmutation of matter. They are humanity's celestial alchemists, and to this degree, they accomplish tangible miracles in the transformation of a human spirit or in the transmutation of matter. While the alchemists haven't been able to transform men into perfect immortal creatures, the angels have. Elijah was transformed into archangel Sandalphon, and Enoch into archangel Metatron.

Beauty belongs to the celestial world; these verses by Charles Baudelaire summarize the angels' alchemistic work in a single brilliant stanza:

"Angels dressed in gold, purple, and hyacinth,
O you, bear witness that I've done my duty,
Like a perfect alchemist and like a sainted soul,
From everything I've extracted the quintessence,

You gave me your mud and I've turned it into gold."

Whatever the alchemistic field of research (physics, chemistry, the composition of matter, philosophy, research on the Panacea, research on immortality, putting an end to the corruption of matter, youthfulness, superman, and transmutation), the angels have always been interested in the human soul's quest for spiritual elevation. They have always supported human research looking to elevate consciousness and guarantee the immortality of the soul. The elevation of consciousness appears to be the primary objective that the angels propose to humans. Elevation is an improvement that never reaches perfection, since this characteristic belongs only to God. In the New Testament (1 Peter 5:10), it says: "And the God of all grace, who called you to his eternal glory in Christ, will himself restore you after you have suffered a little while; he will make you firm, strong, and steadfast."

The alchemic quest to transmute lead into gold is really a search for the manifestation of God in matter. Through the transmutation of matter, the alchemist searches for divine perfection. Victor Hugo confirms it: "For gold is not a metal, gold is light...Gold is the sun; to make gold is to be a God."

The search for God in the alchemic quest is one of the fundamental aspects of alchemy. According to Wilmshurst: "Alchemy is philosophy; it is the philosophy, the seeking out of the Sophia in the soul. Alchemy consists first and foremost in the regeneration of the soul, which can only be its deification."

The angels provide spiritual elevation to those who practice conscious alchemy and who perfect their soul and spirit.

2 - Transmuting Consciousness

Performing angelic invocations produces miracles in everyday life and encourages personal fulfillment. When you are accustomed to the angels' presence and when you meditate in their company, you know that their power is real and effective, and you don't doubt that God sends you his messengers.

People who are connected to angels can have extraordinary experiences regarding the transmutation of consciousness.

This experience is a deep, definitive, and structural transformation of consciousness. Like the alchemists who transformed lead into gold, you will transform your consciousness into gold and divine light. The transformation takes places in the anatomic structure of your consciousness in the same way that atoms of lead transform into atoms of gold.

The transmutation of your consciousness starts with faith in divine perfection, love, and the light of God. Every day, the messenger angels will bring you new opportunities to perfect yourself. They will teach you how to modify your old ways of thinking, your preconceived ideas, your obligations, and your limitations caused by fear and insecurity. The transmutation of consciousness prepares you to receive the illumination and love of God.

There are 10 steps in the transmutation of consciousness.

1.Tolerance – The black light.
2.Respect – The brown light.
3.Openness – The gray light.
4.The end of fear – The blue light.
5.Love and peace – The green light.
6.The light – The yellow light.
7.Intuition – The purple light.
8.Trust – The white light.
9.Strength – The red light.
10.Wisdom – The orange light.

3 - Tolerance – The Black Light – Archangel Tsaphkiel
Stop judging yourself and others. Trusting the angels and meditating

will bring you angelic comfort. Don't criticize the people whose actions and behavior you don't approve of. Detach yourself from judgment and you shall be freer and happier. Your consciousness will no longer be weighed down by negative energies and you will enter the first light in your consciousness.

In the Bible, Old Testament, the Pentateuch (Deuteronomy 1:17), it says: "Do not show partiality in judging: hear both small and great alike, do not be afraid of anyone, for judgment belongs to God. If any case seems too hard, bring it to me, and I will hear it."

When you are happy to be tolerant and without judgment, light a black candle in honor of angel Tsaphkiel and give thanks:

Very holy archangel Tsaphkiel,
I'm committing myself to always live with tolerance for others,
And for myself.
Very holy archangel Tsaphkiel,
I thank you for your support and your help,
I shall be eternally grateful,
Amen.

4 - Respect – The Brown Light – Archangel Sandalphon

The second step in the transmutation of consciousness is to respect others and to teach respect to your children. When you respect others, you are respectful to yourself. Be delicate with others, be soft, affectionate, and caring. Respect begins with positive actions and kind words.

Keep yourself from intervening in the lives of others. Lend advice if you wish, but don't demand results. The lives of others do not belong to you. Know how to withhold yourself when other people make choices that you don't approve of. Be yourself and let others act according to their will. When you feel respectful of others, and you respect yourself, light a brown candle in honor of angel Sandalphon and give thanks:

Very holy archangel Sandalphon,
I'm committing myself to live with respect for others,
And for myself.
Very holy archangel Sandalphon,
I shall be eternally grateful,
Amen.

5 - Openness – The Gray Light – Archangel Raziel

The openness of your spirit allows you to reap the benefits of angelic miracles in every domain of your life. The angels' power and divine light impact you more than mental calculations and worries.

Be open, be ready to receive divine gifts through the intermediary of angels. Open your heart to goodness and love.

Being open forces you to stop trying to control your life and the events in your existence. By acting this way, you will open yourself to the miracles of angels, to happy surprises, and to unexpected encounters. When you are open and ready to receive the angels' gifts, light a gray candle or a black candle, and a white candle in honor of angel Raziel and give thanks:

Very holy archangel Raziel,
I'm committing myself to always living openly,
In angelic trust,
I'm opening my arms receptively.
Very holy archangel Raziel,
I shall be eternally grateful,
Amen.

6 - The End of Fear – The Blue Light – Archangel Tsadkiel

Consciousness can be transformed when you are no longer paralyzed by fear. You can then take risks and launch new projects.

Wise men of all ages, the initiated, and mystics have learned how to control their fear; they let their intuition and their desire to attain the infinite guide them. With angel Tsadkiel's help, you will control your fears and remove your limitations. In the Bible, Old Testament, the Poetic Books (Psalm 27:1), it says: "The LORD is my light and my salvation, whom shall I fear? The LORD is the stronghold of my life, of whom shall I be afraid?"

When you control your fear, and you act with boldness and determination, light a blue candle and give thanks:

Very holy archangel Tsadkiel,
I'm committing myself not to obey fear,
I'm committing myself to be free and happy,
Very holy archangel Tsadkiel,
I shall be eternally grateful,
Amen.

7 - Love and Peace – The Green Light – Archangel Haniel

Living with love is a very important step in spiritual elevation. God is love and his messengers bring divine love to men. Opening your heart to love transforms existence. In the Bible, Old Testament, the Poetic Books (Canticles 8:6): "Set me as a seal upon thine heart, as a seal upon thine arm: for Love is strong as Death; Jealousy is cruel as Hell; the flames thereof are ardent flames: a sacred lightning bolt."

When you live with love, your life is transformed. You open your heart to angelic vibration. Your inner beauty radiates. Negative energies stay away. Negative people avoid you. You are ready to meet your soul mate, to build a fulfilling and happy life. It's never too late to open your heart to love. It's never too late to change. When universal, eternal, and infinite love enters in you, you are born again.

When you taste love and your heart is filled with its radiant energy, light a green candle and give thanks:

Very holy archangel Haniel,
I'm committing myself to open my heart to love,
I'm committing myself to live with love,
And to radiate with love,
Very holy archangel Haniel,
I shall be eternally grateful,
Amen.

8 - Light – The Yellow Light – Archangel Raphael

Letting the divine light radiate in you opens your heart to angelic energies. Your consciousness crosses a higher step. In the Bible, Old Testament, the Poetic Books, it says: "Several people say: Who will show us happiness?

Let the light of your face rise over us, O Lord!"

Light brings happiness. When you let light into your heart, you will receive innumerable benefits. Physical pain is attenuated, and you develop great confidence in yourself. You find success. Light brings out your qualities, and radiates love. When you are in the light, light a yellow candle and give thanks:

Very holy archangel Raphael,
I'm opening my heart to the light,
I'm shining the light and radiating love,
I shall be eternally grateful,
Amen.

9 - Intuition – The Purple Light – Archangel Gabriel

Developing intuition opens the path to angelic elevation. This new step of consciousness is essential in understanding hidden things. The transmutation of consciousness goes through intuition and mediumship. Archangel Gabriel guides the initiated on the path of intuitive consciousness, opening it up to the angelic vibration of protection and transformation.

When you feel your intuition and consciousness opening themselves up to universal dimension, light a purple candle and give thanks:

Very holy archangel Gabriel
I'm opening up my spirit to mediumship,
I'm opening up my consciousness to the higher vibration,
I rise each day,
I shall be eternally grateful,
Amen.

10 - Trust – The White Light – Archangel Metatron

The essential step of elevation can only take place with absolute trust in angels and the Lord who commands them. Trust gages loyalty and effectiveness in every situation of existence, whether human or angelic. Without trust, there can be no well-being or sharing. In the Bible, Old Testament, the Pentateuch (Exodus 23:20), it says: "I am sending an angel ahead of you to guard you along the way and to bring you to the place I have prepared." If you have complete trust, your consciousness is united with the angel and with God, and divine protection is infinite. When you feel absolute trust in angels and you feel as though you're being guided, light a white candle and give thanks:

Very holy archangel Metatron,
I'm granting you my complete trust,
I will follow your light and I will receive your love,
I shall be eternally grateful,
Amen.

11 - Strength – The Red Light – Archangel Kamael

Without strength, consciousness is useless. The penultimate step in awakening consciousness is having the strength to develop self-confidence, to animate energy, to create the willpower and courage to put all the other energies into effect. This strength is indispensable to the achievement of our mission on Earth and for the success of our projects.

In the Bible (Psalm 103:20), it is written that the angels have the strength: "Praise the LORD, you his angels, you mighty ones who do his bidding, who obey his word."

When you are strong, courageous, and willing, when your life is moving in the direction you want it to, light a red candle, and give thanks:

Holy archangel Kamael,
I have the strength,
I put this strength into effect,
For the fulfillment of my life,
I shall be eternally grateful,
Amen.

12 - Wisdom – The Orange Light – Archangel Michael

The last step in the transmutation of consciousness goes through wisdom, which reunites all the other steps and brings about discernment and intelligence. No one is truly conscious without wisdom. In the Bible, Old Testament, the Historical Books (1 Kings 5:12), it says: "The LORD gave Solomon wisdom, just as he had promised him, and there was peace between Hiram and Solomon, and they made a formal alliance."

Wisdom allows you to obtain results. It is essential for peace and the practice of love.

When you assimilate the transmutation of consciousness and wisdom drives you to act in a just manner, light an orange candle and give thanks:

Very holy archangel Michael,

I possess wisdom,
I create peace around me,
Love is in me,
My consciousness has been transmuted,
I shall be eternally grateful,
Amen.

After you've crossed these 10 steps in the transmutation of consciousness, you will have attained wisdom and spiritual elevation. You will be a radiant and happy person who spreads love and goodness. All of the angels' sincerest wishes accompany you on this road to joy.

13 - The Angelic Connection to the Akashic Records

"Akasha" is a Sanskrit word meaning ether. The archives of humanity are located beyond time or space, in ether, which angels have access to.

The Akashic Records contain universal knowledge of the past, present, and future, as well as the history of every person's past life and the events of their current life. Accessing the Akashic Records establishes connection with the initial source of humanity and the primordial energies of our first existence. It also allows us to better understand our mistakes and helps us make progress after we've analyzed our past lives. We can also discover our objective in life, and then make the right choices. Opening the Akashic records also helps us understand the great evolution of humanity and gives us the opportunity to take part in the destiny of the planet.

If we ask for it, the angels can grant us access to the archives of humanity, which allows us to understand who we really are, and how we can serve and elevate our consciousness.

The Akashic Records can be accessed through the mind, expansions of consciousness, out of body experiences, hypnosis, or meditation. They can also be accessed through an angel devoted to a particular field or through the intermediary of a birth angel or guardian angel.

Metatron is the curator of the planet's archives and of human souls. In the Talmud, Metatron is the intermediary between the human plane and the divine plane. He is located in the Sefirah of Keter at the top of the Sefirotic tree. The texts of the Zohar claim that Metatron equals the width of the world in size. His enormousness legitimizes his role as the universal curator of the library of humanity. Metatron receives requests from angels that you summon and opens the door of the Akashic Records to them. The following angels are in charge of transmitting information from the great library of humanity:

- *Och for intuition and mediumship.*

- *Chamuel for your love life.*

- *Michael for finding the right way and awakening consciousness.*

- *Raphael for healing karmic wounds.*

- *Haniel for improving relationships with others.*

- *Auriel for choice and discernment.*

- *Raziel for finding wisdom.*

- *Gabriel for destiny and the objective of life.*

- *Tsaphkiel for out of body experiences.*

- *Uriel for the revelation of prophecies and the mysteries of the afterlife.*

- *Jophiel for knowledge of past lives.*

When you invoke angels to open the doors of the Akashic Records, it's important to formulate a specific request, as if you wish to take out a book from a library. Here are some questions you can ask:

- *What are my objectives in life?*

- *What can my past lives teach me?*

- *Should I perform a karmic cleansing?*

- *How can I replenish my energies?*

- *Will I meet my soul mate?*

- *How can I avoid making the same sentimental mistakes?*

- *What is my path in life?*

- *What will help me make progress?*

- *What is my path for awakening?*

- *How can I heal my emotional wounds?*

- *How can I cure my anxieties?*

- *What job really suits me?*

- *What are my real passions?*

14 - The Egregore

The word "egregore" comes from the Greek "egregorein" or "egregoros," which means "to watch over." According to Western occultist tradition, the egregore is a psychic force produced by the accumulation of energy by different people belonging to the same group. Some occultists think that an egregore produced by people who obey the same ideal or belief can become its own entity, a spiritual being, a thought form, or a creature of the ether. Egregores of charity, egregores of fanaticism, egregores of religious faith, egregores of politics, of ecology, and many other categories, would then exist.

Egregores can also appear during prayers, ritualistic ceremonies, energetic treatments, or shamanic, Masonic, or angelic rituals.

These egregore-creating phenomena take place when people engender important energy. The aggregation of this energy is crystallized into a single force capable of acting upon nature, events, or people.

The angelic egregore happens while simultaneously inviting several angels of the higher celestial hierarchy. Summoning an angelic egregore is a high-level meditation with many implications, and requires substantial experience in communicating with angels. The result is absolutely extraordinary. The energy obtained allows for the evolution of consciousness toward higher and higher levels. It increases inner balance, activates energies already in place, develops the capacity to teach the awakening of consciousness, and unleashes the wonderful joy of living.

15 – Ceremony of the Angelic Egregore
(Approximately one hour)

The meditation of the angelic egregore is a magical operation that demands strict respect for the ritual's requirements. The angels invoked come from the higher spheres of the celestial hierarchy and the energy they produce has a very high vibratory frequency. It is absolutely essential that you are able to support this kind of energy, and use it positively or to do good.

Material
- *A silver candle.*
- *A transparent or white candlestick.*
- *Four large black candles, round or square.*
- *Four large white candles, round or square.*
- *Four orange candles.*
- *A perfume burner.*
- *Charcoal.*
- *Grain incense made of pontifical incense, olibanum, and myrrh.*
- *Comfortable white clothes made of natural fabric.*
- *A white meditation cushion.*

- *A white chalice filled with cooking salt.*

- *A chalice filled with water.*

- *A white feather.*

Ceremony

1. Before the ceremony, skip a meal. Perform this ceremony preferably around midnight.

2. Start with personal purification, by taking a shower or an angelic bath.

3. Put on the white clothes.

4. Fumigate the room with incense, and then air it out.

5. Draw a square on the ground with the cooking salt, approximately 5 ft squared, inside of which you will put the meditation cushion.

6. Place your candles around the square of cooking salt in the following way: the four orange candles in the four corners. Place the four white candles about two inches from the orange candles, toward the inside of the square. Place the four black candles about four inches from the white candles. There should be four squares on the ground made of cooking salt and candles. Place the candlestick with the silver candle on the inside of the square, facing north. Place the chalice filled with water and the white feather on its right.

7. Enter the square of salt. Sit down on the cushion cross-legged or in the lotus position. Light the candles.

8. Begin general relaxation.

9. Take in a deep breath and then exhale without inhaling again for seven seconds. Breathe like this three times.

10. Feel the love for you. You are bathing in radiant white light.

11. Feel the love for your friends and family. The light becomes more and more vivid.

12. Feel the unconditional love for humanity. The light is astonishing.

13. You feel the love for the angels. The light is warm.

14. You feel the love for God. The sun seems to be heating up and shining

over you. You are illuminated. You are in the illumination.

15. Summon the angels of the egregore:

Holy archangel Tsaphkiel,
Holy archangel Raziel,
Holy archangel Kamael,
Holy archangel Metatron,
I feel the illumination and the beauty of your love,
I am receiving your sacred egregore,
I am receiving divine love and the light of the Lord.

16. Open your arms and palms toward the sky to receive the angelic gift.

17. Feel your hands tingling. You are haloed in light. Enjoy this magical moment. Illumination is the angels' most beautiful gift.

18. Cross your arms over your heart, with your hands on your shoulders, to keep the angelic egregore in you.

19. Lower your head as a sign of humility.

20. Give thanks with these words:

Very holy archangels,
Let my heart always honor your love,
Very holy archangels,
I thank you for all eternity,
Amen.

21. Slowly regain ordinary consciousness.

22. Get up.

23. Salute the angels by standing up, with your palms together over your heart and turn to the north, then to the east, then to the south, and then to the west.

24. Put out the silver candle with a snuffer before opening the square of salt.

Effects of the Ceremony

After this angelic celebration, you won't be the same as before. The illumination and love of the angels are wonderful gifts that must be honored with respect and dignity. To do that, you can meditate on the following verse from the Bible, Old Testament, the Poetic Books (Proverbs 3:3): "Let love and faithfulness never leave you; bind them around your neck, write them on the tablet of your heart."

This ceremony is for people who wish to make progress at every level of their existence, and become righteous and radiant beings.

16 – The Elixir of Immortality

Alchemists of all traditions have tried to make the elixir of immortality, which they call the "panacea."

The term "panacea" comes from the Greek "pan," meaning "all," and "akos," meaning "remedy." To the alchemists, the panacea is an elixir that prolongs life. In their efforts to compose the elixir of immortality, the alchemists of the Middle Ages came up with a substance made from the quintessence of wine and prepared with alcohol that was distilled thousands of times. They added gold, thinking the mix they obtained would restore health and enable people to live longer.

In the New Testament, the Gospels (Luke 20:36), it says: "they can no longer die; for they are like the angels: they are God's children since they are children of the resurrection."

According to legend, the famous alchemist Nicolas Flamel discovered an elixir of youth that he used on himself and his wife. The Count of Saint Germain also apparently succeeded in making an elixir of longevity that prolonged his life for several centuries.

Unfortunately, no one has discovered the elixir of immortality to this day. And if alchemists continue doing research through secret distillations in their athanors, it's because their concoctions have not yet proven effective. Man will never give up in his quest for immortality. His mortality will forever push him in search of immortality. The angels propose an alternative to the humans' disappointing failure in prolonging life beyond death or getting rid of the process of physical destruction. Following anatomical death, the psychopompic angels carry the soul toward the light. No one claims that the soul must be reincarnated several times. No one says that it will enter the divine light for all eternity.

No matter what you believe regarding life after death, the angel's work doesn't change. It consists of transmuting a soul incarnated in a terrestrial body into a pure spirit adapted to the celestial plane.

Certain angels help the souls of the deceased leave their bodies. These souls either return to Earth for reincarnation or remain in the light of immortality.

To Greek philosophers, it is obvious that souls that come and go from the body in different incarnations experience transmutations. Anaxagoras talks about how the All contains anything that emanates from and returns to the All. Plato thinks that the great One containing all souls releases souls that are incarnated. These souls return to the One after death.

Hermes Trismegistus' Emerald Tablet, the ultimate alchemist text, confirms the Greco-Alexandrian concept of immortality. It says: "And since all things exist in and emanate from the ONE who is the ultimate Cause, so all things are born after their kind from this ONE." The New Testament extols the human virtues that open up the path to immortality. In the Bible, New Testament, the Epistles of Paul (Romans 2:7): "Eternal life to those who by perseverance in doing good strive for glory, honor, and incorruptibility."

But the role of angels doesn't end with the guarantee of the soul's immortality. They allow men to become aware of this immortality. Men's vision of existence changes when they are aware of the soul's immortality; their psychological structure is transformed; their fear of death is relieved. Men understand that they are not prisoners of matter and that one day angels will bring their immortal souls to more serene places. Becoming aware of the soul's immortality is not always easy. In a rational and materialistic world, the soul's survival is not always recognized, and people accompanied by angels don't always find their place in society. And yet, universal consciousness is in the process of evolving. A growing number of people become engaged with angels to transform their existence and to participate in the emergence of a new more serene and more harmonious humanity.

Making the elixir of immortality with angels brings the promise of eternal life. In the Bible, Old Testament, the Prophets (Habakkuk 1:12), it says: "Are you not from everlasting, O LORD, my God, my Holy One? We will not die!"

Angels are responsible for the soul's journey after death. Trusting them is the first step in becoming immortal. This trust annihilates old psychological patterns about the fear of death. It relieves metaphysical anxiety and emotional disturbances linked to the fear of dying. A transmutation of personality is possible by making an elixir of immortality with angels.

Having the elixir of immortality completely transforms our outlook on life and death. Existential anxiety is relieved. Consciousness is awakened, and the desire for spiritual elevation becomes a priority in life.

17 - Making the Elixir of Immortality
(Approximately one hour)

Making the elixir of immortality is a delicate operation reserved for people already accustomed to communicating with angels. It's a magical operation of high spiritual value. If you have the elixir of immortality, you mustn't transport it, open it, or divulge its secrets to others. It's the highest magical operation you can possibly perform with angels. Having this elixir creates a transmutation in its beholder. Day by day, consciousness is elevated, and universal love and angelic light enters one's personal vibration. The aura changes color and shines with renewed radiance. Positive events happen in the material world, favoring spiritual progression. Financial hardship ends. The effulgence of angelic love attracts a great number of people in search of spirituality toward the person who has the elixir of immortality.

Making this elixir should be done under the authority of archangel Raziel, the angel of secret regions and the head of supreme mysteries.

The name Raziel is reminiscent of the secrets of God, and the knowledge of mysteries. According to Rabbinic tradition, Raziel wrote a book "in which all celestial and terrestrial knowledge is written."

No one other than yourself should ever get their hands on the elixir of immortality. It must never be made twice by the same person, since once it's made, it's eternal. Take your time to make this elixir. Make yourself available, and be in good physical shape, relaxed, and determined.

It's recommended that you perform this ceremony during a waxing moon, at 11 o'clock at night, on a Wednesday. You must be alone and absolutely certain of not being disturbed. Air out the room for at least two hours before performing the ceremony.

Making the Elixir of Immortality

Material
- *Angelic music.*

- *A perfume burner.*

- *Incense charcoal tablets.*

- *Grain incense made of benzoin, myrrh, or mastic.*

- *A lapis-lazuli.*

- *A long blue candle.*

- *A white or silver candlestick.*

- *Four white candles, round or square.*

- *A white chalice filled with cooking salt.*

- *A comfortable white outfit made of natural fabric.*

- *An angelic altar.*

- *A white or blue tablecloth.*

- *A vial of spring water or, if you have a garden, a vial of morning dew.*

- *A transparent glass cup.*

- *Thyme essential oil.*

- *A few dried thyme leaves.*

Making the Elixir

1. You must fast before performing the ceremony. It's recommended that you skip dinner.

2. Begin with personal purification by taking a shower or an angelic bath.

3. Put on the white clothes.

4. Prepare the angelic altar on which you will make the elixir.

5. Cover the altar in a white or blue tablecloth.

6. Play the angelic music.

7. Fumigate the room with incense. Don't air it out.

8. Place the following material on the altar: the chalice filled with cooking salt, the vial of spring water or morning dew, the thyme essential oil, the glass cup, the thyme leaves, the four white candles, the blue candle in the candlestick, the lapis-lazuli.

9. Place the four white candles in each of the four cardinal directions of the altar. Draw a line between these candles with the cooking salt. You get a complete square.

10. Place the transparent glass cup in the center of the square. Light the candles.

11. Place the lapis-lazuli at the bottom of the glass cup and say the following words:

Very holy archangel Raziel,

I'm invoking your presence,
Come assist me for my ceremony,
Let your light and love illuminate my heart.

12. Place the long candle behind the glass cup and light it.
13. Cover the lapis-lazuli with the thyme leaves and seven drops of thyme essential oil. Join your palms together in front of your heart and say the following words:

Very holy archangel Raziel,
My soul belongs to you,
I am an infinite and immortal being,
I have been, I am and I will be,
Lead me toward the eternal light,
Light my path amongst men,
Let it be so, now and forever.

14. Empty the vial of spring water or morning dew into the glass cup. Open your arms, with your palms facing the sky and say the following words:

Very holy archangel Raziel,
Devote the elixir of my immortality,
Give me your love and your light,
Carry my soul to the Lord when my time comes,
Grant me eternity, all eternity,
Amen.

15. Face the altar and present yourself in front of the cup of elixir with your palms joined over your heart and thank angel Raziel by saying the following words:

Very holy archangel Raziel,

My thanks are eternal.

16. Take a sip of the elixir. Don't drink any more than a sip.
17. Take down your angelic altar, and put out the candles, starting with the long blue candle.
18. Go to bed without eating and thank angel Raziel once more before you fall asleep.

Effects of the Ceremony

This meditation is for people who wish to entrust the angels with the important responsibility of making their soul immortal.

Chapter 23

The Angel That You Need

"*Holy Angels, our advocates, our brothers, our counselors, our defenders, our enlighteners, our friends, our guides, our helpers, our intercessors - Pray for us.*"
-Mother Teresa of Calcutta

1 - The Angels of Love

Everyone dreams of having a balanced and harmonious love life. When you call upon the angels of love, you can follow the practical rituals of this Bible of angels with the angels indicated below or you can choose the angel you wish to invoke in relation to your date of birth or in relation to a specific request.

In the field of love, you can invoke angels to solicit romantic encounters or to create opportunities for you to meet the person you wish to see again. But the angels of love will never intervene in a way that goes against a person's desires.

2 - To Meet Your Soul Mate

Main angel: Anael
Related Angels: Raphael, Seraphiel, Metatron, Cherubiel

3 - To Have a Harmonious Relationship

Main angel: Anael

Related angels: Itqal, Ariel, Tahdiel

4 - Angels of Sexuality

Main angel: Anael
Related angels: Aba, Abadiloth, Amabiel, Rachiel

5 - To Follow Your Passion

Main angel: Jelial
Related angels: Uriel, Theliel, Opiel

6 - To Attract a Woman's Love

Main angel: Breschas
Related angels: Donquel, Miniel, Ahabiel, Hanniniel, Opiel, Salbabiel, Theliel

7 - Angels of Fidelity

Main angel: Jeliel
Related angels: Michael, Iezalel, Chavakhiah, Menadel, Muriel, Pahaliah, Zachariel, Tezalel

8 - Angels of Romantic Encounters

Main angel: Anael
Related angels: Theliel, Raphael, Cherubiel, Seraphiel, Uriel, Ariel, Rahmiel, Arbiel, Graniel, Metatron, Habiel, Hasdiel, Mehahel, Lahabiel

9 - Angels of Commitment

Main angel: Habbiel
Related angels: Rahabiel, Phaniel, Chardiel

10 - To No Longer Feel Abandoned

Main angel: Chamuel

Related angels: Haziel, Poyel, Ariel

11 - To Cure Jealousy

Main angel: Raphael
Related angels: Lauviah, Hekamiah, Mihael

12 - To Have Confidence

Main angel: Gabriel
Related angels: Heman, Yerathel, Reiyel, Sealiah

13 - Angels of Marriage

Main angel: Anael
Related angels: Chamuel, Habbiel, Ariel

14 - Angels of Patience

Main angel: Achaiah
Related angels: Raphael, Ariel

15 - To Recover from a Break-Up or Separation

Main angel: Raphael
Related angels: Uriel, Metatron

16 - Angels of Forgiveness

Main angel: Tsadkiel
Related angels: Haziel, Michael, Rachmiel, Hoesediel, Jael, Uzziel

17 - Angels of Friendship

Main angel: Mirh
Related angels: Itqal, Sachiel, Sidqiel, Tadhiel

18 - Family Angels

Family angels bring precious help to maintain family harmony, to help recomposed families live happily, or to ease relations between members of the same family. Summon these angels to favor or solicit pregnancy, or to protect maternity.

Family angels comfort people in mourning.

19 - Angels of Family Harmony

Main angel: Ariel

Related angels: Seraphiel, Cherubiel, Tahdiel, Hagiel, Itqal, Sadriel

20 - Angels of Family Peace

Main angel: Peniel

Related angels: Anael, Melchisedech, Hagiel, Theliel, Jeremiel

21 - Angels of the Fecundity

Main angel: Samandiriel

Related angels: Yushamin, Akriel, Armisael, Habuiah, Mihael

22 - To Choose a Child's Gender

Main angel: Sandalphon

Related angels: Akriel, Armisael, Mihael

23 - Angels of Conception

Main angel: Lailah

Related angels: Sandalphon, Mebahiah

24 - Protective Angels of Pregnancy

Main angel: Chaniel

Related angels: Kaniel, Ofiel, Padiel, Shebniel, Tahariel, Variel

25 - Angels of Birth

Main angel: Gabriel

Related angels: Ietuqiel, Ahaniel, Omael, Armiasael, Briel, Chachmiel,

Chaskiel, Gazriel, Griel, Lailah

26 - Angels of Parents

Main angel: Rehael
Related angels: Chavakhiah, Sandalphon

27 - Protective Angels of Children

Main angel: Rumiel
Related angels: Gediel, Kadmiel, Sarasael
28-Angels of Mourning
Main angel: Yehudiah
Related angels: Adriel, Alad, Gabriel, Metatron, Kofziel, Ophiel, Sanasiel, Suriel, Hemah

29 - Angels Who Accompany the Dying

Main angel: Mumiah
Related angels: Omael, Jabamiah

30 - Angels of the Soul's Separation from the Body

Main angel: Metatron
Related angels: Remiel, Azrael, Sauriel

31 - Psychopompic Angels (Who Lead Souls toward the Light)

Main angel: Metatron
Related angels: Sandalphon, Johiel, Ramiel

32 - Angels of the Last Judgment

Main angel: Uriel
Related angels: Arakiel, Remiel, Samiel, Aziel

33 - Angels of Resurrection

Main angel: Gabriel
Related angels: Aputel, Chafriel, Chamuel

34 - Angels of Immortality

Main angel: Raziel
Related angels: Michael, Gabriel, Samiel

35 - Angels of Work

36 - Angels of Job Searching

Main angel: Lauviah
Related angels: Oriphiel, Nuriel

37 - Angels of Job Stability

Main angel: Sandalphon
Related angels: Lauviah, Oriphiel

38 - Angels of Professional Success

Main angel: Michael
Related angels: Oriphiel, Remiel, Tsadkiel, Nuriel, Harabiel, Maltiel, Nachiel, Shamshiel, Lauviah

39 - Angels of Intelligence and Effectiveness

Main angel: Jophiel
Related angels: Tsadkiel, Zachriel, Zuriel, Chismael, Elimiel, Hagiel, Gradiel, Haludiel, Zophiel, Machasiel, Anael

40 - Angels of Professional Opportunity

Main angel: Ananchel
Related angels: Barachiel, Oriphiel

41 - Angels of Power

Main angel: Tsaphkiel
Related: Gabriel, Cherubiel, Eschiel, Zazriel, Ebuhuel, Elubatel, Esabiel

42 - Angels of Commerce

Main angel: Poiel
Related angels: Michael, Teiaiel, Veualiah, Shamshiel, Lelahel, Kabshiel, Hananiel, Harahel, Hamatiel

43 - Protective Angels of Business and Contracts

Main angel: Tsadkiel
Related angels: Vasiariah, Hiniel, Sarphiel, Makiel, Haniel, Qafsiel, Sitael

44 - To Succeed in Scientific Research

Main angel: Raphael
Related angels: Mahtiel, Hariel, Anael, Cerviel, Machasiel, Lelahel, Seraphiel, Hodiel, Miel, Kabniel, Tarpiel, Zophiel, Kokaviel, Radueriel, Exael, Umabel

45 - Angels of the Writing Profession and Artists

Main angel: Metatron
Related angels: Shamiel, Radueriel, Tarmiel

46 - Angels of Teaching

Main angel: Zaphkiel
Related angels: Raziel, Jophiel, Gabriel, Raphael, Metatron, Maltiel, Kamael, Cerviel, Hochmel, Mehiel, Peliel

47 - Angels of Knowledge

Main angel: Raphael

Related angels: Zachariel, Hahaiah, Harahel

48 – Angels of Money and Finances

Angels of Moneymaking
Main angel: Raziel
Related angels: Phanuel, Poiel, Lauviah

49 – Angels of Heritage

Main angel: Tsadkiel
Related angels: Raziel, Hannuel, Pagiel

50 – Angels of Good Luck in Gambling

Main angel: Barachiel
Related angels: Uriel, Rubiel

51 – To Ask for Wealth and Prosperity

Main angel: Tsadkiel
Related angels: Kamael, Teiael, Shamshiel, Hamatiel

52 – Angels of Financial Success

Main angel: Tsadkiel
Related angels: Uriel, Raziel

53 – Angels of Luxury

Main angel: Teiazel
Related angels: Veualiah, Shamshiel

54 – To Stay in Good Health

Main angel: Raphael
Related angels: Rehael, Suriel, Sabrael

55 - To Ask for Healing

Main angel: Raphael

Related angels: Suriel, Assiel, Ariel, Mumiah, Rehael, Sabrael

56 - Angels of Longevity

Main angel: Seheiah

Related angels: Raphael, Mumiah, Rehael, Eiael

57 - To Fight Against Sickness

Main angel: Raphael

Related angels: Adonael, Rehael

58 - To Fight Against Depression

Main angel: Raphael

Related angels: Tsadkiel, Seraphiel, Aftiel

59 - Angels of Providence and Assurances

Main angel: Michael

Related angels: Raphael, Sapiel, Adad

60 - Angels of Sports

Main angel: Kamael

Related angels: Geburael, Nuriel, Arafiel

61 - Angels of Practical Life

62 - Angels of Travel

Main angel: Raphael

Related angels: Ezgadi, Nadiel

63 - Angels of Moving

Main angel: Raphael
Related angels: Nadiel, Metatron

64 - Protective Angels of the House

Main angel: Haniel
Related angels: Michael, Gamiel

65 - Angels Fighting Against Curses

Main angel: Shamriel
Related angels: Abrid, Gurid, Phanuel

66 - To Recover Lost Objects

Main angel: Raphael
Related angels: Rochel, Haniel, Raziel

67 - Angels of Pets

Main angel: Hariel
Related angels: Uriel, Behemiel

68 - Angels of Nature, the Garden, and Plants

Main angel: Cahetel
Related angels: Lecabel, Maktiel, Seeliah, Sofiel, Habuhiah

69 - Angels of Goodness and Spiritual Elevation

Main angel: Cherubiel
Related angels: Seraphiel, Tsadkiel, Aebel, Anush, Michael, Shetel, Adoyahel, Arzel, Hamaya, Pachriel, Suriel, Hahayel, Carmax, Elyon, Ayscher, Azzael, Ezriel, Gemaliel, Salathiel

70 - Angels of Beneficence, Charity, and Generosity

Main angel: Seraphiel

Related angels: Temeluch, Hadarmiel

71 - Angels of Wisdom

Main angel: Metatron
Related Angels: Zagzagel, Hadar

72 - Angels of Spiritual Development

Main angel: Cherubiel
Related angels: Seraphiel, Raphael, Gabriel, Michael, Iahhel

73 - Angels of Meditation

Main angel: Raphael
Related angels: Cherubiel, Seraphiel, Shateiel

74 - Angels of Purity

Main angel: Cherubiel
Related angels: Seraphiel, Tahariel

75 - Angels of Compassion

Main angel: Raphael
Related angels: Haziel, Rachmiel, Halacho, Rahmiel

76 - Angels of Peace and Temperance

Main angel: Tsadkiel
Related angels: Seraphiel, Michael, Raphael, Gabriel, Metatron,
Phanuel, Jael, Hakamiah

77 - Angels of Forgiveness and Mercy

Main angel: Jeremiel
Related angels: Uriel, Tsadkiel, Remiel, Rahmiel

78 - Protective Angels of the Innocent

Main angel: Michael

Related angels: Gabriel, Prukiel, Hukiel, Sadayel, Harschiel

79 - Angels of Harmony and Personal Balance

Main angel: Ariel

Related angels: Cherubiel, Seraphiel, Hagiel, Itqal, Sadriel, Cassiel, Hasdiel, Phanuel

80 - To Enter Into the Divine Light

Main angel: Raphael

Related angels: Gabriel, Uriel, Shamshiel

81 - Angels of Humanitarian Causes

Main angel: Cherubiel

Related angels: Seraphiel, Raphael, Haamiah, Nemamiah, Shetel, Aebel, Anush

82 - Angels of Justice

Main angel: Tsadkiel

Related angels: Raguel, Ahadiel, Sarakiel, Amitiel, Peniel, Quelamia, Ielahiah, Asaliah, Kamael, Azza, Daniel, Hakamiah

83 - Protective Angels against Evil

Main angel: Seraphiel

Related angels: Sandalphon, Michael, Shalmiel, Garshanel, Haniel, Buchuel, Azriel, Natiel, Shamshiel, Amriel, Antiel, Markiel, Busthariel, Nuriel, Takifiel, Akzariel, Harariel, Hiel, Hasriel

84 - Protective Angels of the Planet

Main angel: Uriel

Related angels: Haamiah, Maktiel, Samuel, Shetel, Aebel, Anush,

Oriphiel

85 – Personal Angels

86 – Angels of Destiny

Main angel: Sandalphon
Related angels: Cherubiel, Seraphiel, Oriel

87 – Protective Angels of Destiny

Main angel: Uriel
Related angels: Raphael, Gabriel, Michael

88 – To Acquire Power

Main angel: Metatron
Related angels: Afriel, Guriel, Hofniel, Shamshiel, Nachiel, Arafiel, Dagiel, Gamiel, Remiel, Sarphiel

89 – To Feel Unconditional Love

Main angel: Anael
Related angels: Cherubiel, Seraphiel, Raphael, Metatron, Uriel, Theliel, Mehahel, Phaniel, Lahabiel, Ariel, Rahabiel, Hasdiel, Arbiel, Habiel, Graniel, Hagiel, Noguel, Chardiel, Rahmiel, Chamuel

90 – To Heal Emotions

Main angel: Chamuel
Related angels: Raphael, Seraphiel, Cherubiel, Anael, Metatron, Ariel

91 – To Find the Love of Life

Main angel: Tsadkiel
Related angels: Seraphiel, Cherubiel, Metatron, Raphael

92 - Angels for the Education of Children

Main angel: Jophiel

Related angels: Ofiel, Chamuel, Raphael

93 - To Make Your Desires Come True

Main angel: Vehuiah

Related angels: Corael, Hannuel, Pagiel

94 - Protective Angels of Dreams

Main angel: Gabriel

Related angels: Anael, Gethel

95 - Angels of Inner Transformation

Main angel: Och

Related angels: Uriel, Sabiel

96 - To Know the Great Secrets of Life

Main angel: Gabriel

Related angels: Uriel, Cherubiel, Eiael, Sabbathiel (Michael), Aha, Pastor, Sabiel, Abariel

97 - To Preside Over Angelic Ceremonies

Main angel: Azrael

Related angels: Harschiel, Sarphiel

98 - Angels of Divination and Clairvoyance

Main angel: Raziel

Related angels: Uriel, Eistibus, Neciel, Ieiaiel, Kadriel, Ramiel, Teiaiel

99 - Angels of Intuition

Main angel: Uriel

Related angels: Seraphiel, Kyriel, Leliel, Anachiel, Kalmiya, Muriel,

Ramiel, Elimiel, Och

100 - Angels of the Subconscious

Main angel: Uriel
Related angels: Gabriel, Furmiel, Gethel, Kyriel, Naromiel, Requiel

101 - Angels of the Awakening of Consciousness

Main angel: Gabriel
Related angels: Raziel, Uriel

Conclusion

*M*ay the angels be with you. May the angels bring you love, beauty, light, and happiness.

May the angels illuminate the world with goodness and peace.

They kept me company throughout the process of writing this book, giving me the courage and willpower to work with everlasting passion.

The angels are not invisible creatures. If you connect to their vibration, they will come to you, love will enter your life, and success and prosperity will fulfill all of your desires.

Marie-Ange Faugérolas

The Rituals

Meditations

Visualizations

Prayers

Ceremonies

Bath

Massage

Invocations

Solicitations

1-Angelic Solicitation, p. 265
2-Solicitation to Prepare Your Future with the Angels
(15 minutes), p. 351
3-Angelic Solicitation with an Icosahedron (10 minutes), p. 495
4-Angelic Solicitation to Obtain an Immediate Answer
(15 minutes), p. 527

Angelic Altars

1-Angelic Altar of the Zodiac for Gathering Yourself and for
Saying Requests, p. 392
2-Angelic Altar for Inner Transformation, p. 209

Requests

Request to Make Your Dreams Come True (15 minutes), p. 398

Treatments

1-Treatment with a Pendulum (15 minutes), p. 216
2-Treatment to Eliminate Negative Energies, p. 220
3-Treatment for the Sacred Awakening of Consciousness
(30 minutes), p. 204
4-Treatment to Energize the Chakras with a Pendulum
(15 minutes), p. 216

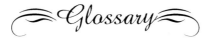

Glossary

Alchemy

Occult science of Greco-Egyptian origin that blends different techniques of physics and chemistry to achieve the Great Work and the transmutation of matter.

Angel

A celestial creature whose origin comes from the Greek word "aggelos," which means "messenger." Angels are the intermediaries between the celestial plane and the terrestrial plane. They are pure spirits, but can take human form, and most often have wings, when they appear to humans. Angels have diverse functions related to humans, who they protect and illuminate with divine love.

Angelology

This term means the study of angels. Angelology was developed through the exegesis of ancient manuscripts and the historical exploration of the different traditions of the peoples of the Bible.

Apocryphal

Apocryphal texts copy, modify, or complete the texts recognized by religions.

Archangels

Kabbalistic tradition recognizes the 10 archangels of the Sefirot as the main archangels. In the Book of Revelation, John announces that seven angels stand before God. They are the highest archangels of the celestial hierarchy.

The Book of Enoch names seven archangels: Uriel, Raguel, Michael, Seraqael, Gabriel, and Raphael.

There are a great number of archangels other than the highest archangels of the celestial hierarchy or the more commonly referenced archangels. They all belong to the choirs of the hierarchy located above the angels of the third choir in the third angelic hierarchy.

Akashic Records

The records of humanity located in the etheric plane, timeless and without a defined space. These archives contain all of the information concerning the history of humanity, the past, the present, and the future. They are accessible to angels and to people with awakened consciousness and a high vibratory rate.

Athanor

A large container capable of doing slow combustions used for alchemic transmutations.

Aura

The term "aura" is a Latin word for "breath" and "atmosphere." The aura of a person is a subtle concept meaning the energy that surrounds the human body. It's composed of seven layers, and the closest layer to the physical body is called the etheric body.

Ayurvedic Medicine

A kind of medicine originating from India, based on holistic medicine and natural treatments.

Books of Enoch

The three books of Enoch are attributed to Enoch, Noah's great-grandfather. These books are considered apocryphal by the Christian Church. They are a precious source of information on angels, the archangels, and the prophetic visions.

Buddhism

Philosophy, spirituality, and religion that first appeared in India in the VI century B.C., with the illumination of Siddhartha Gautama, who became Buddha. The spiritual path leads to awakening by renouncing ego and sufferance.

Celestial Hierarchy

The celestial hierarchy is the very structured organization of the angelic plane. It was established according to Celestial Hierarchy, by Dionysius the Areopagite, the works of Thomas Aquinas, and according to the texts of the Old and New Testament. The angelic plane is composed of nine choirs of angels divided into three separate hierarchies. The Seraphim, the Cherubim, and the Thrones are in the first hierarchy. The Dominations, the Virtues, and the Powers are in the second hierarchy. The third hierarchy is made up of the angels that are closest to the terrestrial plane: the Principalities, the Archangels, and all the angels.

Chakras

The term "chakra" comes from a Sanskrit word that means "wheel" or "disk." The Chakras are subtle wheels of energy that contribute to physical and emotional well-being. The energy of the Kundalini circulates in the Chakras. Opening the Chakras contributes to spiritual awakening.

Chaldeans

Semitic people located south-west of Babylon. They were dominant from the IX to the VI century B.C., and fought the Assyrians.

Channeling

A spiritual channel that creates an opening between the terrestrial plane and the angelic plane. It allows us to contact angels, and to ask for their help, assistance, or comfort through spiritualistic practices like automatic writing, materialized apparitions, or vibratory contact.

Chi or Qi

"Qi" is a Chinese word that's pronounced "tchi," meaning "vapor, fluid, energy." The Qi is an energy that circulates in the universe and inside the body.

Etheric Body

The etheric body is the first layer of the aura, filled with subtle energy. It's connected to the physical body that it protects and feeds energy to. The seven Chakras are in the etheric body.

Egregore

The egregore is an energy emitted by a group of people. This energy is very powerful. Prayers, group meditations, and gatherings create an egregore that heals or saves people, social groups, or causes.

Gematria

The science of numeric symbols and the codification of numbers.

Guardian Angel

Guardian angels are entrusted with protecting someone from the day they are born until their death. They are omnipresent and every human can call upon them for comfort and advice whenever they feel the need. The protection of guardian angels covers health, sentimental relationships, success, and helps keep negative people and energies away.

Holistic Medicine

Holistic medicine is a global medicine that treats individuals on a physical, psychological, and emotional level.

Kabbalah

The Kabbalah is a mystical school of thought originating from Judaism. Its sources are the Books of Enoch, the Sefer Yetzirah, the

Book of Creation, and the Zohar, the Book of Splendor. The Kabbalah offers symbolic and spiritual interpretations of the Bible. The Sefirotic tree of life is the angelic and spiritual symbol of the human ascension toward God.

Kundalini

The Kundalini is an energy located in the sacrum. Traditionally, it's represented as a coiled snake. As the Kundalini ascends each Chakra, it activates energy and provokes spiritual awakening.

Mesopotamia

Region of the Middle-East located between the Tigris and the Euphrates, with Assyria to the north and Babylon to the South.

Sefirot

The 10 Sefirot symbolize the 10 primordial numbers. The word "Sefirot" comes from the Hebrew root SFR, meaning "to count" or "to enumerate." The 10 Sefirot guide men on the path that leads to God. Each Sefirah is an emanation of divine energy. The goal is to attain the tenth Sefirah of Keter to meet the manifestation of the divine.

Subtle Energy

The seven layers of the aura are composed of this invisible, but particularly effective, energy. It circulates in the Chakras. You can test this subtle energy by stretching out your hands, with your palms facing the sky. After a few moments, you should feel a tingling sensation and a feeling of weight on your hands.

Talmud

Text of Judaism founded on the transcription of oral Rabbinic traditions that teach and define the rules of Jewish religious and civil life. The two fundamental texts of the Talmud are the Mishnah and the Gemara.

Transmutation

Chemical transformation of a substance into another substance. The alchemists worked on the transmutation of metals.

Tree of Life

In Kabbalah, the tree of life is a symbol of the hierarchical organization of the celestial plane. It's composed of the 10 Sefirot, which represent the initiatory steps that must be crossed to attain the higher Sefirah of Keter where the divine is manifested.

Vibratory Rate

The vibratory rate is the quantity of subtle energy a person has to awaken consciousness, open up their Chakras, to call the angels, or to receive angelic messages. Practicing angelic meditations, opening up the Chakras, and communication with the angelic plane raises the vibratory rate. Raising the vibratory rate can also be achieved through goodness, generosity and compassion. The higher a person's vibratory rate is, the more this person can connect with angels and bring about miracles in their existence.

Zohar (Sefer ha-Zohar), Book of Splendor

The Zohar establishes communication between men and God through the intermediary of the 10 Sefirot.

Zoroastrianism

Zoroastrianism is also called "mazdeism," a monotheistic religion whose God is Ahura Mazda. The prophet of Zoroastrianism is Zoroaster (Zarathoustra). This religion was developed in the I century B.C., in Iran. The Persians adopted Zoroastrianism until the rise of Islam.

Index

419, 428, 429, 433, 448, 455, 459, 475, 476, 487, 509, 534, 536-539, 546-548, 553, 581, 585

Binah, 103, 104, 106, 110, 112, 116

Boaz, 106

Bodhisattvas, 76

Book of Mormon, 79

Book of the Dead, 121

Brahma, 77, 100, 121, 487

Buddha, 76, 380, 583

Buddhism, 76, 455, 583

C

Candle, 54, 56, 108, 149-153, 156, 157, 165, 166, 177-179, 183-186, 191, 194, 205, 207, 209, 212, 215, 216, 218-220, 222, 224-226, 228-230, 232, 234-236, 239-245, 247-250, 253, 254, 258, 259, 261, 266, 269, 273, 280, 288, 289, 290, 291, 298, 300, 302, 303, 305, 306, 309-311, 313, 314, 316, 317, 319-322, 331, 334, 340, 341, 343, 345-352, 357, 361-363, 367-370, 372, 373, 375, 376, 379, 381, 383, 386, 391-393, 399, 400, 419-430, 432, 448, 449, 451, 453, 454, 457, 462, 465, 468, 498, 499, 527, 534-539, 543-545, 549-551

Catholic Church, 58, 79, 326

Celestial choirs, 124

Ceremony, 168, 257, 258, 268, 284, 285, 289, 290, 360, 360-362, 368-372, 374, 543, 544, 546, 549-552

Chakra, 116, 117, 150, 152, 180-195, 198, 199, 205, 206, 215-218, 221, 223, 226, 228, 229, 235, 237, 241, 244, 247, 272, 298-303, 309, 310, 322, 323, 331, 335, 347, 360, 465, 468, 478, 493-497, 499, 501-507, 509-521, 523-527, 583, 585

Chakra, fifth, 189, 497, 499, 502, 505, 506, 510, 525, 527

Chakra, fourth, 187-189, 497, 499, 509, 513-515, 521, 524

Chakra, root, 116, 182, 183, 194, 198, 215, 216, 229, 237, 310, 360, 496, 499, 511, 516, 523, 526, 527

Chakra, second, 184, 194, 198, 217, 309, 496, 499, 519

Chakra, seventh, 192, 195, 199, 497, 499, 504, 507, 517

Chakra, sixth, 190-192, 199, 465, 497, 499, 512, 515, 518

Chakra, third, 185, 186, 198, 496, 499

Chaldean, 67, 102, 121, 126, 332

Channeling, 277, 278, 583

Cherubim, 81, 83, 84, 91, 98, 125-128, 141, 142, 147, 332, 407, 583

Choirs, nine, 123, 124, 147, 583

Christianity, 56, 79, 92, 121, 135, 342

Colors of angels, 273, 445

Creation, 56, 62, 65, 75, 100-102, 112, 116, 117, 132, 147, 184, 209, 285, 330, 375, 389, 421, 448, 449, 530, 585

Crystals, 35, 52, 64, 196, 198, 261, 273, 284, 355, 487, 488, 491, 492, 496, 497, 500, 509, 520, 527

D

Daath, 103, 104

Daniel, 46, 69, 84, 98, 136, 338, 405, 564

Devas, 77, 121

Devote, 132, 262, 272, 293, 312, 393, 490, 495, 500, 528, 551

Diamond, 150, 232, 336, 337, 353, 354, 362, 376, 468, 497, 500, 508

Diffusers, 432

Dionysius, the Areopagite, 58, 67, 83, 123, 124, 127-132, 583

Dominations, 84, 92, 128, 129, 183, 332, 583

Drums, 176, 360

E

Earth, 42, 74, 75, 79, 85, 87, 109, 122, 126, 128, 138, 139, 141, 142, 175, 177, 179, 183, 210, 238, 246, 306, 310, 333, 358, 359, 360, 364, 380, 381, 385, 419, 448, 450, 451, 461, 464, 487, 488, 522, 525

Egypt, 56, 98, 210, 475, 529, 530

Ein Sof, 101, 115

Elijah, 59, 84, 134, 531

Elixir of immortality, 546, 548, 549, 576

Emotion, 43, 100, 112, 135, 151, 161, 167, 169-172, 179, 194, 221, 223, 225, 230, 233, 244, 255, 298, 321, 327, 360, 365, 377, 392, 399, 424, 428, 435, 445

Enoch, 57, 59, 65, 84, 86, 88, 94, 97, 122, 129, 132, 134, 140, 333, 531, 582, 583, 584

Essential oils, 273, 290, 291, 431, 432, 434, 436-441, 443

Eternity, 59, 296, 299, 545, 547, 551

Etheric body, 209-211, 213, 218, 219, 337, 347, 501-503, 505-507, 509-526, 582, 584

Eve, 62, 91, 97, 129, 139

Ezekiel, 66, 74, 83, 98, 126, 128, 142, 487, 488

F

Fast, 257, 550

Feather, 63, 159, 307, 453, 467, 468, 544

Fire, 54, 65-67, 74, 75, 84, 87, 91, 98, 122, 125, 134, 139, 170, 171, 192, 199, 210, 253, 342, 375, 387, 419, 472, 475

Five senses, 372

Flame, 67, 98, 125, 170, 177, 186, 237, 242, 280, 330, 331, 419, 451

Flower, 77, 286, 362, 457, 462

Four worlds, 111

Free will, 135, 276

G

Gabriel, 52, 68, 69, 76, 77, 82, 92, 103-105, 108, 109, 111, 116, 122, 127, 130, 132-134, 139, 213, 214, 222, 223, 234, 235, 280, 325, 329, 338-342, 348, 351, 352, 372, 373, 375-378, 390, 391, 395, 407-417, 426, 429, 442, 446, 447, 463-465, 483, 484, 517, 537, 538, 541, 555-559, 563-567, 582

Garden of Eden, 91, 93, 98, 126, 487

Gematria, 99, 100, 584

Gemini, 333, 410, 502, 505, 507, 513, 514, 516, 517, 524, 525

Gemstone elixir, 490

General relaxation, 152, 185, 213, 215, 219, 222, 244, 247, 261, 266, 267, 270, 321, 322, 337, 346, 347, 349, 351, 353, 363, 370, 544

Gongs, 176

Greek, 45, 53, 59, 73, 82, 92, 101, 124, 132, 143, 285, 488, 504, 542, 546, 547, 581

Gregory the Great, 124, 133

H

Haendel, George Friedrich, 62

Haydn, Joseph, 62

Healing, 41, 45, 59, 154, 201-204, 207-209, 216, 217, 219, 221, 226-231, 233, 236, 244, 245, 249, 250, 251, 254, 258-260, 263, 265, 268, 270, 279, 333-335, 358, 406, 425, 428, 440, 441, 460, 462, 463, 469, 471, 477, 482, 483, 489, 521, 541, 561

Heaven, 41, 42, 55, 62, 65, 69, 70, 74-76, 78, 84, 85, 87, 89, 90, 97, 99, 121-123, 130, 135, 138-142, 158, 177, 179, 238, 246, 254, 310, 322, 323, 341, 365,

371, 380, 382-384, 391, 403, 419, 452, 464, 488

List of the Angels and Archangels in the Bible of Angels

A

Aba, 554

Aha, 566

Abadiloth, 554

Abariel, 566

Abdizuel, 412

Abrid, 562

Abrinael, 412

Achaiah, 404, 555

Adad, 561

Adnachiel, 412

Adonael, 561

Adoyahel, 562

Adriel, 412, 557

Aebel, 562, 564

Aftiel, 561

Afriel, 565

Agibiel, 412

Ahabiel, 554

Ahadiel, 564

Ahaniel, 556

Akriel, 556

Akzariel, 564

Alad, 557

Aladiah, 404

Amael, 132, 408

Ambiel, 411

Amitiel, 564

Amnediel, 412

Amnixiel, 413

Amriel, 564

Amutiel, 412

Anachiel, 566

Anael, 131, 163, 165, 166, 167, 225, 226, 299, 329, 412-416, 422, 521, 553-556, 558, 559

Anafiel, 515

Ananchel, 558

Anauel, 405

Aniel, 405, 427

Anixiel, 412

Antiel, 564

Anush, 562, 564

Aputel, 558

Arbiel, 554, 565

Ardifiel, 412

Arkhas, 428

Dirachiel, 412

Donquel, 554

E

Ebuhuel, 559

Eiael, 561

Eiaieil,

Eistibus, 566

Eleniah,

Elimiel, 558, 567

Elion,

Elubatel, 559

Enediel, 412

Ergediel, 412

Ertrosi, 130, 408

Esabiel, 423, 425, 559

Eschiel, 559

Exael, 559

Ezgadi, 561

Ezriel, 562

F

Furmiel, 567, 601

G

Gabriel, 52, 68, 69, 76, 77, 82, 92, 103-105, 108, 109, 111, 122, 127, 130, 132-134, 139, 213, 214, 222, 223, 234, 235, 280, 325, 329, 338-342, 348, 351, 352, 372, 373, 375-378, 390, 391, 395, 406-417, 426, 429, 442, 446, 447, 463-465, 483, 484, 517, 537, 538, 541, 555-559, 563-567, 582, 601

Gadamel, 521

Gamiel, 562, 565

Garshanel, 564

Gaviel, 522

Gazriel, 422, 557

Geburael, 561

Geburathiel, 422

Gediel, 557

Geliel, 412

Gemaliel, 562

Geniel, 412

Gethel, 566, 567

Gradiel, 558

Graniel, 554, 565

Griel, 557

Gurid, 562

Guriel, 565

H

Haaiah, 404

Haamiah, 405, 564

Habaiah

Habiel, 554, 565

Habbiel, 521, 554, 555

Habuhiah, 406, 562

Hadar, 563

Hadarmiel, 563

Hagiel, 187, 188, 396, 397, 410, 556, 564, 565

Hahahel, 405

Hahaiah, 404, 426, 560

Hahasiah, 405

Hahayel, 562

Haheuiah, 404, 489

Haiaiel, 406

Hakamiah, 563, 564

Halacho, 563

Haludiel, 558

Hamaliel, 130, 408, 411

Hamatiel, 559, 560

Hamaya, 425, 562

Haniel, 103-105, 111, 130-133, 213, 214, 249, 303, 406, 408, 409, 424, 440, 441, 446, 447, 458, 459, 460, 482, 536, 537, 541

Hananiel, 559

Hanniniel, 554

Hannuel, 560, 566

Harael, 405

Harahel, 559, 560

Harariel, 564

Hardaniel, 429

Hariel, 404, 559, 562

Harschiel, 564, 566

Hasdiel, 214, 215, 554, 564, 565

Hashmal, 129, 408

Haskmal

Hasriel, 564

Haziel, 404, 426, 555, 563

Heckamiah, 404

Hekamiah, 555

Hemah, 557

Heman, 555

Hiel, 564

Hiniel, 559

Hodiel, 204-206, 559

Hochmel, 559

Hoesediel, 555

Hofniel, 565

Hukiel, 564

I

Iahhel, 563

Ielahiah, 564

Ietuqiel, 556

Iezalel, 554

Imamiah, 405

Israfel, 132

Itqal, 424, 554-556, 564

J

Jabamiah, 557

Jael, 555, 563

Jagniel, 139

Jazeriel, 412

Jehoel, 125, 407, 430

Jehudiel, 409

Johiel, 251, 252, 557

Jelial, 521, 554

Jeliel, 404, 554

Jerazol, 422

Jeremiel, 409, 556, 563

Jophiel, 75, 128, 184, 185, 407, 496, 499, 519, 541, 558, 559, 566

K

Kabniel, 559

Kabshiel, 430, 559

Kadmiel, 557

Kamael, 103, 104, 111, 130, 133, 213, 214, 243, 280, 292, 293, 314, 397, 406, 408-411, 428, 439, 446, 447, 471, 472, 481, 538, 539, 545, 559-561, 564

Kadriel, 566

Kalmiya, 566

Kemuel, 125, 407

Kaniel, 556

Kofziel, 557

Kokaviel, 559

Kyriel, 412, 566

L

Lahabiel, 554, 565

Lailah, 556, 557

Lauviah, 555, 558, 560, 404, 426

Lecabel, 405, 562

Lehahiah, 405

Lelahel, 404, 425, 559

Leliel, 566

Leuviah, 404

M

Machasiel, 558, 559

Mahasiah, 404

Mahtiel, 559

Makiel, 559

Maktiel, 562, 564

Malahidael, 411

Malashiel, 75

Maltiel, 558, 559

Manakel, 406

Markiel, 564

Mebahel, 404

Mebahiah, 405, 556

Mehahel, 554, 565

Mehiel, 406, 559

Melahel, 360, 404

Melchisedech, 556

Melioth, 423

Menadel, 405, 424, 554

Metatron, 59, 75, 84, 103, 104, 109, 110, 111, 113, 122, 123, 125, 133, 134, 163, 165-167, 178, 179, 213, 214, 229, 231, 283, 321, 370, 400, 446

Michael, 53, 75, 76, 81, 86, 87, 90-92, 103-105, 109-111, 129, 132-134, 136, 140, 205, 222-224, 238-242, 280, 325,

Quelamia, 564

R

Rabacgel
Rachmiel, 555, 563
Radueriel, 559
Rahabiel, 554, 565
Rahmiel, 302, 554, 563, 565
Raguel, 132, 254, 255, 409, 525, 564, 582
Raphel, 75
Raphael, 33, 43, 44, 52, 57, 68, 69, 78, 81, 92, 103, 104, 105, 111, 127, 132-134, 139, 163, 165-167, 213, 216-223, 226, 227, 232, 233, 247, 248, 253, 254, 280, 310, 311, 325, 329, 332-335, 338, 351, 358, 359, 363, 364, 371-373, 389-391, 400, 406, 407, 409-411, 413-417, 425, 429, 441, 446, 447, 460-463, 471, 483, 537, 541, 553-555, 559-566, 582
Raziel, 75, 98, 103, 104, 110, 111, 113, 128, 133, 190-192, 280, 406, 407, 409, 424, 437, 446, 447, 451, 452, 454, 497, 499, 511, 512, 514, 535, 541, 545, 549, 551, 552, 558-560, 562, 566, 567
Rehael, 405, 425, 557, 560, 561

Reiyel, 555
Remiel, 557, 558, 563, 565
Requel, 131, 132, 408
Requiel, 412, 567
Rhamiel, 186, 187, 497, 499, 505
Rikbiel, 429
Rochel, 406, 562
Rubiel, 560
Rumiel, 557

S

Sabbathiel (Michael), 239, 342, 566
Sabrael, 560, 561
Sabriel, 130, 408
Sachiel, 413-416, 555
Sadayel, 564
Sadriel, 556, 564
Sahriel
Salathiel, 562
Salbabiel, 554
Samael, 329, 409, 413-416
Samandiriel, 556
Sammael, 410
Samuel, 409, 564
Sandalphon, 59, 75, 84, 103-105, 108, 109, 111, 133, 134, 140, 178, 179, 280, 348, 406, 409, 422, 442, 443, 446, 447, 449-451, 484, 485, 531, 534, 535, 556-558, 564, 565

World of Angels
Publishing

11948 Ventura Blvd,
Studio City CA 91604
USA

Visit Theworldofangels.com for more information